Brothers Apart

Stanford Studies in Middle Eastern and Islamic Societies and Cultures

Brothers Apart

**PALESTINIAN CITIZENS OF ISRAEL
AND THE ARAB WORLD**

Maha Nassar

Stanford University Press
Stanford, California

Stanford University Press
Stanford, California

© 2017 by the Board of Trustees of the Leland Stanford Junior University. All rights reserved.

No part of this book may be reproduced or transmitted in any form or by any means, electronic or mechanical, including photocopying and recording, or in any information storage or retrieval system without the prior written permission of Stanford University Press.

Printed in the United States of America on acid-free, archival-quality paper

Library of Congress Cataloging-in-Publication Data

Names: Nassar, Maha, author.
Title: Brothers apart : Palestinian citizens of Israel and the Arab world / Maha Nassar.
Other titles: Stanford studies in Middle Eastern and Islamic societies and cultures.
Description: Stanford, California : Stanford University Press, 2017. | Series: Stanford studies in Middle Eastern and Islamic societies and cultures | Includes bibliographical references and index.
Identifiers: LCCN 2016055465 (print) | LCCN 2016056607 (ebook) | ISBN 9781503602496 (cloth : alk. paper) | ISBN 9781503603165 (pbk. : alk. paper) | ISBN 9781503603189
Subjects: LCSH: Palestinian Arabs—Israel—Intellectual life—20th century. | Palestinian Arabs—Israel—Ethnic identity—History—20th century. | Politics and literature—Palestine—History—20th century. | Palestine—Relations—Arab countries. | Arab countries—Relations—Palestine. | Israel—History—1948–1967.
Classification: LCC DS113.7 .N378 2017 (print) | LCC DS113.7 (ebook) | DDC 305.8992/7405694—dc23
LC record available at https://lccn.loc.gov/2016055465

To my parents, Tawfik Nassar and Khawla Dajani Nassar
With love and gratitude

CONTENTS

	Acknowledgments	ix
	Introduction	1
1	Strategies of Resistance	15
2	Competing Narratives	46
3	Debates on Decolonization	78
4	Palestinian Spokesmen	114
5	Complicated Heroes	146
	Conclusion	181
	Notes	191
	Bibliography	233
	Index	257

ACKNOWLEDGMENTS

First, I especially thank the librarians and staff members of the numerous collections I visited in the United States and the Middle East who helped me locate and access so many of the texts that I analyze here. They are all too often the unsung heroes of academic research. Thanks in particular go to Marlis Saleh and staff at the Joseph Regenstein Library at the University of Chicago, where this project originated. Thanks, too, go to Atifa Rawan and staff at the University of Arizona's Main Library, where it was completed. During my research, I was aided by staff members at the Nami Jafet Memorial Library at the American University of Beirut, the Library of the Institute for Palestine Studies (Beirut), the National Library of Israel, the Peace Library at the Givat Haviva Institute, the Widener Library at Harvard University, and the Doe Memorial Library at the University of California, Berkeley. Mary Wilke at the Center for Research Libraries in Chicago facilitated the purchase of microfilm copies of the newspaper *al-Yawm*, making it available to US-based researchers for the first time.

Over the last several years I have benefited immensely from the insights and generosity of Palestinian and Arab intellectuals who helped me sharpen my thinking and gave me new insights into the complex and nuanced conditions of the Palestinians inside the Green Line. My late uncle, historian and political thinker Ahmad Sidqi al-Dajani, first opened my eyes to the intra-Arab debates regarding this community. The late author Fouzi El-Asmar generously shared with me his complete collection of *al-Fajr* and *al-Ard*, while Hanna Ibrahim graciously gave me his personal copy of his out-of-print memoir. Hanna Abu Hanna, Salem Jubran, and the other interviewees who shared their time, their memories, and often their books with me likewise made this book much richer in its details and insight.

The University of Chicago and the University of Arizona have been my two main intellectual homes for nearly twenty years. At the University of Chicago, I benefited tremendously from the mentorship of Rashid Khalidi and Holly

Shissler, both of whom helped guide me through the early stages of this project. Fred Donner, Wadad Kadi, Ariela Finkelstein, and the late Farouk Mustafa sharpened further my analytical and translational skills. I also benefited from the intellectual environment provided by Rana Barakat, Abigail Jacobson, Mezna Qato, Roschanak Shaeri, and Rochdi Younsi. At the University of Arizona, my colleagues in the School of Middle Eastern and North African Studies (MENAS), including Anne Betteridge, Samira Farwaneh, Benjamin Fortna, Adel Gamal, Leila Hudson, Amy Newhall, Yaseen Noorani, Sonia Shiri, Charles Smith, and Kamran Talattof, have strengthened this work with their attentive questions, constructive feedback, and opportunities to share my work. I have also enjoyed enlightening conversations with Arizona colleagues Sama Alshaibi, Carine Bourget, Julia Clancy-Smith, Faten Ghosn, Sandy Marshall, Brian Silverstein, and Ed Wright. The groundbreaking work of graduate students Britain Eakin, Brooke Lober, and Alex Karaman has furthered my thinking on important aspects of contemporary Palestine. My research has also benefited from institutional funding at the University of Arizona, in particular an SBSRI Research Professorship, a Junior Faculty Research Leave, and a Provost Author Support Fund award. And I will forever be grateful to the late Michael Bonine for his unwavering mentorship.

Kate Wahl and Joel Beinin at Stanford University Press have provided wonderful support over the years. Their advice and suggestions, coupled with the incisive and meticulous comments of the two anonymous reviewers, were extraordinarily helpful in strengthening the arguments and fleshing out the details of this book.

I have presented my research in a number of venues, including at the annual meetings of the Middle East Studies Association and the American Historical Association. The questions and comments I received there helped me think more deeply about my subject. The feedback I received from Beshara Doumani, Zachary Lockman, Ilan Pappé, and the other participants at the 2015 New Directions in Palestinian Studies symposium at Brown University was particularly valuable in helping me clarify the points I wanted to make. I have also benefited in ways both large and small from the incisive comments, questions, and help in tracking down sources provided by numerous friends and colleagues. They include Orit Bashkin, Amahl Bishara, Aomar Boum, Hamid Dabashi, Leena Dallasheh, Marda Dunsky, Ziad Fahmy, James Gelvin, Adina Hoffman, Ian Lustick, Norma Mendoza-Denton, Ibrahim Muhawi, Shira Robinson, Sherene Seikaly, Yasir Suleiman, and Farzin Vejdani. I am especially grateful to Aomar

Boum, Benjamin Fortna, and Mezna Qato for reading and providing thoughtful feedback on the entire manuscript. Special thanks, too, go to Mezna for more than thirty years of friendship and for always pushing me to think more clearly and compassionately about what matters most.

I am blessed to have the inspiration and support of my family. My parents, Tawfik Nassar and Khawla Dajani Nassar, nurtured my early fascination with all things Palestinian, and they encouraged me to pursue my academic studies accordingly. My siblings and their spouses—Ida Nassar, Rochdi Younsi, Alaa Nassar, Dalia Qubbaj-Nassar, Salma Nassar, and Basil Salem—are refreshing sources of humor and sustenance. My cousin Omar Dajani helped facilitate my first trip to my parents' birthplace, which proved to be invaluable on so many levels. My in-laws, Ellen and Hank Lucas, and Jon Lucas and Erin Walsh, have provided valuable perspective. My husband, Scott Lucas, has been my steadfast companion during this long journey. Through it all, his love, generosity, and keen insights have helped me in more ways than I can possibly lay out here. Our children, Ali and Salma, recently joined us on this journey, providing incredible joy and much-needed laughter. I hope they will see the day when everyone in the Holy Land—and in the world—lives in peace as equals.

Brothers Apart

INTRODUCTION

As Rashid Husayn (Rashid Hussein) boarded the plane, he was full of nervous excitement. In July 1959 the twenty-three-year-old poet-journalist embarked on his first overseas trip to attend the Seventh World Festival of Youth and Students in Vienna, where seventeen thousand leftist activists from around the globe were gathering to celebrate "brotherhood and peace." He was especially eager to meet some of the thirteen hundred delegates from Arab countries since, as a Palestinian citizen of Israel, he had been cut off from the region for more than a decade.[1] The ongoing hostilities between Israel and the Arab states meant that Israeli citizens—Jewish and Palestinian alike—were, with rare exception, forbidden from traveling to Arab countries. International gatherings in Europe and the Soviet Union provided a rare opportunity for politically connected Palestinians in Israel to meet face-to-face with their Arab counterparts.

But attending the festival was also fraught with dilemmas. Husayn and his fellow Palestinians were going as part of a formal Jewish-Arab delegation that Israeli government officials hoped would reinforce their portrayal of Israel as a beacon of progressive democracy, complete with a content Arab minority accorded their full rights. Yet many of those same Palestinians were at the forefront of an ongoing struggle *against* the state, in particular its harsh military government that controlled their movement, confiscated their land, restricted their political expression, and hindered their economic development. At the same time, it was unclear whether the other Arab delegates would even be interested in meeting Husayn; they were, after all, some of Israel's most vociferous critics. Four years earlier, at the Sixth Festival in Moscow, Arab delegates passed out pamphlets denouncing Israeli policies and calling for the state's elimination.² Would Arab delegates condemn the Palestinian minority as traitors to the Arab cause, as they had in Moscow? Husayn also faced tensions within his own delegation. Although he was politically independent, Husayn wrote regularly for the Arabic publications of Mapam (Mifleget Hapoalim Hameuhedet; United Workers' Party), a leftist-Zionist political party. But several of the other delegates belonged to the Communist Party of Israel (CPI), a strong critic of Mapam. Three months earlier, Husayn and CPI members debated in their respective journals how to view the recent Arab revolutions. Would Husayn have to fend off attacks from within his own delegation?

Most of Husayn's concerns were allayed on his arrival in Vienna. Members of his delegation put their differences aside during the festival, while the other Arab attendees were receptive to learning about the expressions of anticolonial solidarity taking place in Israel. When Husayn and his fellow delegates eagerly showed their Algerian counterparts photos of a demonstration in Nazareth calling for Algeria's independence and the release of prisoner Djamila Bouhired, the Algerians thanked them for their support.³ Several of them also discussed eagerly the latest developments in Iraq with some of that country's six hundred participants who were themselves in attendance for the first time. One Iraqi intellectual hailed the periodicals that Husayn and his colleagues distributed as meeting "the highest standards for Arabic journals."⁴

While heartened by the expressions of support from most of his fellow Arabs, Husayn was disappointed by the reaction he received from some members of the Lebanese delegation. They were so incensed at seeing Palestinians walk behind the Israeli flag during the festival's opening procession that afterward they marched over to Husayn and other Palestinian members of the Israeli delegation, loudly accusing them of being traitors to the Palestinian cause and to the Arab world. Later that evening, Husayn overheard a couple of delegates, with their distinctive Lebanese accents, chatting at the hotel bar where he was having a cup of coffee. He ordered a couple of cups for them, but before taking a sip, they asked where he was from. When Husayn replied that he was an "Arab from Israel," they cursed him as a traitor and stormed off.⁵

In reporting the incident to his readers back home, Husayn made it clear that "we would be mistaken to take the Lebanese delegation as representative of the Arabs as a whole."⁶ But he was nonetheless troubled by what he had encountered. After returning to his office in Tel Aviv, Husayn published an open letter to "my brothers in Lebanon" in the local Arabic monthly, *al-Fajr* (The dawn). In it, he urged the Lebanese to recognize that, despite his Israeli passport, he and his fellow Palestinian citizens of Israel were Arabs too. "It is shameful," Husayn wrote, "that we have to swear and give oaths of allegiance in order to prove to you our Arabness. We are the remainder of the Palestinian people, your neighbors in tents." Husayn also insisted that he and his fellow Palestinians in Israel were still deeply connected to the Arab world. "Your delegation called us 'traitors,'" he recalled ruefully. "If only you knew how much these 'traitors' cheered during the heroism of Port Said, during the Iraqi Revolution, and during your revolution— yours, O Lebanon! If only you knew, dear friend, how we danced and gave candy to children after every victory of the Arab people against the enemies of our people."[7] Tellingly, Husayn affirmed his solidarity with the Lebanese and Arab people, not by recalling their common language or heritage but by invoking a set of shared experiences that Arabs throughout the region—including in Israel—had hailed as recent triumphs in the Arab struggle against Western hegemony.[8] And he did so on the pages of an Arabic literary journal, published in Israel, that he hoped would eventually reach the hands of his fellow Arabs.

Husayn's affirmation of solidarity with the major Arab causes of the day and his plea for understanding from his "brothers" in Lebanon speak to the central questions that drive this study. How did Palestinian citizens of Israel attempt to foster cultural and intellectual connections to the Arab world in the 1950s and 1960s, during a time of profound political and geographic isolation? How did Arab intellectuals and political leaders in the region respond to these attempts, and how did their responses change over time? How did regional and global political developments, particularly during the heady days of decolonization, reverberate back into Palestinian communities in Israel? More broadly, what do these dynamics tell us about the transnational circulations of decolonizing discourses produced and consumed through written texts, and what role do these texts play in creating new political vocabularies and solidarities? In this book, I argue that a critical examination of Palestinian and Arab writings, found in newspapers, journals, poetry, literary collections, and memoirs, sheds light on these important questions. In doing so, I locate the cultural and intellectual history of Palestinian citizens of Israel, including their resistance against state policies and the Zionist logic that underpinned them, within the larger context of Palestinian, Arab, and international struggles for decolonization.

ISOLATING THE PALESTINIANS

The making of the Palestinian minority in Israel was a direct, if unintended, consequence of the tumultuous events of 1947–1949, a period that has become known in Palestinian collective memory as the *Nakba* (catastrophe). Over several months of intense fighting, the well-organized military forces of a relatively small Jewish population (about 650,000) in British Mandate Palestine overwhelmed the forces of an Arab population more than twice its size and subsequently defeated the armies of several Arab states. As a result, the Palestinian Arab community was dramatically altered from one that constituted more than two-thirds of the population of Palestine to one that was defeated, dispersed, and dispossessed.[9] More than half of the nearly 1.4 million Palestinian Arabs were driven or fled from their homes,[10] including nearly all of the political, intellectual, and cultural elites; most of the urban population;[11] and the rural inhabitants of more than four hundred villages.[12]

But not everyone left. About 160,000 Palestinians remained within the 1949 Armistice Lines, forming a small minority (about 13 percent) within the newly established state. Often separated from family members during the chaos of the conflict, many of them were internally displaced while others were briefly exiled out of the country before making their way back into the self-declared Jewish state. Israeli leaders, seeking to minimize the number of non-Jews in the country, nonetheless recognized that expelling the remaining Palestinian population en masse was untenable given the international pressure they were already facing to repatriate the refugees.[13] Therefore, they were eager to create a mechanism that would distinguish those Palestinians who were to remain in Israel from those who had left and therefore would not be allowed to return.[14] Initially only some Palestinians residing within the 1949 Armistice Lines (the so-called Green Line) obtained citizenship. Following passage of the 1952 Citizenship Law, a majority of Palestinians living in Israel received the status of citizen, though it was not of equal standing with that of Jewish Israelis.[15] And as the porous borders between Israel and its neighbors grew more impermeable,[16] the dislocations, separations, and military rule that Palestinians had thought were temporary wartime measures became entrenched.

In describing the dramatically altered circumstances of the Palestinians in Israel, famed novelist and literary critic Anton Shammas wrote, "The state of Israel put us in isolation."[17] This isolation took two forms: First, Palestinians faced physical and cultural isolation within Israel. In contrast to Jewish citizens who could travel freely throughout the country, until 1966 Palestinian citizens of Israel were under the watchful eye of a military-run bureaucratic regime that limited where they could live, work, and travel.[18] On the cultural front, the authorities sought to cultivate "Arab Israeli" subjects who were divided internally along political and sectarian lines, cut off from their Palestinian Arab heritage, and solely dependent on the state for their cultural nourishment. The second type of isolation they faced was physical and cultural isolation from the Arab world. In the wake of Israel's establishment, the Arab League enforced a boycott of all Israeli goods and citizens,[19] while Israel banned its own citizens from traveling to Arab countries and restricted Palestinian citizens' access to textual material from the Arab world, citing fears of incitement.[20]

STRATEGIES OF RESISTANCE

To blunt the effects of this internal and external isolation, Palestinian intellectuals, party organizers, and cultural producers adopted several distinct, yet overlapping, strategies of resistance that drew on strategies developed during the Mandate period. In the immediate aftermath of the 1948 Arab-Israeli War the first strategy that CPI members in particular adopted was simply bringing people together, whether for protests or for cultural festivals. But such physical gatherings were difficult to hold given the tight restrictions on movement that Palestinians faced, so the CPI simultaneously adopted a second, more discursively centered strategy: utilizing local Arabic newspapers and journals to challenge Israeli stereotypes, to acquaint readers with Arab civilizational heritage and international literature, and to comment on major events at home and abroad from a decidedly communist viewpoint.

In the second half of the 1950s, revolutionary fervor in the Arab world led Palestinian intellectuals inside the Green Line to cast their gaze toward Egypt and Iraq. Egyptian president Gamal Abdel Nasser's defiant stance during the Suez Crisis and his immensely popular radio broadcasts, coupled with Iraq's overthrow of the pro-Western Hashemite monarchy, ushered in a brief period of hope and camaraderie throughout the region. This buoyant spirit reverberated in Israel as Palestinian communist and pan-Arab nationalist intellectuals put aside their differences and adopted a third strategy: establishing nonpartisan organizations to speak against the state's isolating policies with a united voice. To accommodate the growing range of political viewpoints emerging at this time, intellectuals also established new Arabic newspapers and journals to comment on the local, regional, and international news of the day. While the subsequent fallout between the communists and nationalists in the Arab world led to sometimes acrimonious exchanges on the pages of their respective publications, their shared political vocabulary stressing cultural emancipation and dignity for all linked them discursively to the region and to the broader decolonizing world.

This linkage worried Israeli officials, who feared that allowing Palestinian citizens to acquire regional Arabic print material could incite the "Arab minority." But those Palestinians also recognized that access to such material was crucial to sustaining their shared discursive formations with the region. Thus, they adopted a fourth strategy: sneaking regional Arabic newspapers, literary journals, books, and poetry collections into the hands of the growing Palestinian intelligentsia. These texts were crucial for exposing a younger generation of Palestinians educated in the Israeli school system to alternative viewpoints that celebrated their cultural heritage and political outlook. As a result, despite the difficulty of establishing direct contact with Arabs in the region, many Palestinian citizens of Israel nonetheless followed intensely wider global debates through the consumption and circulation of Arabic print material. In the mid-1960s this strategy was reversed, as texts produced in Israel were increasingly smuggled out to neighboring countries, where they played a key role in acquainting Arab intellectuals with the struggles of Palestinians inside the Green Line.

A central question being debated throughout this period was the role that literature should play in mobilizing people to the cause of justice at home and abroad. The rise of socialist realism, literary commitment, and platform poetry in the Arab world inspired several Palestinian writers in Israel to turn to a fifth strategy: composing, publishing, and reciting politically themed poems. The CPI publications were central in promoting such poetry because they published local, regional, and global voices that spoke of a shared solidarity. Meanwhile, poetry festivals became occasions for Palestinians in the country to challenge their physical isolation from one another and from the region. Performers and audience members alike often had to defy travel bans and circumvent police cordons just to attend the events. Once there, poets often recited verses that positioned their community within a wider Palestinian, Arab, and global decolonizing milieu. As younger Palestinian poets such as Mahmoud Darwish and Samih al-Qasim came to dominate the literary scene in the 1960s, their poems not only played an important role in fostering a shared national consciousness among Palestinians in Israel but would later emerge as a central means of alerting Arabs in the region to the conditions—and to the defiance—of their community.

Darwish and Qasim were part of a younger cohort of Palestinian intellectuals who were eager to reach an audience outside the Israeli state. Some of these intellectuals had previously made contact with their Arab counterparts through a sixth strategy: attending international conferences and festivals. But their main interlocutors were other Arab leftists who were themselves often marginalized or persecuted in their home countries, limiting the overall impact of those gatherings. By the 1960s, some of the more nationalist-oriented Palestinian intellectuals adopted a seventh strategy: sending memoranda to international bodies describing their conditions in Israel. The 1964 Ard memorandum received especially wide attention, thanks in large part to a growing body of Palestinian nationalist organizers in exile who were eager to raise awareness about this beleaguered—and overlooked—community.

Despite these efforts, until 1967 the Palestinians in Israel went almost entirely unnoticed in the Arab world. Most Arab intellectuals deemed them to be passive victims of Israeli tyranny at best and traitors to the Palestinian cause at worst. But the June 1967 War, with its massive, humiliating defeat of Arab forces and Israel's occupation of the remainder of historic Palestine, altered that perception. Arab intellectuals now turned to the Palestinians in Israel, especially the image of the poet-resister, for a glimmer of hope. The 1968 World Youth Festival in Sofia, Bulgaria, where Darwish and Qasim met face-to-face for the first time with their Arab contemporaries, proved to be an important turning point in this Arab "discovery" of Palestinians who were actively resisting their oppression inside the Green Line.

This discovery came at a time when the Palestinian armed resistance movement was reaching new heights, leading Israeli leaders to worry about the growing connections between Palestinians in Israel and the Arab world. As a result, state security apparatuses stepped up their efforts to prevent contact between Palestinian intellectuals in Israel, in the occupied territories, and abroad. Ultimately this led to some intellectuals and political organizers being banished to neighboring Arab states; it also led to the self-imposed exile of Darwish, who moved to Cairo in 1971. Thus, an eighth and final strategy (albeit not always a freely chosen one) was to physically leave the country. Yet even after their discovery and celebration in the Arab world, and even after several of them took up residence in Arab capitals, Palestinian citizens of Israel often found that they still had an uneasy relationship with their Arab counterparts. This tension continues to some extent to this day, and it is part of what makes this story so important for comprehending the transnational dynamics of the region.

LOOKING BEYOND THE NATION-STATE

Despite the deep, multilayered engagements that Palestinian intellectuals in Israel had with developments in the Arab world and beyond, scholars have largely examined this group through the analytical lens of the nation-state. Early studies focused on economic and social transformations among rural Palestinians, often presuming the Israeli state was a modernizing force for good.[21] In the late 1970s, a new wave of scholarship began to situate this community more clearly within Israeli matrices of control. Elia Zuriek argued that Palestinians in Israel faced a form of "internal colonialism," while subsequent studies, grounded largely in social science methodologies, determined the means by which Israeli policies effectively controlled, marginalized, and excluded the Palestinian minority.[22] As Palestinian citizens stepped up their oppositional political activities in the 1970s, some social scientists grew concerned with whether this group identified more closely with Israel or with the Palestinians, and the implications of this identification for the Israeli state.[23] Even sociological works that take seriously the more nuanced and complex worldviews of Palestinians in Israel have tended nonetheless to gloss over the historical period before and immediately after 1967.[24] Yet without a thorough analysis of the intellectual and cultural transformations that I lay out in the following pages, there can be little accounting for how or why these contemporary worldviews emerged.

A number of recent historical studies have shed light on forms of Palestinian resistance against Israeli systems of oppression during the early years of statehood, attending more explicitly to Palestinian subjectivity.[25] While these works have made important contributions to the historical record, they, too, examine this community largely within the framework of the Israeli state. My study builds on these works, but it also departs from them by focusing on the perspectives of intellectuals and cultural producers in order to understand more fully their relationship not only with the Israeli state but also with each other and with intellectual developments in the Arab region and the decolonizing world. This analytical lens takes heed of what Palestinian American scholar Ibrahim Abu-Lughod warned regarding the "pitfalls of Palestiniology": that is, viewing Palestinians' historical development primarily through the lens of their struggles against the Zionists and the British. While conceding that scholars must take into account the "entanglement" of Palestinian and Zionist societies, Abu-Lughod cautioned that such an approach not only narrows the range of historical questions deemed worthy of study but also risks occluding Palestinian voices.[26] This book ameliorates some of these imbalances in the scholarship by demonstrating how Palestinians in Israel turned to written texts, both to contest the state and its dominant Zionist paradigms at home and to reach out to (and sometimes challenge) their ethno-national brethren abroad.

Applying a transnational analytical framework to the study of Palestinian writings during this period requires a creative approach to procuring sources. This is especially true since Palestinians have no fully functioning national archive of their own;[27] their main documentary repositories have been shut down, seized, or destroyed;[28] and the postwar files of Arab state archives remain largely inaccessible to researchers.[29] Moreover, official Israeli state and party archives have tended to define members of this community within the parameters of the state, often obscuring their agency and worldviews.[30] As a result, the newspapers, journals, poetry collections, memoirs, and other documentary sources examined here come from an amalgam of collections held in libraries and by individuals in the United States and the Middle East, reflecting the ongoing Palestinian condition of dislocation and exile. In addition, interviews conducted with several key figures from this period shed light on the political and material conditions that gave rise to the production and consumption of these texts.

ON TEXTS AND AUDIENCES

To analyze these texts in ways that can shed light on larger historical processes, I pay close attention to what Edward Said termed the "worldliness" of texts, keeping in mind that they "are always enmeshed in circumstance, time, place and society."[31] I also heed Raymond Williams's call to examine the "conditions of practice" that go into producing a piece of art or literature.[32] As a result, I devote considerable attention to the material conditions in which these texts were produced, including the political events that gave rise to them. Doing so allows me to undertake an analysis on multiple spatial and temporal scales to highlight their role in the strategies of resistance elucidated previously.

Such an analysis also sheds light on the multiple audiences these texts had over time and space. Prior to 1948, members of the Palestinian Arab intelligentsia were deeply integrated into the broader Arab cultural and intellectual milieu. Their engagement with the anticolonial discourses that circulated throughout Beirut, Damascus, Cairo, Baghdad, and beyond resulted in the production and consumption of texts that were part of an imagined pan-Arab audience. The profound dislocations that resulted from the 1948 Nakba, even among Palestinians who ultimately became citizens of Israel, attenuated to some degree this pan-Arab horizon. Intellectuals focused initially on reaching out to their fellow Palestinians in Israel and to government officials to secure their position within the new state while still affirming their Arab heritage and identity.

During the second half of the 1950s, as a buoyant pan-Arab nationalism took hold in the region, Palestinian intellectuals in Israel embedded within their cultural and political writings a more expansive spatial and temporal horizon that, while still accounting for their isolation, was aimed at possible future audiences beyond the borders of the state. Their cognizance of this futurity can be seen in the eagerness with which Palestinian delegates in Vienna distributed back issues of their publications to Arab delegates and reported to readers back home the positive reception those publications received. Husayn's open letter to his "brothers in Lebanon"—knowing full well that they were unlikely to read his plea immediately but might do so sometime later—is another example of this future-oriented temporal horizon. With the rise of the Palestinian national movement in the 1960s, Palestinian intellectuals and cultural producers in Israel were more cognizant of their position within a broader Palestinian milieu and thus developed a discourse that was aimed more specifically at their fellow Palestinians. After the 1967 war these multiple audiences came together as Palestinians on both sides of the Green Line were able to physically reconnect with one another and as Arab intellectuals paid greater attention to the Palestinians in Israel than they had before.

INTELLECTUALS ACROSS GENERATIONS

In accounting for the worldliness of these texts, I also attend to the backgrounds of the authors that produced them. Most of the figures I discuss in this book functioned in society as Gramscian "organic intellectuals,"[33] who came from working-class backgrounds and/or were deeply invested in improving the lives of the working class and peasants (who were the majority of the Palestinians in Israel at this time[34]). My use of the term "intellectual" to describe these individuals also reflects their own self-identification as *muthaqqafun* (intellectuals). Like them, I use this term to refer to high school and college graduates, teachers, writers, journalists, attorneys, and party organizers who wrote poetry and prose aimed at improving the conditions of their society. The close etymological link in Arabic between "intellectual" (*muthaqqaf*) and "culture" (*thaqafa*) further underscores the need to examine their intellectual and cultural writings together. To be sure, "traditional intellectuals" could be found among the Palestinians in Israel, mainly in government-run institutions. But their textual output was much more modest and less influential than that of their more critical counterparts.[35]

Despite the shared interests of these organic intellectuals, clear distinctions existed between an older generation who came of age during the pre-1948 period and a younger generation who came of age in the Israeli state. Members of the older generation hailed largely from Christian (primarily Orthodox) working-class or middle-class family backgrounds and grew up in relative material comfort in urban or town settings. They were also among the few Palestinians who were able to obtain a high school degree and, in some cases, went on to college in neighboring countries. These opportunities led them to develop a strong connection with the regional intelligentsia, often resulting in the development of a pan-Arab nationalist orientation with a leftist bent.

The younger generation of intellectuals was more diverse, with members hailing from Muslim, Christian, and Druze families and often from working-class or rural peasant backgrounds. They generally came of age under Israeli rule, which, on the one hand, expanded educational opportunities for Palestinian citizens in rural areas but, on the other hand, restricted their access to regional Arab discourses. Because they were unable to travel to neighboring countries, this generation's engagement with Palestinians and Arabs beyond the Green Line was mediated almost exclusively through texts, whether produced locally or smuggled in from abroad. And as these texts increasingly questioned widely held truisms about internationalism and pan-Arab nationalism—while still championing Third World solidarity and Palestinian liberation—cleavages emerged between the older and younger intellectuals about how best to alleviate the burdens their community faced.

In short, members of each generation inhabited what historical anthropologist David Scott terms a distinct "moral-political location" that informed the conceptual and practical questions they sought to tackle.[36] Building on sociologist Karl Mannheim's conceptualization of generations as social forms, Scott calls on contemporary observers to step outside the "epistemological privilege of the present" and to recognize that earlier generations of intellectuals were proposing specific answers to moral, political, and social challenges that reflected the particular temporal location that they inhabited.[37] Not only does this approach help us uncover how shifting political and material circumstances influenced the writings of these specific intellectuals, but it also sheds light on how we may understand the ways in which ideas are shaped and reworked across generations more broadly.

Despite these generational shifts, both the older and younger Palestinian intellectuals at this time shared a preference for producing cultural texts in Arabic rather than Hebrew. While many politically engaged intellectuals, particularly in the CPI and Mapam, communicated with their Jewish colleagues in Hebrew and composed political tracts for their respective party's Hebrew press outlets, they used Arabic for the vast majority of their culture work, especially when reaching out to Palestinians and other Arabs.[38] Their use of Arabic also signaled their engagement with the Arab modernist project in the 1950s and 1960s, which was in many ways quite distinct from its European counterpart. As intellectual historian and literary scholar Yaseen Noorani notes, Arab modernists excoriated the colonial underpinnings and neocolonial conditions of the mid-twentieth century while also critiquing those Arab social values they deemed to be in the service of the status quo. As a result, they developed a literary and artistic aesthetic that stressed visual autonomy and self-sacrifice, viewing the production of creative work itself within the context of revolutionary nationalism.[39] The writings I examine here were certainly influenced by the broader Arab modernist project, but they were not merely derivative of it. Rather, Palestinian intellectuals and cultural producers in Israel made significant contributions to Arab modernism in ways that have not yet been appreciated fully. Darwish and Qasim were but two of a host of writers who contributed to a literary aesthetic that stressed cultural emancipation and pride in their identity and heritage. Understanding the local, regional, and global conditions that gave rise to these texts can therefore shed light on these larger processes of cultural decolonization.

DECOLONIZING CITIZENS

Some readers will be surprised by my positioning of these works within the context of decolonization, arguing that Palestinians in Israel are citizens of a postcolonial state and as such are accorded basic rights—including the right to vote and hold political office—that colonial subjects are typically denied.[40] Some may also object that the individuals I examine here rarely, if ever, referred to themselves explicitly as colonial subjects. Both points are correct. An explicit invocation of colonial subjectivity was beyond the pale of acceptable political discourse in Israel, and not all Palestinian intellectuals were comfortable with the colonial analogy. Some fully accommodated themselves to Zionist narratives, portraying themselves as part of a loyal minority grateful for the benefits bestowed on them by a relatively liberal democratic state. Even those organic intellectuals who saw parallels between their conditions in Israel and those of other colonized populations by and large rejected the prevailing decolonizing logic of the time, which called for armed struggle to achieve national independence in the form of a sovereign state.

However, by introducing the conceptual framework of the "liberal settler" state, historian Shira Robinson calls on us to broaden our understanding of colonialism to account for the fact that modes of liberal thought can and did coexist with colonial practices, as demonstrated by Israel's policies toward its Palestinian citizens.[41] It then follows that we should also embrace a more expansive conceptual framework of decolonization that accounts for the various ways in which marginalized groups sought to make sense of their political, cultural, and material conditions. As the following pages reveal, Palestinian intellectuals in Israel turned frequently to the struggles of decolonization then taking place in the Arab world and beyond to make legible their own conditions and seek out an effective path for improving their lives and their community, even if they did not call for national independence or secession from the Israeli state.[42]

In adopting this broader concept of decolonization, I build on a recent body of scholarship that pushes our understanding of decolonization beyond the grip of national liberation. Drawing on the cosmopolitanism and universalism found in the writings of Négritude cofounders Leopold Senghor and Aimé Césaire, historical anthropologist Gary Wilder calls on scholars of decolonization to "inquire into the range of political forms that were imagined and fashioned" in the postwar era.[43] While these imaginings often included national independence, this was not always the case. Expanding our understanding of decolonization beyond national liberation also accounts for the varied forms of supranational imaginaries, most notably Third Worldism, in which politically engaged peoples living under a range of colonial, semicolonial, and nominally independent legal statuses still considered themselves to be part of a larger struggle for full decolonization.[44] This analytical approach also extends our periodization of the decolonizing era well past the attainment of formal independence to show how the transnational circulation of literary texts from the 1930s through the 1950s impacted the decolonizing discourses of the following decade.[45] Moreover, by attending to the writings of this period, I demonstrate that Palestinian intellectuals spoke back to concepts of decolonization long before the recent emergence of scholarship that foregrounds the settler-colonial paradigm in discussions of Israel-Palestine.[46]

Examining these texts within the context of decolonization also helps us comprehend the evolving debates about what term best describes this community. For decades, the terms "Arab Israelis" and "Arabs in Israel" had been the most common appellations, reflecting both the official Israeli designation of this group as a fully integrated minority and the pan-Arab inclinations of the intellectuals themselves. More recently, growing numbers of Palestinian citizens of Israel have preferred the terms "Palestinians in Israel" and "Palestinian Arabs in Israel,"[47] viewing the term "Arab Israeli" as one that denies their Palestinian national affiliation and functions as a form of settler-colonial erasure.[48] Many of the more nationally conscious intellectuals and activists refer to themselves (and are referred to by other Arabs) as "Palestinians Inside/Inside People" (*Filastiniyun fi'l-dakhil/ahl al-dakhil*) or "48 Arabs/48 Palestinians," both of which refer to those Palestinians living on land inside the Green Line, which became part of the Israeli state in 1948. While the term "Arab Israeli" is still commonly used in Israel, recently scholars have preferred using a combination of these other terms that take into account this group's own subjectivity and outlook.

In short, I argue that despite the double erasure that Palestinians in Israel faced from the Israeli state and the Arab world, intellectuals within this community insisted that they were a part of the global projects of cultural and political decolonization. By shedding light on these overlooked vicissitudes of Palestinian history, I establish the role that the production and circulation of written texts play in developing new political vocabularies that transcend multiple spatial and temporal planes. In doing so, I hope to deprovincialize the Palestinian citizens of Israel and write them back into Palestinian, Arab, and global history.

1 STRATEGIES OF RESISTANCE

Before he was a communist party organizer, an Israeli Knesset member, or a world-renowned novelist, Emile Habibi was a young Palestinian taking in the social, cultural, and political crosscurrents of British Mandate Haifa. Born in 1921 and raised in a Protestant home, Habibi spent his early years in local government schools, where his teachers encouraged the voracious reader to immerse himself in the classics of Arabic poetry and prose, to master the intricacies of Arabic grammar, and to study the Qurʾan to appreciate its linguistic and cultural influences. His older brothers, who labored in Haifa's rapidly expanding railroad and oil industries, used to invite communist coworkers to meet secretly in their family home, familiarizing Habibi with basic Marxist tenets.[1] As a student at Acre's government high school and later at St. Luke's missionary high school in Haifa,[2] Habibi participated in the nationalist anticolonial protests that were part of the 1936–1939 Arab Revolt. After completing high school in 1939, Habibi began working with one of his brothers in an oil refinery and, along with a number of other recent high school graduates from Haifa, joined the Palestine Communist Party (PCP). Habibi was attracted to the PCP's framing of the Arab Revolt as a nationalist, anticolonial struggle that was aimed primarily at the British government, as well as its call for cooperation between Arab and Jewish laborers.[3]

But the ambitious Habibi soon grew restless with manual labor, seeing himself as an intellectual and literary "knight concealed in workman's clothes."[4] Through the Arabic periodicals that came to Palestine from Cairo, Beirut, and beyond, Habibi familiarized himself with an array of intellectual currents. He read about the modernizing, pro-Western Egyptian literary doyens Taha Husayn and ʿAbbas al-ʿAqqad,[5] as well as Russian authors known for their radical outlooks, such as Leo Tolstoy, Anton Chekhov, and Vladimir Mayakovsky, whose works had been available in Arabic translation for decades.[6] As his interest in communist thought grew, Habibi was drawn to Lebanese critics Marun ʿAbbud, Raʾ if Khuri (Raif Khoury), and other contributors to the Beirut-based leftist monthly *al-Tariq* (The path).[7] In 1942 Habibi had an opportunity to engage in more intellectual pursuits when he was hired as a radio host for the Palestine Broadcasting Service (PBS) in Jerusalem. His two-year term nourished his deep interest in Arabic literature and culture, as authors and musicians from Iraq to Egypt came to Palestine to appear on the radio and perform in the social clubs that dotted Palestinian cities.[8] Habibi's solidifying leftist views also led him to criticize Husayn and al-ʿAqqad as espousing outdated views at a time when strong, progressive, anticolonial voices were needed to end European hegemony over Arab lands. When al-ʿAqqad held literary salons in Palestine, Habibi disrupted them and challenged vociferously the elderly Egyptian's conservative positions.[9] Habibi also took to the pen to express his own evolving leftist views.

Habibi's formative experiences during the interwar period suggest several factors that would become central to the social, cultural, and political development among Palestinians in Israel. In particular Habibi's keen interest in a wide array of local and regional cultural works reveals the pivotal role that they played in constructing a nationalist, anticolonial pan-Arab imaginary that called for an end to British rule in Palestine, while simultaneously rejecting the notion that Palestinian Arabs were engaged in an ethno-religious struggle against Jews.[10] After the 1948 war Habibi would continue to insist that colonial domination and "bourgeois nationalism" (by which he meant a deliberate attempt to divide people along ethnic and religious lines to forestall their united, class-based struggle against the bourgeoisie) were the main obstacles to peace and justice in the region.[11]

The magnitude of the changes that occurred in 1948 has often led historians to mark this year as a moment of rupture. Yet viewing 1948 solely as a dividing line in the periodization of Palestinian history can obscure important continuities that spanned that auspicious year.[12] This is especially true in the realms of cultural and intellectual history, where the discourses and strategies that Arabs in Palestine and in the region developed as far back as the late nineteenth century continued despite the dramatic changes to their political circumstances.[13] To make sense of how and why, in the immediate aftermath of the Nakba, Palestinians in Israel with strong leftist and anticolonial orientations were so quick to mobilize within the new state and to reach out to their fellow Arabs beyond it, it is necessary to understand the social, political, cultural, and intellectual milieu in which they were steeped before that fateful year.

A central question that galvanized Palestinian Arabs during the interwar period was how to wrest control of their country from British colonial rulers who, along with the French, had carved up the region and prevented the establishment of an independent, unified Arab state. Many Arab nationalists considered British rule in Palestine to be especially pernicious, as it not only hindered Palestinian Arab political and economic development but also paved the way for the establishment of Zionist settlements that displaced thousands of Palestinian Arabs.[14] Members of the traditional Palestinian Arab leadership, drawn mainly from the landed notable class, initially petitioned the British for more meaningful political representation and a curb on Jewish immigration. When that approach failed, some of these leaders, most famously the mufti Hajj Amin al-Husayni, increasingly framed their struggle in terms of ethno-religious strife between Arabs and Jews who were competing with one another for control over Palestine.[15]

But a number of politically conscious Palestinian Arabs objected to this analysis, arguing that it ignored the central role that British colonialism played in obstructing their development. Stemming mainly from a professional class that included journalists, educators, civil servants, and lawyers, these intellectuals developed an anticolonial discourse that named British rule as the primary obstacle in their quest for independence. Especially notable was the Istiqlal (Independence) Party, which in the 1930s played a pivotal role in mobilizing Palestinians toward nationalist activities that culminated in the general strike of 1936.[16] Although the Istiqlalists were ultimately unable to wrest political power from the grip of the traditional elite, they utilized emergent forms of cultural and political expression to position Palestine and the surrounding Arab countries as being engaged in a collective struggle for independence from British and French colonial rule. This nationalist-anticolonial formulation was subsequently adopted by several Palestinian Arab communist leaders who placed it more firmly within an internationalist framework that carried over into the post-1948 period.

In this chapter I trace the spatial and temporal horizons that shaped members of the Arab intelligentsia in Palestine prior to 1948. In particular, I highlight how the strategies of resistance that they developed during this period impacted the worldviews of three men—Hanna Naqqara, Emile Habibi, and Hanna Abu Hanna—who became central figures in the Israeli Communist Party. Born over the span of sixteen years (1912–1928), they were shaped by the Mandate period in distinct ways. But they were all influenced by several key developments, including (1) the rise of nationalist- and socialist-minded teachers who actively subverted British colonial discourses by emphasizing Palestinian Arab connections to the land of Palestine and to a rich Arab civilizational heritage; (2) the emergence of the local press as a means of mass mobilization that linked Palestinian Arabs to one another and to the region; (3) the spread of politically themed poetry that drew on nationalist and socialist themes to denounce the political elite and celebrate the power of the people; (4) the utilization of social clubs and radio programming to expose a wider array of Palestinian Arabs to local and regional cultural developments as well as contemporary ideological, cultural, and political debates; and (5) a rise in leftist-inflected nationalist discourses that linked Palestinian Arab intellectuals to their counterparts in neighboring countries. A crucial factor that linked all of these developments was the increased production, consumption, and circulation of texts, including newspapers, journals, books, and leaflets, which allowed politically conscious individuals like Naqqara, Habibi, and Abu Hanna to tap into regional and global conversations that had both pedagogical and oppositional purposes.

As a result of these transformations, by the early 1940s all three men had developed a strong belief that their calls for Palestinian liberation must be foregrounded in an anticolonial imaginary that positioned their struggle for independence within broader campaigns for freedom and social justice in the Arab world and beyond. They envisioned a region of socialist-democratic states, including Palestine, in which people of all religions and ethnicities would live in equality. This call, with its overlapping visions of pan-Arab (*qawmi*) nationalism, Palestinian (*watani*) patriotism, and global internationalism, drew on intellectual and cultural leftist formations that had begun to emerge in Egypt and the Levant as early as the late nineteenth century. Although leftist organizations were marginal in Palestinian society overall, their relative strength in Haifa and Nazareth during the 1940s would prove essential to the reconstitution of Palestinian intellectual and cultural life in Israel after 1948.

PALESTINE AND ITS NEIGHBORS

For centuries, Palestine had been an integral, yet distinct, part of the Arab East.[17] Following the Muslim conquests of those areas in the seventh century, successive Umayyad and Abbasid administrations employed the term "Jund Filastin" (District of Palestine[18]) to denote the geographic area extending roughly from the Jordan River in the east to the Mediterranean Sea in the west, and from the Sinai Desert in the south up to a line a few miles north of the modern-day boundaries of the West Bank. Although the administrative use of this term fell out of favor beginning in 1250 CE, its popular usage continued, as seen in historical studies, travelogues, and religious texts from the fifteenth through the twentieth centuries. Not only did these works continue to use the term "Filastin" in ways that corresponded to the old administrative boundaries of Jund Filastin; they also distinguished this land from its neighbors Sham (Damascus/Syria) and Misr (Cairo/Egypt).[19]

Part of this distinctiveness stemmed from Palestine's religious prestige for the three major Abrahamic traditions. Numerous biblical references to Jerusalem, Hebron, Bethlehem, and Nazareth led Jews and Christians to revere the area for centuries, while Qur'anic references to Palestine as a "holy land" and to the environs of the Aqsa Mosque as "blessed" led Muslim writers to develop an extensive body of work dedicated to elucidating the "merits of Jerusalem" and of Palestine more broadly.[20] At the same time, the idea of Jerusalem as the center of the world integrated Palestine into the region. Sitting astride major trade and pilgrimage routes, Palestine saw wayfarers and visitors from across the region and around the world cross into its lands. In addition, numerous social, economic, educational, and religious networks were established in Palestine, tying its inhabitants to neighbors farther afield.

During the nineteenth century, Palestinian Arab society underwent a series of economic, social, and political changes that further integrated it into the surrounding region. As Egypt and the Arab East were incorporated into the European-dominated world economy, regional trade networks linked merchants in Palestine to those in surrounding trading centers such as Cairo, Beirut, and Damascus.[21] Ottoman administrative redistricting in the nineteenth century led the northern areas of Palestine (including Haifa and Nazareth) to be placed under the auspices of the Beirut district (*vilayet*), which facilitated trade, social, and intellectual exchanges between northern Palestine and the international trading hub of Beirut. Technological developments in the late nineteenth century, including the steamship and railroad, further connected the inhabitants of Palestine to those in surrounding areas. Merchants from Syria and Egypt could more easily trade in Palestinian markets, while Muslim pilgrims from North Africa and the Levant visited the Aqsa Mosque in Jerusalem and the Ibrahimi Mosque (Tomb of the Patriarchs) in Hebron on their way to perform the hajj in Mecca.[22] By the turn of the twentieth century, residents of Palestine were intimately tied economically and socially to the surrounding regions, giving them increased access to the emergent cultural and intellectual expressions.

THE NAHDA, ARABISM, AND THE CIRCULATION OF RADICAL SOCIALIST IDEAS

As a broad Arab cultural and intellectual project that emphasized Arab literary and cultural modernization, the *Nahda* (renaissance) ushered in a rise in the reading and writing of texts, especially books, journals, and newspapers, in the late nineteenth century.[23] Several strands of thought emerged from this project: One was a reformist, modernist strand that became associated with Arabism (Arab cultural pride) and later Arab nationalism. It combined German-inspired Romantic nationalism with a positivist outlook and a deep sense of ethnic and linguistic pride to argue that Arabs could regain their former greatness as a world civilization while remaining true to their identity by adopting selectively those aspects of Western civilization, such as scientific and technological advances, from which they could benefit.[24] A second strand emerged among a new middle class of Syrian intellectuals residing mainly in Cairo, Alexandria, and Beirut. They tapped into the emergent global leftist radicalism of the fin de siècle era and adapted socialist, anarchist, and anticolonial discourses to their local context to call for "social justice, workers' rights, mass secular education, and anticlericalism, and more broadly a general challenge to the existing social and political order at home and abroad."[25] Their calls overlapped—and sometimes competed—with those of more nationalist-minded reformers, a split that would continue into the interwar period.

Proponents of both strands of thought took to the press to communicate their message: From 1860 on, Arabic periodicals grew steadily in the urban cultural centers of Istanbul, Cairo, Alexandria, and Beirut, where they eventually made their way to Palestine. The prestigious Cairo-based journals *al-Hilal* (The crescent) and *al-Muqtataf* (The selected) played an especially pivotal role in introducing readers to both the liberal modernist and the radical socialist ideas that were being debated on their pages.[26] By the turn of the twentieth century, these journals and others were delivered to Palestine, and its residents wrote back to the journals, asking questions, responding to queries, and submitting their own essays.[27] To be sure, the number of literate Arabs in Palestine at this time was small,[28] and the number of people who read *al-Hilal* and *al-Muqtataf* was likely minuscule.[29] Nonetheless, the delivery of regional publications to the few libraries in Palestine paved the way for the ideas of both the reform-minded nationalists and the radical socialists to gain a foothold in the country.[30]

In addition, local print media were on the rise, further enhancing the cultural landscape in Palestine. Jerusalem-based publishing houses printed religious texts, translations, and some original works, while publishing houses in Nazareth produced local newspapers and magazines.[31] Palestinian writers were often involved in both the composition and publication of literary reviews, translations of European works, and original pieces of fiction and poetry. Arabic translations of Russian literature were especially popular prior to World War I, in part because two prominent Arab writers of the early twentieth century, Mikhail Nuʿayma (Naimy) and Khalil Baydas, were graduates of the Russian Teacher's College (also known as the Seminary) in Nazareth.[32] This rise in the production and consumption of published texts also corresponded to increasing educational opportunities, as the late Ottoman period saw an expansion of government primary schools;[33] the establishment of two government high schools;[34] the rise of private, Arab-run secondary schools;[35] and a growth in French, Russian, and British missionary schools at the primary and secondary levels.[36] Together these schools educated only a minority of children in Palestine,[37] though this small cohort would become core figures within the emergent print culture of Palestine.

The last decade of the Ottoman Empire was seminal in the rise of Arab nationalist thought in Palestine. The initial euphoria that accompanied the 1908 Ottoman constitutional revolution was soon tempered as Arab supporters grew disenchanted with the centralization policies of the ruling party.[38] In response, local notables and intellectuals intensified their calls for greater Arab autonomy, citing Arabs' shared linguistic and historical ties as justification.[39] The proliferation of newspapers and journals in Palestine, Syria, Lebanon, and Iraq during this period,[40] along with the still-popular press outlets in Egypt,[41] circulated these ideas further. The multiplicity of political orientations in local publications allowed for a broad range of views to be heard, and articles deemed especially salient would be reprinted in other papers, facilitating the circulation of nationalist, socialist, anticolonial, and other political vocabularies throughout the region.

While print runs and literacy rates in Palestine remained low during this period,[42] they do not necessarily tell the whole story. Newspapers often passed through numerous hands and were read aloud in public places such as cafés, allowing the information they contained to reach far beyond the readers themselves.[43] Moreover, the expansion of public and private schools in the late Ottoman period—established mainly in cities and large towns—meant that literacy rates rose much more rapidly in urban than in rural areas.[44] This was particularly true in Haifa, where the high concentration of private and missionary schools would lead the city to become a key site in Palestinian cultural and intellectual activity.[45]

During the final years of the Ottoman Empire, the advent of greater educational opportunities and the growing proliferation of the press helped facilitate the early stages of an imagined community in Palestine.[46] Yet the movement of people and ideas into and out of Palestine also meant that the spatial horizons of this imagined community extended beyond the Ottoman administrative districts of Jerusalem and Beirut. At the same time, as Zionist and British interest in Palestine increased, intellectuals began to pay closer attention to the ways in which the discourses they were hearing from these two groups bore a striking resemblance to colonial discourses heard elsewhere in the region and around the world.

RESPONDING TO ZIONIST AND BRITISH COLONIAL DISCOURSES

Colonial discourse, what Caribbean scholar Asselin Charles defines as "the verbal expression of the West's will and right to power," witnessed a revival in the late nineteenth and early twentieth centuries.[47] These discourses manifested themselves in the Arab world through orientalist tropes that characterized Arabs as backward, unfit to rule over themselves, and in need of a Western savior. Such tropes were used to justify French settler-colonialism in Algeria, the establishment of French protectorates in Morocco and Tunisia, the Italian occupation and colonization of Libya, the British occupation of Egypt and the Sudan, and the establishment of the British Trucial States of the Persian Gulf. In response, Ottoman rulers prior to World War I fought even harder to maintain the empire's rule over their remaining territories of the Arab East.

Zionist leaders and settlers also utilized colonial discourses to justify their project of establishing Jewish settlements in Palestine.[48] The popular Zionist slogan that deemed Palestine "a land without a people for a people without a land" led early settlers to look past the abundance of people actually living in

Palestine (the vast majority of whom were Arab Muslims[49]) and to describe the area as "neglected," "desolate," and "ownerless."[50] When Zionists did acknowledge the presence of Arab inhabitants, they often portrayed them as an ephemeral group that could be given "employment in the transit countries" or "transported from the Palestinian hill country to the Transjordanian plateau."[51] These sentiments corresponded to the second wave of Zionist immigration to Palestine between 1905 and 1914, where increased Zionist land purchases from absentee landlords, coupled with the growing assertiveness of Zionist settlers, led to a sharp rise in the expulsions of Palestinian Arab peasants, particularly as stipulations in sale contracts often required the removal of existing tenants.[52] As peasants resisted their expulsions more and more vociferously, the local and regional press raised their profiles, seeking to draw in Arab intellectuals and political leaders to champion their cause. The 1910 case of the al-Fula tenant farmers points to an early example of the ways in which the regional press could transform an ostensibly local dispute to a regional cause célèbre.[53]

Meanwhile, British policy makers applied colonial discourses that had been developed elsewhere in the empire to the Palestinian context. Colonial administrators, many of whom had served previously in India and/or Egypt, portrayed the native population as being backward, hostile, and unfit to rule themselves.[54] In 1915, Anglo-Zionist activist Herbert Samuel, who would later become Britain's first high commissioner in Palestine, penned a secret report urging the British to endorse the establishment of a Jewish national home in Palestine, arguing it was the best way to protect British colonial interests and facilitate the spread of civilization in the region. Missing in Samuel's report was any acknowledgment of the national aspirations of the Palestinian Arabs, who were not even mentioned by name but were referred to as the "native" or "non-Jewish" population of Palestine.[55] This language made its way into the 1917 Balfour Declaration, in which British foreign secretary Arthur James Balfour formally announced Britain's intention of facilitating the establishment of a "national home for the Jewish people" in Palestine, while according only civil and religious rights to the "non-Jewish communities."[56] Arab nationalists were dismayed by the declaration's denial of their aspirations for sovereignty and denounced it immediately.

After the fall of the Ottoman Empire in 1918, Arab nationalists called for a united, independent Arab state that would encompass most of Greater Syria, including Palestine.[57] Instead, the League of Nations covenant called for communities in the former Ottoman lands to become Class A Mandates, in theory a temporary condition in which they would receive "administrative advice and assistance by a Mandatory until such time as they are able to stand alone."[58] But not all Class A Mandates were created equal: The British Mandates of Iraq and Transjordan (which had been separated from the Palestine Mandate in 1922[59]), with their Hashemite rulers Faysal and ʿAbdallah, respectively, enjoyed the most autonomy, followed by the French Mandates of Syria and Lebanon, which faced additional restrictions. Despite important differences between them, the terms of all these Mandates nonetheless called on the British or French authorities to "take into account the rights, interests and wishes of all the population inhabiting the said territory."[60] However, the terms of the Palestine Mandate incorporated the language of the Balfour Declaration nearly verbatim and therefore did not even pay lip service to the "rights, interests and wishes" of the majority population.[61] In doing so, the Palestine Mandate placed unique encumbrances on the ability of Palestinian Arabs to build institutions that could lay the groundwork for eventual sovereignty.[62]

Even as the Palestinian Arabs' struggle for national independence shared many similarities with those of the surrounding countries, the exceptional terms of their Mandate put them in a remarkably difficult situation. Therefore, they needed to craft a nationalist, anticolonial discourse and a political program that took into account their commonalities with other Arabs while simultaneously facing a rival nationalist group that asserted its own claims over the territory. Over the next two decades, Palestinians developed strategies of resistance that were disseminated through schools, press outlets, poetry, social clubs, and even radio programming, all aimed at countering these colonial discourses. By turning our attention to the impact of these political outlooks on Naqqara, Habibi, and Abu Hanna, we can see how, by the eve of the 1948 war, they each developed a leftist, nationalist, anticolonial stance that was uniquely Palestinian yet intimately tied to the Arab world. We can also gain insight into how they carried these strategies of resistance over into the post-1948 period since they encountered many of the same challenges to their social, political, and economic development that they faced under British rule.

EDUCATING A PALESTINIAN ARAB SUBJECT

With an uneven expansion of government schools, especially in rural areas,[63] the British Mandate period saw the rise of private, "national" secondary schools to compensate for the shortfall and to compete with missionary schools already in place. Consciously seeking to inculcate a sense of national identity within their students, the directors and teachers of these schools played a key role in disseminating an anticolonial discourse that stressed Palestinian patriotism, pan-Arab nationalism, a love of Arabic literature and civilization, and the need to protect their country from Zionist and British encroachment. A key institution in this project was al-Najah national school, founded in Nablus in 1921. Its first director, Muhammad 'Izzat Darwazah, used to gather students every morning before school to sing patriotic songs, and on Tuesdays he gave short lectures on moral, religious, or nationalist themes to middle school students. Older students from al-Najah often took the lead in organizing political demonstrations and strikes against the British, bringing out students from government and missionary schools to join them on the streets.[64] While missionary schools continued to garner a lot of prestige, the growing nationalist sentiment expressed by students in the national schools impacted many of them, occasionally leading to tensions between students and administrators.

Such was the case with Hanna Naqqara, who was born in 1912 to a Greek Orthodox family in the northern Galilean village of al-Rama. Naqqara's father had moved the family to Haifa in 1918, hoping to find work in one of Britain's new industrial projects. He was moderately successful, which allowed the young Naqqara to attend private missionary schools in Haifa, then transfer to the prestigious St. George's School in Jerusalem in 1923. The school was founded by a British Anglican missionary order and seen as a means of cultivating civil servants, and Naqqara's father believed St. George's would provide his son with the training he needed for a stable bureaucratic career.[65]

But it was not to be. In April 1925 students from Jerusalem's government and national schools called for a strike and poured onto the streets of the city to protest the arrival of Arthur Balfour (author of the eponymous and much-reviled declaration) in Palestine to attend the grand opening of Hebrew University. When the protesters reached the gates of St. George's and urged its students to join them, school administrators blocked the entrance and forbade anyone from participating. Naqqara, who was only thirteen at the time, did not yet grasp who Balfour was or why students were protesting his visit. But the incident left a deep impression on him, and for the first time he paid attention to the older students as they discussed Balfour, British colonialism, and Zionist settlement. He also took note of the older St. George's students who defied the administrators and snuck out of school to join the protests.[66]

Dissatisfied with what he felt increasingly was a colonial education, in 1926 Naqqara took the extraordinary step of leaving St. George's against his father's wishes and transferring to the National College in Aley, Lebanon, where its secular, nationalist spirit was more amenable to the young man's emergent political views. With an explicit embrace of the area's four main religious groups (Muslim, Christian, Druze, and Jewish) and a motto that declared, "Religion is for God, and the nation is for all," the National College in Aley attracted budding nationalists from throughout the Arab East. Naqqara's classmates, who hailed from Lebanon, Syria, Jordan, Iraq, and different parts of Palestine, all followed the anticolonial uprisings in their respective countries and organized solidarity activities to demonstrate support for their fellow Arabs. These activities, coupled with the personal friendships Naqqara formed with students from throughout the region, led him to conclude that they were all united in a larger struggle against imperial powers and that they should not consider religious differences as an obstacle to that unity.[67]

Moreover, the school's vice principal and Arabic teacher, leftist writer-critic Marun ʿAbbud, made sure that students appreciated the richness of the Arabic language and literature. ʿAbbud invited Naqqara to join the school's literary club, where members discussed the works of famed classical poets such as al-Mutanabbi and contemporary writers such as al-ʿAqqad.[68] Naqqara took this spirit with him when he graduated on to the nearby American University of Beirut (AUB), itself a center of Arab nationalist activities.[69] But without a scholarship, Naqqara was compelled to transfer a year later to the less expensive University of Damascus, where he continued to be involved in nationalist causes and to nurture his love of Arabic literature until he obtained a law degree in 1933.[70]

Taken together, these glimpses into Naqqara's experiences at St. George's, the National College in Aley, AUB, and the University of Damascus not only illustrate the strong overlap between nation-state patriotism and pan-Arab nationalism that shaped students' outlook at this time. They also indicate the pedagogical impulse of educators to instill in students a deep appreciation of the Arabic textual tradition, which they saw as essential to fostering a nationalist spirit. In the 1920s and 1930s, as several graduates from AUB and other regional universities took up teaching posts in Palestine, this spirit would be introduced to growing numbers of Palestinian students, who themselves eventually formed a generational cohort that was more politically mobilized and textually engaged than their predecessors.

CIRCULATING NATIONALIST HISTORIES

The Palestine Mandate's preamble recognized "the historical connection of the Jewish people with Palestine" as "the grounds for reconstituting their national home in that country," but it offered no such recognition of the historical connection that Palestinian Arabs had to the land.[71] As a wave of Zionist archaeological and historical projects emerged in the early twentieth century asserting ancient Jewish claims over the area as a basis for their national project,[72] Palestinian Arab educators produced works that were aimed at countering these narratives and promoting their own people's rootedness in the territory. Reflecting the overlapping pan-Arab nationalist and Palestinian patriotic spirit prevalent at this time, authors sought to enhance students' pride in Arab culture and civilization while insisting on their specific, long-standing ties to Palestinian land.[73]

A key element of this project was writing and publishing history textbooks. At the outset of the Mandate, most of the textbooks used in Palestine's government and national schools were imported from Egypt (and to a lesser extent from Syria and Lebanon), but they focused mainly on literary topics and paid little attention to history. To fill this gap, several nationalist-minded educators in Palestine wrote textbooks on Arab and Palestinian history that sought to foster pan-Arab nationalist and Palestinian patriotic sentiment. Survey textbooks built on the then-popular "Semitic wave" theory of American orientalist Henry Breasted, who argued that the migrations from the Arabian Peninsula to the lands of Egypt, Iraq, and Greater Syria thousands of years ago tied Arabs together in primordial ways that predated the advent of Islam. They also carried strong anticolonial themes, denouncing the ancient Persians, Byzantines, Crusaders, and western Europeans as imperial hegemons.[74] Textbooks devoted specifically to Palestinian history defined the parameters of the Palestinian state (which corresponded to the borders of Mandate Palestine) and advanced a narrative that insisted on the constant presence of a people who had for centuries called Palestine their home.[75]

Many of the educators who wrote these textbooks were also actively engaged in nationalist political activities, which sometimes led them to clash with their British supervisors. One example is Darwish al-Miqdadi, author of the popular textbooks *History of the Arab Nation* and *Our History through Stories*. An AUB graduate who began his post at the prestigious government Men's Teacher Training College in 1922,[76] Miqdadi urged his students to participate in the 1925 demonstrations protesting Balfour's visit to Palestine, whereupon he was temporarily suspended.[77] One year later, Miqdadi again clashed with

British authorities after he refused to place his Arab Boy Scout troop within the Baden-Powell scouting network, calling the organization "colonialist in spirit."[78] While Miqdadi was one of the more outspoken educators to confront British administrators, he represented a trend that would continue throughout the Mandate period and into the days of Israeli statehood: teachers in government schools who sought to instill an anticolonial spirit in their students that actively subverted the government's civilizing mission.

As the link between educators, students, and political protest expanded in subsequent years, British authorities concluded that they needed to have firmer control over government school curricula. The Education Ordinance of 1933 placed curricular decisions for government schools in the hands of the director of education, who also kept careful watch over the activities of schoolteachers. Shortly thereafter, a new curriculum was introduced that placed Palestinian history within a larger pan-Arab context, though it rejected material that would encourage the formulation of a distinct Palestinian patriotism.[79] Palestinian educators and students accused the British of promoting a policy of "stultification" (*tajhil*) that kept students ignorant of their history and culture.[80] In their view, textbooks that laid out a generalized Arab history were not enough—they needed to be accompanied by a pedagogical sense of purpose aimed at enhancing Palestinians' distinctive identity and ties to the land. In response, several educators penned their own books that highlighted the intimate ties between Palestinian Arabs and specific locales in Palestine.[81] At the heart of these efforts was a recognition by all parties that education, access to specific (and sometimes competing) texts, and growing political awareness were all closely intertwined, especially since students were often at the forefront of nationalist demonstrations. Through the increasing number of student-led protests like the one Naqqara had witnessed, students, graduates, and political organizers pushed to spread their message to an even wider audience.

THE PRESS AND MASS POLITICS

As British rule and Zionist land purchases in Palestine persisted during the 1920s, the traditional Palestinian elites were in a state of paralysis. Their petitions to the British for a meaningful Arab legislative body that would be elected by Palestine's current inhabitants fell on deaf ears; instead, the elites wrangled among themselves over various political appointments that were made (and often manipulated) by the British rulers. Local Arabic newspapers of the early to mid-1920s reflected this factionalism: editors from each paper argued over who was best able to persuade the British of the justness of the Palestinian cause.[82]

The 1929 riots marked a turning point in this state of affairs. After several months of mounting frustration over the rise in evictions of Palestinian Arabs (coverage of which increasingly made its way into the local Arabic press[83]), Zionist provocations at the Western Wall in Jerusalem that August led to a series of clashes between Arabs, Jews, and the British police. British authorities and the Hebrew press focused on instances of brutal Arab attacks on unarmed Jews in Hebron and Safed.[84] Meanwhile, the Arab press highlighted cases of Jewish and British attacks on unarmed Palestinians;[85] they also reported on several local demonstrations that condemned British colonialism and Zionist encroachment but did not end in mob attacks.[86] These demonstrations marked the advent of mass political mobilization in Palestine and a shift in the role of the local Arab newspapers. From 1929 onward, they came to function more explicitly as a means of rallying popular support around a national cause, connecting Palestinian Arabs to one another and to the region, and opposing colonial discourses that characterized Palestinians as lacking any legitimate political grievances.[87]

The Istiqlal Party, formed in 1932, was particularly adept at utilizing the press to mobilize Palestinian Arabs. Seeking to introduce a more explicit anticolonial discourse into the public sphere, the party turned to the press to call for noncooperation with the British, which was modeled closely on Gandhi's program in India. Istiqlal leaders also worked with Arab Boy Scout troops, athletic clubs, peasants, and the growing number of wage laborers in the industrializing cities of Haifa and Jaffa.[88] Together they held a series of demonstrations in 1933 calling for Britain to curtail the spike in Jewish immigration to Palestine, which had led to a sharp rise in Arab unemployment and displacement. The pro-Istiqlal newspaper *al-ʿArab* stressed that protesters had directed their criticisms almost exclusively at British policies, while a British intelligence report noted that "definite orders were given by the leaders that Jews were not to be attacked."[89]

The British authorities viewed the rise of Palestinian Arab mass politics—and the changing tone of the newspapers that accompanied it—with alarm. In January 1933 a Press Ordinance was issued that controlled both the licensing and content of publications in Palestine. The ordinance gave the high commissioner wide-ranging discretionary powers to suspend any newspaper for any period of time if he deemed it likely to "endanger the public peace." The high commissioner also had the power to block the importation of any foreign newspaper that he feared was potentially seditious.[90] Despite the restrictions imposed on journalists and editors by the ordinance, the pivotal role of the press as a means of solidarity building would continue to evolve over the following years.

The press's role in connecting Palestinian Arabs to one another was especially clear during the 1936–1939 Arab Revolt.[91] Newspaper editors not only advertised the call for a general strike in April 1936, but they also participated in it by suspending their publications for two days in a show of solidarity.[92] Two years later, the rebels called for a ban on the red-felt *tarbush* (fez) and for the universal adoption of the *kufiya* (keffiyeh) to make it more difficult for the British to distinguish between *tarbush*-wearing urban men and their *kufiya*-wearing rebel brothers. The papers were so effective in conveying the message that within one week the *tarbush* reportedly disappeared from the streets of Palestinian towns and cities.[93] Despite ongoing low literacy rates and difficulty with access,[94] newspapers nonetheless made otherwise isolated rural villagers feel like they were part of the larger struggle.[95] ʿAli ʿUthman, who in 1936 was a sixteen-year-old resident of the central Palestinian village of Beit Safafa, recalled walking long distances to buy a newspaper and bringing it back to read aloud to his neighbors. They beamed with pride when they heard the name of their village in the context of the revolt.[96] Thus, newspapers served in part to connect otherwise isolated rural Palestinians to the national cause, providing them with a sense of empowerment and allegiance.

The press also played a crucial role in connecting Palestine to other parts of the Arab world. Regional coverage of the revolt, along with reports of solidarity demonstrations in neighboring Arab countries, let politically active Palestinian Arabs know that their actions were being supported by their fellow Arabs, providing a measure of reassurance.[97] The British, too, were aware of this dynamic and tried to blunt the newspapers' impact. On several occasions the government blocked outright the importation of regional papers, citing the 1933 Press Ordinance as justification.[98] In an effort to undermine regional support, government agents planted stories in friendly Damascus- and Beirut-based papers accusing exiled Palestinian Arab leaders of pocketing donations that were being collected in support of the revolt.[99] Throughout the rest of the Mandate period, British authorities used the Press Ordinance (with limited success) to control both content and access in order to undermine support for the revolt. After 1948, Israeli authorities would continue to invoke this ordinance to limit Palestinian access to regional papers.[100]

During the 1930s, the increased stridency of the local and regional press, coupled with its utilization as a means of popular mobilization, helped cultivate a Palestinian public sphere that linked urban and rural populations with their counterparts in surrounding countries.[101] Yet low literacy rates, difficulties with access and circulation, and the rapidly changing events on the ground all gave the reports and political commentary found in newspapers a measure of ephemerality. As a result, some nationally conscious Palestinian Arabs used their literary talents to develop the contours of an anticolonial discourse they hoped could achieve greater permanence, even as the press continued to spread their message to a wider audience.

ADDRESSING THE PEOPLE: EARLY RESISTANCE POETRY

The tone and content of Arabic poetry in Palestine underwent significant shifts during the early twentieth century, reflecting the political urgency of the times. In the aftermath of the 1908 Young Turk Revolution, poets moved away from composing ornate verses that praised rulers and patrons, utilizing instead more direct language aimed at drawing in larger audiences. With the rise of mass politics, Arab poets in Palestine and elsewhere increasingly wrote and recited verses that criticized political leaders and urged people to mobilize toward a brighter future.[102] These themes formed the basis of what would later come to be known as resistance poetry.

Foremost among these early resistance poets in Palestine were Ibrahim Tuqan (1905–1941), Abu Salma ('Abd al-Karim Karmi, 1909–1984), and 'Abd al-Rahim Mahmud (1913–1948). Born less than a decade apart, all three poets were deeply affected by the tumultuous political uprisings of the early to mid-1920s and subsequently became active in nationalist literary and cultural circles. By composing and reciting poems that expressed strong anticolonial views and sharp criticism of the traditional elite, these men played a central role in popularizing poetry that embraced more direct political commentary while retaining elements of elevated Arabic verse.[103]

As Palestinian fears over Zionist settlement increased at the end of the 1920s, Tuqan turned to verse to help his people make sense of the rapidly unfolding events around them. In 1928 he recited a poem at al-Najah's commencement ceremony, where family members, local leaders, and political organizers gathered to celebrate the graduation of some of Palestine's best and brightest Arab students. Tuqan opened his poem with the lines, "Hold back your tears / Cries and wails will not help you. / A nation is being bought and sold." As he spoke of the role that the Arab landowning elite was playing in undermining their national clams, Tuqan also expressed confidence that the youth, the "hope of tomorrow," would join together for the sake of the nation (*watan*) and to safeguard its future.[104] Some of the youth in attendance were so moved by Tuqan's poem that they repeated it to others, while its publication in a local newspaper facilitated its spread even further.[105] Although reciting politically themed poems had been in practice for years, Tuqan's invocation of mass mobilization as the savior of the nation popularized a theme that would become increasingly prominent in Palestinian Arab poetry. Over the years, this combination of oral and textual transmission would also lead Tuqan's poem to become a cultural touchstone for Palestinian Arabs around the country.

Two years later Tuqan returned to al-Najah's commencement ceremony and recited what would become another one of his most famous poems, "Red Tuesday." Palestinians throughout the country had been shaken by the recent hangings of Muhammad Jamjum, Fu'ad Hijazi, and 'Ata al-Zayr by the British authorities for their role in the 1929 uprisings, despite pleas from many quarters that their lives be spared.[106] With the executions taking place amid an enforced media blackout,[107] Tuqan's poem placed the deaths of the three men within a larger narrative of anticolonial resistance, reassuring his audience that the deaths of the three men had not been in vain.[108] Echoes of Tuqan's verses reverberated immediately throughout al-Najah's campus, and nationalist-minded Palestinian Arabs committed his verses to memory. Tuqan's poem also inspired Mahmud, then a student al-Najah, to undertake the writing of political poetry more seriously.[109] Mahmud subsequently become famous in the late 1930s for his poems celebrating Palestinian Arabs who took part in the Arab Revolt—poems that were often published in the local press.[110]

In addition to ascribing meaning to local events, some of the poetry during this period became a means of placing the Palestinian Arabs' collective struggle within a larger spatial and temporal imaginary. In 1937 Abu Salma wrote a scathing attack on the monarchs of Egypt, Jordan, Saudi Arabia, Yemen, and Iraq. They had promised to deliver tangible results to the Palestinian Arabs if the latter suspended their general strike in fall 1936 and allowed the kings to intercede on their behalf with the British. But the monarchs, who relied to varying degrees on the British to secure their thrones, failed to gain any meaningful concessions from the colonial power. Abu Salma began his poem by locating the Palestinians' struggle within an expansive temporal horizon that linked his people's condition to that of exploited peoples throughout history:

"Spread across the flame of the poem / the lament of slaves to slaves / a lament that echoes through time / tomorrow until forever. / They said "kings," but they don't / rule over even a bitter melon." Abu Salma then honed in on the present, devoting the next five stanzas to censures of each Arab king's servility to the British. But he ended with a hopeful nod toward the future, looking to the Arab peoples (*shuʿub*) to liberate the masses from imperial oppressors and their petty rulers.[111] Abu Salma's populist message, with its linkage of the Palestinian Arabs to other exploited peoples, its condemnation of the ruling elite, and its celebration of popular strength, echoed many of the radical, socialist, and anticolonial themes found in fin de siècle cultural works that had been circulated around the world and in Beirut, Cairo, and Alexandria.[112] As a result, the work of Abu Salma in particular served as a bridge that introduced a younger generation of intellectuals to these concepts. They would then elaborate on these themes in the post-1948 period.

Abu Salma did not recite this highly charged poem at a graduation ceremony, or anywhere else. Initially he wrote it anonymously, whereupon it was printed in leaflets and surreptitiously distributed to the rebels and their supporters as a cri de coeur.[113] The poem's anonymity and circulation through leaflets conveyed an aura of universality: Naqqara later recalled (with a bit of rhetorical flourish) that during the revolt, Abu Salma's poem was uttered on "nearly every lip and tongue."[114] This means of distribution reflects the oral and aural impact that followed the poem's initial textual appearance, allowing both the literate and illiterate to take part. Abu Salma's poem also showed other aspiring poets how well-crafted verses that commented on major events of the day could achieve a measure of durability that press commentaries simply could not.

Moreover, popular, politically themed poetry introduced younger Palestinian Arabs to discourses that were missing from their school curriculum. Such was the case with Hanna Abu Hanna, born in 1928 to an Orthodox family in the village of al-Rayna near Nazareth and an elementary school student during the revolt. He recalled his nationalist-minded schoolteachers introducing him to Tuqan's famous poem "Hold Back Your Tears," which had first appeared a decade earlier.[115] But Abu Hanna's Arabic teachers also stressed that poetry was not just about sloganeering: for poems to have a truly lasting effect, they needed to also have a high aesthetic quality. Echoing Nahda-era themes that stressed pride in Arabic language and literature, Abu Hanna's teachers called on students to appreciate classical poetry—and cultural works more broadly—as a means of connecting to and learning from their civilizational heritage. As a student in Nazareth's government high school, Abu Hanna joined the Culture Club, where students and teachers met biweekly to discuss the works of famous Arab cultural figures and to perform original compositions in front of their peers. Abu Hanna won several prizes for his works, nurturing his love for Arabic literature and opening his eyes to its social and political value.[116]

The late 1920s and 1930s witnessed the development of poetry with nationalist and radical socialist messages that excoriated imperialist powers and the servile Arab elite while celebrating populist resistance. These messages were part of a larger oppositional project aimed at condemning British colonial rule, as well as a pedagogical project that sought to inculcate in younger Palestinian Arabs a sense of anticolonial defiance and a deep appreciation of the masters of Arabic letters. Abu Hanna and others of his generation were deeply affected by these projects, which would be elaborated on in the 1940s and carried over into the post-1948 period.

THE FLOURISHING OF INTELLECTUAL LIFE IN THE 1940S

At first glance, World War II would seem to be an inauspicious time for Palestinian intellectual life to flourish. Britain's military planners considered Palestine to be a key strategic base in their war effort, and to that end the colonial government imposed a series of austerity measures that placed disproportionate hardships on the Palestinian social and economic sectors.[117] Political activities were restricted, and the delivery of regional newspapers to Palestine, even to libraries, was frequently disrupted.[118] Despite (and in some ways because of) British wartime measures, cultural and intellectual outlets expanded significantly during this period. This was especially true in the urban centers of Jerusalem, Jaffa, and Haifa and in the Galilean town of Nazareth, where increased access to schooling and print material for city and town dwellers contributed to an overall rise in Palestinian literacy.[119] Examining the growing vibrancy of cultural and intellectual life in these four locales sheds light on how Haifa and Nazareth in particular emerged as bases for Palestinian cultural and intellectual life—and for leftist politics—after 1948.

Throughout the late Ottoman and Mandate periods, Jerusalem and Jaffa had been two of the most important political and intellectual centers in Palestine. Jerusalem's wealth of national, missionary, and government high schools drew in high-achieving students from around the country. Moreover, the Arab College in Jerusalem (one of only two government upper-secondary educational institutions and one of only two teacher training colleges) witnessed a steady growth in the number of students and graduates, especially during the 1940s.[120] Jerusalem was also home to several popular libraries and bookstores that brought regional and European print material to Palestine,[121] while Jaffa held the offices of the two most popular Arabic dailies, *Filastin* and *al-Difaʿ*.[122] For those who could not afford to buy all the material they wished to read, both cities also housed numerous bookshops that offered lending services for a modest fee.[123]

The advent of radio broadcast stations enhanced the reputations of Jerusalem and Jaffa as Palestinian cultural hubs, in part because of their ability to convey textual materials to a broader listening audience. In March 1936 the British authorities launched the PBS in Jerusalem, both to counter what they saw as the anti-British sentiment that dominated the newspapers and to provide (presumably less subversive) cultural and educational programming. Yet the station's first two Arabic subdirectors, nationalist poet Ibrahim Tuqan and former Istiqlal leader ʿAjaj Nuwayhid, steered the Arabic cultural broadcasts toward programs that aimed to instill in their audience a sense of pride in Arab history, civilization, language, and literature.[124] The establishment of the Near East Broadcasting Service (NEBS) in Jaffa in 1942 further boosted that city's reputation as a cultural center, with local and regional writers and musicians coming to Jaffa to perform on NEBS programs.[125] Habibi fondly remembered his experience as a PBS host in Jerusalem (1942–1943) as a time in which he "lived in the midst of litterateurs."[126] Abu Hanna was proud to have participated in the *Student's Corner* program on NEBS, where he and his friends reenacted famous scenes from Arab history on air.[127] Their involvement with the local radio stations introduced them to national and regional cultural and intellectual figures who passed through and familiarized them with the latest literary developments.

At the same time, British backing of these stations meant that only literary and cultural figures sanctioned by the government were invited to appear.[128] Prominent on the PBS guest list were famed Egyptian writers Taha Husayn and al-ʿAqqad,[129] both known for their pro-Western orientation. Writers and critics who espoused strong anticolonial views, including the growing number of leftist intellectuals in Syria and Lebanon, did not appear on these programs. Despite their exclusion from radio broadcasts, the writings of leftist thinkers still managed to reach Palestinian Arabs through the circulation of books and journals that were sold and lent out in bookstores and through the growing number of social clubs emerging in the country.

Social clubs began sprouting up in the Arab East in the late nineteenth century,[130] and by the 1940s, an estimated thirty such clubs had been established in Palestine alone.[131] These clubs served as a place for current and aspiring members of the Palestinian intelligentsia to gather, exchange ideas, and listen to presentations by prominent and up-and-coming thinkers. While a student at the Arab College in the mid-1940s, Abu Hanna would visit one of Jerusalem's most prestigious clubs, the Young Men's Christian Association (YMCA), whose towering building just west of the Old City hosted lectures by famous authors on book tours, along with musical and other cultural performances.[132]

Haifa and Nazareth likewise boasted robust social club scenes. In the 1940s Naqqara and Abu Salma established the Arab Orthodox Club in Haifa where Abu Salma invited writers, artists, and political commentators from Egypt, Lebanon, Syria, and Iraq to address a full hall that often numbered well over a hundred people.[133] Social clubs in Nazareth, like their counterparts in Haifa, arranged for speakers (mainly men, along with a few women[134]) to give lectures that were frequently timed around the anniversaries of major historical events to promote awareness of and pride in Arab culture and civilization. These clubs also served as venues for writers to hold literary salons with their admirers. During his breaks at home from the Arab College, Abu Hanna would attend the Nazareth salons of 'Abd al-Rahim Mahmud, whose participation in the revolt and eloquent verses had earned him a reputation as an inspiring nationalist poet.[135] Abu Hanna and his friends listened intently as Mahmud discussed topics ranging from Arabic literary theories to current political developments. Mahmud's pro-Soviet interpretation of global events provoked even more questions in the college student,[136] and they enhanced Nazareth's reputation as a welcoming place for leftist political expression.

THE EMERGENCE OF LEFTIST DISCOURSES IN PALESTINE

While leftist discourses had been in circulation in the region since the Nahda era,[137] communist organizing emerged in Palestine in 1919, with the largest communist groups coming together in 1923 to form the PCP. The following year, the PCP was recognized by the Third International (Comintern) as the official section in Palestine, securing it greater dominance vis-à-vis rival communist groups.[138] The party's opposition to Zionism as a bourgeois nationalist movement put it at odds with the dominant Zionist Histadrut labor union, yet its overwhelmingly Jewish composition hampered its ability to mobilize among Arab laborers in Haifa and surrounding areas.[139]

Urged by the Comintern to "Arabize" its ranks, in 1925 the PCP offered then-seventeen-year-old Najati Sidqi a scholarship to attend the Communist University of the Toilers of the East (KUTV), becoming the first Levantine Arab to do so.[140] Founded in 1921, the KUTV brought in approximately seven hundred students from more than fifty countries annually for a two-year course of study that included lessons in history, political science, economics, organizing, public speaking, and journalism.[141] During his second year at KUTV, Sidqi was joined by Arab students from Morocco, Algeria, Tunisia, Palestine, and Syria, as well as by an inaugural group of African Americans, all of whom took classes together in the university's English-language program.[142] The multinational composition of the classes, coupled with the Comintern's insistence that celebrating the national cultures of colonized peoples did not contradict proletarian internationalism,[143] led students to explore further the cultural dimensions of their shared anticolonial struggles. KUTV students also honed their journalistic skills by launching newspapers in their national languages: the Arab students launched a wall newspaper titled *al-Hurriya* (Freedom) in 1926 in Moscow, where they formulated a political outlook that positioned both pan-Arab and nation-state nationalisms within a broader internationalist framework.[144]

After returning home, KUTV graduates Sidqi and Khalid Bakdash (who would soon become leader of the Syrian Communist Party) put their journalistic skills to use, writing for newly established literary journals that allowed them to share their views with people in and outside their respective countries.[145] Sidqi had a regular column in the Damascus-based communist journal *al-Tali'a*, where he wrote columns on topics common to nationalist and radical socialist intellectuals of the era, including Darwinism, Arab nationalism, and Abbasid cultural history.[146] In doing so, Sidqi and his comrades developed further Arab anticolonial discourses that presented cultural pride and a strong commitment to economic and social justice as the foundations for a new political order.[147] Although Sidqi quit the PCP in 1939, his subsequent position as the NEBS director of Arabic cultural programming allowed him to convey these ideas to the next generation of Palestinian Arabs, including Abu Hanna and his friends who appeared on the *Students' Corner* program during Sidqi's tenure there.[148]

With the expansion of communist parties in Syria, Lebanon, Iraq, and Egypt during the 1930s, the PCP was able to make some inroads among Palestinian students and laborers.[149] Although the revolt brought Palestinian labor activities to a halt,[150] the PCP's endorsement of it as an anticolonial struggle that need not sow ethno-religious divisions between Arabs and Jews attracted a number of high school students and graduates. Habibi was a member of this cohort, as were his contemporaries Emile Tuma (1919–1985) and Tawfiq Tubi (1922–2011). Tuma and Tubi were from relatively well-to-do Greek Orthodox families in Haifa, and both completed high school at the prestigious Anglican Bishop Gobat School in Jerusalem, where their Arabic literature teacher, the well-known leftist Lebanese writer Raif Khoury introduced them to Marxist thought as part of a strong anticolonial, antifascist, and anti-Nazi orientation.[151] Like Habibi, Tuma and Tubi joined the PCP after graduating from high school (in 1939 and 1940, respectively).[152] Khuri's intellectual imprint would be seen on the writings of all three comrades for decades to come.

This influx of younger, more educated members into the PCP's ranks came just as Palestinian Arab society was starting to recover from Britain's brutal suppression of the revolt and the onset of World War II. During the revolt, British forces killed, injured, jailed, or expelled an estimated 10 percent of the adult male Palestinian Arab population.[153] Communists were not spared: The heightened Anglo-Soviet tensions of the interwar period, coupled with the strong overlap of leftist and anticolonial political orientations, meant that Palestinian Arab leftists who were active in the revolt likewise sought to evade British capture. Several of them went into exile in Iraq, which enjoyed a relatively freer political environment since being granted formal independence in 1932 and which boasted a small but defiant group of communists who welcomed their comrades from Palestine.[154] Anglo-Soviet rapprochement following the Nazi invasion of the Soviet Union in 1941 led Mandate officials to grant a general amnesty to exiled Palestinian Arabs who had participated in the revolt, paving the way for several of them to return.[155] Although the PCP was still not recognized as a legal party, by the early 1940s it had more room to maneuver politically.[156]

But tensions soon surfaced. Arab and Jewish members clashed over the question of cooperation with Labor Zionists, and Arab members disagreed among themselves about the extent to which they should recruit intellectuals and laborers.[157] As the Comintern was dissolved in May 1943 and the PCP was splitting along national lines, Habibi and some of his comrades traveled to Damascus to seek the counsel of Bakdash. The Syrian Communist Party leader advised them to set up an independent Arab organization that did not have an explicitly communist name but still embraced a leftist, nationalist, anticolonial message that could appeal to a wide array of Palestinian Arabs.¹⁵⁸ This advice was modeled on the situation in Syria and Lebanon, where several leftist groups (including but not limited to the communists) coalesced around a shared set of beliefs that emphasized "bread, freedom, independence" and the defeat of fascism. A central figure in that coalition was Tubi and Tuma's former high school teacher Raʿif Khuri, who by this time had cofounded the League against Nazism and Fascism in Syria and Lebanon and had written frequently in the league's journal, *al-Tariq* (of which Habibi was an avid reader).¹⁵⁹ Khuri, who was not a Communist Party member, worked with an array of nationalist, leftist, and labor groups to call for the downfall of fascism, independence from France, and social justice for all. Bakdash suggested Habibi and his colleagues take a similar approach.

THE NATIONAL LIBERATION LEAGUE

Habibi followed Bakdash's advice and, together with Tuma, Tubi, and Fuʾad Nassar,¹⁶⁰ founded the National Liberation League (NLL) in early 1944. The NLL described itself as a "socialist democratic party" seeking the "national liberation of Palestine,"¹⁶¹ and its leaders drew on their connections with left-leaning groups in Palestine to attract laborers, students, and intellectuals.¹⁶² The NLL's message of social justice, workers' rights, and independence resonated with a growing number of Palestinian Arabs. It was particularly strong in Haifa, where railroad companies, oil refineries, and other large firms employed thousands of wage laborers, and in Nazareth, many of whose inhabitants commuted daily to Haifa as part of the city's labor force or worked in the town's small factories and workshops.¹⁶³ Both Haifa and Nazareth also had a robust history of Arab labor organizing that stretched back over a decade.¹⁶⁴

The NLL's rising popularity was also due in large measure to the increased availability of textual material in Arabic and English that introduced members of the Palestinian Arab intelligentsia to leftist and communist ideas. After returning from Iraq in 1943, Nassar resettled in his hometown of Nazareth and opened a small bookshop that carried leftist books and journals he had imported from Iraq and Lebanon. Abu Hanna recalled dropping by the store with a friend while on break from the Arab College, where they listened to a group of older leftists discussing political and philosophical matters as the students perused the shelves. Abu Hanna bought two books and took them home, but then he "found himself facing unfamiliar terms: 'proletariat,' 'dialectical materialism.'" Abu Hanna later recalled that as he struggled to make sense of the texts, he was gradually drawn to the leftist concepts about which he was reading.¹⁶⁵

Meanwhile in Haifa, Bulus Farah, a senior NLL member,[166] opened a bookshop of his own specializing in English-language Soviet and Marxist material that until recently had been banned from entering the country.[167] This proliferation of leftist-oriented texts in the 1940s attracted the attention of a growing number of Palestinian Arab intellectuals who identified broadly with the NLL's message but did not consider themselves to be socialists. This included Naqqara, who by this time was well known as a nationalist-oriented—but politically independent—attorney who had defended Palestinian Arabs accused of rebel activity during the revolt and later represented workers in labor disputes. His close interactions with Arab laborers, coupled with his already strong anticolonial outlook, led him to Farah's bookstore in Haifa. As Naqqara read communist texts and as he spent more time with NLL organizers, he became a league sympathizer.[168] Both Abu Hanna and Naqqara recalled specifically their encounters with leftist texts, coupled with face-to-face conversations with leftist thinkers, as foundational moments in their intellectual development. These dynamics shed light on the interplay between oral and textual engagements as a means by which such discourses were circulated.

To further boost the circulation of these ideas, NLL leaders believed they needed to establish a local newspaper that explicitly linked their struggle for independence with a broader anticolonial, antifascist, socialist message. In May 1944, Nassar, Tuma, and Habibi launched the weekly Arabic newspaper *al-Ittihad* (The union) to communicate the party's views on political and labor matters. They served as editors and contributors, utilizing the paper as a platform to champion workers' rights and criticize "bourgeois nationalist" leadership at the national, regional, and international levels.[169] The paper introduced readers to the basic tenets of Marxist thought, defended the Soviet Union and its policies in the Middle East, condemned fascism and Nazism, and reported on independence movements throughout the world. While readership levels are difficult to gauge during this period, at the very least the establishment of *al-Ittihad* familiarized NLL leaders with the minutiae of running a newspaper and honed their journalistic skills, which they would reprise after 1948.

Seeking to make further inroads in the cultural realm, several NLL figures also worked closely within the nonpartisan League of Arab Intellectuals to relaunch the monthly magazine *al-Ghad* (The morrow) in 1945, transforming it into the NLL's theoretical organ.[170] During its two-year run *al-Ghad* introduced readers to the Marxist "theory of stages" (which prioritized Arab national liberation over the establishment of socialist economic systems) and to episodes in Islamic history that were portrayed as early examples of social justice and national independence. The journal also laid out the tenets of literary socialist realism, publishing poetry and fiction by Palestinian, regional, and international writers that connected "literature to life."[171] This literary approach was given an added boost by Abu Salma and ʿAbd al-Rahim Mahmud, whose poems appeared frequently in the journal.[172]

With regard to Palestine, *al-Ghad* criticized the traditional leadership's refusal to recognize British colonialism—rather than Jewish immigration—as the primary obstacle in their struggle for independence. Rejecting the traditional slogan of "Arab Palestine," the journal called instead for a "democratic Palestinian state" that would guarantee Jewish political rights along with the rights of all people. But *al-Ghad* also criticized the Zionist movement as an extension of British imperialism that sowed divisions between Arabs and Jews, thereby thwarting their efforts to usher in "a just economic order" in Palestine.[173] The NLL's vision of Arab-Jewish brotherhood was very much in keeping with the views expressed in *al-Tariq* and other leftist journals in the region. But this vision would soon be put to the test as NLL leaders witnessed firsthand the traumas and dislocations of the Nakba.

THE ROAD TO ISOLATION

After waves of attacks by Zionist militant groups, in 1947 the British announced they were handing over the "Question of Palestine" to the newly founded United Nations. The UN Special Committee on Palestine (UNSCOP) proposed partitioning the country, which passed in the General Assembly on November 29, 1947.[174] The Partition Plan called for a Jewish state to be established along a coastal strip of land from south of Jaffa up to Acre, with corridors connecting it to a large swath of land around Lake Tiberias in the north and to the Negev Desert in the south. The proposed Arab state would consist of the hilly interior portion of the country, with corridors connecting it to the Galilee in the north and to a coastal strip around Gaza in the south. Jerusalem was to be an international city.

Reactions to the proposed partition of the country could not have been starker. Jewish communities around the world hailed the plan as an important step toward international legitimacy, while Arabs, particularly those in Palestine, received the news with dismay. Even though Palestinian Arabs constituted more than two-thirds of the population, their proposed state comprised only 45 percent of the total area of Mandate Palestine.[175] The Jewish state would comprise more than half the territory, even though Jewish land ownership stood at around 7 percent.[176] In addition, while the proposed Arab state was almost demographically homogeneous, the Jewish state was slated to contain more than five hundred thousand Palestinian Arabs who would either have to live as a minority in the new state or leave.[177]

Soviet support of the UN plan forced the NLL to reassess its previous opposition to partition. The party initially maintained that Palestine should remain "united and undivided in democratic unity,"[178] and *al-Ittihad* published a statement by Bakdash opposing partition.[179] But a few weeks later, under pressure from pro-Soviet NLL leaders (most notably Habibi), the party reversed its position, arguing that while unity was ideal, political circumstances were not ripe for such a solution and that the UN Partition Plan offered the best chance to expel British colonial forces.[180] By endorsing the plan, the NLL also implicitly recognized a future Jewish state, a stance that paved the way for its eventual incorporation into the Israeli political system. But its position was at odds with that of most Arabs in Palestine and in the region who opposed partition, which would later contribute to suspicions about the party's fealty to Arab and Palestinian nationalist causes.

Fighting in Palestine broke out the day after the UN vote. Local Palestinian Arab irregulars defended their towns, villages, and cities as Zionist forces sought to take over, by force if necessary, those parts of the country allocated to them. Fighting intensified in the spring of 1948, and the poorly armed and trained Arab irregulars lost one battle after another to the better-trained and better-equipped Zionist forces. As Haifa, Jaffa, and other cities, towns, and villages fell, and as news of massacres spread,[181] Palestinian Arabs in the line of fire were either directly expelled from their homes or fled in fear. Thousands took refuge with relatives living in quieter areas, sometimes just a few miles away, while thousands more fled or were forced into neighboring Arab countries. By the time Israel declared its independence on May 14, 1948, the number of displaced Palestinians stood between 250,000 and 350,000.[182]

The public outcry in the Arab world over the plight of the Palestinian refugees, coupled with rivalries among the various Arab monarchs and strongmen, led to the deployment of four armies, ostensibly to protect the Palestinians and defeat the newly established Israeli state.[183] But poor training and coordination meant that after a few initial Arab victories in early summer, Israeli forces were able to consolidate their control over the coastal areas and expand into areas that had been allocated to the Arab state. As they did so, they continued to expel Palestinian inhabitants or pressure them to leave.[184] By the time the last armistice agreement was signed in July 1949,[185] more than half of the nearly 1.4 million Arabs living in Palestine had been uprooted from their homes.

Among Haifa's displaced Palestinians were Naqqara and Habibi, who in August 1948 found themselves stranded in Beirut.[186] Habibi soon managed to sneak back into Haifa in the car of a physician who had permission to cross the Israeli-Lebanese front line.[187] Naqqara, who had a wife and two young children in Beirut, took what he thought would be a safer route and bought a plane ticket from Beirut to Haifa.[188] But on landing at Haifa's airport, he and the other Palestinian passengers on board were immediately detained, interrogated, and jailed by the new Israeli authorities on grounds of "infiltration."[189] The seasoned attorney represented the detainees in their demand to be released, even launching a hunger strike to push their cause.[190] When Naqqara was discharged three months later, he returned to his apartment in the German Colony neighborhood of Haifa only to find it had been completely looted by Haganah forces during his absence.[191] The looting was part of a larger Israeli military order to clear out the possessions of the nearly seventy thousand Palestinians who fled or were expelled from the city to make room for incoming Jewish immigrants.[192] In addition, the four to five thousand Palestinians remaining in Haifa's mixed neighborhoods were ordered to relocate to the Wadi Nisnas area on the outskirts of the city.[193] Habibi and Naqqara's experiences of exile, their difficult journeys home, and the ongoing dislocation and dispossession they faced on their return illustrate the pervasiveness of the Nakba and its impact on even those Palestinians who ultimately became citizens of Israel. These shared experiences would lead the two men and others to call for the return of refugees and the restoration of their property rights very shortly after conclusion of the war.[194]

Palestinians who did not face the prospect of exile, such as Abu Hanna, nonetheless also witnessed the refugee crisis firsthand. In 1948 he was a high school teacher in Nazareth, a town whose location in the heart of the proposed Arab state and whose religious significance for Christians worldwide led it to be spared the forced expulsions visited on other Palestinian areas.[195] As a result, throughout 1948 and into 1949, an estimated twenty thousand displaced Palestinians poured into this town of about fifteen thousand residents,[196] hoping for a reprieve from the fighting.[197]

This internal refugee crisis proved to be an important early moment of popular mobilization in which Palestinians in the Galilee who had recently come under Israeli military rule reprised the tactics of protest that they had exercised during the Mandate era. Abu Hanna recalled one day in fall 1948 when the army cordoned off the eastern quarter of Nazareth to identify "infiltrators" (mainly internal refugees[198]) and expel them. A group of left-leaning high school students who were close to Abu Hanna launched a protest march from the town's center to its troubled quarter, calling for the army to leave the inhabitants alone. As students from the local government high school were joined by those from nearby private and missionary schools, their large numbers took the police force by surprise, and, after a brief standoff, the cordon was lifted and the expulsions called off. Protesters, refugees, and residents cheered their victory against the military government, but a few months later all the government high school teachers, including Abu Hanna, received letters of dismissal.[199] As Abu Hanna and other NLL leaders soon concluded, the anticolonial discourses they had developed in opposition to British rule would still be relevant to their daily lives.

CONCLUSION

For Palestinian Arabs prior to 1948, developing discourses and strategies of resistance required a multifaceted approach. Like Arabs in surrounding countries, they pushed back against western colonial and orientalist discourses, but unlike other inhabitants of the Arab East, they also had to contend with a Zionist settler-colonial movement that claimed ancient rights over the land in which they sought independence. As a result, a newly mobilized group of nationalist- and leftist-minded Palestinian Arab intellectuals disseminated an anticolonial discourse rooted in Nahda-era calls for social justice, sovereignty, and pan-Arab cultural pride. As British rule became entrenched in Palestine and as Zionist immigration increased, these intellectuals stressed local ties to the land and opposition to the displacements that resulted from the new settlements. They also developed strategies of resistance that included popular protests and the dissemination of anticolonial discourses orally and textually through schools, books, the press, poetry, social clubs, and radio programs.

By the 1940s, leftist voices were increasingly added to the mix, aided by an expansion of the Palestinian Arab intelligentsia, greater access to textual material about leftist and communist thought, and a more vibrant public sphere in which to discuss these ideas. The NLL, which combined Marxist and Arab nationalist tenets, provided an operational network in which these ideas could be used both to confront the British authorities through direct political action and to raise awareness within the Palestinian Arab community through their publications. While the traditional Palestinian Arab leadership still called for an "Arab Palestine," these intellectuals hoped to see an independent, democratic Palestinian state in which all religious and ethnic groups would enjoy equal rights and freedoms.

The 1948 war dashed those hopes and scattered the Palestinian people. In all the major cities that came under Israeli rule, including Jerusalem, Jaffa, and Haifa, the vast majority of Palestinian residents were systematically forced out. While a small percentage of them managed to return and obtain Israeli citizenship, they continued to experience loss and displacement even after the guns fell silent. But Haifa's post-1948 trajectory differed somewhat from that of other depopulated cities. The composition of Haifa's local Palestinian leadership, which included several NLL members who had recognized the Jewish state, coupled with Israel's reluctance to antagonize the Soviet Union by prosecuting local communist organizers,[200] gave the NLL leaders who remained in or returned to the city a bit more room to maneuver than they might have had otherwise. In addition, Haifa's proximity to the Galilee (and especially to Nazareth), where large numbers of Palestinians remained,[201] would eventually lead the northern coastal city to regain some of its earlier vitality while also contributing to Nazareth's growth as a cultural and political hub.

Under these new and unexpected circumstances, Israeli government officials adopted wholesale many of the colonial laws that British authorities had promulgated. They also continued to deploy Zionist colonial discourses that portrayed Palestinians as either security threats or as in need of the state's uplifting hand. In response, Naqqara, Habibi, Abu Hanna, and many other intellectuals adapted the discourses and strategies of resistance they had helped develop in the Mandate era to their new condition as a Palestinian Arab minority in a self-proclaimed Jewish state.

2 COMPETING NARRATIVES

In August 1950, Haifa attorney Ilyas Kusa (Elias Koussa) submitted a letter to the official Israeli Arabic newspaper, *al-Yawm* (Today), objecting to British journalist Jon Kimche's account of the Palestinians in Israel, which had recently appeared in the *Jerusalem Post*, the English-language daily. Kusa, a Christian Palestinian who had served on Haifa's governing council during the Mandate period and had recently obtained Israeli citizenship,[1] criticized Kimche's condescending tone and his use of the term "suspect minority" to describe the Palestinians who remained. Kusa insisted that the Palestinian minority had nothing to do with the ongoing tensions between Israel and the Arab states and that if Israel persisted in its discriminatory practices against his community merely because of what other Arab leaders did or said, this would amount to collective punishment and a violation of Israel's professed democratic principles. Challenging Kimche to support his allegations, Kusa wrote, "There is not a single piece of evidence that supports the notion that the Arab minority is a threat to the country's peace."[2]

Al-Yawm editor in chief Michael Assaf took umbrage at what he saw as Kusa's denial of reality. A German-trained Jewish orientalist who immigrated to Palestine from Poland in the 1930s, Assaf used his Arabic training to cite several regional newspapers in which Arab political leaders were quoted as threatening the newly founded Jewish state, arguing that this provided incontrovertible proof that "suspect minority" was an apt description. Chastising the offended attorney, Assaf wrote: "[Kusa] must not try to present the past as if it did not happen. All the Arabs of Palestine (and, of course, Mr. Kusa is among them) were opposed to peace with the Jews. [Kusa should not act] as if Hajj Amin [al-

Husayni] wasn't their representative and that the Arabs of Palestine did not cooperate with him in any way to oppress the Jews." While Assaf conceded that there were shortcomings in Israel's treatment of the Palestinians, he called on the minority group to refrain from making hyperbolic claims: "O Arabs: ask for all your rights and defend them. But ask for them with seriousness, with composure, with judiciousness and with patience."[3]

This exchange between Kusa and Assaf highlights one of the central challenges that Palestinian citizens of Israel faced in the immediate aftermath of the Nakba. They were eager to remain on their land and to secure their position within the new state, but much of the Israeli establishment viewed them as a fifth column, arguing that they—along with the rest of the Palestinian Arabs—had opposed the 1947 Partition Plan in overwhelming numbers and had objected to the founding of the Jewish state. Assaf's rejoinder to Kusa reflected the beliefs of many establishment figures that the Palestinians in Israel would have to more forthrightly disavow their connections to the Palestinians and Arabs as a whole if they wished to have their demands taken seriously.

The exchange also reflects the unexpected situation that arose out of the ashes of the 1948 war. The expulsion and flight of some 750,000 Palestinian Arabs meant that the Israeli state was much more demographically homogeneous than Zionist leaders had initially envisioned, but the army's conquest of territory that had been designated as part of the Arab state under the Partition Plan suddenly placed tens of thousands of additional Palestinians under Israeli rule. Eager to secure their territorial gains while maintaining an overwhelming Jewish majority,[4] Israeli leaders debated what to do with the roughly one hundred thousand Palestinians in the newly conquered lands. More than 80 percent of the remaining Palestinians resided in the northern region of the Galilee, while roughly 10 percent were in the central coastal plain stretching from Jaffa to Ramleh, and another 10 percent comprised Bedouins living in the Naqab (Negev) desert in the south.[5] Jordan's 1949 ceding to Israel of the Little Triangle (a strip of land bordering the northern West Bank) placed an additional twenty-eight thousand Palestinians under Israeli rule,[6] while the constant stream of refugees slipping back, especially overland from Lebanon into the Galilee,[7] meant that by the end of 1952 the Palestinian population in Israel rose to an estimated 179,000, the vast majority of whom were concentrated in the north.[8]

Facing international pressure to grant the Palestinian minority equal rights, and facing domestic pressure to minimize the number of Palestinians living in the state, the Israeli government initially launched what it dubbed a "war on infiltration" to try to prevent refugees from returning to their lands.[9] But as thousands of Palestinians persisted in finding ways to get back into the state, the authorities turned to Mandate-era laws to impose a system of military governance that regulated which Palestinians would be allowed to stay in the country and which ones would be forced to leave.[10] In areas with high concentrations of Palestinians—the Galilee in the north, the Triangle and coastal areas in the center, and the Naqab in the south—a military commander was appointed to serve as governor. The military governor was vested with the power to impose a total or partial curfew on any person or area, declare certain areas to be "closed" and therefore off-limits to Palestinians, confiscate privately held property, place individuals under police supervision (forcing them to report to the police station daily), and place individuals under administration detention without trial or charge for an indefinite period of time.[11] This onerous regime, which governed the lives of the vast majority of Palestinian citizens, remained in place officially until 1966. The few Palestinians who lived in the "mixed" cities/towns of Haifa, Acre, Jaffa, and Ramleh were ordered to relocate to designated Arab-only neighborhoods, where they, too, were initially subject to military rule.[12] As a result, the previously expansive spatial horizons of many Palestinian intellectuals and political organizers were largely attenuated as they focused on overcoming their internal isolation from one another and on securing their presence on their land.

For decades scholars have glossed over this period as one of loss and quiescence,[13] though more recent research has uncovered instances of Palestinian collaboration with and active resistance against the new authorities.[14] Historian Leena Dallasheh eschews the collaboration-resistance dichotomy and argues that Palestinians pursued a variety of strategies in response to Israeli colonial policies. Some opted for "reluctant accommodation" while still seeking ways to circumvent Israeli hegemony; others took a stance of "militant confrontation" while still choosing to cooperate at times with state authorities.[15] Conceptualizing a spectrum of accommodationist and confrontationist stances also helps us understand the multiple discursive strategies undertaken by members of the Palestinian intelligentsia to contest their new condition of isolation within Israel.

CONFRONTING AND ACCOMMODATING ISOLATION

With a long history of organizing demonstrations against the Mandate government, Palestinian leftists in Israel once again turned to protests to oppose Israeli policies. But unlike the 1948 demonstrations in Nazareth, which had successfully prevented the Israeli military from expelling refugees who had taken shelter there, subsequent protests were met with considerably more force.[16] In addition, ongoing travel restrictions, along with the threatened and/or actual revocation of highly coveted work permits as punishment for political activity, meant that bringing people together for large-scale protests was, during the earliest years of the state, exceedingly difficult. At the same time, Palestinian intellectuals recognized that the Israeli authorities were deploying a number of colonial discourses to justify their policies of isolation. Therefore, the question of how to deal with the Palestinians' conditions of isolation was embedded within a wider set of discursive contestations with the Israeli state.

The first contestation, as the Kusa-Assaf exchange highlights, was the question of Palestinian loyalty to Israel. Many Palestinian intellectuals initially accommodated themselves to Israeli demands, hoping that once they reassured anxious Israelis about their fidelity to the state, the threat of expulsion would be lifted and their conditions would be eased. But others took a more confrontational stance, rejecting the notion that they needed to ingratiate themselves to the authorities or reject all ties to the region in order to secure their rights within the state. This latter group consisted largely of NLL members and sympathizers who had rejoined the Jewish communists to form the CPI in October 1948. As members of the only legal, non-Zionist political party that gave Arab and Jewish members equal standing, they had a bit more political room in which to maneuver. As a result, they placed the Palestinian struggle for equal rights in a larger context of decolonization, insisting that Israel shun the influence of "Anglo-American imperialism" and join the body of postcolonial states around the world seeking greater political independence.

But these communist intellectuals could not reject Israeli framings altogether, especially given the political suspicions they faced. Moreover, by joining the predominantly Jewish CPI, the party's Palestinian leaders were often forced to take stances that were within the Israeli political consensus but were at odds with those of other Arabs and Palestinians. Most of the latter viewed Israel as a fundamentally illegitimate colonial enterprise in the heart of the Arab nation. Yet Palestinian CPI leaders not only recognized the Israeli state as legitimate but initially fell in line with the party's platform, which in 1952 recognized Israel's expansion into the territories that had been designated as part of the Arab state and opposed "any attempt to raise the question of borders."[17] Moreover, CPI leaders disavowed expressions of pan-Arab (*qawmi*) nationalism, arguing that such rhetoric was counterproductive in an era of servile Arab political leadership. To formulate a cohesive platform that bridged the gap between confrontation and accommodation, they implicitly framed their calls for equal rights in terms of territorial (*watani*) patriotism,[18] which sought to integrate Palestinian citizens into the Israeli body politic while avoiding thorny questions regarding Israel's legitimacy. In doing so, they appealed to Palestinian laborers and left-leaning intellectuals who did not wish to adopt a fully accommodationist stance vis-à-vis the state and were drawn to the strong internationalist viewpoints of the party.[19]

Along with these debates about state-minority relations was a second discursive contestation around the question of Israel's role in facilitating the cultural and intellectual development of its Palestinian citizens. State officials and establishment figures continued to invoke the colonial discourses of the pre-1948 era to claim that the "Arab minority" was a traditional society in need of a modern, Western-oriented outlook that could counteract Arab nationalist or leftist proclivities.[20] Some Palestinians echoed these modernizing discourses on the pages of *al-Yawm* and the monthly journal *al-Mujtamaʿ* (The society), crediting the state either explicitly or implicitly with uplifting the Palestinian minority. But those affiliated with the CPI rejected these modernizing discourses, turning to the party's weekly newspaper *al-Ittihad* and its monthly literary journal, *al-Jadid* (The new) to argue that Arabs already possessed a strong national identity, a rich civilizational legacy, and a modern progressive outlook. Therefore, they argued, there was no need for the Israeli state to introduce them to modernity.

Related to these two contestations was a third one regarding the role of the Israeli state in promoting—or hindering—Arab-Jewish relations. Israeli demands that Palestinians turn away from the region were informed by a Zionist outlook that viewed Arab nationalist and leftist criticisms of Israel as motivated primarily by anti-Jewish hatred. According to this logic, only when Palestinians in Israel rejected completely the hate-filled rhetoric emanating from the Arab world would they live in peace with Jewish Israelis and serve as a model of Arab-Jewish harmony for the region and the world. A few Palestinians who were close to the establishment adopted this logic. But a robust set of critiques came from CPI members—Arab and Jewish alike. They argued that the state's discriminatory practices were the driving force behind the suspicions between Arabs and Jews. They called instead for an intercommunal brotherhood attuned to class struggles that would build progressive, secular societies in their country and around the world. CPI leaders also challenged their physical segregation from one another by organizing Arab-Jewish brotherhood festivals.

Looming large over all these contestations was Iraq: more specifically, the question of what impact that country's writers and intellectuals would have on Palestinians in Israel. Intellectual and political ties between Palestinian and Iraqi leftists stretched back for decades, and in the aftermath of the 1948 war Iraq was home to some of the most pioneering literary figures of the Arab world. Aspiring Palestinian writers—especially poets—were eager to learn more about the innovations of the "free verse" movement in Iraq and the role that poetry was playing in that country's populist mobilizations. While they could not import material directly from Iraq, leftist Iraqi Jewish intellectuals who arrived in Israel as part of the mass migration of Iraqi Jews brought some of these highly coveted works with them.[21] Meanwhile, Iraqi Jews of varying Zionist orientations disseminated official Israeli discourses that stressed the state's role in cultivating positive relations with Palestinian citizens. While both leftist and Zionist Jewish intellectuals shifted to writing in Hebrew beginning in the late 1950s,[22] during these early years they were integral players in these debates.

Taken together, these contestations shed light on both the ruptures and continuities that Palestinians in Israel faced in the immediate post-1948 period. On the one hand, they were suddenly cut off from the majority of their people and isolated politically, socially, culturally, and intellectually. The steady stream of regional newspapers and journals that came to Palestine prior to the outbreak of hostilities was halted, and the vast majority of bookstores and publishing houses that had existed prior to 1948 were closed and/or looted. Bulus Farah recalls that when he returned to his bookstore in central Haifa one month after being forced into the "ghetto" of Wadi Nisnas, he found that his storage room had been "plundered and laid to waste."[23] On the other hand, many Palestinian intellectuals adapted the strategies of resistance (and accommodation) they had developed during the pre-1948 period to criticize their isolation and call for greater integration into the state and the region.

Textual production and consumption continued to play a key role in implementing these strategies. In the absence of direct contact with their Arab counterparts, Palestinian intellectuals focused on expanding their "textual encounters" with the region to bypass the restrictions imposed on them, to connect temporally to the legacy of Nahda- and Mandate-era Arab nationalist and leftist discourses, and to connect spatially to the cultural and intellectual developments that were emerging beyond the increasingly impermeable borders of the state.[24] There was also a clear pedagogical impetus in cultivating these textual encounters, as intellectuals affiliated with the state and with the CPI competed with each other for the hearts and minds of a small but growing number of Palestinian youth who were attending school but who had little to no exposure to the robust Arab intellectual discussions that had flourished in Palestine just a few years before catastrophe befell them. At stake was the question of whether the Palestinians in Israel would become loyal, modern "Arab Israeli" citizens who were grateful to the state that uplifted them, or whether they would become bold and modern Palestinian Arabs who were proud of their rich cultural and civilizational legacy and who saw themselves as part of a global fight against imperialism.

CULTIVATING LOYALTY

Having ruled out the mass expulsion of Palestinian Arabs who remained in Israel after 1949,[25] and with a flood of Arabic-speaking Jews immigrating to Israel,[26] bureaucrats in the Prime Minister's Office of Arab Affairs and in the Histadrut's Department of Arab Affairs looked for ways to induce these communities to turn inward, toward the state, rather than gaze out longingly past the barbed wire. In particular, authorities worried that, left unchecked, regional Arabic media outlets could incite the Palestinian minority,[27] and they could forestall Arab-Jewish immigrants' acclimation to a Hebrew environment. Seeking to "meet the cultural needs of Israel's Arab citizens, as well as give accurate news to Arab listeners in the neighboring countries,"[28] the government launched a two-hour Arabic program on the official Voice of Israel radio station.[29] The programming consisted of Qur'anic recitations, musical performances, light entertainment, and three daily news bulletins that presented national, regional, and international news from an Israeli perspective.[30]

The authorities also scrambled to fill the gap left by the loss of Arabic newspapers in the country. After the fall of Jaffa in May 1948, the editors of the two most popular Arabic dailies, *Filastin* and *al-Difaʿ*, were forced to leave their equipment and newsprint behind as they fled to East Jerusalem.[31] With the major Palestinian Arab newspapers gone, government officials decided to produce their own Arabic newspaper that could present the government's positions and convince Arab readers—both Palestinian and Jewish—to look to the state as a beneficent ruler. To that end, Bechor Shitrit, minister of minorities from May 1948 to June 1949, directed his Department of Information, Culture and Education to launch the daily newspaper *al-Yawm* in October 1948.[32] Having taken over the offices and printing press of *Filastin*,[33] the newly appointed *al-Yawm* editor, Michael Assaf, and his team got to work.

Beginning rather modestly as a two-page tabloid, *al-Yawm* soon grew to four tabloid pages, and it served as the mouthpiece of the ruling Mapai (Mifleget Poʿalei [Eretz] Yisraʾel; Workers' Party of [the Land of] Israel). State employees and teachers had a mandatory subscription, automatically deducted from their paychecks,[34] which boosted the paper's circulation figures and revenue stream.[35] Despite these efforts, by the late 1950s the paper "was treated as a laughingstock by the same intelligentsia that it was supposed to serve and give expression to."[36] Nonetheless, an examination of *al-Yawm*'s early issues reveals how it served as one of the first systematic attempts by the government to convince Palestinian readers that the state of Israel was a force for good in their lives. It also sheds light on how establishment figures viewed the Palestinians overall and what they thought Palestinian citizens wanted from their new government. These officials assumed that touting the material improvements that the Israeli government made for villagers would go a long way toward winning their gratitude, so the paper reported regularly on schools being opened and roads being paved in rural villages.

As the Palestinian refugee issue was being debated in the international community, *al-Yawm* also attempted to convince readers that Palestinian refugees needed to be resettled in the surrounding Arab countries rather than repatriated to their original homes and lands in the state of Israel.[37] Echoing what would become a popular Zionist mantra, *al-Yawm* insisted that Arab losses were due to the shortsighted actions of their leaders, who ordered Palestinians to evacuate so that the Arab armies could march in and destroy the nascent Jewish state. The paper also regularly printed selected news clippings from *Filastin* and *al-Difaʿ* (both of which had resumed publication in East Jerusalem) that reinforced official Israeli views. One boldface headline, reprinted from a 1949 *Filastin* article, declared, "The Return of the Refugees Will Not Solve Their Problem." The author argued that Israel's absorption of large numbers of Jewish refugees meant that Palestinians would not be able to find work even if they returned.[38] By selectively mediating the news and views that Palestinians were allowed to receive, Israeli officials utilized *al-Yawm* to promote the message that Palestinian refugee repatriation was untenable.[39]

But *al-Yawm* also became a vehicle of protest. Since its launch, Palestinians had written to the paper to voice their frustration over a variety of Israeli policies, and some of those letters were published in a section moderated by Assaf called the "Free Platform" (Al-minbar al-hurr). A prevalent source of discontent was the 1950 Absentee Property Law, which allowed a government-appointed custodian of absentee property to confiscate any piece of land whose owner was deemed an "absentee" (i.e., a refugee).[40] Several Palestinians wrote to the paper, after their petitions to the custodian went unanswered, disputing the government's designation of them as absentees when they were in fact present in the state.[41] One petitioner, Nicola Saba, demanded to know why his three properties were confiscated when he had ample documentation proving his ownership and his constant presence in Israel. Presuming government incompetence (rather than malice), Saba asked, "Do the Knesset members know what happens in this office? And if they know, why haven't they taken the necessary steps to improve its administration? Where are the state inspectors?"[42] Saba's letter takes the Israeli state at its word that it seeks to treat all its citizens equally. Saba, Kusa and other members of Palestine's traditional Arab elite framed their appeals to the Israelis in much the same way they had appealed to the British before 1948: by calling on the government to uphold its stated claims of democracy.

Assaf's replies to these letters (and he almost always insisted on having the last word) showed him to believe that printing such letters was itself enough proof of Israel's democratic character, even if the specific complaints were unaddressed.[43] But as more land was confiscated and other demands went unmet, Assaf's responses proved increasingly unpersuasive to those Palestinians who continued to write letters. And as the "Free Platform" section began appearing less frequently,[44] the government's policies were called more forcefully into question by *al-Yawm*'s communist rival.

AGAINST IMPERIALISM

On September 30, 1948, schoolteacher Nimr Murqus read a leaflet that had been secretly placed on his door in Nazareth, despite a military-imposed curfew.[45] It was a joint communiqué signed by the NLL and the communist parties of Iraq, Syria, and Lebanon that proclaimed, "The Palestine war was a direct result of the fierce struggle between England and the United States, who caused the war in order to exploit it to settle accounts between them.... The Palestine war revealed finally and completely the betrayal of the reactionary rulers in the

Arab states and their complete submission to foreign imperialism."[46] Calling for the establishment of an Arab state in Palestine, a return of the refugees to their homes, and the Arab peoples to unite against imperialism and its agents, the statement promised that by working together, and with the support of the Soviet Union, Arabs could achieve independence and democracy.[47]

The communiqué marked the opening bid by communists in and outside Israel to challenge the Israeli state's framing of the conflict in terms of Arab hostility against a peace-loving Jewish state. Drawing on leftist rhetoric espoused during the late Mandate period, they placed the conflict within a broader history of imperialist machinations in which Arab and Israeli state leaders were pawns in a larger global struggle. While the communiqué's content staked out a political platform for party cadres, its distribution to Palestinians in the form of a leaflet was aimed at winning the hearts and minds of a wider range of Palestinians by helping them make sense of the traumatic events they confronted. Murqus, who had received a strong nationalist education in primary school during the 1936–1939 revolt and had been increasingly drawn to Arab leftist writings in the mid-1940s, recalled that after reading the leaflet, "I felt I had received a precious gift" that had "unlocked to me the secret behind the misfortune that had befallen me and my people."[48] Soon thereafter, he joined the party.

By placing the 1948 war in the context of Anglo-American imperialism (an outlook shared with Jewish communists in Israel) the NLL paved the way for its members to be incorporated into the CPI. The NLL's newspaper, *al-Ittihad*, which had been suspended by the British in January 1948, was relaunched as the official Arabic paper of the CPI in October, two weeks prior to *al-Yawm*'s debut. Early issues of the newspaper listed Tawfiq Tubi as the owner and chief editor, though Habibi wrote most of the paper's editorials.[49] As a CPI-sponsored publication,[50] the paper adhered to the party's official platform and did not question the fundamental existence of the Israeli state, but it did express consistent opposition to government policies that discriminated against and isolated the Palestinian minority, destabilized the region, and aligned Israel with Western imperial interests. In contrast to Israel's claims that it sought harmony between Arabs and Jews, *al-Ittihad* argued forcefully that the state's discriminatory policies sowed animosity between the two peoples, which only played into imperialism's hands by isolating Israel further from the region.[51]

But the CPI did not just criticize Israel. In keeping with the party's official positions (and with Arab leftist-nationalist positions before that), *al-Ittihad*'s editorial line criticized the Arab League and the traditional Palestinian leadership as being in the pockets of imperialist forces. The paper was especially critical of Jordanian king ʿAbdallah's annexation of the "Arab part of Palestine" (i.e., the West Bank). It drew on information gleaned from the trickle of regional leftist papers that could enter the country to report on antigovernment protests there,[52] as well as on the conditions of the "Palestinians in the shadow of Anglo-Hashemite occupation."[53] In contrast to *al-Yawm*'s portrayal of the refugees as merely lamenting their sorrowful state, *al-Ittihad* depicted them as actively engaged in a broader struggle against multiple strands of imperial hegemony. Internationally, *al-Ittihad* positioned itself as a champion of the masses worldwide, drawing on wire services and Soviet propaganda to report and comment on anticolonial movements from around the world. Thus, despite the huge ruptures brought about by the events of 1948, *al-Ittihad*'s editors saw this new situation as part of a global struggle that had a long history preceding it. Focusing on these larger dynamics allowed them to criticize vociferously Israel's domestic and international policies while avoiding the rhetorical trap of singling out Israel as illegitimate, which would have resembled too closely the pan-Arab nationalist political line.

Even though *al-Ittihad* did not single out Israel for rebuke, its criticisms of state policy led the paper to face particularly harsh scrutiny from the government. While all major newspapers in Israel (both Hebrew and Arabic) were subject to military censorship, they were also governed by an agreement between the Editors' Committee, composed of the editors of the major daily newspapers and the military authorities. This agreement, known as the "Censorship Accord," gave papers considerable latitude in publishing political news items and commentary. Editors of *al-Ittihad* were not members of the Editors' Committee and were therefore subject to greater restrictions and more punitive treatment for violations.[54] Israeli authorities decided not to revoke *al-Ittihad*'s publishing license (a politically unsavory option given its support from the Soviet Union and its Arab and Jewish membership), but they applied censorship laws more stringently and punished violations more harshly than they did for other papers.[55]

In addition to censoring the paper's content, the authorities also tried to limit *al-Ittihad*'s reach, especially to Palestinians. Military rulers threatened to revoke the work permits of those caught with the newspaper, and they often held up or refused to grant travel permits to party comrades who distributed the paper.[56] CPI members circumvented the restrictions as best they could. Tubi recalled that one party comrade who managed to obtain a travel permit to visit relatives would board the train and drop off a bundle of papers at an intermediary stop, and another comrade would pick up the bundle and distribute the paper in his village. Eventually the military rulers discovered this scheme and put an end to it, though the practice was subsequently revived.[57] During these early years, the villagers of the Triangle area were especially hard to reach: "Reading *al-Ittihad* there," according to Tubi, "was a miracle."[58] Despite the threats, obstacles, and low circulation rates, *al-Ittihad*'s message gradually reached growing numbers of Palestinian citizens, including intellectuals and laborers, the old and—increasingly—the young. After Siham Daoud's father was accused of reading *al-Ittihad* and fired from his job as a field hand on grounds of being a communist, the young Daoud would secretly buy the paper and read it to her father (since he was illiterate). Though she did not fully grasp the concepts she was reading about, like Habibi and Abu Hanna before her, her early exposure to the political vocabularies of resistance and class struggle resonated with her and eventually drew her into political activities,[59] whereupon she became a leading cultural and political figure in her own right.[60]

As *al-Ittihad*'s editorial line censured Israel in ways that echoed its earlier criticisms of the British, the state's attempted suppression of the paper unwittingly reinforced the parallels between the two regimes. The British, too, had censored the content and restricted access to papers deemed to be seditious and had tried to cultivate loyal Arab subjects who would turn away from the nationalist and leftist discourses circulating in the region. The material difficulties under which the CPI operated, including censorship of its newspapers and punitive actions taken against those associated with the party,[61] reinforced the CPI framing of Israel as a lackey of British imperialists. It also contributed to the communists' view that the fall of Palestine was not an isolated event but part of a larger struggle between the forces of imperialism and the forces of progress. And just as that struggle had a political dimension that went back decades, it had a cultural component as well.

BEING MODERN, BECOMING MODERN

While much of the discussion in *al-Yawm* and *al-Ittihad* centered on questions of state-minority relations and regional political developments, there was an underlying cultural debate that built on, and expanded, debates that had been taking place in the region prior to 1948. As the CPI launched *al-Jadid* in November 1953, and Nazarene journalist Michel Haddad founded the nominally independent (but Mapai-funded[62]) monthly cultural journal *al-Mujtamaʿ* in

October 1954,[63] these cultural debates multiplied. While at first glance the literary and cultural content of the publications appear similar—with their essays about Arab cultural and historical figures and samples of local and regional poetry—a closer examination reveals that these journals had fundamentally different answers to a central question that had been animating Arab intellectual debates since the Nahda era. This question was, in the words of intellectual historian Yoav Di-Capua, "Can Arabs have an authentic existence, and is it possible for them to become modern on their own terms?"[64]

For CPI writers, the answer was a resounding yes. Echoing interwar leftist discourses, they argued that the Arab people already possessed a modern, progressive culture that was being shackled by the reactionary forces of imperialism and its cronies. In other words, they argued that the fights for political freedom and cultural emancipation were in fact one and the same. This convergence can be seen in the post-1948 career of Naqqara. He had become a tireless attorney defending Palestinian land rights in Israel, joined the CPI in 1950, and soon assumed a role in its leadership.[65] In 1953 he was also appointed to be *al-Jadid*'s first editor in chief, where he drew on his previous engagements with Arab leftist thought to declare in the journal's inaugural issue: "We, the editors of *al-Jadid*, believe that the people are continuing in their struggle [for justice], that the necessary weapons for this struggle are available, and that literature, like organization, is one of these necessary weapons."[66] Building on the views of his former teacher Marun ʿAbbud, Naqqara called for politically committed literature that accurately reflected the social realities of the downtrodden. By drawing on the rich body of premodern and contemporary Arabic literature to help the masses in their struggle against oppression, Naqqara argued, Arabs could indeed have an authentic and modern existence that would also help them achieve their political goals.

But for establishment writers and their affiliates, the answer to this question of Arabs and modernity was quite different. Reflecting official Israeli narratives, they described Arab society as traditional, even backward, and in need of greater exposure to Western liberal thought to help it become more modern. *Al-Yawm*'s literature page was one means of conveying this message: it published local and regional poems with a Romantic outlook and select essays by liberal thinkers, especially Taha Husayn and ʿAbbas al-ʿAqqad, calling for Arab writers to embrace the modern world and eschew dogmatic (i.e., leftist) political content in their creative productions.[67] Haddad's journal *al-Mujtamaʿ* was another means: the editor in chief's inaugural essay staked out his positivist outlook, describing the journal as "lighting the path for those whose eyes remain veiled by ancient times, so that they may see their society in the light of reality, shake off the dust and fairy tales of the past, and join us on the path of proper culture towards a better society."[68] Both publications depicted an Arab society that was mired in old-fashioned ways of thinking and in need of enlightenment from the elite. While true that the vast majority of Palestinians in Israel in the early 1950s did in fact come from rural, largely traditional, societies, there was no acknowledgment in either publication that there were Palestinians, particularly on the left, who were calling for progressive reforms that celebrated their heritage and incorporated elements of their culture into the modernist project.

Rather, both *al-Yawm* and *al-Mujtamaʿ* positioned the Israeli state as the key conduit for Arab modernity. In January 1955 *al-Mujtamaʿ* published an article on Arab culture in Israel in which schoolteacher ʿAdnan Abu al-Saʿud lamented the widespread ignorance and lack of cooperative spirit among his fellow Arabs. "Today we have become part of Israeli society," he declared. "We must take from this society the advances that have come to it."[69] Abu al-Saʿud's call to adopt Israeli cultural traits (defined as the Ashkenazi elite's socialist practices) neither acknowledged the presence of any modern dimensions of Arab thought nor expressed any concern with the questions of authenticity that were dominant in the region at this time. It is difficult to ascertain whether he was unaware of these questions or simply did not consider them worthy of mention.[70] It is also unclear to what extent Abu al-Saʿud genuinely held the beliefs he espoused and to what extent his essay was a performative act in which he sought to assure the Israeli intelligence officials overseeing the Arab school system of his obeisance to the state.[71]

These contrasting visions for fashioning a modern Arab self were manifested in different ways on the pages of *al-Yawm* and *al-Mujtamaʿ*, on the one hand, and *al-Ittihad* and *al-Jadid*, on the other. Through an examination of their respective writings, we see a discursive contestation that in many ways was a continuation of Mandate-era struggles in Palestine and the region. On one side was a colonial discourse that viewed Palestinians in Israel as having a traditional culture and in need of the Israeli elite's tutelage to help them become proper, modern, Western-oriented citizens. On the other side was an anticolonial discourse that viewed the Palestinians in Israel as already sharing with other Arabs a modern, dynamic culture that was being stifled along with their political rights. Advocates of this latter view called on their readers to turn outward, to see the connection with the broader Arab region and with other colonized people around the world.

EDUCATING ARABS, DEFINING ARABS

As they were during the Mandate period, these debates were often played out in the realm of education. Israeli officials were eager to have their "minority" students identify with the state while maintaining aspects of a (depoliticized) Arab identity. As a result, students were segregated into Jewish and Arab sectors, and teachers hired to work in the Arab schools were chosen more on the basis of their loyalty to the state than their qualifications or abilities in instruction.[72] Moreover, even though Arabic was retained as the language of instruction, the state-mandated curriculum emphasized the great works of Jewish civilization and Jewish ties to the land while minimizing lessons on Arab history, culture, and civilization.[73] That curricular mandate, coupled with an overall lack of quality schooling for Palestinian children, set the stage for schools to become a battleground in debates over state-minority relations, over the role of the state in educating its Palestinian citizens, and more broadly over what it meant to be an Arab in the modern world.

But first, students had to get to school. The Mandate authorities had not kept up with Palestinian demands to establish schools in rural areas, so many of the villages that came under Israeli rule did not have adequate educational facilities. Moreover, the new authorities initially lacked a system that could match the few remaining Palestinian teachers to schools that were in need of them. Nimr Murqus, for example, was repeatedly turned away from teaching posts in 1948–1949, despite his prior teaching experience.[74] The state gradually built and opened schools in villages, and the percentage of Palestinian children attending school eventually rose. But with only about half of Palestinian school-age children in elementary school by the mid-1950s, enrollment rates still lagged far behind those in the Jewish sector.[75]

Israeli authorities (and some Palestinians) alleged that cultural factors—including a traditional educational system that stressed rote memorization and parents who would rather send their children to the fields than to the classroom—were the main culprits.[76] Palestinians across the political spectrum objected vehemently to such explanations, arguing that unlike the Jewish school system, the lack of Israeli investment in the Arab school system accounted for the bulk of the difference.[77] CPI intellectuals further argued that the Israeli state-mandated curriculum was designed to leave Arab students more ignorant, rather than more knowledgeable, of their cultural background, history, and identity.[78]

To fill this gap, they turned to their own Arabic publications, especially *al-Jadid*, to put forth a series of arguments countering what they saw as incorrect and dangerous claims. One contentious debate was about the very definition of who was "an Arab citizen of Israel." Israeli orientalists, who in the prestate period had tried to sow divisions among Palestinians,[79] took up positions in the state bureaucracy after 1948, where they continued to support state policies designed to weaken any unified political opposition from the Arab minority.[80] One such policy was aimed as setting Druze citizens apart from the rest of the Palestinian minority, in part by conscripting them into the army and discouraging them from identifying as Muslims.[81] To help shore up this policy and lend it intellectual weight, some orientalists propagated the claim that the Druze were a unique people, distinct from Arabs and Muslims in both lineage and religious practice.[82]

CPI veterans took to the pages of *al-Jadid* to object to these claims that they saw as isolating the Arab people from one another. Trotskyite theorist Jabra Niqula (Jabra Nicola) in particular challenged Israeli assertions that the Druze were neither Muslim nor Arab but a distinct ethno-religious group. Niqula, who was himself of Christian Orthodox extraction but was quite familiar with the tenets of Islam,[83] picked apart the experts' claims one by one. He argued that just because the Druze prayed in separate houses of worship did not mean that they were outside the purview of Islam, especially since the Druze perform the hajj to Mecca. Moreover, Niqula argued, by trying to determine who was Muslim based on observable acts of worship, Israeli orientalists had overlooked a central Islamic theological principle: "Upholding obligatory acts like prayer, fasting and pilgrimage are not conditions of faith, and it is not permissible to declare anyone who says the declaration of faith [*shahada*] to be an infidel."[84] As for the claim that the Druze were not Arab but "a blend of Persian origin with Kurdish blood, mixed in with the blood of ancient Arab tribes of the Persian Gulf and Arabian Peninsula," Niqula asked sardonically, "How does that differ from any other Arab?" He stressed that the Druze were simply one group of many that make up the rich fabric of the Arab nation (*al-umma al-ʿarabiyya*), a nation whose identity is not based on bloodline but on "a common language, a common land, a common economy, and a common personal composition that manifests itself in a common culture."[85]

By asserting this expansive definition of Muslim and Arab identities, Niqula was positioning his claims within the purview of early twentieth-century Arab nationalist thought.⁸⁶ But more than that, he was also seeking both to resist the internal isolation of the Palestinians in Israel by asserting their shared identity and to overcome their external isolation by emphasizing their connection with the larger Arab nation, despite being physically cut off from it. Moreover, by demonstrating his own knowledge of Arab and Muslim history, and by pointing out subtle theological nuances that Israeli orientalists had apparently missed, he sought to undercut the authority of those experts who claimed the unique ability to define the contours of Palestinian and Arab identity.

"KNOW YOUR HERITAGE"

As part of their project of challenging Israeli orientalist portrayals and instilling a sense of pride in their readers, the editors at *al-Jadid* sought to promote an alternative historical paradigm that promoted an Arab national identity. Between 1953 and 1956 the journal ran twenty-five articles under the heading "Know Your Heritage" (Iʿrif turathak). Each article highlighted a specific historical figure or event from Arab history and offered lessons for contemporary readers. Niqula authored many of the pieces in this section, which included essays on well-known philosophers and writers from the Arab classical period such as Ibn Tufayl, Jahiz, al-Mutanabbi, and al-Maʿarri. Celebrating these prominent figures of Arab civilization allowed Niqula and other contributors to assert a rationalist legacy of Arab-Islamic history that was in keeping with early twentieth-century Arab nationalist narratives.⁸⁷

There was also a clear revolutionary subtext to these essays. Mirroring the theses of Mandate-era Marxist Palestinian thinker Bandali Jawzi, they described episodes of rebellion in early Islamic history from the perspective of those who rebelled against exploitative rulers.⁸⁸ Tuma drew on his previous experience at *al-Ghad* to pen essays that described the revolt against the third caliph, ʿUthman, and the revolts of the Zanj and Qaramites using a Marxist vocabulary that depicted the rebels as avant-garde, egalitarian revolutionaries who turned the tables on corrupt leaders.⁸⁹ Although such interpretations were well outside mainstream Sunni Muslim depictions of these events, they represented a continuation of earlier Arab leftist efforts to secularize Islamic history and assert its relevance in an increasingly restive anticolonial environment.⁹⁰

This effort to blend the themes of class solidarity and Arab pride were most visible in *al-Jadid*'s studies of the modern period, such as its profile of pan-Islamic modernist Jamal al-Din al-Afghani. The journal celebrated the reformer's influence, crediting him with "awakening" the feelings of independence and liberation among the Egyptian people and encouraging them to rise up against their corrupt ruler, Khedive Ismaʿil. Again echoing leftist Mandate-era analyses, the essay portrayed al-Afghani as a closet Marxist and quoted speeches in which al-Afghani called on the peasants to stand up to the elite, eliding his speeches that stressed pan-Islamic solidarity.[91] Such depictions served to not only acquaint a new generation of readers with these figures from recent history but also to tie them to the legacy of early twentieth-century anticolonial thought.

By reviving analyses of premodern and modern history found in Mandate-era Arab discourses, these essays introduced readers to popular leftist theories that posited Arab civilization as having modern resonance and significance. In doing so, they contested both the temporal isolation Palestinians under Israeli rule faced from their own past and their spatial isolation from contemporary leftist intellectual discourses. In keeping with Soviet formulations, these authors avoided drawing direct parallels with their own condition in Israel, which also allowed them to maneuver within the highly circumscribed political atmosphere that existed at this time and still counter Israeli colonial discourses.

In contrast to the revolutionary depictions of Arab history found in *al-Jadid*, the weekly literature page of *al-Yawm* portrayed Arab heritage primarily as a traditional culture that was gradually being influenced by the advent of various modernization (and Westernization) projects. Early essays touched on the lives and works of late nineteenth- and early twentieth-century liberal Islamic thinkers such as Muhammad ʿAbduh, Qasim Amin, and Muhammad Husayn Haikal, presenting them as gradualist, modernizing reformers who sought to improve societies that were mired in tradition and backwardness.[92] Since premodern Arab civilization was not seen as having much relevance in contemporary society, few pieces on classical writers appeared. Those that did, such as the celebration of ninth-century "wine poet" Abu Nuwas,[93] were treated as interesting cultural tidbits with little bearing on modern-day issues. Some contemporary poets from Egypt, Syria, and Iraq made an appearance, mainly expressing Romantic sentiments. Such pieces followed *al-Yawm*'s overall tone, which generally avoided the sense of urgency found on the pages of its communist rival.

Both *al-Yawm* and *al-Jadid* sought to attract readers by running essays on interesting Arab intellectual figures and movements from history, thereby continuing the intellectual debates seen in earlier years. While *al-Yawm* drew on trends in Arab liberal thought to present a positivist view of history that stressed key pro-Western reformers as the exemplars of modernization, *al-Jadid* invoked leftist discourses of the interwar years to argue for the need to understand the revolutionary aspects of their heritage so that Palestinians could be proud of their Arab identity and prepared to engage with contemporary struggles for justice. One such struggle was rapidly unfolding in Iraq.

IRAQ AS A SOURCE OF INSPIRATION

Given the strong connection that Palestinian intellectuals had with regional and global cultural trends prior to 1948, the loss of access to material from the Arab world was particularly severe . Since the end of the war, Israeli government officials had banned Palestinians from importing print material from the Arab world, fearing it to be potentially seditious. But they could not stop access altogether: Palestinians persisted in sneaking issues of regional publications into Israel through various means, such as smuggling books through the Mandelbaum Gate leading to East Jerusalem, which Palestinian Christians could cross once a year during Christmas.[94] In addition, Palestinian teachers at the Kafr Yasif high school who had connections to American Quaker educators in the region could receive Arabic books through the mail, which they would then quietly share with students.[95] Yet such instances provided only a trickle of access compared to what had come into the country before.

An improvement in this situation soon came, thanks to some of the 120,000–130,000 Jewish Iraqi immigrants who came to Israel between 1951 and 1952. Many of the new arrivals were journalists and writers, and they brought with them books and periodicals recently published in Iraq and the Arab world. Some also brought with them a deep knowledge of and engagement with contemporary leftist Arab political and cultural discourses that resonated with Palestinian CPI members.[96] Many Iraqis who had been active in the Communist Party of Iraq and were more comfortable expressing themselves in Arabic than in Hebrew soon found a new home writing for the Arabic publications of the CPI, especially *al-Jadid*.[97] Meanwhile, the persistent belief among most of the Israeli establishment that the state also needed to uplift its benighted Mizrahi citizens was particularly ironic since Iraqi Jews were some of the most educated and polyglot immigrants who arrived in Israel during this period.[98] Given such attitudes, Palestinian and Jewish writers affiliated with the CPI worked together to produce a counterhegemonic discourse closely linked to emergent global and regional trends that presented Arab culture as a dynamic and modern force.

This discourse was especially widespread in the realm of literature. Despite the ongoing prevalence of Romanticism in Arabic literature, Soviet-inspired socialist realism had been gaining steady traction in Arab leftist intellectual circles since the 1940s.[99] The calamities of 1948 accelerated this trend, forcing a wide swath of Arab intellectuals to revisit the value of Romanticism and question the "art-for-art's sake" approach to literature. While the loss of Palestine shook the entire Arab world to its core, it was not the only event that unsettled the region. That year also saw large anticolonial and antielite uprisings by peasants, students, and workers in Egypt, Syria, Lebanon, and especially in Iraq, where communists spearheaded a month-long series of massive anticolonial demonstrations that January. Known as the *Wathba* (leap), protesters gathered on Baghdad's main streets and bridges to denounce both Britain's extended control over their country's affairs and Iraqi rulers' continued acquiescence to foreign control. The police's quelling of the protests was especially brutal: an estimated three hundred to four hundred protesters were killed, while thousands more were rounded up and jailed.[100]

Notable at the Wathba demonstrations was the presence of two Iraqi poets: Muhammad Mahdi al-Jawahiri and Badr Shakir al-Sayyab. They had both been active in communist circles, and they both took it upon themselves to be at the forefront of the demonstrations, reciting verses that moved the crowds to tears and immediately became popular rallying cries. Jawahiri's elegy for his brother, among the first killed in the Wathba, commemorated him as a son of Iraq, verbalized Iraqis' frustration at the ongoing British colonial presence in their country, and reassured them that their sacrifices would not be in vain. Such poems were subsequently published in leftist newspapers in Iraq and elsewhere, further extending the reach of his words. Jawahiri's eloquent verses were quickly committed to memory, becoming an anthem of Iraqi patriotic and anticolonial sentiment.[101]

Jawahiri and Sayyab's participation in the Wathba was not the first case of poets joining political rallies. Palestinians such as Tuqan had been rallying crowds through their verses as far back as the 1920s. But the Iraqi poets represented an early sign of a new trend in Arabic literature: the rise of platform poetry. Unlike earlier poetry that adhered to the strict meter and rhyme schemes of traditional Arabic poetry, platform poetry adopted more direct language, simpler rhyme schemes, and a more pronounced rhythm. These changes were more suitable for delivery on large platforms in front of massive crowds, many of whom were illiterate. Since the primary goal of platform poetry was to imbue the audience with patriotic feelings and stir them to action, poets usually invoked several specific, recurring images. These images included the resistance of the oppressed against the oppressor, the inevitability of the coming revolution, the immortality of the nation, the ground-shaking chants of the people, and the wrath of their anger at the tyrant's injustices.[102] Jawahiri and Sayyab's activism within communist circles familiarized them with the tenets of socialist realism, particularly its insistence that authors depict class struggle in ways that championed the oppressed and always ended on a note of optimistic triumph.[103]

While Jawahiri (the more senior of the two poets) wrote verses in the neoclassical form that still adhered to the metrical and rhythmic conventions of Arabic poetry, Sayyab pioneered what became known as "free verse" poetry (*al-shiʿr al-hurr*). By introducing variable rhyme schemes and line lengths, free verse poetry hued more closely to familiar speech patterns, allowing the poet to create a more direct connection with the audience.[104] Along with Iraqi free verse pioneers Nazik al-Malaʾika and ʿAbd al-Wahhab al-Bayati, they introduced direct, clear, and powerful language that would soar to the heights of popularity in the Arab world—and among Palestinians in Israel.

These trends were part of a larger shift in Arabic literature that came to be known as the advent of "committed literature" (*adab al-iltizam*). Taha Husayn first coined the term in 1947 to describe Jean-Paul Sartre's concept of *littérature engagée*, but Marxist writers quickly adopted it to describe the socialist realist approach to writing that the Soviet Union had been promoting for decades. In the early 1950s, pan-Arab nationalist writers sought to imbue the term with more of the existentialist ideas promoted by Sartre. Beginning in 1953, nationalists and Marxists, as well as conservative and Romantic writers, all found a forum in which to exchange their views: the prestigious Beirut-based literary monthly, *al-Adab* (Literatures). Despite the disagreements between the socialist realist and existentialist proponents of committed literature, they agreed on several basic principles. Above all was the duty of Arab cultural producers to create work that would benefit their society, particularly in the ongoing struggle against imperialism. They also shared a desire to build a modern, Arab progressive society whose members would take pride in their heritage, culture, and civilization.

With Iraq emerging as an epicenter of avant-garde poetic developments in the late 1940s,[105] it was fortuitous that Iraqi Jewish cultural producers arrived in Israel at a time when their Palestinian counterparts were starved for the latest print material from the region. Especially instrumental in this regard was Sasson Somekh. As a teenager he had been attuned to Baghdad's rich cultural and intellectual scene, befriending Iraqi free verse poets Bayati and Sayyab. One of the few books that Somekh managed to take with him when leaving Iraq was a signed copy of Bayati's latest free verse poetry collection.[106] Thanks in part to Somekh's efforts, the work of Bayati and other free verse poets would come to have a profound influence on Palestinian poets in Israel.

BUILDING SOLIDARITY AND DEFIANCE THROUGH VERSE

This new literature from Iraq was just one factor in the development of Palestinian poetry in Israel. Since the Mandate era, leftist intellectuals had championed the socialist realist approach to literature promoted by the Soviet Union. Poets like Abu Salma and ʿAbd al-Rahim Mahmud had promoted an amalgamation of nationalist and leftist themes in the NLL's journal, *al-Ghad*, and they had recited moving poems in front of large crowds. But in the early, uncertain months after the 1948 war, a key requirement of platform poetry—a large audience—was exceedingly rare. Nonetheless, within a month after resuming publication, *al-Ittihad* took up the mantle of promoting such poetry, where it could find it. In November 1948 the paper ran its first poem, a dedication to Russia's October Revolution by Hanna Abu Hanna, who had recited it at Nazareth's Empire Cinema as part of a CPI rally celebrating the thirty-first anniversary of the Soviet Union. Recalling how the czar's palace was destroyed by the people, Abu Hanna triumphantly concluded, "Today we hoist our banner over the highlands."[107] Abu Hanna's style was in keeping with the neoclassical rhyme schemes of early twentieth-century Arabic poetry, while the content mirrored that commonly found in socialist realist works of earlier years. But Abu Hanna's recitation of such a poem so soon after the fall of Nazareth—and more significantly the poem's publication in *al-Ittihad*—signaled a conscious effort on the part of CPI leaders to revive the political and social function of Arabic political poetry to register people's opposition to the ruling elite and give them a sense of hope that their future would be brighter.

This effort at revival can be seen even more clearly in the second poem to run in *al-Ittihad*, a direct a reprint of Abu Salma's famous 1937 poem, "To the Arab Kings." The paper's editors reported that they had received several requests to reprint "the poem that spoke of the people's indignation in 1937 [and] continues today to express that same indignation."[108] With its condemnation of Arab monarchs as lackeys of imperialism and its promise of popular revolution, Abu Salma's poem provided a historical precedent to the CPI's core anti-imperialist message. It is unclear whether or not *al-Ittihad* actually received requests to republish the poem; it is entirely likely that CPI leaders simply took it upon themselves to do so. Yet by introducing the poem in that way, the paper's editors signaled their desire to draw a direct line between the conditions that gave rise to the popular nationalist and anticolonial sentiments during the Arab revolt and the contemporary situation they were facing. Running the poem in its entirety also indicated the early determination of *al-Ittihad*'s editors to reprise the political function of poetry as a means of consciousness raising and political mobilization, despite the devastation brought about by the Nakba.

But *al-Ittihad*'s editors did not just draw on poetry written by Palestinians to rally people. In order to locate their community within the international struggle for justice, they also ran Arabic translations of works by literary figures who had gained global fame in previous decades, in part through their appearance in the Soviet-sponsored bimonthly journal, *International Literature*. The English-language version of the journal, distributed to communist parties around the world, featured pieces by leftist-oriented Black American poets such as Langston Hughes and Countee Cullen, as well as translations of non-anglophone figures, including Russian writers Maxim Gorky and Vladimir Mayakovsky, Chilean poet-diplomat Pablo Neruda, Spanish poet and dramatist Federico García Lorca, and Turkish poet Nâzim Hikmet.[109] *Al-Ittihad*'s Arabic translations of these works, which were a regular feature in the paper, generally ran without commentary. But by simply publishing them, the paper's editors sought to position their readers within a larger progressive movement that extended far beyond the state. They may have also intended for such poems to serve as a model that could inspire readers to compose socialist realist works themselves.

Al-Ittihad adopted a more direct pedagogical approach with its coverage of contemporary Arab literary trends. In March 1950, the paper reprinted Jawahiri's famous elegy to his brother that had rallied Iraqis two years earlier.[110] This and other works by regional Arab poets called on the workers and proletariat of the world, especially those of Asia and Africa, to rise up and overthrow the imperial hegemons. The publication of such works not only sought to inculcate feelings of pro-communist sympathy and pan-Arab solidarity but also to put into practice the CPI's belief that literature should inspire people with a feeling of hopefulness and empowerment. These themes would also appear in the small but growing number of locally produced poems that began appearing on the pages of *al-Ittihad* and *al-Jadid* a few years later.

In a further effort to encourage their readers to create their own revolutionary works in line with those of Iraq, CPI activists offered analyses of contemporary literary trends, especially those coming out of Iraq. One of the earliest such studies was Ibrahim Khayyat's 1951 study of Jawahiri and Sayyab that drew a relationship between the Iraqi poets' growing popularity and their ability to express effectively the pain and hope of their people who are living in a time of crisis. Khayyat, an Iraqi Jewish student at Hebrew University, stressed that a revolutionary poet is aware that "the reason for this distress and this suffering is imperialism, and he is well aware that silence will not resolve his crisis, so he revolts against it and against the silent mediators." He contrasted such figures with "poets of love and passion, of pain and hopelessness, of abandonment and deprivation, who flee from reality." According to Khayyat, Iraqis "scorn" them.[111] While he certainly oversimplified the poetic landscape, Khayyat's emphasis on poetry naming imperialism as the source of people's suffering in order for it to be considered revolutionary was a key distinguishing feature of socialist realism. It, too, would have a significant impact on Palestinian poetry that emerged in Israel within a few years.

By the early 1950s, as the belief in the need for committed literature grew quickly among Arab intellectuals in the region,[112] Palestinian CPI leaders likewise pointed to the need for a more in-depth discussion of literature than could be sustained on the pages of their weekly newspaper. In November 1953, just a few months after the launch of *al-Adab* in Beirut, CPI activists debuted the monthly journal *al-Jadid*, calling for many of the same goals as the Beirut monthly but with a more clearly Marxist-inspired orientation. In his keynote address at a January 1954 conference, convened to discuss *al-Jadid*'s duty to society, Emile Habibi called on the participants to promote "a literature of the people" that would instill in them a conscious awareness of "the essential conflict in society between those who obtain a morsel through the sweat of their brow and the those who steal that morsel." With so much at stake, Habibi argued, "we do not want literature that is floating in the clouds, but rather literature that is one of the weapons of the people's struggle; [a struggle that is] against colonialism and its local cronies and in favor of national liberation, independence and peace."[113] Habibi's vision was very much in keeping with the CPI's strong anticolonial message, as well as the regional and global trends of committed literature. By calling for locally produced literature that both portrayed the hurdles faced by their community and created a sense of solidarity among the working classes around the world, he insisted on linking local and global struggles.

Habibi's call was already being taken up by a younger cohort of Palestinians in Israel who were standing up to the Israeli military and using their literary talents to express anticolonial solidarity. Abu Hanna was part of this cohort, as was his contemporary Tawfiq Zayyad, born in 1929 to a working-class Muslim family in Nazareth. As a student in that town's municipal high school in the 1940s, Zayyad was introduced by his teachers to leftist-nationalist thought and protest, whereupon he began reading *al-Ittihad* and leading student protests against the British. Soon after Nazareth came under Israeli rule, Zayyad revived his community activism. He escorted workers to the military governor's office to demand work permits and organized a sit-in to prevent the military from forcibly removing the displaced villagers who had sought shelter in Nazareth's eastern quarter.[114] In addition to his political work, Zayyad sought to galvanize his community with poems that celebrated regional popular triumphs, such as Iran's 1951 communist-led oil workers' strikes calling for the nationalization of the Anglo-Iranian Oil Company,[115] as well as Egypt's massive protests that same year against the British military presence there.[116] These poems, which reinforced the idea of the masses overthrowing the tyrannical lackeys of Western imperialists, conveyed Zayyad's Marxist political outlook that encouraged Palestinians to join with other workers in Israel and beyond in the struggle for social justice and equality in their respective nations.

In addition, Zayyad's ongoing confrontations with the authorities reinforced the parallels that he and his supporters saw between Israeli rulers and the region's pro-Western counterparts. When he was elected to Nazareth's municipal council in 1954, Zayyad objected to the presence of Nazareth's military chief of police at the council meeting.[117] His stance led to his arrest and torture in the infamous Tiberias prison, where he was hung from the door frame by his wrists and beaten repeatedly by several policemen. According to the testimony of other prisoners who witnessed the event, Zayyad remained defiant throughout the ordeal, even spitting in the face of one of the officers, which provoked another round of beatings. After being held for more than a year, Zayyad was finally tried on charges of disturbing the peace and sentenced to forty days in prison.[118] Zayyad believed that confronting the Israeli state over its treatment of Palestinians went hand in hand with raising awareness about other instances of popular mobilization in the region. In doing so, he sought to instill a sense of empowerment within a community that was largely disempowered by the overwhelming force and exhausting restrictions put in place by the Israeli military regime. Utilizing poetry in this way also allowed Zayyad to build on pre-1948 and contemporary cultural precedents to link the Palestinians in Israel to regional anticolonial struggles.

Zayyad's combination of politics and poetry illustrates one clear answer to the questions regarding the role of the Israeli state in Palestinians' cultural development. Zayyad and other writers affiliated with *al-Ittihad* and *al-Jadid* emphasized a leftist, anticolonial discourse that sought to link Palestinians in Israel to a rich and dynamic Arab literary and political heritage, as well as to contemporary populist mobilizations in the region and the world. For them, poetry was a means of rebelling against the status quo and the structures of oppression they faced. Meanwhile, those affiliated with *al-Yawm* and *al-Mujtamaʿ* framed Arab culture in terms of a Romantic, apolitical literary legacy and promoted a modernizing discourse that credited the state with uplifting its Palestinian citizens. As CPI poet-leaders were increasingly prosecuted by Israel for their defiance, these seemingly theoretical debates quickly gained added urgency. They also became enlivened with the growing involvement of Iraqi Jewish immigrants who brought to the fore their own unique insights to the questions at hand.

BROTHERS AND OTHERS

In addition to questions of loyalty and the role of the state in Palestinians' cultural advancement, a third overlapping site of contestation was the question of whether the Israeli state fostered or undermined positive relationships between Arabs and Jews. Mizrahi intellectuals, particularly from Iraq, played an especially prominent role in these debates: Several figures with a Zionist outlook joined the editorial boards of *al-Yawm* and *al-Mujtamaʿ* to push the state's line that it was the key promoter of intercommunal harmony. Meanwhile, intellectuals who were skeptical of the Zionist project and retained fond memories of their diverse friendships in Iraq and a deep love of progressive Arabic literature, were not as eager to toe the official line.[119] Some of the intellectuals from this latter group wrote for *al-Ittihad* and *al-Jadid*, where they challenged the state's positioning of Arabs and Jews as inherently hostile toward one another and emphasized that friendship between the two groups needed to be based on mutual admiration and respect.

Sasson Somekh again played a pivotal role in this regard and, along with poet David Semah,[120] sought to utilize their growing proficiency in Hebrew to bridge the gap between Arab and Jewish cultures in a way that did not presume the superiority of one over the other. In March 1954, Somekh and Semah wrote a letter to *al-Jadid* in which they proposed:

> to convene a group of friends to be at the core of a literary circle associated with *al-Jadid*, with the goal of bringing us closer to activist Arabic literature

and exposing a set of young people to a socially committed literature.... Our intention is to strengthen the solidarity and camaraderie between the two peoples—Jewish and Arab; and the two literatures—Hebrew and Arabic. This will be done through mutual translation of the two languages and familiarization of the Jewish readership with Arabic literature, and the Arab public with Hebrew literature.[121]

Somekh and Semah's interest in strengthening the ties between socially progressive Jewish writers in Israel and their Palestinian counterparts, coupled with their emphasis on mutual respect and understanding between the two cultures, stood in stark contrast to the one-way transmission of knowledge posited by the state and its affiliated intellectuals.

At the first gathering of Somekh and Semah's group, dubbed the "Friends of Progressive Arabic Literature in Tel Aviv," about a dozen of their writer-friends gathered in June 1954 on Semah's apartment balcony, where they met with *al-Jadid* editor Jabra Niqula and Iraqi Jewish short-story writer Sami Michael, both of whom had come down from Haifa.[122] Together they discussed the need for socially committed literature that could reach people in both communities and the role of language choice in building progressive literature.[123] Niqula appears to have been the only Palestinian at the meeting,[124] though as the most senior member, he more than held his own as he "spoke about the 'principles' of proletarian literature, and about the importance of language, the mother tongue, in the literary act."[125] The positive outcome of that meeting led Somekh to join *al-Jadid*, where he published socialist realist poetry and wrote a column, "Message from Tel Aviv," that familiarized readers with trends in Hebrew culture.[126] His decidedly leftist outlook led him to criticize Zionist cultural productions and to call for greater literary commitment from all writers to foster stronger ties between the communities.

Other Iraqi Jewish CPI-affiliated intellectuals likewise saw Zionism as the main obstacle to the development of friendlier relations between Arabs and Jews. Sami Michael argued that Zionism had thrust many Israelis into an "intellectual crisis" because it had "led them to become self-absorbed and helpless." Michael concluded that this Zionist-induced selfishness prevented them from recognizing the possibilities for mutual respect and cooperation with their Palestinian compatriots.[127] Ibrahim Khayyat took a more historical view, praising early twentieth-century Iraqi poet Maʿruf al-Rusafi, who had called on Muslims, Jews, and Christians to band together as brothers against threats coming from the Ottomans and the British. Khayyat expressed disappointment at the more recent intercommunal violence between Arabs and Jews in Iraq, which he attributed to the anger Iraqis felt as they suffered the wrath of British colonialism—anger they misdirected toward their Jewish brethren.[128] Khayyat was likely referring to the 1941 Farhud, in which Iraqi protests condemning the British takeover of the country following the Rashid Ali al-Kaylani revolt turned into riots and mob attacks that killed 180 Jews (though there were also many instances of Muslim Iraqis protecting their Jewish neighbors).[129] Both Michael and Khayyat sought to counter the official Israeli narrative that positioned Arabs as inherently hostile toward Jews; instead they argued that by aligning with imperialist forces and shunning progressive ones, the state's Zionist ideologues were the main impediment to Arabs and Jews working together for peace and justice.

While Iraqi Jewish intellectuals writing for CPI's publications stressed a progressive, anticolonial, class-based global solidarity as the foundation for brotherhood between Arabs and Jews, those associated with *al-Yawm* and *al-Mujtamaʿ* framed their calls for brotherhood as being best achieved under auspices of the state. Salim Shaʿshuʿ, an Iraqi Jewish poet-journalist,[130] was particularly emphatic in calling on Palestinians to view the state as the purveyor of positive interactions between Arabs and Jews.[131] The first issue of *Al-Mujtamaʿ* showcased a friendly exchange of letters between Shaʿshuʿ and the journal's general secretary, Palestinian poet and teacher Jamal Qaʿwar, that stressed the importance of printing such letters to "bring together differing viewpoints" and to build a more peaceful society.[132] This framing of intercommunal brotherhood refrained from discussing the structures of oppression that had an adverse effect on the Palestinian. According to this view, the tensions between Palestinians and Jews in Israel were due to cultural misunderstandings, and simply recognizing the goodwill of people on both sides would create a more peaceful society.

In early 1955 both the CPI and establishment figures tried to promote their respective views of intercommunal brotherhood through festivals. In February the CPI branches in Jerusalem, Tel Aviv, and Haifa joined regional communist activists who reportedly held rallies in Nablus, Amman, Cairo, Baghdad, and Basra, all calling for "peace between the Arab region and Israel" based on a shared belief in social justice.[133] The branch activists followed up the effort one month later, when Jewish CPI members were welcomed by Palestinians in the Galilean villages of ʿIbillin and Tamra, where they broke bread and shared in traditional Arab and Jewish line dances (the *dabka* and *hora*). In ʿIbillin a local folk troupe sang a song in colloquial Arabic composed for the occasion: "Our friendship is blessed / through our joint *dabka* / . . . / Long live the unity of the two peoples / and the peoples of the world. / Marching toward serenity / to reach our happiness."[134] At a Tel Aviv brotherhood festival in April, featured speaker Abu Hanna asserted that Arab-Jewish coexistence had existed throughout history, and he presented examples of great literature in both cultures to show their compatibility."[135] *Al-Jadid*'s full coverage of the brotherhood festivals, complete with photos (a rarity at this time), coupled with its endorsement of the Friends of Progressive Arabic Literature in Tel Aviv,[136] illustrate the journal's efforts to position brotherhood between Arabs and Jews as the natural sentiment between the two peoples, a sentiment disrupted by bourgeois nationalists who sought to divide and segregate them.

While poetic performances were a central feature of these gatherings, they were generally peripheral within the larger program. Seeking to promote poetry in a more systematic way, in March 1955 Haddad founded the League of Arabic Poets (Rabitat Shuʿaraʾ al-ʿArabiyya),[137] headed by himself and Shaʿshuʿ and comprising two Iraqi Jewish teachers, six Palestinian teachers, five high school students, and a journalist.[138] The league called for many of the same goals as those promoted by the Friends of Progressive Literature and the CPI. They, too, argued that boosting Arabic literary production in Israel was an excellent means to promote friendship between the two peoples. But Haddad's generally cautious approach to political matters, combined with the strong Zionist outlook of Shaʿshuʿ, led the league to ally with the Histadrut, which led to the exclusion of leftist poets such as Abu Hanna and Zayyad.[139] This attempt to steer local Arabic poetry toward a state-sanctioned understanding of friendship between Arabs and Jews soon caused dissent within the league, especially as members with leftist sympathies found themselves excluded from the league's first literary festival in May. The festival featured a dozen Palestinian and Iraqi Jewish speakers who showcased Romantic-style poetry and presented their views about the positive role intellectuals could play in improving relations between Arabs and Jews in Israel and beyond.[140] But the festival had a strong whiff of government interference around it: In addition to excluding CPI-affiliated poets, festival planners disinvited league member ʿIsa Lubani because he had campaigned with the communists at a recent teachers' union election,[141] and they insisted that ʿIsam al-ʿAbbasi, journalist and league member,[142] could recite only Romantic poetry.[143] The league's insistence that promoting intercommunal brotherhood necessitated avoiding any criticism of the state struck many of its members as too restrictive; as a result, despite the league's promise to serve as the first outlet in Israel dedicated to bringing Palestinians and Jews in Israel together through their shared love of poetry, the debacle led most of the league's Palestinian members to look elsewhere for a literary and intellectual home.

As occurred in other discursive contestations under way at this time, communist and establishment figures had very different views regarding the basis on which friendship, solidarity, and humanism between Arabs and Jews should be formed. For the CPI, Arabs and Jews must look beyond the suffocating Zionist ideology of the state and seek inspiration from the long historical legacy of intercommunal brotherhood in the Arab world to chart a path toward a more democratic future. Establishment writers viewed positively official Israeli efforts to inculcate a sense of brotherhood between Arabs and Jews and therefore saw no need to look beyond the state for inspiration. As the CPI and establishment figures set up organizations to put their ideas into practice, they turned to the promotion of Arabic literature—especially poetry—to attract the growing number of young intellectuals to their respective sides. But they would soon find that many of the younger intellectuals had their own ideas about how to promote Arab intellectual and cultural life in the country.

CONCLUSION

With Palestinians in Israel cut off from the region, and with their movements restricted within the state, intellectuals and political organizers turned to textual productions to raise consciousness within their own community and to contest the state's isolating policies. But Israeli authorities were also eager to cultivate an "Arab Israeli" subject who turned inward, toward the state, and rejected the region's nationalist and leftist discourses. As a result, by 1955 two competing narratives came to dominate the Arab public sphere in Israel. One narrative, propagated by the government and establishment figures, stressed the need for Palestinian citizens to look to the state for the betterment of their society. Echoing colonial discourses of the pre-1948 period, they demanded that Palestinians demonstrate their gratitude for the slow but steady improvement in their lives and that they disavow communists and Arab nationalists, who were portrayed as undermining Arab-Jewish harmony. Some Palestinian intellectuals adopted various accommodationist stances toward this framing, and they turned to the establishment publications such as *al-Yawm* and *al-*

Mujtamaʿ to reassure anxious Israelis of their loyalty, to press Israel to live up to its stated democratic ideals, and sometimes to subtly question Zionist narratives by pointing to the ongoing difficulties that Palestinians in Israel faced.

The second narrative, disseminated primarily by CPI-affiliated intellectuals, drew on the legacy of Arab leftist discourses to adopt a more confrontationist stance that pushed back against these Israeli demands. While not questioning the legitimacy of the state itself, they nonetheless placed the onus on Israel to disavow its ties to Anglo-American imperialist forces, and they emphasized the need to look beyond the borders of the state for cultural and intellectual nourishment. Drawing on tropes popularized in the interwar period by Arab nationalists, as well as by socialist realist ideologies propagated by the Soviet Union, they stressed that their community was part of a global struggle for social justice, decolonization, and national pride. Only when these goals were achieved could Arabs and Jews in Israel live together harmoniously without fear that imperial powers would divide and conquer them.

The press continued to be a key medium in the dissemination of these competing narratives as rival Arabic newspapers and journals sought to win the hearts and minds of the Palestinian community in Israel. Poetry, whether on the pages of the local press or at the smattering of local festivals that were held, gradually began to reappear. While much of the official cultural production in the country was overseen by the establishment, whether through the literature page of *al-Yawm* or at the festivals sponsored by the League of Arabic Poets, the CPI's newspaper *al-Ittihad* and its journal *al-Jadid* quickly emerged as key venues for the promotion of a Palestinian counternarrative. Despite the heavy censorship and harassment of the authorities, these publications would gather support—and expand their readership—in the coming years.

Given this multifaceted environment, it would be oversimplistic to view the Palestinian intellectuals in terms of static confrontationist-versus-accommodationist camps. As frustrations mounted over Palestinians' unmet needs, some who had initially adopted an accommodating stance toward the state became more confrontational. Attorney Kusa, for example, grew increasingly vociferous in his criticisms of Israel, eventually leading the military government to disbar him.[144] Other intellectuals continued to maneuver as best they could given the difficult circumstances they faced. Qaʿwar, a poet and schoolteacher employed by the Ministry of Education who had participated in several Histadrut-sponsored literary events, nonetheless refrained from writing poetry that was obsequious to the state and described in poignant detail the anguish his community faced.[145] Some Palestinians saw Qaʿwar's stance as being necessitated by his position as a schoolteacher, since government employees were seen as having "a sword of terror constantly hanging over their heads."[146] Meanwhile, intellectuals with leftist sympathies, like al-ʿAbbasi and Lubani, were nonetheless willing to give an establishment-affiliated group like the League of Arabic Poets a chance, perhaps in the hope that their shared interest in promoting Arabic poetry could overcome their different political stances. Although they would break from the league the following year, their early willingness to work within it highlights the fluid positions that several Palestinian intellectuals had at this time.

In the coming years, the rise of an Arab revolutionary spirit and the call for Third World solidarity would reinvigorate the spatial and temporal imaginaries of Palestinian intellectuals in Israel. As they became embroiled in the region's political and cultural debates, they looked for ways to speak back to their Arab counterparts, even as they faced ongoing isolation within the state and (they would soon learn) profound misunderstandings from the very people with whom they wished to connect. And as the Israeli state became more anxious to stem the tide of anticolonial sentiment among an increasingly restive minority, Palestinian intellectuals would have to once again adapt their strategies of resistance to address the rapidly changing environment they faced.

3 DEBATES ON DECOLONIZATION

On the morning of May 1, 1958, hundreds of demonstrators converged on the streets of Nazareth to take part in the CPI's annual May Day demonstration. Party organizers led marchers in a call and response demanding an end to the military government and its policies of land confiscation and "national discrimination" (*al-itdihad al-qawmi*).[1] Two protesters hoisted a large banner that read in Arabic, "Victory for the Algerian people's struggle against French brutality!"[2] As a sign of things to come, some participants added a chant that was popular throughout the Arab world but was studiously avoided by CPI leaders: "Long live Abdel Nasser!"[3]

The May Day rally came at a time when Arabs throughout the Middle East viewed the ascendency of Egyptian president Gamal Abdel Nasser and the Algerian war of independence as signs of hope for a brighter future. But Israeli authorities worried that Palestinian citizens might be inspired to adopt their own insurrection against the state, shattering Israel's carefully crafted self-image as an enlightened democracy with a content Arab minority.[4] In a departure from previous years, the Galilee's military governor denied the CPI's request to hold a May Day rally that morning because, he claimed, "This year there was a different atmosphere."[5] Anticipating the CPI's defiance, Israeli military police fanned out across Nazareth the night before the rally, arrested CPI leaders, barred hundreds of Palestinians from surrounding villages from entering the town, and stood in riot gear along the city's main thoroughfare to ensure that the two authorized processions—those of the Histadrut and Mapam—would pass through without incident. The heavy-handed security presence led to clashes between rock-throwing youth and the military police, and later that day between police and CPI demonstrators.[6] Dozens of Palestinians and a few policemen were injured, and more than three hundred protesters were arrested.[7]

The Nazareth clashes drew international attention to the presence of Palestinian discontent in the Jewish state, although interpretations of what happened that day differed sharply. Israeli officials and sympathetic Western journalists portrayed the incident as the result of a few communist agitators seeking to undermine the camaraderie that existed between Arabs and Jews in the state by importing venomous attitudes from abroad.[8] Arab news outlets, including the popular *Voice of the Arabs* radio broadcast from Cairo, presented the clashes as an undeniable example of Israeli brutality against the Arab minority that was akin to the brutality of other colonial regimes against native populations.[9] As different as these claims were, both portrayed the Palestinians as passive victims of larger regional forces. But they overlooked the ways that this community was actively engaged with the overlapping Palestinian, Arab, and Third World anticolonial discourses and struggles. Palestinian intellectuals inside the Green Line certainly emphasized the interconnectivity of these causes. As one commentator declared, "With their steadfastness [*sumud*] in the face of this assault, the Nazarenes have done a great service for the cause of their Palestinian people and for the cause of freedom and peace in the region."[10]

Outside observers also missed the ways in which both the Palestinians and the Israeli authorities regarded cultural production—especially poetry—as an important political tool. When journalist-poet ʿIsam al-ʿAbbasi was denied permission to enter Nazareth and recite his poem at the CPI rally, *al-Ittihad* published it the next day on its front page, triumphantly declaring that even though the authorities prevented al-ʿAbbasi from reaching the demonstration, "they cannot prevent [his] poem from reaching the workers of Nazareth and the Galilee." The poem's opening lines, "Arabism flows through the workers of Nazareth / And the chants of their processions are strong," illustrated al-ʿAbbasi's desire to locate his community's protest within the wider Arab revolutionary trends.[11] Its invocation of "Arabism" (*ʿuruba*) also signaled the ascendency of pan-Arab nationalism in a community where communist internationalism had been the dominant mode of oppositional discourse.

In the late 1950s Egypt's stand at Suez, Algeria's war of independence, the formation of the United Arab Republic, and Iraq's overthrow of its pro-Western monarchy appeared to signal the end of colonial rule in the region. Yet Palestinian citizens continued to face a host of discriminatory Israeli policies. The juxtaposition between the signs of hope from abroad and the suffocation they felt at home led intellectuals in particular to look for ways to more emphatically position themselves as part of the wider anticolonial struggle for dignity and justice. Veteran organizers, intellectuals, and cultural agents were joined by a younger generation of intellectuals entering the scene. Born between the mid-1930s and the early 1940s, this younger cohort generally came into political awareness during the 1948 Nakba and spent their teenage years under Israeli rule. Hailing primarily from rural backgrounds and educated under the watchful eye of the authorities, they were intimately aware of the difficulties that farmers, refugees, students, and others in their community faced.

As these younger intellectuals grew impatient with the restrictions of military rule, they worked with their older counterparts to adapt previous strategies of resistance to this increasingly restive environment. Reflecting the spirit of cooperation between communists and nationalists in the Arab world at this time, they formed nonpartisan organizations that could speak with a single voice against the ongoing military regime. They also took advantage of the slight easing of travel restrictions in order to mobilize the Palestinians in Israel at rallies and demonstrations in which they demanded an end to the military government, land grabs, and discrimination they faced internally and called for the liberation of colonized peoples elsewhere in the world. Literary productions continued to feature prominently as a strategy for expanding the spatial and temporal horizons of Palestinians in Israel. Reflecting the growing ranks of the Palestinian intelligentsia, *al-Ittihad* and *al-Jadid* published the works of local writers who were putting into practice the socially committed literature that Habibi and Naqqara had called for a few years earlier. Local poetry festivals emerged as particularly acute sites of resistance, with poets and audience members having to elude military cordons just to attend. In addition, the festivals provided an occasion for poets to rhetorically connect their community to the broader decolonizing world.

Many of these poets and intellectuals drew inspiration from contemporary Arab socialist realist writings, so they were eager to access recent journals, newspapers, and books from the region. But the ongoing Israeli restrictions on access to such material meant that they had to get creative in figuring out how to procure it. In addition, international efforts to put Third World solidarity into practice through international festivals and conferences gave some Palestinian intellectuals an opportunity to meet face-to-face with other Arabs and to exchange print material, as Rashid Husayn did at the 1959 World Youth Festival in Vienna. But such encounters also revealed the ignorance that many Arabs had about the Palestinians inside the Green Line, reminding those intellectuals who did manage to attend such events just how isolated they were.

Taken together, these strategies reveal that by the late 1950s, most politically active Palestinian intellectuals were no longer interested in appealing to the Israeli state for an amelioration of their condition. Rather, they sought to rally Palestinians in their community and to tap into the revolutionary spirit of the Third World to demand their full civil and national rights. They also looked for ways to connect to their Arab counterparts and to challenge the widespread perception of them as passive victims or, worse, as traitors to the Arab cause.

But the Arab world itself was divided between pan-Arab nationalists, who called for a unified, independent Arab state under Nasser's leadership, and Arab communists, who called for a broader coalition of independent states to achieve global social justice. As pan-Arab nationalists and communists became increasingly hostile toward one another at the end of the 1950s, their rivalries reverberated among the Palestinian intellectuals in Israel. Some intellectuals opposed the CPI's class-based analysis of regional developments and directly challenged the party's positioning of itself as the preeminent champion of the Palestinian minority. Thus, while their deep engagement in regional events brought Palestinian communists and pan-Arab nationalists together at the Nazareth May Day rally, their close attunement to these wider developments would also, for a brief time, tear them apart.

By following closely the regional and global debates regarding the best means of decolonization and by engaging in their own parallel debates at home, Palestinian intellectuals in Israel articulated new "geographies of liberation,"[12] which discursively connected Nazareth, Cairo, Algiers, Baghdad, and beyond as all sharing in the larger struggle for freedom and dignity. With political protests circumscribed, the verse took on a greater role in facilitating Palestinian expressions of support for revolutionary movements. The proliferation of poetry festivals, coupled with the rise of local Arabic publications, led cultural producers to create a "horizontal solidarity" between Palestinians in Israel, Arabs, and others in the decolonizing world.[13] Analyzing this expanded spatial and temporal horizon not only demonstrates the links between a vibrant Palestinian public sphere in Israel and its counterparts in the region, but it also accounts for a generational shift that would ultimately push Palestinian politics and culture into uncharted waters.

LOOKING FOR HOPE, CONFRONTING A MASSACRE

By 1956, a growing number of Palestinian intellectuals were fed up with the seemingly interminable Israeli military government. Particularly egregious was the Ratner Commission report, issued that February, which called for continued military rule and rejected the return of Palestinian refugees on security grounds.[14] Tuma denounced the report as a "conspiracy theory" that denied Palestinians agency and negated their connection to the land.[15] Yet he felt compelled to issue his condemnation using his regular pen name (Ibn Khaldun), indicating the fraught political climate in which he and his colleagues continued to operate. But in a sign of things to come, the CPI-led protests against Ratner and the military government also began attracting a growing number of noncommunist Palestinian citizens who were likewise calling for an end to the military regime.[16]

Palestinian intellectuals and cultural producers were also frustrated with ongoing efforts by government and establishment figures to thwart their expressions of solidarity with other Arabs seeking greater independence from colonial rule. Hanna Ibrahim embodied these frustrations well. Born in 1927 in the northern Galilean village of al-Biʿna, he had graduated from Acre's government high school and had been one of the young intellectuals drawn to the NLL in the 1940s. No longer able to find a desk job after 1948, he cut stone in a quarry to support his growing family, though he kept up his love of writing poetry and short stories.[17] When the League of Arabic Poets announced it was seeking contributions to its second poetry festival, Ibrahim submitted a title that clearly celebrated the Jordanian people's anticolonial protests of the previous winter.[18] Festival organizers rejected Ibrahim's poem on the grounds that it was too political, reflecting the establishment's ongoing aversion to anticolonial expressions.[19] While having his poem rejected from a festival was a relatively minor nuisance, when combined with the daily inequities of living under military rule, it added to Ibrahim's mounting impatience with the status quo.[20]

It was this sense of impatience—shared by many other people under colonial and semicolonial rule—that President Nasser successfully tapped into.[21] Following the Free Officers revolution that deposed the unpopular Egyptian monarch, Nasser's opposition in 1955 to the British-led military alliance known as the Baghdad Pact appealed to nationalist-minded Arabs, while his leadership at that year's Afro-Asian (Bandung) Conference calling for nonalignment and Third World solidarity led many outside the Arab world to look to him for inspiration as well.[22] Palestinians in the CPI were split. For Murqus, the fact that the 1952 revolution "swept away the regime of a corrupt, regressive ruler in the largest Arab country was enough to fill us with joy."[23] At the same time, many CPI leaders shared with other Arab communists deep misgivings over Nasser's reluctance to adopt socialist economic policies and grew alarmed over his repression of communist organizers in Egypt.[24] But Nasser's growing popularity in the wake of Bandung, along with his opposition to the Baghdad Pact and his arms deal with Czechoslovakia in September 1955, forced CPI leaders to join their Arab comrades and offer at least qualified support of the Egyptian president's unabashed anticolonial stance.[25]

For Palestinians who felt suffocated by Israeli military rule, listening to Nasser's speeches over the radio was a lifeline that bonded them to the region. As Haifa-based schoolteacher and poet Najwa Qaʿwar Farah explained: "To the majority of Arabs who remained in Israel, he was sent by God. Our ears were glued to the radio when President Nasser of Egypt spoke. Shops were closed and people rushed to their homes and congregated round that magical apparatus to listen to him."[26] Abu Hanna recalled that in Nazareth,

> that powerful voice filled the squares, streets, alleyways, roofs and hearts. Movement stopped on the streets and in the houses of the cities and villages.... He makes the rounds, entering every place without a permit from the military government, as the compass of hope points to him. He is the first leader in the Arab world whose voice speaks of dignity, speaks of pride. He speaks in the name of Arabism from the [Atlantic] Ocean to the [Persian] Gulf, and people can sense his noble intentions.[27]

Like other Arab listeners, Palestinians in Haifa, Nazareth, and elsewhere inside the Green Line heard in Nasser's speeches a sense of hope for true independence that could alleviate the suffering they endured under a Western-backed regime.

Although Nasser projected a revolutionary image of anti-imperialism and pan-Arab nationalism, his primary concern was always Egypt and ensuring Egyptian leadership over the Arab world. Uninterested in engaging Israel militarily over the Palestine question, on several occasions before 1956 he attempted to restrain Palestinian raids on Israel and even appeared to be open to negotiations.[28] But with Israeli prime minister David Ben-Gurion coming to view Nasser as a threat, the British wanting to ensure that the Suez Canal remained under international control, and the French believing he was the main impetus behind the ongoing Algerian revolution, hawkish leaders in all three countries sought to put Nasser in his place.[29] The opportunity came in the summer of 1956 when US secretary of state John Foster Dulles abruptly withdrew an aid package that Egypt needed to build the Aswan Dam and provide the country with much-needed irrigation and hydroelectricity. The move was clearly intended to humiliate Nasser, and Arabs anxiously waited to see how he would respond. Nasser's answer came a week later, on July 26, in a speech broadcast throughout the Middle East and listened to by millions. In it, Nasser argued that because Egyptians had dug the Suez Canal "with our lives, our skulls, our bones, [and] our blood," it belonged to the Egyptian people, and therefore its profits would be used to build the Aswan Dam.[30] Nasser's nationalization of the Suez Canal was a clear appeal to Arab pride, and the announcement was received ecstatically throughout the region.

Nasser's defiant stance proved to be a formative moment in the political consciousness of many young Palestinians in Israel, whether they went on to align more closely with pan-Arab nationalist groups or the CPI. Fouzi El-Asmar, who was born in 1937 to a Christian family and would later write for pan-Arab nationalist publications, recalled gathering around the radio with his high school classmates in Nazareth, listening intently to Nasser's speech. When they heard the nationalization decree, according to El-Asmar, "all those present jumped to their feet with cries of joy and hugged one another."[31] Salim Jubran, born in 1941 to a Muslim family in Nazareth, was also a high school student at the time. Though he soon began writing for CPI publications, he had been so moved by Nasser's nationalization speech that he procured a cassette tape of it so he could listen repeatedly to the "sincere leader whose hands were clean."[32]

Nasser's nationalization decree not only inspired great joy among those in the region; it also triggered the planning of a joint Anglo-French-Israeli attack on Egypt. On the night of October 29, Israeli forces launched an air and ground invasion of Egypt's Sinai Peninsula. Ben-Gurion and his military advisers hoped to destabilize the Egyptian regime and expand Israeli territory to establish what they considered more defensible borders.[33] A few days later, the British and French launched an assault on the northern canal city of Port Said to shore up Israel's rapid territorial gains and regain control of the Suez. But paratroopers were met with fierce resistance as Egyptian troops shed their uniforms and joined the popular resistance on the ground.[34] Meanwhile, the United States, the Soviet Union, and much of the rest of the world denounced the attack as unwarranted and a violation of Egyptian sovereignty. The combination of Port Said's defiance and mounting international pressure compelled

British and French forces to retreat in December, while Israel completed its withdrawal in March 1957. The Suez Crisis confirmed Arab nationalists' suspicions that even in an era of ostensibly independent nation-states, the great powers still intended to dominate the region.[35] Yet Nasser's ability to resist the military wrath of two imperial forces and their junior ally led him to gain tremendous prestige.[36] Jubran believed that Palestinians in Israel "loved [Nasser] more than anyone else" because the Egyptian leader "crystallized [the idea that] pan-Arab national consciousness was an instrument in the confrontation with Israel."[37] In this celebratory atmosphere only the communist leaders demurred, but they could do little more than issue muted criticisms of the Arab hero.

While the world was riveted to events in Egypt, another incident, this one in Israel, went almost entirely unnoticed. Just after sunset on October 29, on the eve of the Sinai invasion, Israeli border police killed forty-nine Palestinian men, women, and children, mainly on the outskirts of the border village of Kafr Qasim, for unknowingly violating a sunset curfew that had been hastily imposed just a few hours earlier. News of the Kafr Qasim massacre, which the government initially tried to suppress, spread like wildfire.[38] The shock and outrage among Palestinian citizens at their government's disregard for their lives led to the emergence of more robust opposition to government policies. Since the massacre occurred in response to orders given to quiet the Jordanian border in preparation for the Suez offensive, Palestinian intellectuals viewed both the massacre and the attack on Egypt as twin examples of a broader Western-Israeli assault against the Arabs.

The CPI played a central role in discursively linking what was ostensibly a local tragedy to broader regional developments. In November 1956 *al-Ittihad* noted that, despite Israeli attempts to "quell the Arabs both here and in the Sinai," the government "did not take into account the solidarity of the peoples of the world and the resistance of the people of Port Said."[39] One month later, CPI Knesset member Tawfiq Tubi challenged the government's line that the Kafr Qasim massacre was simply a tragic mistake: "The roots of this massacre go back to odious, racist policies that the ruling spheres in Israel have undertaken since its establishment," Tubi said. Citing previous instances in which Palestinian civilians were killed by Zionist or Israeli forces, he asked, "How many massacres have been arranged against harmless Arab residents in numerous villages during 1947–48 and after in Dayr Yasin . . . and elsewhere?[40] Doesn't this policy continue under the cloak of 'retaliation' and 'punishing infiltrators' in Qibya, Nahalayn, Gaza and Khan Yunis?"[41] By placing the events at Kafr

Qasim within the context of previous attacks against Palestinians, Tubi cast the massacre as one part of a larger campaign waged by Israel against the Palestinians, thereby positioning the Kafr Qasim killings within the Palestinian people's collective memory. Poetry that emerged in response to the Kafr Qasim massacre also played a key role in this discursive linking.[42]

FESTIVALS AND INTELLECTUALS

Even before the Kafr Qasim massacre had shaken them to their core, Palestinian intellectuals chafed at the ongoing inequities between Palestinian and Jewish Israelis. Qaʿwar Farah recalled being invited to speak about the great tenth-century Arab poet al-Mutanabbi at a conference hosted by the League of Arabic Poets, but she "came to feel that a cultural relationship [between Arabs and Jews] should only exist between equals because it would otherwise be a cover-up for the oppressor, a means of hiding the fact that lands and rights were being taken away."[43] As more Palestinians grew unwilling to abide by the league's parameters, a split emerged largely along national lines. Establishment figures and their affiliates (mainly Iraqi Jewish intellectuals) formed a new group called the League of Arabic Pens, while most of the Palestinian members steered the League of Arabic Poets toward a stance that spoke more directly to their community's experiences of repression and isolation. One sign of that stance was that they soon renamed their group the League of *Arab* Poets (Rabitat Shuʿaraʾ al-ʿArab) to reflect their national and pan-Arab identity.[44]

This new orientation was on display at the Second Nazareth Poetry Festival in March 1957. With a roster that now included CPI members and sympathizers, many of the poems followed the precepts of committed literature, emphasizing the bitter experiences and the steadfastness of the Palestinian people. ʿIsa Lubani's "Sad Nights and a Smiling Dawn" recounted the experiences of a heartbroken and exiled Palestinian father, his martyred son, and his starving baby. Yet the narrator vowed: "We will return to the fertile land, the land of my stolen village / the land of my fathers, the legacy of my forebears."[45] Lubani's simple, defiant insistence on return would become an increasingly common literary theme in the coming months and years, signaling the growing salience of the refugee cause despite the fact that the possibility of refugee return seemed further away than ever.[46]

The Nazareth festival was one of a number of poetry festivals that attracted poets of various political stances. On July 14, 1957, several hundred men, women, and children gathered at the Culture and Sports Club in the western

Galilean town of Kafr Yasif, where they filled the outdoor square and spilled over onto the balconies and roofs of nearby houses as they listened for over three hours to a dozen poets recite from their work.[47] Land was a major theme of the evening: Hanna Abu Hanna denounced the theft of land from the Abu al-Hayja family in the village of ʿAyn Hawd,[48] while Jamal Qaʿwar hailed the peasants' determination to remain on their land, despite it being snatched from them.[49] The populist atmosphere stood in sharp contrast to the Romantic sentiments heard at the previous, establishment-oriented literary events.

For many audience members, the highlight of the evening was the appearance of Rashid Husayn. Born in 1936 to a Muslim family in the Triangle village of Musmus, he had attended high school in Nazareth with the help of an affluent uncle. As a student Husayn achieved notoriety with his poem celebrating the Bandung moment ("I Am from Asia"), which he was asked to recite repeatedly in local cafés and on street corners.[50] After finishing high school, Husayn returned to Musmus and worked as an elementary school teacher, though he continued to be a sought-after poet at the expanding festival scene. That July evening, with the Israeli military having cordoned off Kafr Yasif to try to restrict the size and scope of the festival, Husayn, who had traveled thirty-seven miles (sixty kilometers) from his hometown just to attend, snuck in through the fields behind the village. Once onstage, he declared to thunderous applause: "Today I come when we are all prisoners / When will I come when we are all free?"[51] The audience was reportedly moved to tears as Husayn recited his second poem, in the form of a letter from his cousin in Jordan describing the refugees' harsh conditions and their longing to return.[52] The difficulties in reaching the festival illustrate how such events became sites of resistance against the physical isolation faced by Palestinians living in different parts of the country.

The rise of poetry festivals—with their verses that articulated the cruel realities of Palestinians on both sides of the Green Line—signaled a growing recognition that poetry could have an immediate political function among Palestinian citizens that it did not have in the immediate aftermath of the Nakba. With military rule still firmly entrenched, Palestinian intellectuals and political organizers needed a way to rally their people toward a sense of collective spirit as a precursor to pushing for greater mobilization. In a community that was still largely illiterate but had a strong oral literary tradition, poetry festivals were an ideal vehicle for politically conscious Palestinians to connect with people who yearned for a sense of hope. As Hanna Ibrahim later explained, "The strong language, the strong meter, the musical rhyme that transferred zeal to people was necessary and important to gather people and unite them around a cause."[53] Festivals had a practical benefit as well: because most poets were too poor to publish their own bound collections and Israeli censorship made even the CPI reticent to publish material that was too strongly worded, festivals became the primary means by which poets could share their most defiant verses directly with their audience.[54]

Fearing that such verses could be translated into a threat against the state, Israeli officials stepped up their efforts to limit access to the festivals by intimidating attendees, revoking participants' travel permits, and threatening to fire (the majority of) poets who made their living as teachers.[55] The socialist realist message of many poems further worried establishment figures. Writing about the Kafr Yasif festival in *al-Yawm*, editor Michael Assaf suggested the poets' harsh words constituted a betrayal of the state, though he condescendingly allowed them some leeway since "the poet is a man of emotion and not a man of logic." Refusing to acknowledge the legitimacy of the grievances expressed, Assaf wondered instead whether some of the poets had simply "become Moscow's tail in Israel."[56] Assaf's confused reaction to the festival, seeing it as both a dangerous threat and the mere ramblings of emotionally overwrought men, reflected the inability of Israeli establishment figures to deal with Palestinians seeking to empower their people through verses that spoke clearly and eloquently to their shared fears and hopes.

The sense of empowerment had a strong influence on younger Palestinians, including two—Mahmoud Darwish and Samih al-Qasim—who would, in the following decades, become *the* leading luminaries of the Palestinian cultural scene. Darwish was born in March 1941 to a Muslim family in the northern Galilean village of Birwa, fled to Lebanon with his family in 1948, and snuck back across the border a couple of years later. They moved to the town of Dayr al-Asad near the remains of their destroyed village, but as "infiltrators," they initially lived in constant fear of expulsion. When Darwish was in second grade, his principal hid him in a closet whenever an inspector from the Education Ministry came by so he could hide the boy's undocumented status.[57] As a result, Darwish felt more out of place in Israel than in Lebanon because, in his words, "there is no logic" to making someone a refugee in his own country.[58] Qasim was born in 1939 to a Druze family from the Galilean village of al-Rama, a few miles east of Darwish's birthplace. In 1948 he witnessed the Haganah order the expulsion of most of al-Rama's Christian residents while allowing Druze residents to stay.[59] Only after Qasim's father and other senior Druze figures intervened did the authorities allow the Christian villagers to return.[60] The secular, Arab nationalist education Qasim received as an elementary school student in the mid-1940s stood in sharp contrast to Israeli attempts to sow sectarian divisions among the Palestinians, which later led Qasim to resist government policies that singled out him and other Druze citizens for special treatment.

By the mid-1950s, both young men became increasingly aware of the power and salience of poetry. Qasim entered Nazareth's government high school just as Rashid Husayn burst onto the cultural scene with his ode to Asia.[61] Meanwhile, as an eighth-grader Darwish, whose poetic talents were already starting to show, was asked to recite a poem for his school's Israeli Independence Day festival. He recalled: "For the first time in my life, I stood in front of the microphone in my shorts and read a poem that was a cry from an Arab child to a Jewish child: . . . 'You have a house; I have no house because I am a refugee. You have holidays and celebrations; I have no holiday or celebration. Why don't we play together?'"[62] Darwish was promptly summoned by the local military governor, who threatened to revoke his father's quarry work permit if Darwish continued to recite such poems.[63] Both events were formative: while Qasim witnessed the power of the verse to inspire his community, Darwish learned how even the naïve sentiments of a middle school student could be perceived by the state as a threat.[64] The military governor's threats pushed the young Darwish to retreat into Romantic poetry for a while, but his habitual reading of *al-Ittihad* and *al-Jadid* "ignited within [me] a desire to connect directly with reality."[65] Poetry festivals also inspired Darwish to turn to more socially relevant material. At the first festival he attended, Darwish heard Abu Hanna recite a poem that "was received with incomparable excitement due to its stylistic grace, its deep simplicity and its revolutionary content."[66] Darwish, along with Qasim, would soon join Abu Hanna onstage with verses of their own that would likewise be received with enthusiasm.

As poetry festivals were inspiring young poets, some Palestinian intellectuals sought to establish nonpartisan organizations that could serve as a vehicle for those of differing political orientations to come together. But because so few Palestinians attained high levels of formal education,[67] it was unclear who should even be considered an intellectual. As the League of Arab Poets expanded to become League of Arab Writers and Intellectuals (Rabitat al-Udabaʾ waʾl-Muthaqqafin al-ʿArab) in summer 1957, members discussed this point. With the prodding of Habib Qahwaji, a nationalist-minded teacher who had objected to the earlier league's ties to the Histadrut,[68] the new group decided to recognize as an intellectual "whosoever seeks through speech, thought, pen and work to counteract the social problems in which he lives and to strive to find solutions to those problems."[69] In adopting such an expansive description, the league stressed intellectuals' collective responsibility toward their people, eschewing any specific educational markers. While their definition was an acknowledgment of the still-low number of formally educated Palestinians in the country, it also signaled a deep awareness that for intellectuals to matter in society, they needed to be connected to it.

Since members hailed from multiple political and social backgrounds, the League of Arab Writers and Intellectuals wished to stress its openness to people of all views. At its first Preparatory Committee conference in Haifa in September 1957, board member ʿIsam al-ʿAbbasi declared, "The League's members are free in their ideas, views, writings and productions, whether they are rightists or leftists, believers or heretics."[70] To be sure, the CPI publications still dominated the cultural and intellectual scene. Former *al-Mujtamaʿ* contributor ʿAdnan Abu Saʿud observed that writers were "flocking" to *al-Ittihad* and *al-Jadid* and "fleeing" from *al-Yawm* and *al-Mujtamaʿ* because the latter were stuck in "ivory towers" while the former presented the realities of people's lived experiences.[71] Abu Saʿud's change of heart from two years earlier, when he implored Palestinians in Israel to turn to the state as a wellspring of modernization, reflected the ascendency of committed literature as the most salient form of literary expression, especially in the aftermath of the Suez Crisis and the Kafr Qasim massacre. Little did Abu Saʿud or any of the intellectuals know what revolutionary fervor would greet them the following year.

REVOLUTIONS ABROAD, DEMONSTRATIONS AT HOME

The Israeli military governor had been correct in describing the lead-up to the 1958 May Day as having "a different atmosphere" than in previous years. During the preceding four months, the formation of the United Arab Republic, the visibility of the Algerian revolution in the international arena, and a renewed Histadrut push to showcase its "loyal Arab minority" as part of Israel's tenth-anniversary celebrations led politically conscious Palestinians to express their mounting sense of defiance. As a result, during that year's CPI May Day demonstration, which included many noncommunist intellectuals and organizers, protesters were more explicit than before in linking their struggle against Israeli state policies with global anticolonial struggles using language that embraced both communist and pan-Arab nationalist discourses.

Photo 1. Tawfiq Tubi (far left), Hanna Naqqara (far right), and colleagues distributing *al-Ittihad*, 1960s. Courtesy of Naila Naqqara.

This change reflected the high-water mark of Nasser-led pan-Arab nationalism in the region. Seeking to expand Nasser's influence, Egypt had increased the airtime of its flagship radio program, *Voice of the Arabs*, from three hours per day to seven.[72] The program aired Nasser's full speeches (which could run for more than two hours) while its popular host, Ahmad Saʿid, commented on the news of the day. Together Nasser and Saʿid shaped the views of millions of Arab listeners, showering praise on those who worked toward Arab unity and mocking those, especially the region's monarchs, who deferred to their Western sponsors. Meanwhile in Syria, supporters of the socialist, pan-Arab Baʿth Party also called for Arab unity to curtail Western meddling in their government and to prevent the rise of that country's Communist Party.[73]

These two strands of pan-Arab ideology came together in February 1958 when Syria and Egypt joined to form the United Arab Republic (UAR). Although the UAR was ultimately short lived, at first Arabs throughout the region believed it represented a real united force that extended beyond mere rhetoric. Palestinians of various political leanings in Israel hoped that such unity could alter the political dynamics in the region and improve their conditions at home. Speaking at a rally in the Galilean village of ʿArraba less than two weeks after the UAR's formation, Habibi welcomed the union as a sign of resistance against "those who oppress the Arab people, stole their land,

and deny their right to self-determination."[74] Murqus recalled that the formation of the UAR "gave fresh momentum to the nationalist spirit among our people."[75]

Also inspiring Palestinians during that spring was the ongoing Algerian war for independence against French settler-colonial rule. By 1958 news of France's ruthless campaign to quell the insurgency had spread throughout the world, leading Algeria to become the symbol of Third World revolution.[76] Palestinians in Israel had been following news from Algeria since the war began, thanks to the extensive coverage it received on Radio Cairo and on the pages of *al-Ittihad*.[77] As *al-Ittihad* focused on the widespread imprisonment, torture, and execution of Algerian fighters,[78] and as Israel sided with France in voting against a UN resolution calling for Algerian independence,[79] the CPI arranged a gathering on March 1 to protest Israel's vote and affirm Palestinians' solidarity with the Algerian people. The protest itself was part of an international day of solidarity with Algeria that had been announced by the Conference of Asian-African Solidarity in Cairo earlier that year, whose declaration of intent reflected the broader anti-imperialism of this period.[80]

Israeli officials, fearful that the Palestinians under their rule could launch their own Algerian-style insurrection,[81] clamped down. Authorities denied a permit to hold the Algeria Solidarity rally in Nazareth's Empire Cinema (the town's largest venue), forcing organizers to move to the smaller Communist Youth Center, which in turn found its electricity cut off on the evening of the event. Israeli police also encircled the town with checkpoints and harassed those trying to attend.[82] Despite the police barricades and cramped quarters, *al-Ittihad* reported that hundreds of people from Nazareth and nearby villages attended, gathering on top of rooftops and balconies to listen to speeches and poems in support of the Algerians. Habibi denounced Israel's UN vote and called on the French government to "halt the filthy, aggressive war on the Algerian people." In a tribute to Algerian fighter Jamila Bouhired, whose torture by French troops had been particularly notorious, Abu Hanna declared, "O Jamila! / You are the liberation songs on Algeria's horizons / The victory tunes on the weapon of every avenger."[83] In contrast to Abu Hanna's anticolonial poetry of the early 1950s that spoke in generalized, abstract terms of workers around the world uniting, his tribute to Jamila connected Palestinians to a specific cause in a concrete, personified way that was more easily relatable than some of his earlier verses. Abu Hanna's literary evolution not only highlights the salience of more direct anticolonial poetry in this restive environment but also demonstrates the central role that poetry played in contributing to Palestinians' expanding political horizons.

This versified revolutionary fervor came as Israeli officials sought to turn the state's tenth-anniversary celebrations into an international public relations extravaganza that highlighted, among other things, the country's content Arab minority.[84] Seeking to cultivate more intellectuals who were loyal to the state, the Histadrut sponsored its own poetry festival in April 1958, awarding prizes to the top contributors. In the proceedings of the festival, timed to correspond with Israel's anniversary celebrations, Histadrut director of Arab affairs Eliahu Agassi doubled down on the state's colonial discourses. He explained that since Israel was a model of "economic, agricultural, health, cultural, social and democratic progress," each Arab citizen ought to join the state to serve "as an example of understanding and harmony between Israel and her neighbors."[85] In a bid to reinforce this view, the Histadrut granted second-place prize to school principal ʿAbdallah Muhammad Yunis, who declared, "Peace, o people, is better than your battles / that separated us from our families. / Hasten to peace my people / for our souls have grown weary from the torture of war."[86] By blaming Arab recalcitrance for the plight of Palestinian refugees and the isolation of Palestinian citizens within the country, Yunis's poem reinforced Israel's self-image as an innocent, peace-seeking state surrounded by implacably hostile Arabs.

But such a message was still a tough sell for Palestinians entering their second decade under Israeli rule, and young poets were much more eager to follow Abu Hanna's example than Yunis's. The same month as the Histadrut festival, seventeen-year-old Darwish made his debut at a very different poetry festival in Acre. With a poem titled "Sister," he addressed his younger sister as he spoke intimately of refugees' suffering. But he ended on a hopeful note, declaring, "No matter how much misery mingled with poison is poured upon us / We will return, sister—we will return to the old country!"[87] Darwish's childhood experiences as a refugee in Lebanon undoubtedly influenced his choice of topic, though his defiance and timing (on Israeli Independence Day) also reflected a changing political and cultural landscape in which he felt empowered enough to defy the threats of the military governor and insist on his people's return. Three months later nineteen-year-old Qasim participated in his first poetry festival, expressing his admiration of the Algerian people's struggle against the French.[88] Darwish joined him with a poem of his own that was dedicated to "every martyr in every battle for freedom."[89] While the poems were not remarkable in their aesthetic qualities, they point to the salience that these topics had for aspiring poets and their audience. As Darwish later admitted, it would "have been impossible to have stood up at a festival and recited a love poem."[90] The reason is that, for Palestinians under Israeli rule, poetry festivals were seen as key sites for resisting their internal and external isolation. Naqqara's clarion call that literature serve as a "weapon" in the people's struggle for justice had been heeded.

The revolutionary fervor of that summer received another boost on July 14 when a group of disaffected army officers overthrew the conservative, pro-British Hashemite monarchy of Iraq, replacing it with a new republic that had a nationalist-leftist orientation.[91] Pan-Arab nationalists and communists alike had held the Hashemite rulers of Iraq in particular contempt for their accession to the Baghdad Pact, their brutal crackdown on the Wathba, and their betrayal of the Palestinians in 1948 by sending a weak and leaderless contingent of fighters.[92] The overthrow of such a regime was an especially hopeful sign, but of what? For communists like Hanna Ibrahim, the changing regime signaled "that the end of imperialism and its lackeys was near and that socialism and the realization of our dreams had come."[93] But pan-Arab nationalists in the region believed that the Iraqi revolution—coming a mere five months after the establishment of the UAR—signaled the next step in Arab unity under Nasser's leadership.[94] With the events in Iraq coming at a time of strong communist-nationalist alliance at home and in the region, the spirit of cooperation continued in the immediate aftermath of the coup. But the differing visions of what the postrevolutionary region should look like soon led to tensions.

PAN-ARAB VERSUS COMMUNIST VISIONS OF THE REGION

The creation of the UAR and the Iraqi revolution appeared to signal an irreversible shift in the Arab political order. Palestinians under Israeli rule in particular hoped that Arab political unity could help them combat state policies of discrimination and marginalization. As the broadcasts of Radio Baghdad and Radio Cairo extolled the virtues of Arab independence and revolution, Israel's ongoing detention of the May Day protest leaders, coupled with the decision to try them in a military rather than a civilian court, left Palestinian activists in the country—nationalist and communist alike—infuriated. The immediate urgency of securing the release of the prisoners, coupled with the regional spirit of cooperation, pushed Palestinian communist and nationalist activists to come together to form the Popular Front in July 1958. Although the Popular Front's demands were largely domestic,[95] its coalition of communist and nationalist members illustrated how the political dynamics in the Arab world reverberated among Palestinian intellectuals and political organizers at home.

The Popular Front's emergence also triggered reassessments among the two main Israeli political parties that had sought to position themselves as champions of the Palestinian minority. Palestinian CPI leaders had grown alarmed at Nasser's ban on political parties in the UAR, and they were disappointed at his reluctance to adopt more robust socialist economic reforms. But they knew full well that they could not attack Nasser outright, lest they alienate themselves from their main base of support. They therefore praised the spirit of Arab revolution while refraining from giving direct credit to Nasser himself. Mapam had previously made some overtures to Palestinian citizens, in part through its weekly newspaper, *al-Mirsad* (launched in October 1952).[96] But by the late 1950s, as some of the party's "Arabists" (specialists in Arab affairs) realized there was a cohort of nationalist intellectuals who could not bring themselves to join the CPI, they persuaded party leaders that Mapam could garner more Palestinian votes by providing a platform for these intellectuals. As a result, the party expanded the number of Palestinian writers on staff for *al-Mirsad*. More important, it helped launch the monthly cultural journal *al-Fajr*, which was modeled on the format of *al-Jadid* and other regional journals. By assuring nationalist-minded writers that they did not need to join to work for the journal, and by setting aside half the editorial board members for non-Mapam members, *al-Fajr*'s wide-ranging platform attracted a substantial audience during its four-year run and helped spread the tenets of pan-Arab nationalism even further among Palestinian intellectuals and cultural agents in the country.[97]

Al-Fajr's debut in October 1958 was timely, as the spirit of unity between Egypt and Iraq was already dissipating. Over the previous several months Iraqi leader Qasim had built ties with the country's communists and an amalgam of Kurds, Shiʿa, and other minority groups who worried about their political standing were Iraq to join an expanded (Arab- and Sunni-dominated) UAR. Meanwhile, Khalid Bakdash, head of the Syrian communists, demanded greater autonomy for Syria and a looser UAR federation, a move that triggered Nasser to denounce the Syrian communists in a widely broadcast speech that December.[98] The tensions left Palestinian intellectuals in a quandary: Should they support Qasim and his revolutionary, pro-communist stance, or should they rally around the more popular Nasser?

Initially CPI leaders tried to have it both ways. As the UAR celebrated its first anniversary in February 1959, Habibi still lauded the republic as "a harbinger of greater Arab unity," though he warned that "imperialism . . . has redoubled its effort to return to its previous position" of dominance by sowing discord.[99] Habibi urged Arabs everywhere to remain united, but his fears materialized one month later when, after some minor tussles at a series of rallies and counter-rallies in the northern Iraqi city of Mosul, a group of pro-Nasser Iraqi military personnel issued an open call to revolt against Qasim on March 8. The Iraqi Air Force (led by a member of the Communist Party) bombed the headquarters of the rebellious brigade, and clashes in Mosul erupted between pan-Arab nationalists on one side and government forces supported by communists, Shiʿa, and Kurds on the other. By the time reinforcements arrived to quell the violence four days later, approximately two hundred people had been killed.[100]

The violence in Mosul caused irreparable damage to relations between Iraq and the UAR, and the high number of casualties forced Arabs throughout the region to choose between two factions that were both supposed to be at the forefront of the Arab anticolonial movement. While the majority of Arabs backed Nasser and criticized the Iraqi government's ruthlessness in putting down the revolt, Arab communists (including most of the CPI's top leadership) insisted on supporting Qasim. A banner headline in *al-Ittihad* on March 10 (before the total death toll was known) declared triumphantly, "The recalcitrant orphans of the past era in Iraq have received their due."[101] The article portrayed Nasser as an agent of imperialism, surreptitiously trying to overthrow the legitimate rulers of Iraq.

Meanwhile, Nasser and his supporters attacked the communists just as vehemently. *Voice of the Arabs* host Ahmad Saʿid accused the Arab communist parties of undermining Arab unity, backstabbing Nasser, and being agents of imperialism.[102] *Al-Fajr* also weighed in on the events of Mosul, with editor Rashid Husayn arguing that the Iraqi regime's use of such brutality showed that Qasim and his communist backers lacked popular legitimacy.[103] Husayn's accusation marked the opening salvo in a protracted debate between Husayn and Abu Hanna over how to frame the political contestations taking place around them.

Writing in *al-Jadid*, Abu Hanna took umbrage at Husayn's criticisms of the Iraqi revolution and of communism more generally. He reminded Husayn that "before Nasser appeared, the communists here struggled for the sake of the people, their future and their comfort, and they made sacrifices for the sake of all the people, which they continue to do today."[104] Abu Hanna's line of argument crystallized the dilemma that the communists faced. As a CPI organizer, Abu Hanna, who was himself an admirer of Nasser, nonetheless continued to frame the Palestinians' struggle against the state as the CPI had done for more than a decade. By using the language of nation-state nationalism, he argued that the party's valiant efforts to achieve equal rights within Israel signaled its unmatched leadership. But the political landscape was changing: Husayn represented an ascendant pan-Arab framing of the political landscape that prioritized overcoming Palestinians' isolation from the Arab world as the best means of achieving true freedom. By linking the CPI with regional communist parties—parties that were being attacked as obstacles to Arab unity—Husayn portrayed the communists as an impediment to the Arab cause.[105] Throughout the spring of 1959, Husayn and Abu Hanna wrote rebuttals and counter-rebuttals on the pages of their respective journals, with little resolution.[106] Despite their insistence that the debate was not personal, it took an enormous toll on the friendship between two poets. Just two years earlier, they had shared the stage at poetry festivals throughout the country, where they both called on audience members to imagine the resplendent day when colonialism and Western-backed tyranny was finally eradicated from the region.[107] Now that the day seemed within reach, new challenges arose.

The bitter recriminations between the two camps were especially hard for the communists. Tawfiq Zayyad felt betrayed at hearing Nasser charge that communists were Zionist agents, especially when Zayyad had suffered repeatedly at the hands of Israeli jailers who had accused him of supporting the Egyptian leader.[108] As Zayyad wrote:

They hung me from an iron rod and claimed, "Nasserite," "enemy sympathizer"

And today, o Gamal, I am the "agent" whose "sins" fill the earth and sky?
Today I am the "partisan," the "mercenary," the "enemy" of your people and mine?
Shut up! Your words are mere lyrics, planting poison in hearts and minds
We have heard it all before, long ago and in recent times.[109]

Such a direct attack on Nasser was rarely seen at this time, even among CPI leaders. Zayyad's bitterness reflected the dark underside of being so closely invested in Arab political developments: he saw Nasser's condemnations of the region's Arab communists as a direct assault on him and felt compelled to reply. Zayyad's indignation also illustrated CPI leaders' frustration at the lack of Arab understanding about the unique challenges they faced. Israeli officials viewed both communists and pan-Arab nationalists as twin threats that needed to be neutralized, so a rift between the two groups would only strengthen the state's hand.

And it did. With the Israeli election season approaching in fall 1959, the ruling Mapai party concluded that it could exploit the rift between Nasser and the communists to its benefit. Official media outlets, including the *Voice of Israel* and *al-Yawm*, reproduced Nasser's accusations against the communists, while Acre's chief of police drove his jeep through the narrow alleyways of the old city, using his megaphone to blare at full blast the segments of Nasser's speeches that denounced the communists.[110] Meanwhile on Radio Cairo, Ahmad Sa'id accused the communists of playing into the hands of the Arabs' enemies, seeking to impose a foreign ideology, and having contempt for all that is dear to Arabs and Muslims. Sa'id even alleged that the Iraqi communists tore up pages of the Qur'an out of their disdain for Islam.[111]

Such accusations, far-fetched though they were, held sway among at least some Palestinian citizens. As the CPI tried to rally support in Palestinian communities ahead of the polls, they experienced firsthand the impact of the Egyptian broadcasts. When Hanna Ibrahim made a campaign stop outside a small mosque one afternoon, hoping to persuade some villagers to vote for his party, one congregant waved Ibrahim away, telling him, "Leave us alone, man. We don't want to vote for the communists." When Ibrahim beseeched the man to listen for a minute before making up his mind, the latter replied contemptuously, "You tear up the Qur'an and you want us to listen to you?" Recalling the incident nearly forty years later, Ibrahim ruefully asked, "Was the word of a stonecutter from al-Bi'na equal to the words of Ahmad Sa'id and the broadcasts of *Voice of the Arabs*?"[112]

It turned out the answer was no, and the CPI lost three of its previous six Knesset seats.[113] In his post-election analysis, Habibi cited Israeli government propaganda efforts and "the repeated attacks against the communists launched by leaders of the UAR" as the primary reasons for the CPI's poor showing.[114] Habibi did not concede that the CPI's backing of Qasim in a rapidly changing Arab political environment played a role, nor did he acknowledge the influence of the pro-Nasser Ard movement that had made its debut at the height of election season. Although the Ard movement's appearance on the political scene was short lived, its unabashed championing of Nasser and pan-Arab nationalism would have a lasting impact on the Palestinian political and cultural landscape in Israel.

THE ARD MOVEMENT: PALESTINIAN LIBERATION THROUGH PAN-ARAB UNITY

In addition to echoing the rivalries between communists and pan-Arab nationalists in the Arab world, the Ard movement's debut reflected four additional developments related more specifically to the Palestinian political scene. First, the Arab National Movement (ANM), which was founded by (predominantly Palestinian) students at the American University of Beirut in 1951 and called for pan-Arab unity as the only viable path for Palestinian liberation, had recently made significant inroads in the dozens of UN-run schools in the countries surrounding Israel, drawing support from the Palestinian refugees' growing intelligentsia.[115] Second, Palestinian students in Egypt and other Arab countries founded the General Union of Palestinian Students (GUPS) in 1959, emphasizing the responsibility of nationally conscious Palestinians to instill a sense of identity and pride among its youth.[116] Around the same time, Palestinians in Kuwait launched Fatah (an Arabic reverse acronym for the Palestinian Liberation Movement), which, though still marginal at the time, propagated the idea that revolutionary armed struggle was the only means by which to assert Palestinian agency and to oust the Israeli regime.[117]

The fourth development was the emergence of the Palestine issue as part of the Nasser-Qasim rivalry. At the thirty-third session of the Arab League Council on March 29, 1959 (less than a month after the Mosul uprising), Nasser introduced the idea of establishing a "Palestinian entity" (*al-kayan al-filastini*), thereby directly acknowledging a distinct Palestinian people. Nasser also began declaring regularly that "unity is the road to Palestine,"[118] and he hosted the first General Congress of GUPS in Cairo that November.[119] In response, Qasim announced plans to set up a Palestine "liberation regiment" in June 1959, and in December he called for the establishment of an "immortal Palestinian republic."[120] But neither of Qasim's declarations provided much detail, and they failed to hold sway among the majority of Palestinians who were already pro-Nasser.

With the expanding rivalry between Nasser and Qasim, cleavages within the Popular Front—originally a base of cooperation between Palestinian communists and nationalists—quickly came to the surface. In an early effort to diffuse tensions, nationalist member Habib Qahwaji and a few of his colleagues petitioned the Front's Central Committee in spring 1959 to pass a resolution calling on all members to cease commenting on the rivalry between Iraq and the UAR. According to Qahwaji, the CPI members argued that since Arab communists in the region were coming under attack from the nationalists, the CPI felt it had no choice but to return the favor.[121] Believing the CPI held disproportionate sway within the Popular Front, several nationalist members broke off, forming the core of the Ard movement.[122]

The Ard movement marked a turning point in the Palestinian political scene in Israel. For the first time, a group of Palestinian intellectuals organized around clear pan-Arab nationalist principles and directly linked their isolation in Israel to the post–World War I dividing up of the Arab nation and the 1948 scattering of the Palestinian people. This position was reflected in the opening line of the group's April 1959 founding communiqué: "We are a part of the Palestinian people [al-sha'b al-filastini], who are in turn a part of the Arab nation [al-umma al-'arabiyya]."[123]

But the founders also recognized the unique political environment in which they were operating. According to Qahwaji, they deliberated carefully over the wording of their communiqué and concluded that if they did not recognize Israel explicitly, they would be likely arrested and jailed on charges of subversion.[124] Thus, they simultaneously positioned themselves as a civil rights group that would "struggle within this country for the sake of full equality between Arab and Jew." Reflecting this duality, the communiqué then called on Israel to:

(1) recogn[ize] that the Arab nationalist movement is the established movement of the region
(2) cut itself off completely [qat'an batan] from Zionist thought and the Zionist movement
(3) pursue a policy of positive neutrality and peaceful coexistence
(4) help the Palestinian people, acknowledge their right to self-determination, and allow all those who left this country to return to it.
If Israel pursues these steps, we will consider it to be moving on the correct path toward a just and lasting peace in this area.[125]

On the one hand, the communiqué elucidated several political stances that were nearly identical to those of the CPI, such as equal rights for Arabs and Jews, positive neutrality in the Cold War, and peaceful coexistence between Israel and its neighbors. On the other hand, by calling explicitly for Palestinian self-determination and on Israel to dissociate itself from Zionist ideology, the Ard founders were asserting an unapologetically Palestinian-Arab nationalist narrative that had until that time seen little public expression in Israel. Both the CPI and Mapam, whether implicitly or explicitly, had acceded to the state's Zionist underpinnings and worked within the state's framework to achieve equal rights. In positioning themselves more squarely within pan-Arab and Palestinian nationalist frameworks, the Ard founders displayed a rising self-confidence that hewed more closely to the orientation of Palestinian exile groups such as ANM and GUPS.

Recognizing that a newspaper was crucial to be taken seriously as a political force, Qahwaji and his colleagues began planning the launch of their own weekly. But neither Mapam nor the CPI was interested in helping them out, and the group's application for a publishing permit languished, unanswered, in Israeli ministry offices. To circumvent these obstacles, Qahwaji and his colleagues turned to a little-known law, carried over from the Mandate period, that allowed any citizen to publish a one-time paper without a permit. They decided to publish a series of single-issue papers, each under the sponsorship of a different board member, and they found a Palestinian in Acre with remnants of a printing press who agreed to print the papers.[126] Between October 1959 and January 1960 twelve issues appeared, usually weekly, and they were met with an overwhelmingly enthusiastic response from Palestinians throughout the country, enjoying much higher circulation (estimated to top eight thousand) than any other Arabic publication in the country.[127]

Critics of the Ard movement dismissed its paper as a regurgitation of Nasserist propaganda,[128] but the paper served as more than a mere echo chamber for the UAR's party line.[129] By contrasting their experiences as a Palestinian minority in Israel with the reported successes of the UAR, writers discursively linked their community to the heart of pan-Arab nationalism and, more important, cast their physical isolation from the rest of the Arab world as the primary reason for their poor condition. One such article, contrasting the UAR's Fifth Annual Science Day celebrations with the mediocre state of education in their community, contended that unlike the UAR, where students were encouraged to excel, in Israel the inadequate number of teachers, poor facilities, and high rates of failure on the high school matriculation exam led students to have poor confidence in their abilities and intelligence. This state of affairs was especially tragic, the article concluded, given the high levels of scientific advancement that Arabs had historically achieved.[130] The article's criticisms of Palestinian education under the Israeli state and the invocation of Arab civilizational greatness echoed themes previously invoked by the CPI. But unlike the CPI's treatments of this subject, which compared poor Arab educational facilities with superior Jewish Israeli ones to call for greater equality, the author here explicitly linked a local problem to the larger one of isolation from the Arab world.

While the Ard movement's emphasis on Arab unity connected Palestinians in the country to broader discourses, cofounder Salih Baransi understood well that the Israeli state was not to be discounted. Born in 1928 in the central town of Tayba and a graduate of the nationalist-oriented Nahda high school in Jerusalem, from 1951 to 1958 Baransi worked as a high school Arabic teacher, primarily in Kafr Yasif. But when he became more politically active, the Education Ministry reassigned him to a remote elementary school (a common response to political activism). When Baransi refused to accept the transfer, he was fired.[131] In an article titled "Arab Unity: The Only Way to Solve the Palestinian Issue," Baransi asserted that four conditions needed to be met before the Palestinian issue could be resolved: (1) the expulsion of imperialism from all parts of the Arab nation; (2) nationalist unity parties reaching leadership in each Arab country; (3) organizing countries that have gained independence into a single united entity; and (4) progressive groups reaching leadership in Israel.[132] While the first three points reflected broad pan-Arab nationalist positions, the fourth represented a recognition that without progressive leadership in Israel, Arab unity and independence would not be enough to solve the Palestinian issue. This was a more nuanced view than that of most pan-Arab nationalists outside Israel, and it demonstrated that, in contrast to groups such as GUPS and ANM, the Ard founders acknowledged the reality of Israel's permanence, even if they disputed the state's ideological underpinnings.

Ard's emergence on the political scene precipitated a crisis within the CPI. The new group's calls for educational reform, anti-imperialism, and Arab pride were all causes that the CPI's Palestinian leaders had been championing from a Marxist perspective for more than a decade. But linking these issues more explicitly with Nasser-led pan-Arab nationalism clearly resonated with large numbers of Palestinians inside the Green Line. Making matters worse for the CPI, one of the first calls of the Ard paper was to boycott the 1959 Knesset elections, arguing that the Palestinian citizens needed to show the Israeli public and the world the "failure of other groups from among our people in the past to organize solely along national lines."[133] This not-so-subtle reference to the CPI, coupled with the communists' dismal showing in that election, further demonstrated the salience of the Ard's pro-Nasser, pan-Arab nationalist message in the Palestinian community.

The CPI could not plausibly undermine the Ard movement's nationalist bona fides by associating it with Zionist parties, as it had done with nationalists who wrote for Mapam-affiliated publications. But behind the scenes the party's old guard, particularly Emile Habibi, attacked Ard members vehemently, even as younger party activists, such as Abu Hanna, respected the nationalists' position. Some of the CPI's young guard suspected that the veteran leaders' antipathy toward the nationalists had less to do with ideological disagreements and more to do with the CPI wanting to monopolize the Palestinian political arena.[134] Ard leaders likewise refrained from directly attacking the CPI; instead, they mocked the Iraqi leader Qasim, depicting him as a shortsighted egomaniac unable to see the greater good that Arab unity would bring. One article inveighed, "The day Iraq is freed ... from your buffoonery it will be able to participate in the awakening of the Arab giant."[135] Partisan point scoring aside, of note here is that the author addressed Qasim directly, as if the Iraqi leader—or Iraqis more generally—might one day read his words. This personal tone indicates the expanding spatial horizon of Palestinian intellectuals as they engaged with the region's fractious debates in the hope that their contributions might reach beyond the confines of the state.

There is no indication that the Ard papers reached Iraq, but the group's unabashed enthusiasm for Nasser soon earned it the ire of the Israeli authorities. While waiting for their publishing permit to be approved,[136] the Ard leaders continued to publish single-issue papers, including a particularly audacious one on the December 28, 1959. Appearing on the third anniversary of British and French troop withdrawal from Suez, the paper carried a large, above-the-fold photograph of a beaming Nasser, accompanied by a banner headline hailing the Arabs' "victor" (a play on Nasser's name), who spoke at Port Said on the third anniversary of "Victory Day, the Day the Aggressors Withdrew."[137] Nasser's prominent picture, the triumphant headline, and the framing of the Suez War as an example of imperialist aggression against an Arab hero proved to be too much for the authorities. One week after the issue, on January 4, 1960, the interior minister formally denied the group's request for a publishing license, citing a technicality.[138] When Ard leaders resubmitted their petition, the Interior Ministry again denied the request, this time citing a provision in the Mandate-era Emergency Defense Law that allowed authorities to refuse a petition without giving a reason.[139]

Despite the denial, two more issues were published in January 1960. But when the thirteenth issue went to press in early February, Israeli police stormed the printing office and confiscated the original page layouts and all of the copies that were (quite literally) hot off the press.[140] The raid was accompanied by a wave of arrests: All six members of the editorial board were

Photo 2. December 1959 issue of *al-Ard* with a smiling Nasser on the front page. Courtesy of Laila El-Asmar.

charged with distributing a newspaper without a license, printing a newspaper without submitting it to the district commissioner for approval, and abusing the law that allows for a one-time publication. In June 1960, an appeals court in Haifa sentenced them to three months in jail and a hefty fine.[141] The group tried for another year to obtain permission to publish a paper, to no avail.

The fate of the Ard movement demonstrated the limits of acceptable political discourse in Israel. Palestinian citizens were allowed to complain about Israeli domestic policies, including land confiscation, military rule, and discriminatory laws—all of which the CPI publications did quite a bit—as long as they did so within a framework of seeking equal rights within Israel. But what proved to be unacceptable to Israeli authorities was the unabashed championing of Nasser-led pan-Arab unity as the solution to Palestinians' isolation from the region. While the Ard movement had collapsed for the time being, the ideas it propounded would resurface a few years later and push the CPI to adopt a more unabashedly Palestinian nationalist stance.

ENGAGING ARAB CULTURAL DEBATES

Despite their strong political disagreements, both pan-Arab nationalists and communists believed that in an environment of ongoing imperialism and social inequities, cultural productions needed to display a commitment (*iltizam*) to addressing larger social and political issues that went beyond the whims of the author. This position contrasted with the one espoused by proponents of freedom (*hurriya*), who argued that expecting artists to hew to a political line ruined the artistic quality of their work. Due in large part to the influence of the Beirut-based cultural monthly *al-Adab*, by the late 1950s the commitment position was dominant in progressive Arab literary circles.[142]

Palestinian intellectuals inside the Green Line followed these debates with great interest, but with limited access. Ongoing Israeli restrictions on the importation of Arabic media meant that whoever wished to stay abreast of the latest regional developments had to find ways to circumvent the authorities. While the influx of Iraqi Jews into Israel in the early 1950s had facilitated the CPI's dissemination of works from that country, equally important developments elsewhere in the Arab world remained largely inaccessible. This began to change when Fouzi El-Asmar and other Palestinian intellectuals (with help from Mapam) launched the Arab Book Company in 1958 and began acquiring back issues of Egyptian, Lebanese, and other Arab journals and newspapers from friends in Europe who sent them copies through the mail.[143] In addition, Palestinian students who entered Hebrew University in sizable numbers beginning in 1958 found a treasure trove of historical and contemporary Arabic books, poetry collections, magazines, and newspapers at the university's library. The collections were due in part to Israeli plundering of Palestinian collections during the 1948 war and in part to the up-to-date journal and book acquisitions made by an Israeli purchasing office in Geneva.[144]

While books and journals from the Arab world were not inherently illegal in Israel, Palestinians who obtained such material without permission could raise the suspicion of the authorities. Rashid Husayn learned this lesson the hard way one evening in 1960 when an armed police officer arrived at his house with a search warrant and a single question: Did Husayn "have any printed material from Arab countries?" Confident he had done nothing wrong, Husayn pulled out six issues of the Egyptian newspaper *al-Ahram*, two issues of the Lebanese magazine *al-Sayyad*, and a smattering of Arabic books. The disclosure triggered a call for backup, and soon nine police officers were poring over the hundreds of pieces of printed Arabic material in his small apartment. A criminal investigator asked Husayn how he obtained recent issues of Arabic newspapers and recently published books, to which Husayn replied that he had procured them from the Arab Book Company, which itself received the material legally through the mail. Meanwhile, a group of police officers separated the locally printed material from that published abroad, seizing dozens of books "whose only crime," according to Husayn, "was to be printed in Egypt." After four hours of searches and questioning, Husayn was hauled off by the police, whereupon he spent his first night in jail.[145]

Given the danger of possessing printed material from the Arab world, Palestinians increasingly copied material by hand. Muhammad Mi'ari, a law student at Hebrew University from 1958 to 1962, spent hours in the library copying Arabic poetry collections, which he then passed around to others.[146] Salim Jubran, who was a high school student at the time, recalled copying more than twenty poetry collections that he had borrowed from friends, particularly those of poets known for their literary commitment.[147] The irony of a policy that rendered an Arabic text legal while sitting on a university library shelf and subversive in the hands of a Palestinian citizen was not lost on them, and it made them all the more determined to obtain such material. As an aspiring poet, Jubran recalled eagerly awaiting for whatever issues of *al-Adab* and other Arab journals he could access, "like a lover waits for a beloved."[148]

Recognizing this thirst for information, editors for CPI and Mapam Arabic publications worked to circulate news about regional cultural developments to their readers. They had greater access to publications than individual Palestinians had, due to the joint Jewish-Arab makeup of the editorial boards and the greater ease with which editors (several of whom were current or former Knesset members) could obtain print material from abroad.[149] But the political differences between communists and nationalists, coupled with the political constraints inherent in writing for party-affiliated publications, led to differences in the type of material that was offered. In keeping with its internationalist outlook, *al-Jadid* and *al-Ittihad* continued to reprint works by Arab writers who championed a clear leftist perspective, along with Arabic translations of internationally acclaimed writers, from Neruda to Lorca to Langston Hughes.[150] They also covered regional and international writers' symposia, highlighting, for example, Muhammad Mahdi al-Jawahiri's remarks at the Fourth Arab Writers' Conference on Kuwait in December 1958, in which the Iraqi poet chastised those writers who discuss abstract issues in a detached manner.[151] *Al-Fajr* shied away from addressing issues of literary commitment head-on, but it did reprint the works of Arab figures associated with modernist and free verse poetry.[152] Together, these journals acquainted their readers with ongoing developments in the Arab cultural sphere—developments that local Palestinians would soon put into practice.

Israeli officials looked for ways to counteract the influence of such publications, but it was an uphill battle. *Al-Mujtamaʿ* closed its doors in 1959 because of lack of funds, and although *al-Yawm* was still in circulation, it was widely mocked for its poor quality and ham-handed propaganda.[153] Seeking to remedy this situation, in 1959 the Histadrut revamped the daily and hired as its editor in chief Nissim Rejwan, an Iraqi Jewish journalist with an established reputation in Israel as an expert on Arab affairs.[154] The following year Rejwan expanded the paper's staff to include more Palestinian writers and editors,[155] and he gave former *al-Mujtamaʿ* editor Michel Haddad and former contributor Taha Muhammad ʿAli a weekly column to discuss cultural and literary matters from a noncommitment perspective. Titled "A Window," the column introduced readers to classical and modern Arabic literature, although local Palestinian poetry did not appear and nothing with a political message made its way into the column.[156] While the content was along the same lines of *al-Yawm*'s earlier literature page, younger writers and intellectuals starved for information about the Arab literary scene eagerly read it. Jubran loved reading both modernist Taha Husayn and leftist Marun ʿAbbud. For him, "all publications were beneficial in some way,"[157] because they acquainted him with the cultural and literary debates that had been under way before his time.

Seeking to challenge the dominance of *al-Jadid* and *al-Fajr* on the literary scene, in 1960 the Histadrut launched its own literary monthly, *al-Hadaf* (The goal). The journal's overall objective was to resuscitate Israel's official narrative that the state was a force for good in the lives of its Palestinian citizens, as demonstrated by its technical projects, uplifting of women, desire for peace, and introduction of the great works of Hebrew and Arab writers to a local audience. The journal also emphasized literary freedom (rather than committed literature) and sought to convince readers that injecting literary works with political content would inevitably lead to overly dogmatic work.[158] While Jubran and other young intellectuals may have been interested in reading *al-Hadaf*, its anti-commitment message failed to convince them to join the journal's ranks, as demonstrated by the exceedingly low number of contributions made by local Palestinian writers over its two-year run.

SONGS OF REVOLUTION

Instead, revolution filled the air. The 1960 "Year of Africa," in which fourteen African nations gained formal independence, inspired Arabs to champion decolonization struggles beyond the region. Meanwhile, Israeli officials were eager to present their country as a role model for the decolonizing world, stressing their country's strong collective economic sectors and ruling socialist government. To shore up this reputation, Israeli officials established a broad network of technical assistance and cultural exchange programs with several Asian and African nations and cultivated diplomatic and military ties with pro-Western African leaders.[159] But they were wary of decolonization movements they considered to be too radical, most notably those of the Congo and Algeria, both of which received enthusiastic support from both Arab nationalists and communists for their strong socialist and anti-imperialist stances.

Along with their fellow Arabs, Palestinian intellectuals in Israel participated in political, literary, and intellectual "solidarity discourses" to support in particular the Congolese and Algerian revolutionaries.[160] The CPI championed Congolese leader Patrice Lumumba in his quest to shed Western imperial control, and the party celebrated Congo's formal independence.[161] But the Palestinians' greatest excitement was reserved for the Algerians' ongoing fight for liberty. As the provisional Algerian government in exile stepped up its efforts to build leftist, anti-imperial, pan-African alliances throughout 1960,[162] Palestinians joined in the international celebration of Algerians' steadfastness. In the process, they raised uncomfortable questions about Israel's relationship with Africa. In *al-Fajr*'s special issue on Algeria that September, Rashid Husayn called attention to the revelations of France's use of sexual torture against Algerian revolutionaries Jamila Bouhired and Jamila Boupacha. He then contrasted the global outrage over France's actions in Algeria with "our Foreign Minister Golda Meir, [who] remains cross-legged on her dais, trying to come up with plans to strengthen the bonds of friendship with African countries, as if Algeria is part of Australia rather than a part of Africa!"[163] Husayn sought to point out Israel's tenuous stance in which it championed certain decolonization movements while ignoring the most famous anticolonial cause of the day. Although he studiously avoided comparing Israel to French settler-colonialism outright, and even took for granted Israel's self-styled position as a role model for newly independent African countries, soon other intellectuals would begin drawing clearer connections between Israel and colonial projects.

Poetry continued to serve as the main mode of Palestinian expression of support for Algeria. In the same special issue of *al-Fajr*, guest editor Fouzi El-Asmar reviewed the numerous poems by local Palestinians from across the political spectrum that celebrated Algerian heroism, including works by Habib Qahwaji, Rashid Husayn, Samih al-Qasim, Mahmoud Darwish, Jamal Qaʿwar, Hanna Abu Hanna, and ʿIsam al-ʿAbbasi. The Algerian cause, El-Asmar wrote, "has given us literature to be proud of" and "raised our heads as Arabs."[164] For El-Asmar, being able to tap into the global zeitgeist of solidarity with Algeria was key for Palestinians inside the Green Line to be able to develop a body of work that could reach out beyond borders of the state.

TRAITORS, VICTIMS . . . HEROES?

Despite their deep engagement with these transnational discourses, Palestinians in Israel were largely ignored in the rest of the world. In Western countries, the official Zionist narrative describing a content, if benighted, Arab minority was pervasive. That narrative was also prevalent in the Arab world, where most nationalists seemed to regard any Palestinian who accepted Israeli citizenship as a turncoat. Soviet-sponsored gatherings in Moscow provided some opportunities for contact between CPI activists and their Arab communist counterparts.[165] But the latter were either marginalized or driven underground in their respective countries,[166] making it exceedingly difficult for them to serve as a bridge between Palestinian citizens of Israel and the Arab world.

Rashid Husayn's experience at the 1959 World Youth Festival in Vienna, where Lebanese delegates accused him of being a traitor for accepting Israeli citizenship, was repeated in a more subdued fashion two years later when he went to cover the Conference of Non-Aligned Nations in Belgrade for *al-Mirsad*. Eager to meet other Arab journalists and writers, Husayn walked up to several of them on the first day of the conference and introduced himself. According to Husayn, "Each one of them, without a single exception, hastened to get away upon hearing that I was an Arab from Israel. . . . I could see the suspicion in their eyes, while some of them smiled as if to say, 'An Arab from Israel? We understand.'"[167] While he had fruitful conversations with the nationalist Egyptian journalists Ihsan ʿAbd al-Quddus and Ahmad Bahaʾ al-Din (whose articles had been reprinted in *al-Fajr* two years earlier), Husayn was struck by the overall ignorance about his community that he found among the Arab elite.

When meeting the Tunisian minister of propaganda and information, Husayn had to explain to him that there were in fact Palestinians who still lived in Israel, to which the minister declared that they "ought to leave their homes and come to the Arab states." Husayn pressed him to explain how, at a time when "the Arab states demand the repatriation of the Arab refugees . . . you demand that their number be increased by a quarter of a million?" Stumped for an answer, according to Husayn, the minister changed his mind and agreed with Husayn that the Palestinians should remain where they were.[168]

Palestinian intellectuals in exile, some with relatives inside the Green Line, sought to raise Arab and global consciousness about the Palestinian citizens of Israel by publishing studies about their condition. The first such report, written by US-based Palestinian academic Fayez Sayegh in 1955,[169] laid out the various forms of persecution visited on the Palestinian minority, including discriminatory laws, land confiscations, the destruction of Palestinian towns and villages, and the desecration of Muslim and Christian holy sites.[170] In 1959, Sami Hadawi, a Palestinian land expert and cofounder of the Arab League's Arab Information Center (AIC) in New York,[171] laid out the case that Israel was systematically violating international human rights law through its policies toward the Palestinian minority.[172] While the tone of these studies was quite strident, both authors strove to document as carefully as possible their allegations to avoid being accused of propagandizing. Despite their efforts, such publications had little reach in Arab circles, as Husayn's experiences in Vienna and Belgrade showed.

Seeking to build on the growing international attention the Palestinian cause was receiving at this time, Palestinian intellectuals in Israel also began sending memoranda of their own. In November 1960 ten political organizers (including five from the recently disbanded Ard movement), issued one such memorandum to the UN secretary general laying out Israel's myriad violations of Palestinian rights. Delegates from some Arab countries distributed the memo at the UN, while the AIC republished it in the form of a pamphlet to facilitate further distribution.[173] The document echoed the allegations laid out in Sayegh's report, highlighting instances of Israeli aggression and discrimination. In the coming years, memoranda would play an increasingly important role as a strategy of resistance against Palestinian citizens' ongoing isolation.

While the portrayal of this community as victims of Israeli discrimination was perhaps better than viewing them as traitors, both depictions nonetheless characterized them as passive and disconnected from the Palestinian people and the wider Arab world. But in the early 1960s, a few Palestinians in exile began to call attention to the forms of resistance undertaken by Palestinians inside the Green Line. In 1961 Palestinian historian Ahmad Sidqi al-Dajani delivered a lecture on the condition of the Palestinians in "occupied Palestine" at the Cultural Center in Tripoli, Libya.[174] Drawing on the few available English studies about this group, he argued that far from being passive victims, they displayed a strong national consciousness and engaged in acts of resistance despite the oppressive atmosphere in which they lived. Calling attention to the internally displaced villagers in Kafr Birʿim, who refused government compensation for their stolen lands,[175] and to schoolteachers who instilled a sense of Palestinian cultural identity in their students despite Israel's educational restrictions, Dajani concluded that "there is no doubt that these brothers play a significant role in our struggle against the usurping enemy. . . . Until the day comes when we reunite with our beloved land, we send them greetings of love and admiration."[176] Dajani's appeal to see the Palestinians inside the Green Line as part of the collective Palestinian struggle was still uncommon at this time, but it was a hint of the discursive shifts to come.

CONCLUSION

After the Suez Crisis and Kafr Qasim massacre, Palestinian intellectuals in Israel searched for political and cultural outlets to express their opposition to state policies and their connection to the revolutionary spirit of the decolonizing world. Nonpartisan groups such as the League of Arab Writers and Intellectuals and the Popular Front showed how intimately these intellectuals were tied to the regional optimism of 1958. But the collapse of such groups under the weight of subsequent rivalries between communists and pan-Arab nationalists likewise demonstrated how those regional ties could overwhelm local dynamics.

Cultural outlets, especially poetry festivals, were much more successful at facilitating expressions of belonging among this group of Palestinians, as the spatial horizons that had been attenuated in the immediate aftermath of the Nakba began to expand once again. Veteran and aspiring poets connected with members of their community who were eager to hear about the pain and hope they shared with other Palestinians in exile and with peoples under various forms of colonial and semicolonial rule in Algeria, the Congo, and elsewhere. To be sure, neither the poets nor the political figures expressed their anticolonial sentiments through a call for armed insurrection against Israel or national independence from it. Rather, they formulated a more expansive conceptual framework of decolonization that focused on the ultimate goal: that all people in the world live with dignity and freedom. This was especially true of the younger generation of Palestinian poets, including Darwish and Qasim, who would in the coming years become the leading Palestinian spokesmen to articulate this vision of justice.

While poetry succeeded in helping Palestinians inside the Green Line feel a sense of connection to the region, it did not yet succeed in raising Arab awareness about them. Ongoing Arab misunderstandings and suspicions, coupled with Israeli restrictions on the importation of Arab material and the travel bans imposed on all sides, meant there were few opportunities for Palestinian citizens of Israel to meet other Arabs face-to-face. International gatherings allowed some opportunities to challenge regional stereotypes about them, but they were not enough to change the prevailing image. A few Palestinian intellectuals in exile recognized this as a problem and tried to shed light on this enigmatic community, to little avail.

Israeli officials viewed Palestinian expressions of solidarity with the Arab revolutionaries—especially pro-Nasser ones—as a threat. The Histadrut's attempts to counter literary commitment with "carrots," such as poetry festivals and greater investments in *al-Yawm* and *al-Hadaf*, largely failed. Instead, the authorities resorted increasingly to "sticks." The Ard movement, with the clearest articulation of pan-Arab nationalist and pro-Nasser sentiment at this time, hit up against the limits of acceptable political discourse in Israel: as a result, its leaders were subject to jail sentences and fines. But even the somewhat milder *al-Fajr* faced sanction. Right-wing leaders in Mapam had objected to the journal's special issue on Algeria, and in 1961 they ordered that the journal's editorial staff be combined with that of the more conservative Arabic party weekly, *al-Mirsad*. *Al-Fajr*'s editors were also told they needed to join the party in order to keep working for the journal, while those who did not, including El-Asmar, were fired. Three more issues came out before Mapam leaders ordered that the journal be folded altogether, claiming budgetary constraints.[177]

The closing of *al-Fajr* allowed the CPI to reemerge as the primary repository for Palestinian political and cultural expression in the country. But the party was no longer operating in the same environment it had been five years earlier. The region's fractious debates had exposed readers to a range of political views that challenged the CPI's internationalist outlook and its skepticism of Nasser-led pan-Arab nationalism. Meanwhile, as Palestinian nationalists in exile began to establish institutions that could more effectively disseminate their national narrative, they turned to their Palestinian brothers and sisters inside the Green Line and looked for ways to dispel the ongoing regional misconceptions about this beleaguered group.

4 PALESTINIAN SPOKESMEN

As *al-Jadid* welcomed the approach of its tenth anniversary, twenty-year-old editorial board member Mahmoud Darwish offered his analysis about why it was the only remaining Arabic literary journal in Israel. He challenged those who complained about a communist "monopoly" over Arabic cultural production in the country to ask themselves:

> What do the people of a million refugees want from their literature . . . ? What do the survivors and grandchildren of the martyrs from Dayr Yasin and Kafr Qasim want from their literature . . . ? What about the people whose heroic brothers fought back darkness on the tops of the Aures Mountains [in Algeria], on the soil of Port Said, though the streets of Baghdad, in the untouched regions of Yemen and elsewhere—what do they want from their literature? Simply put, they want a literature that emanates from these wounds and from these victories, not just some cerebral mutterings scattered in the wind.[1]

On one level, Darwish's invocation of Arab anticolonial struggles reflected the legacy of the CPI anticolonial and socialist realist outlook that stressed the need for literature to be "of the people" and to engage with the major decolonizing events of the day. On another level, by referring to his audience as "the people of a million refugees" and by invoking the Dayr Yasin and Kafr Qasim massacres together, Darwish positioned his community as a part of the Palestinian people as a whole. His phrasing signaled the emergence of a subtle, yet profound, discursive shift in Palestinian cultural expression in Israel that centered this community within the collective experiences of Palestinian people more clearly than before.

Darwish was not alone in doing so. During the mid-1960s a generation of Palestinian intellectuals born between the late 1930s and early 1940s and living on both sides of the Green Line came to the fore as the leading spokesmen of the Palestinian national movement. This cohort, who experienced the Nakba during their formative years and who came into political consciousness during the advent of Third World solidarity and the 1958 Arab revolutions, developed a shared political vocabulary that stressed overlapping concepts of leftist anticolonialism, pan-Arab nationalism, and Palestinian cultural pride. As they grew disappointed with the setbacks to the revolutionary order in the wake of the communist-nationalist rivalries and the growing repression of intellectuals at the hands of Arab revolutionary regimes, they turned toward a discourse that emphasized Palestinians' own steadfastness and the liberationist potential within themselves.

To tap into this emergent national framework, these younger Palestinian intellectuals pushed the strategies of resisting isolation pioneered by their predecessors in new directions. First, they revitalized the CPI Arabic publications as forums to weigh in on the political and cultural debates being contested in the region. But in contrast to their predecessors of the 1950s who avoided labeling Israel as "an imperialist base" and called for a clear socialist realist outlook,[2] these writers were more willing to compare Israel—albeit subtly—to other settler-colonial regimes and to push the aesthetic and ideological horizons of Arabic literary production further than before. Second, as these poets continued to recite their works at poetry festivals and other gatherings, they turned increasingly toward more explicitly Palestinian themes that aimed to connect their audience to one another and to other Palestinians. As these poets, especially Darwish and Samih al-Qasim, became more prominent, the Israeli authorities subjected them to various forms of physical confinement to try to curtail their influence, which ultimately had the opposite effect.

With attention to Palestinian rights increasing at the global level, the Ard movement revived a third strategy. In 1964 the group issued a memorandum to the UN and other bodies drawing international attention to Israel's discriminatory practices toward the Palestinian minority. Unlike previous such memoranda that had garnered little interest, this one gained the attention of Palestinians in exile, who were themselves establishing research institutes aimed at producing and disseminating knowledge about matters related to Palestine. Ard cofounder Sabri Jiryis likewise contributed to this endeavor, producing the first academic study to detail Israel's discriminatory practices against its Palestinian citizens, which was subsequently smuggled out of Israel and translated from Hebrew into Arabic by Palestinian intellectuals abroad. Meanwhile, *al-Ittihad*, *al-Jadid*, and other Arabic newspapers, along with poetry anthologies, were also taken out of Israel at increasing rates (though the exact means by which this happened remain unclear). Thus, a fourth strategy for connecting Palestinians in Israel to the Arab world—sneaking texts across the border—was now reversed, as locally produced texts were increasingly being smuggled out.

Scholars of this period have generally discussed these cultural and political developments in atomized ways, focusing, for example, on the early aesthetics of Palestinian resistance poetry,[3] or on early nationalist sentiment among Palestinian citizens of Israel.[4] While each of these topics is indeed worthy of detailed study, examining the intersections of these cultural and political endeavors reveals how the production and circulation of texts, including essays in journals, poems, memoranda, and academic studies, together played a central role, not only in forging relationships between Palestinian intellectuals on either side of the Green Line but also in helping those intellectuals take the lead in articulating a Palestinian anticolonial discourse to Arab and international communities.

LITERARY COMMITMENT IN A POSTREVOLUTIONARY WORLD

The Arab nationalist sentiments and anticolonial revolutions of the late 1950s had wide-ranging repercussions for the cultural developments of the region, especially given the Cold War environment. Fearing that the ascent of Arab nationalism would pave the way for greater Soviet influence in the region,[5] American cold warriors stepped up their promotion of a specific type of pro-Western modernist aesthetic that was intended to challenge socialist realism by emphasizing an individual's personal freedom, unencumbered by social or political constraints.[6] To further that goal, the United States Information Agency (USIA) sponsored Franklin Book Programs, Inc., which sold inexpensive American books, translated into Arabic and other local languages in the Middle East and Southeast Asia, that promoted themes of modernization and Westernization.[7]

Meanwhile, the revolutionary optimism of the late 1950s was being called into question as Arab intellectuals grew dismayed at the UAR's growing repression of the public spheres in Egypt and Syria. Due to the communist-nationalist rift, scores of leftist intellectuals had been arrested and jailed, and by 1960 Nasser had co-opted or suppressed most of the cultural, educational, political, and civic institutions in the two countries (a move toward authoritarianism that continued even after the UAR's split the following year). This disappointing shift led Arab intellectuals and cultural producers to debate more seriously the relationship between political commitment and personal freedom. While in the 1950s both Marxist and pan-Arabist proponents of literary commitment had easily outmaneuvered their opponents who called for an individualistic, "art-for-art's-sake" approach, by the early 1960s, the rivalries of the previous few years, coupled with the oppressive political landscape, led to cleavages between the two strands of commitment.

Those intellectuals sympathetic to the pan-Arab nationalist understandings of literary commitment questioned whether the socialist realist approach, with its ebullient predictions of the victorious people, was still relevant at a time when Arab revolutionary regimes disregarded personal liberties as freely as their colonial and neocolonial predecessors had done.[8] Iraqi poet Badr Shakir al-Sayyab, a leftist-turned-pan-Arab nationalist who had been a pioneer of the modernist-oriented free verse movement, delivered a paper in 1961 denouncing "partisan intellectuals" (primarily communists) whose ideological rigidity led their artistic work to suffer.[9] Marxist critics, led by Lebanese Communist Party leader and editor of the leftist Beirut-based cultural monthly al-Tariq, Husayn Muruwwah, pushed back against this attack, arguing that the calls for greater introversion would dilute the Arab revolutionary project of its vigor.[10]

Due in part to such debates, the Arab literary landscape of the 1960s was considerably more textured than before. While few writers openly sided with the type of Westernization being promoted by Franklin Book Programs, some took up a more existentialist position, arguing that liberating the self from societal repressions was a necessary condition of political freedom.[11] Meanwhile, Iraqi poets Sayyab and Bayati promoted modernist literary forms, albeit from pan-Arab nationalist and leftist political positions, respectively.[12] Their approaches echoed those of other Third World writers who adopted and adapted selective aspects of modernist aesthetics while rejecting the Western political projects that undergirded them.[13]

The editors of al-Jadid continued to weigh in on these debates from a decidedly pro-communist stance,[14] but the previous communist-nationalist disputes had demonstrated to younger intellectuals that socialist realism could not adequately address the challenges they faced. At the same time, a retreat into the individual self through Western-style modernism was not a viable option for them given the ongoing oppression and isolation they faced collectively as Palestinians citizens in a self-defined Jewish state. So the question remained: What kind of literary aesthetic and content could help Palestinians inside the Green Line improve their material conditions and overcome their isolation while still allowing them to represent their authentic selves as writers? For Darwish, Third World modernist writers offered some possible answers.

DARWISH ON DECOLONIZATION

In addition to being the most frequently published poet of this period,[15] Darwish was also a prolific essayist, writing columns in CPI publications that examined the role cultural productions have played in colonial and anticolonial projects both locally and globally. Darwish's long and productive career, coupled with his deep involvement in the Palestinian national movement, led him to become the most famous Palestinian poet of the twentieth century and one of the most studied.[16] Yet surprisingly little attention has been paid to his early essays, particularly those that appeared in *al-Ittihad*. After formally joining the CPI in 1961, he was given a regular column where, from July 1961 to January 1963, he wrote more than forty-five essays that discussed various matters related to literature and politics before moving full-time to the editorial board of *al-Jadid*.[17] Despite being only twenty years old when his essays first ran, Darwish offered remarkably trenchant analysis of cultural debates that had been under way for well over a decade but were undergoing significant changes at this time. By tackling such issues as the relationship between literature and politics and the role of the Israeli state in Palestinian cultural development, Darwish's essays shed light on his formative views regarding the ways in which cultural productions have been used in both colonial and anticolonial projects. They also shed light on his expanding spatial and temporal horizons—horizons that would impact Palestinian cultural and political developments for decades to come.

Darwish's own experiences, as an internal refugee, as a student in the Israeli school system, and as a rising poet and intellectual during the 1958 Arab revolutions, all contributed to his insistence that literature must serve the people in the cause of justice. This insistence came at a time when the buoyant atmosphere of 1958, which had led numerous aspiring poets to try their hand at composing revolutionary verse,[18] was replaced by partisan rancor, leading many of them to question the value of such work. Darwish wrote of receiving a letter from one disappointed would-be poet who proclaimed that it was folly to think that his poems could change the world and that from now on he was going to stick to topics of love and wine. Darwish replied that such a stance betrayed an already selfish attitude in the writer and that the solution for such an "illness" was "to transform the self-centered experience into a collective one." In other words, by immersing oneself among the "working, suffering people, among the peasant of the land and the laborer," Darwish argued that a poet can find "authentic artistic experiences." Darwish also warned that retreating into hedonism only "served the very rulers who prevent him and his people from the very pleasures they want in life."[19]

For Darwish, the call for poets to represent the collective experiences of their society was not part of an abstract literary debate. He worried that America's promotion of an apolitical modernist aesthetic in the Arab world was in fact an attempt to dislodge cultural producers from the front lines of the struggle for justice. Darwish pointed to these political dimensions in a two-part essay on Franklin Book Programs, criticizing what he saw as the program's underlying propagandistic aim to "overwhelm Arab writers and dissuade them from writing authentic Arabic literature that springs from the Arab hopes of liberation" by "flooding the market with books that are cheap in price and in content." Darwish specifically decried the prevalence of books published by Franklin that focused on the individual, to the exclusion of books that tackled wider social issues.[20] The letter Darwish received from the disappointed writer demonstrated to him the need to counteract this individualism with a modernist aesthetic that situated the individual within a broader collective experience that would work toward justice.

While Darwish recognized the broader Cold War dimensions of this struggle, he also made it clear that these debates had implications closer to home. In another essay he argued that for Palestinian writers in Israel, connecting their writings to their political struggles was imperative because "the political problems in our country . . . force [our] literature to walk in the caravan of revolution, not to build a socialist society now, but rather to attain freedom, to be rid of the heavy shackles, and to address the urgent demands of our people."[21] Unlike earlier socialist realist poetry that tended to subsume local struggles beneath a worldwide march toward class-based revolution, Darwish was calling for literature that focused more directly on the specific struggles that Palestinians in his community were undergoing to help ameliorate the immediate problems they faced.

Darwish's sense of urgency regarding this matter came into sharp relief when he and several other CPI party members were arrested on the eve of the August 1961 Knesset elections. According to Darwish, an officer came to his home, questioned him about some of his recent poems, then accused him of incitement and hauled him off to jail. Darwish waited in a cell with forty other men, wondering what he had done, then was released ten days later without charge. It was Darwish's first time in prison, which he described as a "university of dignity and steadfastness." But the dubious circumstances of his arrest, combined with the appalling conditions of prison, reaffirmed the justness of his cause. "Is there anything greater than for us to be inciters against such a government?" Darwish wondered.[22] His inaugural time in prison was another reminder of the lesson he had first learned as an eighth-grader at his school's Israeli Independence Day festival: those who proclaim the humanity of the Palestinians in the face of Israeli discrimination are subject to the sanction of the state.

Meanwhile, the state (primarily through the Histadrut) continued to extend carrots in an attempt to cultivate a new generation of Palestinian cultural producers who would reinforce the state's official narrative. Darwish recognized this project, and he was especially critical of the Histadrut's ongoing sponsorship of literary endeavors that promoted poetry with an individualistic, apolitical outlook as an antidote to the politically conscious poetry he championed. Darwish took issue with comments made by Histadrut director of Arab affairs Eliahu Agassi at a January 1962 poetry festival in which Agassi criticized as "negative" those writers "who wish to live in the past, feed into people's painful memories, and open old wounds." Darwish wanted to know "how literature—any literature—exists without a past," insisting that "literature that is unmoored from its base or heritage will remain lost."[23] Darwish's criticisms of Agassi revived those made by Palestinian intellectuals a decade earlier in response to official Israel discourses that insisted on the need for Palestinian citizens to prove their loyalty to the state by disavowing broader Arab and Palestinian narratives. But Darwish's criticism of Agassi's comments also indicated a larger temporal challenge that the poet saw, which was that Palestinians in Israel were cut off from their past. Darwish attributed the relatively weak literary output of his community to its condition as "an 'orphan' literature who lost his father and remained a small abandoned child, fumbling along his way." In contrast to the dramatic rupture and isolation that Palestinians inside the Green Line faced in the aftermath of the Nakba, Darwish argued, "the major writers of the world were all connected to a cultural chain, and every generation integrated the works and experiences of the previous generation."[24] Since Darwish and the writers of his generation were too young to have personally known the Palestinian and Arab writers of the pre-1948 period, and since they did not learn about the them in school, independent readings of prose and poetry offered the only lifeline they had to connect to their cultural past.

In addition to emphasizing the need for Palestinians to be connected to their past, Darwish wished to place his community's current condition within a larger context of Western colonialism. He repeatedly framed his community's inaccessibility to its past as part of a larger colonial endeavor whose effects could be seen elsewhere in the world. For example, in an essay praising the recent publication of Emile Tuma's history of the Arab national movement and a reprint of the popular eighth-century Arabic literary classic *Kalila wa Dimna*, Darwish noted that the publication of such books by a local Arabic printing house was an important step in combating colonialism. Citing Europe's erasure of precolonial African history as an example, Darwish wrote, "The genius of colonialism is that the first thing it seeks to do is erase the heritage of the people whose resources it covets."[25] Therefore, becoming acquainted with their own heritage, according to Darwish, is a key step in undermining such colonial endeavors. By positioning the debut of these local Arabic works within the larger dynamics of cultural colonialism, Darwish invited his readers to think of the ways in which the colonial erasure of Arab history operates in Israel, even as he studiously avoided explicitly identifying Israel as a colonial power.

Darwish's interest in cultural colonialism also led him to pay particular attention to the role that literature played in decolonization movements. He praised works by modernist Arab poets al-Bayati and Muhammad al-Fayturi, as well as the revolutionary Angolan writers Viriato de Cruz, Mário Pinto de Andrade, and Agostinho Neto, for their role in challenging Western narratives of colonial passivity.[26] But Darwish was most interested in the role of literature in Algeria, devoting several columns in *al-Ittihad* and *al-Jadid* to the Algerian struggle for cultural sovereignty and independence. In particular he admired how francophone Algerian writers who had been cut off from their from Arab heritage contested French rule using the language of the colonial power. In one column Darwish hailed Algerian novelist and teacher Mouloud Feraoun, whose tender portraits of Berber village life and evocative portrayals of anticolonial resistance—all written in French—led to him being killed by French extremists just three days before the cease-fire that marked Algeria's independence. According to Darwish, the power of writers such as Feraoun was their ability to depict vividly an individual's experience and, through that intimate depiction, to "draw portraits for history and for humanity, to expose and holler and inform the world about their issue."[27] By rallying Algerians around their cause and by humanizing them to an international audience, Darwish argued, these writers' contribution to Algerian independence was just as important as that of the revolutionary fighters.

But Darwish also recognized the limits of cultural productions in humanizing an oppressed people. In December 1962 he derided yet another Histadrut-sponsored endeavor, this one dubbed the "Israeli Organization for Understanding and Friendship," that aimed to melt away the "icy relations" between Palestinians and Jews in Israel. Darwish was struck by the hamhandedness of the effort, especially its attempt to efface the state's role in creating tensions between the two groups in the first place. "We are not so stupid as to forget that the political climate in this country is fundamentally affected by the smog coming out of the political 'ice factories' that are funded by the capital of hatred and chauvinism," Darwish wrote. He reminded his readers that the CPI also sought to bring Arabs and Jews closer together, but unlike the government, "we do not support one side at the expense of the other." He insisted that any improvement in the relationship between the two peoples must originate with a change in state policies, but he was not optimistic about that happening. "As long as [Israeli] educational programs pour streams of rubbish about 'barbaric Arabs' into the minds of Jewish students," Darwish concluded, and "as long as young Jews are not exposed to any of the humanistic Arab heritage and literature, neither in school nor in the press, the generation of 'glaciers' will remain."[28] The essay was an admission by Darwish of the steep obstacles that remained for CPI members and other community organizers to overcome the stereotypes that Palestinian citizens faced in Israel and to improve their social conditions. The hopeful brotherhood festivals that had been sponsored by the CPI less than a decade earlier had done little to improve the relations between the two peoples, and more recent efforts to bring Arab and Jewish poets together had likewise been disappointing.[29] As a result, Darwish would increasingly adopt a more confrontational stance in his own poetry while simultaneously casting his attention further afield.

Taken together, Darwish's essays in *al-Ittihad* demonstrate that the discursive contestations between the state and the Palestinian minority over the previous decade had not abated. Yet the ways in which Darwish pushed back against the state's colonial discourses differed significantly from those of his predecessors. He did not believe that polite appeals would affect government policies, like earlier accommodationists had, but he was more pessimistic about the promises of intercommunal harmony than older CPI leaders had been. Instead, as someone who grew up under Israeli rule and had experienced firsthand Israel's sequestration of the Palestinians, he saw the state as being engaged in a project of colonial erasure and isolation akin in some ways to what was taking place in Algeria and elsewhere. While militarized revolution was not the answer, Darwish did see hope in other Third World writers whose works humanized their struggles and enlisted global support for their cause. As Darwish and his colleagues faced a renewed Israeli land grab in the heart of the Galilee in the early 1960s, he would soon test his theories on the relationship between literature and political struggle.

"RECORD, I AM AN ARAB"

In the early 1960s the Israeli government stepped up its efforts to expropriate Palestinian-held land, essentially preventing Palestinians "from owning, leasing or being employed on 92% of the land in the state of Israel."[30] But unlike earlier land grabs, which were often done in an ad hoc manner, the latest efforts came with a specific declaration of intent to "Judaize the Galilee," the area that had by far the largest concentration of Palestinians in the country. To do so, the government forcibly consolidated Palestinians into denser population centers and confiscated their farmlands to build towns in which to settle Jewish immigrants.[31] The most ambitious—and controversial—plan was to establish the Jewish development town of Carmiel, in which 5,100 dunums (about 1,250 acres) of land from the Shaghur region east of Acre were slated for confiscation.[32] Local residents formed organizations to defend their lands and demanded that the state modify Carmiel's proposed borders to lessen the impact on their communities.[33]

News of the widespread expropriations brought a renewed sense of urgency to the land issue among Palestinians in Israel. Darwish in particular played a role in using verse to affirm his people's ties to the land and to push his audiences not to give up hope, even amid the demoralizing circumstances they faced. In one such poem, published in the midst of the Carmiel controversy, Darwish declared his people's collective love of the land: "Our beloved land! / We sing to it / We sing, yet we know the misery of the disheartened / Invaded on the splendor of the singers / But our hopes are fresh / And green, no matter how many years pass."[34] While in years past poets had invoked Palestinians' love of land and the refugees' longing to return, Darwish's recitation of this and other poems at the growing number of conferences and rallies specifically aimed at preventing further land confiscations signaled the revival of poetry as a tool of direct national mobilization, similar to what was seen during the Mandate era. But unlike the neoclassical structures of the earlier poetry, with its set rhyme and meter, Darwish used a modernist free verse aesthetic to rally his community.

But what made Darwish's star rise above those of so many other poets was his ability to speak as an individual while simultaneously speaking for the collective. The most famous example of this talent is his 1963 poem, "Identity Card," which would become one of the most oft-recited poems among Palestinians in Israel, and eventually among the Palestinians as a whole. Spoken in free verse, the narrator tells an Israeli policeman (presumably at a checkpoint),

> Record!
> I am an Arab
> And my identity card is number fifty thousand
> I have eight children
> And the ninth is coming after a summer
> Will you be angry?
> . . . .
> My father descends from the family of the plow
> Not from a privileged class
> And my grandfather was a farmer
> Neither well-bred nor well-born
> He teaches me the pride of the sun
> Before teaching me how to read
> . . . .
> Record!
> I am an Arab
> I am a name without a surname
> And my address—
> I am from an isolated, forgotten village
> And all of its men work in the field and the quarry
> They like communism[35]
> . . . .
> Therefore!
> Record on the top of the first page:

I do not hate people
Nor do I encroach
But if I become hungry
The usurper's flesh will be my food
Beware
Beware
Of my hunger
And my anger![36]

Read in the context of Darwish's life experiences and in conjunction with his earlier essays and poems, "Identity Card" crystallizes several elements of the poet's intellectual and artistic development at this time. In using the first-person singular to articulate the collective suffering of his people, Darwish exemplified a type of Arab modernism that foregrounded the individual's perspective while still embedding it within a larger social cause. The poem makes several nods to Darwish's personal story, including his father's modest background and employment in the quarry, his forgotten village of Birwa, and the confiscation of his family's land. And while Darwish repeatedly used the first-person singular in the refrain, "Record / I am an Arab," the personal experiences he invoked were shared by many Palestinians in the country, contributing to a sense of collectivity.

Also embedded in Darwish's lines were several direct challenges to Israeli colonial discourses. His invocation of his forebears and his ancestors' land not only asserted Palestinians' claims of indigeneity but also reaffirmed their resistance to colonial attempts at erasure. His reference to his grandfather teaching him how to read was a rebuke of the notion that the Israeli state was the only—or even primary—source of enlightenment for Palestinians.[37] Darwish's taunting question, "Are you angry?" asked after informing the policeman of his abundant progeny, illustrated his awareness that, despite Israeli efforts to incorporate the Arab minority into its discourses of democratic enlightenment, the presence—and abundance—of Palestinian citizens who refused to embody their citizenship on Israeli terms was an ongoing source of frustration for the state. His last line warning to "Beware / of my hunger / and my anger!" was more directly defiant of the state than earlier Palestinian socialist realist poetry, which tended to speak collectively of the people's anger rather than through the voice of a single individual. Such language was more personally emboldening, inviting listeners to embrace their individual rage rather than subsume it under a collectivist spirit.

"Identity Card" was an immediate success. The first time Darwish recited it at a festival, audience members demanded an encore, followed by a second and a third.[38] In the weeks, months, and years to come, Darwish was asked to recite "Identity Card" (also known as "Record, I Am an Arab") at festivals, rallies, and conferences again and again. The poem remained a cultural touchstone and an affirmation of Palestinian identity for decades to follow. But at the time it did little to stop the land confiscations or alter the establishment of Carmiel, which opened to great official fanfare on October 29, 1964, the eighth anniversary of the Kafr Qasim massacre.[39] Poetry clearly had its limits in terms of effecting change on the ground, but that did not mean that poets were politically irrelevant.

"POETS, NOT DIPLOMATS"

As Palestinian poets engaged in on-the-ground struggles against the Israeli state, they continued to pay attention to wider cultural debates, particularly about the role that committed literature should play in the postrevolutionary Arab world of the 1960s. While scholars often discuss Darwish and Qasim in tandem, during this period they had noticeably different political orientations that influenced the type of poetry they wrote. Darwish's early works, with their leftist-nationalist orientation, reflected the influence and perspective of the CPI. Meanwhile, Qasim's experiences as a Druze citizen of Israel led him to adopt a strong pan-Arab nationalist commitment more in line with that of other pan-Arab poets such as Badr Shakir al-Sayyab.[40] And unlike Darwish, who joined the CPI in 1961, Qasim did not join any political parties during this period, submitting poems and essays covering a range of topics to *al-Ittihad*, *al-Jadid*, *al-Fajr*, and other publications.[41]

The multiple venues in which Qasim published also reflected the shifting cultural landscape with which veteran CPI editors, who remained firmly in the leftist camp, had to contend. In 1964, these differences in outlook clashed directly on the pages of *al-Ittihad*. Editor Emile Habibi deemed one of Qasim's poems to have such "extreme nationalist viewpoints" that it was inappropriate for publication in his newspaper.[42] Qasim responded with a spirited defense of artistic autonomy titled "Poets, Not Diplomats," in which he argued that while commitment to social justice was important, "the poet who is truly dedicated to his literary work reaches into his heart in order to find his subject, then presents it within the framework of his culture and circumstances."[43] Echoing Sayyab's critique of partisanship leveled three years earlier, Qasim argued that his need to be true to himself outweighed his responsibility to promote a certain political or social viewpoint.

The debate reflected the ongoing influence that regional literary developments had on the local Palestinian cultural scene, and it signaled an emergent generational divide. Habibi's reluctance to publish Qasim's poem revealed a defensiveness that was in part a legacy of the previous communist-nationalist debates; Qasim's insistence on artistic autonomy (while still staying committed to his community's political cause) echoed the calls for greater freedom being issued by Arab intellectuals at the time. Although the disagreement between Habibi and Qasim was pronounced, it is important not to overstate the severity of it: Qasim would go on to have several poems published in *al-Ittihad* and *al-Jadid*, and he would begin writing a column for the journal in 1965. Despite their artistic differences, both men soon recognized they would need to support one another amid an intensified Israeli crackdown on those Palestinian intellectuals and cultural producers who challenged the status quo.

CELEBRITIES UNDER CONFINEMENT

By the early 1960s, Israel had begun to ease some of the most visible aspects of its military rule over Palestinians: it lifted the daytime movement restrictions on Palestinians in the Galilee and Triangle regions, and the Histadrut labor union began admitting Palestinian workers as full members.[44] But subtler, more pernicious forms of repression remained in place and in some cases were expanded. Israeli authorities continued to invoke the British-era Emergency Defense Law that required anyone deemed a security threat to obtain a permit from the military governor to travel from one town to another—permits that were not often forthcoming. Travelers who did not carry the proper permit risked incarceration.

Qasim and Darwish had been on the government's radar since their first poetry collections were published in 1958 and 1960, respectively.[45] Their public activism, including leading a march commemorating the fourth anniversary of the Kafr Qasim massacre in 1960, further added to their reputations as troublemakers.[46] Darwish's decision to join the CPI led him to be swept up in a wave of arrests in 1961, but even the politically unaffiliated Qasim earned the authorities' ire by refusing to enlist in the Israeli military service, as required of male Druze citizens. Moreover, Qasim led an anti-enlistment campaign within the Druze community, arguing that service in the military played into Israel's divide-and-rule strategy that was aimed at preventing the Palestinian minority from working together for greater collective rights. After being jailed over his refusal to enlist, Qasim was forced to teach in the army for two years, but then his supervisors accused him of inciting the soldiers against the government, so he was transferred to a different post.[47]

As a result, by the time each of their second collections came out in 1964, both men had established reputations as talented poets and community leaders who had paid a price for their political commitments. This reputation was further enhanced as their new collections defiantly proclaimed their people's steadfastness and their solidarity with those struggling for freedom around the world.[48] With the appearance of their second collections, both men became sought-after poets; as Qasim explained, "I would recite poetry everywhere—on the streets, in houses, squares, and clubs where the [poetry] collection would be sold."[49] Their rising profile led to further trouble with the authorities: that same year, a government panel was convened to hear renewed accusations against Qasim of "incitement"; the hearing resulted in his being banned from teaching in government schools altogether.[50]

Worried about the impact that poets such as Qasim and Darwish would have on the Palestinian community, from 1964 until well after military rule ended, Israel authorities placed both men under "town arrest" in Haifa. According to the terms of their confinement, they were not allowed to leave Haifa's city limits, even to visit their families in their hometowns.[51] In addition, they had to report to the Haifa police station three times each day to verify they were still in the city. Each night from sunset to sunrise, they were confined to their residences, where they awaited a policeman or soldier to arrive, unannounced and at times that varied from one night to the next, so they could sign a form proving they were home.[52] It was their own special isolation within their community's greater isolation.

They had a bit of a reprieve in 1965 when eighteen-year-old Shawqi Kassis became Darwish's roommate. An admirer of the two poets, Kassis helped them partially circumvent their nighttime confinement. Kassis explained:

> As Samih lived in a nearby building, I often went to his room after work and I would stay there while he took a walk or ran some errands, in violation of the restrictions on his movements. When the soldier or policeman responsible for checking on him would arrive, I would distract him by offering him some of the Arabic food that Umm Qasim (Samih's mother, whom I called Aunt Hana) would have me deliver to him—fresh fruit, different kinds of breads and

Photo 3. Samih al-Qasim (second from left) and Mahmoud Darwish (left) listen to writer Tawfiq Fayyad as he reads from his first novel. Haifa, 1963. Source: The National Album of Muhammad Samih al-Qasim. Copyright The Palestinian Museum. Reprinted with permission.

> pastries, and tasty Arab dishes. I would sign the slip of paper, pretending to be Samih, and the official would depart, happy with what he had eaten. Mahmud began to notice that I was often late coming back to our room in the evening and one day he asked me why. "Charity begins at home," he objected when I told him I was doing my "patriotic" duty vis-à-vis Samih. Mahmud wanted me to do the same for him. I agreed and so I would sign for Samih one night and for Mahmud the next night. I was eighteen years old at the time, and it made me feel as if I too were fighting the good fight, for God and for our homeland.[53]

But the reprieve was temporary. In 1965 Darwish was arrested a second time for leaving Haifa without a permit to participate in a poetry festival at the Hebrew University in Jerusalem and sentenced to another stint in prison.[54]

During his two months of incarceration, Darwish penned much of what would become his third poetry collection, *A Lover from Palestine* (*'Ashiq min Filastin*). The title poem, a plaintive longing for Palestine as if it were a distant beloved, was the first published poem by Darwish that invoked Palestine explicitly: "Her eyes and tattoo are Palestinian / Her name is Palestinian / Her dreams and sorrows are Palestinian."[55] Other poems spoke of the daily inequities and deep loneliness he faced while incarcerated, with poems addressed to his mother, his younger sister, his grandfather, and his father.[56] But there was still a defiant note in much of this poetry, a determination that his people's steadfastness would ensure that justice prevailed. While written at the height of his physical isolation, Darwish's verses spoke to the collective Palestinian experience of longing and exile more explicitly that his previous poems had done, paving the way for his entry into the Arab world. But it would take the efforts of Palestinian intellectuals in exile for that to happen.

"PART OF THE PALESTINIAN ARABS"

Since 1948 Palestinians on both sides of the Green Lines had carefully followed regional political developments. Many politically active Palestinians living in exile were fervent Nasser supporters and had opposed the breakup of the UAR because it had diminished Nasser's political capital. But as it became apparent that the "disunion" was permanent, they soon began looking for alternative ways to revive the notion of a Palestinian national entity. More than a dozen groups were formed over the course of the 1960s; they all shared the belief that Palestine had been unlawfully seized from its rightful inhabitants and that it needed to be liberated for its expelled people to return, but each group had a different attitude regarding the idea of pan-Arab unity and the use of armed struggle. The Palestine Liberation Front (PLF), founded in Beirut in 1961, sought to create an organization that would be part of a pan-Arab liberation movement but would be shielded from the rivalries and ideological disputes that had doomed the UAR. PLF members opposed Fatah's raids into Israeli territory and its goal of "entangling" the Arab states into a confrontation with Israel.[57]

In part to support the multiple Palestinian liberationist efforts and in part to control them, in January 1964 the Arab Summit in Cairo passed a resolution that called for "setting the proper foundations for the organization of the Palestinian people, so that they can play their role in the liberation of their nation and acquire self-determination."[58] That May, some four hundred Palestinians from the West Bank, Gaza Strip, and abroad gathered in East Jerusalem and formally declared the establishment of the Palestine Liberation Organization (PLO). With its intent to establish an army, collect "taxes" from Palestinians in exile, and convene representative political bodies on a regular basis, the statist ambitions of this new organization were clear. Also clear was the overlapping combination of pan-Arab and nation-state orientations that characterized much of the thinking of the PLF and other political activists at this time. The pan-Arab outlook of the PLO was apparent in the first article of the body's charter, which declared, "Palestine is an Arab homeland tied by Arab nationalism to all the Arab countries which together compose the wider Arab homeland." Other articles clarified its nation-state orientation, declaring the country's borders as those of Mandate-era Palestine and affirming the need for the Palestinian people to "preserve its Palestinian character and the components [of that character] and to nurture awareness of its existence and oppose any ventures that might dissolve or weaken it."[59] Through this combination of pan-Arab and nation-state orientations, the PLO's charter reaffirmed the central tenets of Palestinian nationalist thought going back to the Mandate period: that the Palestinians were an integral part of the broader Arab nation and that working toward the liberation of Palestine was necessary to achieve Arab unity. The charter also reflected the view that Palestinians had a distinct national "character" and that they were called on to instill future generations with knowledge about their cultural past and present.

Palestinians overall welcomed the establishment of the PLO, even if they were dubious about its Nasser-appointed leader, Ahmad Shuqayri, who had no popular constituency of his own.[60] But the CPI leadership, which had staked so much of its political capital on the idea of building Arab-Jewish progressive solidarity within the state of Israel, was rather skeptical of the endeavor. Party leaders questioned whether a truly progressive, peace-seeking body could emerge from a conference whose representatives included many of the same members of the traditional elite who oversaw Palestine's loss in 1948 and whose host was the "reactionary" pro-Western monarch of Jordan, King Hussein. *Al-Ittihad* reported on the PLO's May 1964 founding conference without much fanfare, while its official editorial criticized Shuqayri's "regressive and harmful" remarks that conflated Jews and Zionists. The editorial's author (most likely Habibi) also expressed disappointment in a resolution passed at the conference calling on Arab states to restrict Jewish "economic and political activities on behalf of imperialism and Zionism" within their respective borders. According to the author, such declarations sent exactly the wrong message, away from progressive, peaceful cooperation between Arabs and Jews and toward an ethno-national hostility that played into the hands of imperialism, not against it.[61] The editorial's criticism revealed two different understandings of the relationship between Zionism and imperialism. According to the logic of the PLO, Zionism and imperialism were twin evils preventing Palestinians from returning to their land. Therefore, its call for restrictions on Jewish activity in Arab countries reflected their understanding of Jews, Israel, Zionism, and imperialism as forming a Gordian knot of oppression against the Palestinians. In contrast, *al-Ittihad* continued to emphasize the distinction between Jews and Zionism, and between Zionism and imperialism, stressing that while Israel's Zionist logic may further imperialist aims, the solution was to work with progressive Jews to challenge that logic. Lumping Arab Jews in particular with Zionist and imperialist forces was counterproductive, especially given the history of friendship between Arabs and Jews in Israel and elsewhere, and would only serve to confirm Western and Israeli framings of the conflict as being driven by Arab hatred toward Israel.

While there are no clear indications of early public support for the PLO among Palestinians in Israel, a number of political organizers in the country had concluded that their complaints against the authorities could not (or would not) be addressed within the parameters of the state. Salih Baransi, cofounder of the Ard movement, said as much in a 1963 interview in which he listed the numerous Israeli policies that oppressed the Palestinian minority in the political, social, economic and educational spheres. He concluded, "The Arabs began to see in them a sign proving the impossibility of two nations living in peace here. They were also taken to mean, or to show, the intention of the Israeli Government to get rid of the Arab community here and so to add a new large number of homeless distressed Arabs."[62]

These frustrations with Israeli policies, coupled with the rising prominence of Palestinian liberationist discourse in Arab politics, led figures associated with the Ard movement to situate their lack of civil and national rights in Israel within a broader framework of Palestinian nationalism. After it was banned in early 1960, the group's founders had faithfully appealed through the Israeli legal system to have the ban overturned and their grievances redressed. A partial victory came in 1962 when the Israeli Supreme Court allowed the group to register as a company, though it did not grant it the right to publish a paper. When the Ard Company tried again to obtain a publishing license in late 1963, the government again refused, leading to another round of legal battles in which the Supreme Court ultimately sided with the state.[63] Seeing the ban as an attempt to silence them, Ard leaders decided to bypass the Israeli state and take their claims to the international arena.

The result was a carefully worded twelve-page memorandum in which the Ard Group (as it was now called) laid out its major grievances against the state, including the ongoing confiscation of Palestinian lands; discriminatory rule through a military government; lack of investment in schools, infrastructure, and municipal services in Palestinian areas; and denial of basic freedoms, such as the freedom of expression and freedom of assembly, to Palestinian citizens.[64] These grievances reiterated many of those that had been voiced in previous memoranda to the UN, albeit with more detail and documentation. But what was fundamentally different this time was the Ard Group's framing of the issue as being not just as a domestic dispute between the state and its aggrieved minority population but also as part and parcel of the larger Palestinian and Arab nationalist cause. According to the memorandum, "The *al-Ard* Group believes that the Arabs in Israel are part of the Palestinian Arabs who are an integral part of the whole Arab Nation."[65]

At the same time, as a group seeking greater rights within Israel, the Ard Group did not adopt Palestinian nationalist framing wholesale. The memorandum explicitly recognized the State of Israel on the areas allotted to it by the 1947 UN Partition Plan, though it considered the territory beyond that to be illegally occupied. It also called for "Israel's recognition of the Arab national movement, which calls for unity and socialism, as the most progressive and reliable force on which the future of this region depends—an outlook on which the future of Israel herself depends."[66] Despite its recognition of Israel, the Ard Group's incorporation of Palestinian and Arab nationalist formulations into its platform once again pushed against the limits of acceptable political discourse in Israel, and its leaders knew they were making a risky move. In July 1964 they fanned out across Israel and quietly mailed nearly one hundred copies of their memorandum from different postal locations, hoping at least some of them would make it past government censors. They sent copies to UN secretary general U Thant, all the foreign embassies in Israel, all Israeli Knesset members and ministers, and Israeli prime minister Levi Eshkol.[67]

The memorandum caused an uproar in Israel. Government officials and the establishment press excoriated the Ard Group for what they saw as a malicious attack that denied Israel's very right to exist.[68] The memorandum also caused a stir in Palestinian circles in the country: While leaders in Mapam and the CPI accused the government of overreacting, they also took the Ard leaders to task for undermining their own more mainstream efforts to strengthen coexistence between Jews and Palestinians in Israel. Mapam leader Muhammad Watad, an editor at *al-Mirsad*, accused the group of peddling a highly marginalized, "extremist" position vis-à-vis the state that "endangers our very existence."[69] Emile

Habibi tried to downplay the Ard Group's significance, arguing that the government's overreaction had less to do with the stepped-up activities of the group itself and more to do with "the deep revolutionary transformations that have taken place and are taking place in the Arab world around us." Nonetheless, the veteran CPI leader criticized Ard leaders for failing to coordinate their efforts with other political groups and for neglecting to include language that endorsed cooperation between Arabs and Jews, which he believed was necessary to be taken seriously as an advocate for Palestinian rights in the country.[70]

The reactions of Watad and Habibi demonstrate the ongoing relevance of regional debates between pan-Arab and nation-state nationalists to the Palestinian political landscape in Israel. At the heart of the debate was the following question: Which approach would more quickly and effectively lead to an improvement in the lives of Palestinians living inside the Green Line: pan-Arab unity or true Arab-Jewish brotherhood and equality within the state? What made the Ard memorandum so disconcerting to Mapam and the CPI—both of which shared its overall grievances against the state—was the Ard Group's underlying demand that the Palestinians in Israel be considered part and parcel of the Arab nation and that the Israeli government in turn accept pan-Arab unity as the best hope for full decolonization in the region. Palestinian leaders in Mapam and CPI recognized that Jewish Israelis by and large did not see the Arabs in the region as engaged in an ongoing struggle against Western colonialism but rather as fomenting a hostile ideological enmity against them as Israelis. As they saw it, the Ard Group's positioning of Palestinian citizens of Israel as part of the Palestinian people and the larger Arab world played directly into Jewish Israeli fears—present since the founding of the state—that Israel was at risk of being overwhelmed by a concerted, unified Arab attack. Despite the investment of Palestinian CPI and Mapam leaders in Arab political affairs, they nonetheless still believed in the need to work within the existing Israeli political framework, not outside it, to help their community. The Ard memorandum directly challenged this framing.

The controversy continued into fall 1964 as the Ard Group tried to register with the journalists' league as a formal association. As part of its registration papers, the group included a copy of the proposed articles of its association, stating that the association's aims were "to raise the educational, health, economic and political standards of all its members" and "to achieve complete equality and social justice for all classes of people in Israel."[71] But what garnered the most attention—and outrage—among Israeli authorities was a clause stating that the association was also aimed at

> finding a just solution for the Palestinian problem, through its consideration as an indivisible unit—in accordance with the wish of the Palestinian Arab people; a solution which meets its interests and desires, restores to it its political existence, ensures its full legal rights, and regards it as the first possessor of the right to decide its own fate by itself, within the framework of the supreme wishes of the Arab nation.[72]

With language strikingly similar to that found in Articles 3 and 4 of the PLO's 1964 Palestinian National Charter,[73] the Ard Group's description of the "Palestinian Arab people" as being "the first possessor of the right to decide its own fate" marked the first time that a group of Palestinian citizens of Israel unabashedly asserted the primacy of Palestinian self-determination—rather than Israeli goodwill—as being the most viable solution to the conflict.

Israel was swift to respond. The district commissioner denied the Ard Group's petition on the grounds that its call for Palestinian self-determination amounted to a denial of Israel's existence and of the right of Jewish citizens to have a say in their own future. The Ard Group once again appealed to the Supreme Court, with Ard's young cofounder, attorney Sabri Jiryis,[74] arguing that the controversial clause indicated their belief that all matters related to Israel, the Palestinians, and the Arabs were interconnected and that a comprehensive solution to the conflict that addressed all parties' grievances must be sought.[75] On November 11, the court rejected Jiryis's arguments and upheld the ban, citing the clause on Palestinian self-determination as a major factor in its decision.[76] A wave of arrests followed the ruling; several Ard leaders were jailed on charges of seeking to contact the PLO and other hostile Arab entities—charges they vigorously denied. The Ard leaders were conditionally released a few weeks later after several rounds of interrogations and house searches failed to produce any evidence supporting the authorities' claims of contact with the enemy.[77]

The second rise and fall of the Ard Group once again demonstrated the limits imposed on Arab nationalist discourse in Israel, but the political atmosphere of the mid-1960s was quite different from the one four years earlier. Habibi was correct to cite the "deep revolutionary transformations" that were taking place in the region as a major factor in Israel's growing anxieties about the Ard Group. But Habibi was reluctant to admit that a central feature of those transformations was the emergence of an independent, anticolonial liberationist Palestinian mode of self-expression that challenged the premise of his contention—made since 1948—that the solution to the problems that Palestinians in Israel faced could be found in broad anti-imperialist alliances, strong Arab-Jewish camaraderie, and appeals to the Israeli authorities for equal rights. Fundamentally, the Ard Group represented an articulation of the germane and unbreakable bond between Palestinians on either side of the Green Line. More important, the group tapped into an emergent discourse about Palestinian rights that increasingly echoed throughout much of the decolonizing world. This emphatic discourse on self-determination and fundamental rights—including the right of Palestinian refugees to return to their lands and homes—was gradually adopted by the CPI itself, signaling the influence of these nationalist discourses on the internationalist-oriented group.

CHAMPIONING THE RIGHT OF RETURN

The Ard Group's brief reemergence came at a time of increased international attention to the Palestine issue. As newly decolonized countries in Asia, Africa, and Latin America wished to express their opposition to the lingering vestiges of imperialism around the world, the sight of hundreds of thousands of Palestinian refugees languishing in UN refugee camps in the countries surrounding Israel—still waiting to go home—appeared to be one of the most blatant examples of ongoing indigenous displacement by a settler-colonial regime. In September 1964, forty-seven Heads of State or Government of the Non-Aligned Movement passed a resolution at the UN General Assembly to "(1) endorse the full restitution of all the rights of the Arab people of Palestine to their homeland, and their inherent right to self-determination; (2) declare their full support to the Arab people of Palestine in their struggle for liberation from colonialism and racism."[78]

The resolution's affirmation of the "rights of the Arab people of Palestine to their homeland" signaled the body's specific distress with the plight of the Palestinian refugees. Palestinians and their supporters throughout the non-Western world continued to insist that the refugees had an inalienable right to return to the homes from which they fled or had been expelled during the Nakba, often invoking UN General Assembly Resolution 194 (III), which affirmed "that the refugees wishing to return to their homes and live at peace with their neighbors should be permitted to do so at the earliest practicable date."[79] But Israel maintained that a solution to the refugee problem must be part of a broader peace agreement between Israel and the Arab countries that focused on the resettlement of refugees in surrounding countries and compensation for those who lost their lands.[80]

The growing international attention given to Palestinian refugees had clear reverberations in Israel. At a time when the Jewish Israeli body politic was shifting to the right,[81] and when Fatah guerrilla attacks left Israelis feeling vulnerable,[82] the idea of refugee return was unfathomable. Prime Minister Levi Eshkol, who was generally perceived to be less belligerent toward the Arabs than his predecessor, David Ben-Gurion, nonetheless insisted that Israel would not cede any ground on the refugee issue. In May 1965 he warned Knesset members that the return of the refugees would mean "the destruction of the state."[83] Meanwhile, Palestinian CPI leaders who had already begun shifting in the late 1950s from calling for refugee return on humanitarian grounds to embracing refugee return as an inalienable right stepped up their demands that Israeli officials acknowledge the refugees' right of return.[84] At a 1964 international youth forum in Moscow in which delegates "call[ed] for the implementation of the UN [General] Assembly Resolution [194] regarding the right of Palestinian refugees to return to their country," CPI delegate Ghassan Habib declared, "We struggle in Israel for the recognition of the rights of Arab refugees to return to their country."[85] CPI leader and former Knesset member Tawfiq Tubi criticized Eshkol's refusal to countenance the return of refugees as standing in the way of peace. Tubi insisted that the only path forward was for Israel to "acknowledge the rights of the Palestinian Arab people, and above all else the rights of its refugees."[86]

In such an atmosphere, the CPI could not hold together. The growing divide between Jewish and Palestinian members over the refugee issue, along with mounting restlessness among their Palestinian constituency, the challenge of the Ard Group, and the Soviet Union's relaxation of ideological discipline, meant that by the mid-1960s CPI leaders could no longer insist on class solidarity and equal rights within Israel as the overarching goals of their party. By summer 1965 the nationalist orientations among Jewish and Palestinian leaders of CPI had become so considerable that the party split into a Jewish party that retained the Hebrew acronym for the CPI (Maki, Hamiflagah Hakomunistit Hayisra'elit), and a predominantly Palestinian communist party that adopted the name Rakah (Hareshimah Hakomunistit Hehadashah, New Communist List).

Freed from the constraints of trying to champion the Palestinian cause within a joint Arab-Jewish framework, Rakah's run for the November 1965 Knesset elections included an even more robust call for the Palestinian refugees to return to their country than had been seen before. *Al-Ittihad* (which now served as the official paper of Rakah) monitored closely the debates at the UN regarding the insertion of language into a General Assembly resolution that would firm up the international body's commitment to implementing refugee return,[87] and it derided Mapam's Arab members for publicly renouncing the refugees' right to return.[88] While much of the heated rhetoric against Mapam could be attributed to election-season campaigning, Rakah's focus on the right of return for Palestinian refugees nonetheless demonstrates the growing salience its leaders believed the issue had among their constituents.[89] It was also a sign of the growing convergence of outlooks among Palestinian intellectuals on both sides of the Green Line.

PEERING BEYOND THE BARBED WIRE

Despite the many decades in which Palestinian intellectuals in Israel positioned themselves as part of the Palestinian people and the Arab world, they made only an occasional appearance in Arab political discourse. The portrayals of them as traitors to the Arab cause had abated somewhat; by this time they were generally portrayed as passive victims of Israeli discrimination. When US and British journalists asked Nasser at a 1963 press conference why he did not make peace with Israel, the Egyptian leader replied that peace had to be based on justice, yet "today in Israel there are about 2.5 million Israelis and 200,000 Arabs who are treated as second-class citizens, [living] in closed areas that are subjected to a military government." Nasser explained, "There are racist practices against them; they cannot work in the jobs they want, nor can they move from place to place because they are under military rule. So is this justice?"[90] Similarly, an advisory committee at the Arab Summit in January 1964 that looked into Israeli violations of Palestinian rights merely noted in passing that Israel "practices racial discrimination [*al-tamyiz al-ʿunsuri*] against its minority and carries out policies of aggression [against them]."[91] In both these cases, the focus not on Palestinian subjectivity but on the violations that Israel had committed against them was invoked as part of the debate over the righteousness of the Arab side of the Arab-Israeli conflict. While this portrayal was an improvement over the accusation that Palestinians in Israel had turned their backs on their fellow Arabs, such depictions nonetheless betrayed a level of paternalism that discounted Palestinians' own agency.

At the same time that Palestinian intellectuals in exile were seeking to establish bodies that would represent their national interests, they began to seek out more information about the one group of Palestinians about which they knew the least: those inside the Green Line. Some journalists and activists had been monitoring the Israeli Hebrew press, and the media firestorm over the Ard Group's memorandum provided the perfect opportunity for these intellectuals to learn more about the Palestinian minority and their attempts to resist Israeli discrimination.

With its proximity to Israel and its large number of Palestinian activists and intellectuals, Jordan-controlled East Jerusalem became a center for learning and disseminating information about the Ard Group and about the Palestinians in Israel more broadly. Newspapers there reported immediately on the memorandum's contents and the reaction in Israel.[92] *Filastin*, which had been the leading Palestinian newspaper before it was forced to relocate to East Jerusalem in 1948, championed the group as "the first spark of the revolution in Palestine" and one that "deserves our support and attention."[93] Such press reports positioned the Ard activists within an emerging Palestinian national struggle—a framing that was a departure from one that depicted them as passive victims in need of Arab or international rescue.

In addition, Palestinian activists and intellectuals in exile took it upon themselves to serve as the diplomatic conduit between Palestinians in Israel and the broader Arab world. The Jerusalem Bureau of the Arab League, which had opened in March 1964, was one such conduit. The bureau's director was Tawfiq Hasan Wasfi (former Palestine representative to the Arab League), while Palestinian journalist ʿIzzat al-Jabali, who knew Hebrew well, served as assistant director. The staff consisted of Palestinian journalists and intellectuals, and one of their main tasks was to familiarize Arab readers with Israeli affairs, including its treatment of the Palestinian minority. According to Wasfi, they would obtain Israel's main Arabic, English, and Hebrew newspapers through the East Jerusalem mayor's office and then read and translate relevant clippings and distribute reports to the Arab embassies in Amman and to the Arab League secretary general's office in Cairo.[94]

As the Ard leaders were garnering international attention, Palestinian nationalist groups in exile took it upon themselves to raise Arab awareness of this group and its struggle for greater rights. The Jerusalem Bureau sent a memorandum of its own in August 1964 to the Jordanian foreign minister and the embassies of eight Arab states describing the conditions of the Palestinians inside the Green Line and calling on Arab leaders to "turn their attention to the Arab minority in Israel, especially the young Arab intellectuals among them, who have withstood the attacks of the newspapers and broadcasts launched by Israel against them."[95] The Jerusalem Bureau also monitored closely Israeli press reports regarding the November 1964 Supreme Court verdict against the group and the arrests of its leaders.[96] Meanwhile, in December 1964 representatives from the PLO took advantage of their inaugural appearance at the UN General Assembly to distribute copies of the Ard memorandum to members of the international body.[97] Thus, the Ard memorandum allowed Palestinians on both sides of the Green Line who had no direct contact with one another to usher in a new political vocabulary that included more centrally this hitherto marginalized group of Palestinians.

But Palestinian intellectuals in exile also recognized that their national liberation project necessitated a huge academic undertaking. In addition to collecting data about Palestine's lost past and current conditions, it also entailed understanding the complex regional and global political dynamics, especially in a Cold War environment. Perhaps most urgently, the national liberation project required detailed knowledge about Israel: its ideological underpinnings, social makeup, and strategic outlook. To address these needs, two Palestinian research institutions were established in Beirut that were devoted to producing timely, relevant, and politically useful knowledge about Palestine and the Palestinian cause: the nonpartisan Institute for Palestine Studies in 1963 and the PLO-affiliated Palestine Research Center (PRC) in 1965. At a time when the rest of the Arab world showed little interest in learning about Israel, researchers affiliated with these two institutions prioritized the need to understand and disseminate an accurate picture of the Jewish state. The PRC, founded by Palestinian academic Fayez Sayegh, took the lead in this regard, with many of its earliest studies dedicated to understanding Israeli politics and society.[98]

The opportunity for Palestinian intellectuals in exile to learn more specifically about the plight of the Palestinians in Israel—as well as their ongoing efforts to resist their oppression—came in the form of a book-length study by Sabri Jiryis. The book, written in Hebrew and published in Haifa in 1966, laid out in detail the legal undergirding of the military government, such as the laws used to confiscate Palestinian land and curtail their movement. The book's third chapter, provocatively titled "From Dayr Yasin to Kafr Qasim: The Strong-Arm Policy," laid out the details of the Kafr Qasim massacre, transcripts from the trial that spoke to the deliberateness of the killings, and the light sentences given to the perpetrators.[99] By laying out Palestinians' major grievances in the political, educational, and cultural realms, Jiryis's study highlighted the systematic discrimination they faced that belied Israel's self-portrayal as a beacon of democracy in the Middle East.

The book received much negative attention in Israel, with the Hebrew press denouncing the study and its author. But it also attracted the interest of Palestinian intellectuals in exile who were already familiar with Jiryis through his robust defense of the Ard Group two years earlier in front of Israel's High Court. Copies of Jiryis's book were smuggled out to East Jerusalem and Beirut in 1966, where members of the Arab League's Jerusalem Bureau and the PRC translated Jiryis's study into Arabic in 1966 and published it in 1967.[100] The Institute for Palestine Studies also translated the book into English in 1969. Jiryis's intimate knowledge of the Israeli legal and political systems, coupled with his careful documentation of his claims by citing transcripts of Israeli Knesset debates, official gazettes, court decisions, and other legal documents, gave Palestinian researchers much-needed insight and documentary support for their claims of Israeli discrimination. It also affirmed that Palestinians were far from content as citizens of Israel, further linking them discursively to the Palestinians' national project.

"RESISTANCE LITERATURE IN OCCUPIED PALESTINE"

Yet even as Palestinian intellectuals in exile began to become more aware of the political resistance taking place inside Israel, the cultural resistance of this community, especially their poetry, was still largely unknown. The March 1964 special issue of *al-Adab*, for example, dedicated to the theme of "Palestine and Literature," made no mention of the young poets calling out from behind the barbed wire. Contributors to that issue were still discussing the "literature of the Nakba," which had flooded the post-1948 Arab literary scene with themes of loss, yearning, and nostalgia. In that issue's roundtable, respected Palestinian literary critic and American University of Beirut professor Ihsan ʿAbbas called for the "mobilization of literature" that could move the Palestinian issue to the forefront of global consciousness. Despite his close friendship with Habibi during the Mandate period, he showed no signs of awareness that such literature was already emerging in the overlooked fields and villages of historic Palestine, illustrating the ongoing isolation of the Palestinians in Israel.[101]

This lack of awareness started to change as *al-Ittihad* and other Arabic-language papers from Israel were smuggled into regional Arab cities. In addition to informing Palestinian political organizers about the discrimination they faced and their protests on the ground, the publications proved to be a crucial means by which the poetry of this community reached a wider audience. Yusuf al-Khatib, a Damascus-based Palestinian poet and radio broadcaster, recalled reading *al-Ittihad*, *al-Mirsad*, and other newspapers from Israel that had been smuggled into the Syrian capital and being impressed with the poetry published on their pages. Shortly after he founded the *Palestine Broadcast* program on Radio Damascus in mid-1964, he began to read aloud some of the verses on air, likely marking the first time that the words of these poets were heard beyond the Green Line. Many of Khatib's colleagues were initially unimpressed with the verses recited, dismissing them as overly simplistic and unoriginal.[102]

A shift in this assessment came in June 1966 when *al-Adab* published Mahmoud Darwish's poem "A Lover from Palestine,"[103] the first such appearance in a prominent Arabic literary journal. The following month, the journal ran Beirut-based Palestinian novelist and critic Ghassan Kanafani's introduction to his groundbreaking study, *Resistance Literature in Occupied Palestine*.[104] Kanafani declared that his purpose in writing the book was to expose the broader Arab world to "this literature [that] has remained unknown to us during these long years of Diaspora, even though it is the most brilliant aspect of the [Palestinian] struggle."[105] In explaining why so little was known about them, Kanafani astutely described the Palestinians in Israel as facing a "cultural embargo" (*hisar thaqafi*) that was characterized by a lack of access to the latest Arab writings, internal restrictions on their movement, government censorship, and attempts by the establishment to circulate only certain types of literature that did not reflect what the people wanted.[106]

Kanafani then turned to how these Palestinians used poetry to resist the isolation they faced. Comparing them favorably to the Palestinian poets of the 1920s and 1930s, he argued that their populist verses helped mobilize people to reject the status quo.[107] The critic singled out Darwish, Qasim, and Zayyad as achieving great artistic merit, and he praised them for responding to regional and global events of the day "faster than many Arab poets respond to the battles and jolts that have come across the Arab stage in recent years." Not only that, Kanafani declared, "but their poetry evaluates these events from a position of greater hope and steadfastness" than other Arab poetry.[108] He gave as one example Qasim's poem "My Brother Sanaʿaʾ," which was a tribute to the Arab nationalist fighters of North Yemen who were at the time (with Nasser's support) rebelling against Saudi-backed royalists.[109]

But Kanafani was most impressed with the ways in which the poets combined their artistic resistance with political defiance. He noted that Darwish wrote most of the poems in *A Lover from Palestine* while in jail, and he especially praised the title poem for turning the state-promoted Romantic poetry on its head by fusing romantic and nationalist love together.[110] Kanafani also admired the poets' willingness to take to the front lines in resisting their internal isolation, as had happened during the ninth annual commemoration of the Kafr Qasim massacre in 1965. Qasim had gathered with other poets and organizers behind a barricade that had been erected by the police to prevent them from entering the village. Through a megaphone across the barbed wire Qasim declared his solidarity with the people of the besieged village: "Despite the night of obscenities and iniquities / A delegation in struggle has come, o Kafr Qasim / Despite Satan's oppression that churns the sky / Despite the wall of wire squatting on the road / Despite the rancor of the machine gun made famous by the oppressors / We have come, so let the rulers taste shame!"[111] Qasim's affirmation of unity with the residents of Kafr Qasim in the face of barricades, declared in a poem that was subsequently memorized and recited by scores of Galileans, illustrated to Kanafani the ways in which protest and poetry reinforced each other among these besieged Palestinians.

Kanafani's study gave new prominence to the argument that, far from being quiescent, passive victims, Palestinians in "occupied Palestine" were actively resisting Israeli policies and the Zionist ideology that underpinned them. Kanafani's reference to their poetry as being the "most brilliant aspect" of the Palestinians' struggle, coupled with his efforts to inform the broader Arab world about it, also highlights the centrality of texts—both their production and their circulation—in overcoming the political boundaries that divided Palestinians from each other and from the Arab world. Kanafani did not state explicitly how he obtained all these poems; yet his dissemination of them led him, along with other Palestinian intellectuals in exile, to facilitate greater access of information about Palestinian cultural resistance taking place behind the Green Line.

By drawing attention to these resistance poets, Kanafani also connected two strands of Palestinian nationalist discourse, the poetic and the political, while simultaneously linking Palestinians inside the Green Line with Palestinians and Arabs outside it. He thus affirmed Darwish's contention that "the people of a million refugees" and "the survivors and grandchildren of the martyrs from Dayr Yasin and Kafr Qasim" wished to see literature that reflected the "wounds" and "victories" of their people, "not just some cerebral mutterings scattered in the wind." Kanafani's article and book received some attention in Arab literary and intellectual circles when they were first published, but it was not until the June 1967 War the following year that his arguments would achieve wider recognition.

CONCLUSION

During the mid-1960s a younger generation of Palestinian intellectuals, political organizers, and cultural producers in Israel once again adapted strategies of resistance to a rapidly changing environment. Inspired by the proliferation of committed literature and by decolonization movements around the world, Darwish in particular pushed forth a line of argument that tied Israel more directly to other settler-colonial regimes (most notably France in Algeria) than previous writers had done. At the same time, he and other poets adopted more innovative poetic forms and a more personally defiant stance that emphasized their indigeneity and steadfastness, despite the ongoing isolation and oppression they faced.

But the state's massive land grab in the Galilee in the early 1960s made it clear that poems and protests were not enough: If Palestinian citizens wished to impact Israeli actions, there needed to be a change in the international balance of power. Some intellectuals saw an opportunity to do so with the rise of newly decolonized countries in Asia and Africa and the growing political momentum of Palestinian groups in exile. The Ard Group's 1964 memorandum and its subsequent attempt to acquire legal standing within Israel were the clearest attempts yet to tap into this global decolonizing discourse and to situate their demands within the emergent Palestinian national movement.

Despite such efforts, Palestinians in Israel continued to be largely ignored in the Arab world. Earlier stereotypes about them as a content minority and thus as traitors to the Palestinian cause were replaced with portrayals of them as passive victims of Israeli discrimination. While it was a more sympathetic (if patronizing) view, it did not take into account the myriad ways in which Palestinians contested their status as second-class citizens of Israel. As Palestinians in exile began to draw attention to the ways in which Palestinians in Israel used political and cultural means to resist their ongoing isolation, changes in this view started to take place. Palestinian critic Ghassan Kanafani was particularly emphatic in situating the Palestinian poets within a larger temporal and spatial context of Palestinian struggles for justice.

Palestinian poets—particularly those of the younger generation—also positioned themselves more clearly as part of the Palestinian people. Darwish's "A Lover from Palestine" was just one example of their effort to locate themselves within a longer history of Palestinian struggle. This shift was part of a broader social and intellectual transformation that affected even the older poets, such as Zayyad, whose poetry by this time had shifted away from the strong communist internationalism of the 1950s toward more Palestinian-centered verses.[112] As Zayyad noted in 1966, "It is not true, as they say, that we are the poets created by the tragedy in our country—that we began anew." Comparing his contemporaries with the famous trio of poets of the 1930s (Tuqan, Mahmud, and Abu Salma), Zayyad insisted:

> Our revolutionary poetry is an extension of their revolutionary poetry because our battle is an extension of their battle. It is in the same trench: the love of land and people; it has the same enemy: colonialism and its henchmen; it has the same goal: national and social liberation; it employs the same weapon: the sharp word that glimmers in the light. The only difference between us and them is in the historical circumstances [we face].[113]

Zayyad's insistence on the close connection between Palestinian poets in Israel and those who wrote in pre-1948 Palestine illustrates the growing identification of Palestinian intellectuals in Israel with not only with contemporary Palestinians but also with previous generations of Palestinians who had actively opposed foreign colonial rule. In contrast to his poems of the early 1950s that situated his community's efforts within a worldwide class-based revolution, Zayyad was now positioning their struggles more explicitly within the specific history of Palestinian anticolonialism. The shift that Zayyad both traced and embodied mirrors broader transformations that were taking place in the Palestinian cultural landscape in Israel as a whole—transformations that would prove to be central to the eventual Arab "discovery" of them and their resistance against attempted Israeli erasures.

What proved key in this process of discovery was the production and circulation of texts—whether through memoranda issued to international bodies or through newspapers, journals, and academic studies smuggled across the border. But these texts could go only so far: While Palestinian intellectuals in exile took immediate interest in them, Arab intellectuals paid relatively little attention, thereby limiting their impact. It would take the shock of a massive defeat at the hands of the Israeli military for sympathy and admiration of this group to spread further afield.

5 COMPLICATED HEROES

In the hallway outside a large auditorium in Sofia, Bulgaria, famed Egyptian writer and literary critic Yusuf al-Sibaʿi was on the lookout. An Arabic poetry night was being held as part of the Seventh International Festival of Youth and Students in 1968, and Sibaʿi was eager to meet Mahmoud Darwish, whose verses had been featured prominently in some of the leading Arabic literary journals of the region during the previous months. The festival also provided the first opportunity for young Palestinian members of the Rakah delegation, particularly Darwish and Qasim, to travel abroad and meet face-to-face with the Arabs and Palestinians attending the festival. When Sibaʿi was finally introduced to the slim, clean-shaven, twenty-six-year-old Darwish, the Egyptian critic exclaimed in surprise, "You're Mahmoud Darwish? I thought you were fat and had a mustache!"[1]

But not everyone was as eager to meet the famed "poets of resistance." The official Syrian Baʿthist delegation forbade its members from having contact with anyone from the detested "Zionist delegation," including the famed poets. Some of the Syrian delegates even distributed leaflets alleging that the two men at the festival claiming to be Darwish and Qasim were really Mossad agents sent to impersonate the real poets who were locked away in an Israeli prison. The attacks continued despite the objections of Faysal Hurani, a Palestinian member of the Syrian delegation who had read issues of *al-Ittihad* that had been smuggled into Damascus. He knew that Rakah had objected fervently to Israel's actions during the previous summer's war and vocally denounced the Israeli occupation of Arab lands. Hurani pleaded with his fellow delegates to recognize that Rakah was not, in fact, a Zionist party and therefore should not be boycotted.[2]

The two episodes highlight the enigma of the Palestinians in Israel, especially the resistance poets, in the Arab political imaginary following the June 1967 War. The sudden, overwhelming defeat of Arab forces by the Israeli military in just six short days overturned the political and cultural paradigms of scores of intellectuals. As they sought to make sense of such a massive loss, they realized that they needed to have a better understanding of Israeli politics, culture, and society. In this context Kanafani's 1966 celebration of the resistance poets received renewed attention: The poets' defiant verses had demonstrated that Palestinian Arab national identity could withstand two decades of Israeli attempts at erasure and emerge even more defiant than before. As a result, Arab cultural producers celebrated them as a sign of hope amid the despair of the defeat. At the same time, Palestinian intellectuals and activists in exile, several of whom had been familiar with the travails of the Ard movement and with the contents of *al-Ittihad* and other publications before the war, were also eager to reconnect with fellow Palestinians from behind the barbed wire and to serve as a bridge of understanding between them and those Arabs who continued to believe that the Palestinians who remained in Israel were traitors.

The 1968 festival at Sofia was the perfect opportunity to do so. Several dozen Palestinians who were part of the Rakah delegation met with many of the one hundred Palestinian delegates hailing from Egypt, Jordan, Lebanon, and Syria, as well as the roughly four hundred Arab delegates in attendance. Unlike previous world youth festivals that lacked an official Palestinian delegation, and unlike communist international conferences that had only small delegations from Arab countries, the Sofia festival was an opportunity for Palestinian citizens of Israel to meet face-to-face with a significant number of Palestinians and Arabs for the first time in two decades. The Palestinian delegates also played a key role in helping introduce the hitherto isolated Palestinian community to a wider Arab audience through personal introductions and passionately delivered essays published in some of the leading Arab media outlets of the time. These actions, coupled with the efforts of the Rakah delegates to reach out to their fellow Palestinians and Arabs, ushered in the beginning of a new vocabulary of liberation that included more fully this previously excluded group of Palestinians.

But the growing prominence of the resistance poets also led to complex debates in Arab intellectual circles regarding the very definition of Palestinian resistance. As Fatah and other Palestinian militant groups stepped up their use of guerrilla-style attacks against Israel, they drew on the writings of such figures as Frantz Fanon and Che Guevara to explicitly locate the Palestinian struggle for independence within the milieu of Third World armed revolutionary movements.[3] This view was shared by many Arab intellectuals, who argued that armed struggle was the central and most productive mode of Palestinian anticolonial resistance, leading them to question whether the Palestinians in Israel, especially the resistance poets, were truly engaged in resistance. Despite their verses of defiance, these poets held on to their Israeli passports, continued to live under Israeli rule, joined Israeli political parties (albeit non-Zionist ones), wrote of intimate relationships with Jewish Israelis, and refused to join the Palestinian armed struggle. According to this logic, the poets had acquiesced to Israeli colonial rule, diminishing their standing as resistance poets. At the same time, the defeat in 1967 led some Arab intellectuals to conclude that Arabs needed to engage in a total cultural and political revolution to improve their society inside and out. They wondered whether the Palestinian resistance poets were in fact radical enough to be considered true resistance poets since their work did not fundamentally overturn Arab modes of thinking, which they argued was the most urgent task in the wake of the 1967 defeat. For such critics, the so-called resistance poets were not engaged in true political or cultural resistance (*muqawama*) but were writing merely in opposition (*muʿarada*) to the status quo.

These intra-Arab debates about the meaning of resistance and resistance poetry revealed an ongoing lack of awareness about the conditions of the Palestinians living inside the Green Line and the struggles in which they were engaged. The emphasis on national liberation through armed struggle as the only legitimate mode of decolonization overlooked the forms of everyday anticolonial resistance that Palestinians in Israel were engaged in, whether by holding on to their land or by refusing to accede to Zionist wishes that they turn away from their Palestinian Arab culture and identity. Such criticisms also overlooked the extremely difficult position in which Palestinian citizens of Israel found themselves during the years following the 1967 war. As Palestinian militants attacked Israeli civilian targets, security officials and the general public grew fearful that the Palestinian minority would join the revolutionaries. As a result, even though military rule was formally lifted in December 1966, Israeli police forces continued to harass Palestinian citizens, especially the resistance poets, through various forms of confinement and imprisonment. The government also forced Ard cofounders Habib Qahwaji and Sabri Jiryis into exile as a result of their nationalist work.

The regional debates about the validity of Palestinian resistance in Israel, combined with the state's persecution of intellectuals and political organizers, put the resistance poets in a bind. For years they had insisted that they would remain on their land in defiance of Israeli attempts at usurpation and erasure. But some of the very Arabs with whom they identified most closely believed that remaining on their land was not in fact an act of defiance but a form of acquiescence. At the same time, increased surveillance and harassment by the Israeli authorities made it more difficult for them to connect to their fellow Arabs and Palestinians. As a result, in February 1971 Darwish decided to leave Israel altogether, taking up residence in Cairo and then in Beirut, effectively placing himself in exile. His actions forced everyone to think about the price that needed to be paid if Palestinians living inside the Green Line truly wished to overcome their physical isolation from the Arab world.

Previous scholarship examining the encounter between Palestinians in Israel and other Palestinians and Arabs in the wake of the 1967 war has generally focused on how contact between the groups across the Green Line led to a growing political assertiveness among Palestinians in Israel.[4] Analyses of these changes have described them variously as "politicization," "radicalization," and "awakening."[5] While Palestinian citizens of Israel undeniably grew more insistent in their calls for national and civil rights in the years following the 1967 war, such analyses tend to overlook the ways in which this group influenced broader expressions of Palestinian and Arab cultural identity in the aftermath of the war. Between 1968 and 1970 a wave of interviews and profiles examining the resistance poets and the communities from which they hailed appeared in prominent Arab publications; meanwhile, the poets' anthologies were reprinted in Beirut and sold throughout the region. As a result of this newfound interest and exposure, Palestinian and Arab intellectuals gained a deeper understanding of the role that cultural expression could play in anticolonial struggles, debated competing definitions of political and cultural resistance, explored overlapping forms of Palestinian identity, and acquired a greater understanding of Israeli politics and society. Understanding the development of these mutually constitutive elements of Palestinian national expression highlights the broader cultural reverberations of these encounters and moves beyond a focus on the unidirectional impact of regional developments on the political identity of the Palestinians in Israel.

THE SETBACK

The June 1967 Arab-Israeli War fundamentally altered the political and cultural dynamics in Israel, among Palestinians, and in the region. After several weeks of escalating brinkmanship by Nasser, which included closing the Straits of Tiran and ordering the withdrawal of UN peacekeeping troops from the Sinai Peninsula, Israel launched what it claimed was a preemptive strike against Egypt on the morning of June 5. Catching leaders in Cairo by surprise, the Israeli Air Force destroyed most of the Egyptian air fleet while it was still on the ground. King Hussein of Jordan, who found himself drawn into the conflict as a result of a hastily concluded mutual defense pact with Egypt a few weeks earlier, saw the Old City of Jerusalem fall to Israeli forces later that day. Over the next five days, Israel captured the West Bank and the rest of East Jerusalem from Jordan, the Golan Heights from Syria, and the Sinai Peninsula from Egypt, more than tripling the territory under its control.[6]

While Israelis were ecstatic at the sudden, massive victory, Arabs throughout the region were stunned. For years the logic of pan-Arab nationalism was built on the premise that a united Arab military force under the command of an Arab revolutionary hero like Nasser would result in an Arab victory in any future military confrontation with Israel. Radio Cairo had initially broadcast false reports of Arab advances, leading to optimistic projections. But when it became clear a few days later that Israel was the one making the enormous military gains, Arabs were at a loss to explain what was happening. Describing the reaction to the broadcasts heard in the later days of the war, Egyptian critic Jalal Amin recalled, "Rather than breaking down in tears, [an Arab listener] would burst into hysterical laughter, as if the news related to someone else, or was nothing more than a cruel, impossible joke."[7] Palestinians in particular were devastated: not only had war failed to liberate their land, but now more than one million additional Palestinians found themselves under Israeli rule.[8]

Much of the international community denounced Israel's invasion and occupation of Arab lands as a violation of international law. The Soviet Union, Bulgaria, Czechoslovakia, Hungary, Poland, and Yugoslavia all cut off diplomatic ties with Israel on June 10 to register their opposition to Israel's capture of territories that belonged to their allies Egypt and Syria.[9] Even countries that maintained diplomatic ties with Israel nonetheless roundly opposed its conquest of territory despite Israel's claims that it was only holding the land temporarily until a peace agreement could be reached.

As the shock of defeat started to wear off over the next several weeks, Arab political leaders began to search for ways to cope with what they termed "the setback" (*al-naksa*). The first opportunity came at the Arab League Summit in Khartoum, Sudan, in August 1967. There, member states approved the Khartoum Resolution, which subsequently became known as the "three no's": no peace with Israel, no recognition of Israel, and no negotiations with it. But behind what appeared to be Arab intransigence was a recalculation of their stance. While they rejected signing a formal peace treaty with Israel, they did not reject peace altogether; while they rejected de jure recognition of Israel, they did not object to de facto recognition of it; and while they opposed direct negotiations with Israel, they were willing to have a third party mediate in indirect negotiations.[10] The language of the Khartoum Resolution marked a strategic shift in Arab dealings with Israel whereby political leaders moved away from questioning Israel's legitimacy toward a focus on recovering the lands they lost in the June War.[11] But the resolution was phrased in a way that would satisfy the many hard-liners in the Arab world who still did not wish to acknowledge Israel's legitimacy in any way. And while Israeli leaders would later claim they had extended a peace offer to Egypt and Syria in the weeks following the war that included a withdrawal of territories, no such offer was made.[12]

The standoff led to the passage of UN Security Council Resolution 242 that November. It emphasized "the inadmissibility of the acquisition of territory by war" and the "need to work for a just and lasting peace in which every State in the area can live in security." Calling on Israel to withdraw its "armed forces from territories occupied in the recent conflict," the resolution affirmed the "territorial integrity and political independence of every State in the area."[13] As a secondary matter the resolution vaguely affirmed the necessity "for achieving a just settlement of the refugee problem." But absent from the text was any acknowledgment of Palestinian national claims or their rights to the land from which they had been expelled almost twenty years earlier. As a result, the PLO rejected the resolution, seeking to chart an independent course that would oblige all parties in the region to recognize its national claims.

One route toward achieving this recognition, championed most famously by the armed group Fatah, was to step up cross-border raids into Israel and Israeli-controlled territories from bases in Jordan. The group hoped to raise its own prestige and put pressure on Israel to relinquish the territories it had conquered. Seeking to put an end to such raids, on March 21, 1968, Israel launched an attack on the Jordanian town of Karamah to eradicate Fatah from its base there. Fatah guerrillas, with the help of the Jordanian military, inflicted heavy damage on Israeli forces while sustaining heavy losses themselves. Although Israel claimed to have achieved its goal, Fatah remained standing. The fact that the small group was able to withstand the full brunt of an Israeli military assault turned a military defeat into a psychological victory for Palestinians and Arabs throughout the region.[14] The Battle of Karamah nurtured the hope that Palestinian guerrillas could achieve what Arab armies could not: the liberation of Palestine.

Before the war, not all Palestinian political activists believed that Fatah-style guerrilla warfare was the best approach to challenging Israel. But the June defeat, the stand at Karamah, and Fatah's ascension to the PLO leadership left many of them feeling they had no choice but to unite under one umbrella.[15] This was especially true as Arab states became increasingly focused on recovering the territory they had lost in the war rather than on the Palestinian cause. Palestinian nationalists feared that such a piecemeal approach to dealing with Israel, one that focused on states bartering for pieces of land, would ultimately relegate the ongoing refugee crisis and the larger question of Palestinian liberation to the back burner. It was a concern shared by many Palestinians in Israel, though Rakah leaders had a different view of the ongoing strategic reassessments.

PALESTINIANS IN ISRAEL AND THE JUNE WAR

The June War did not shock Palestinian intellectuals in Israel as it had their fellow Arabs. They had been aware of Israel's military strength and were not taken in by Arab propaganda in the lead-up to the war.[16] Instead, they faced arrest. On Sunday, June 4, the day before Israel launched its first strike, Israeli defense minister Yitzhak Rabin ordered the arrest of dozens of Palestinian intellectuals who were deemed a security threat. The first wave included the founders of the Ard movement, including Sabri Jiryis, Habib Qahwaji, and Mansur Kardush, as well as most of Rakah's Palestinian leadership, many of whom were also involved in the publication of *al-Ittihad*. Darwish, whose name had been among the first called that morning, managed to avoid arrest by going underground, where he helped oversee the publication of two issues during the war (on June 6 and 9). Once it became clear that Israel had won the war, he emerged from his hiding place and went home. Five days later, Darwish was taken to Damun prison as part of a new wave of arrests, where he assured the anxious editors still being held that the paper had indeed come out during the war.[17] The arrests were part of a widespread crackdown in the immediate aftermath of the war in which Palestinian neighborhoods were put under strict curfew, and even those who ventured out during times the curfew was lifted risked beatings and torture from the police.[18] Although most of the political prisoners arrested during the war were released by the end of June,[19] the broader clampdowns on Palestinians in Israel continued for the next several months.

Rakah leaders had warned against Israeli military aggression in May and spent the summer repeatedly calling on the government to withdraw from the territories it had occupied during its "aggressive, expansionist war."[20] But they also expressed skepticism that Israel would withdraw of its own accord. Writing two months after the war, senior Rakah leader Saliba Khamis warned *al-Ittihad* readers not to be fooled by Israeli claims that it was only temporarily holding on to the land until a peace treaty was signed. "Everyone is racing into the West Bank, the Gaza Strip and the Syrian hills [Golan Heights] to lay down cornerstones for future projects," Khamis wrote. "The banks are competing, as are the transportation companies, settlement movements, merchants and land brokers" to stake claims on different parts of the territories. Far from a temporary or ad hoc measure, he argued, Israel was systematically laying the groundwork to hold on to the land indefinitely. According to Khamis, the reasons included regional expansion and access to Syrian tributaries into Lake Tiberias, as well as to "compel the Arabs to relinquish the rights of the Palestinian Arab people."[21] Khamis's skepticism of Israeli intent would be prophetic, and it was this type of insider knowledge that would be so useful for Palestinians in exile and others who wished to have greater insight into Israeli actions.

The doubts that Khamis raised regarding Israel's willingness to give up the territories it conquered also help explain Rakah's support for the Arab League's Khartoum Resolution, despite Israel's strong objections to it. For Rakah leaders, as for Arabs throughout the region, the three no's symbolized political resoluteness in the face of military defeat. As Emile Habibi (writing under his pen name Juhayna) explained, the resolution demonstrated that "the Arab countries did not abandon their principles in the face of the military assault that they faced, and they refused to relinquish the legitimate rights of the Palestinian Arabs. They decided they would not enter into peace negotiations with Israel under the shadow of aggression and occupation."[22] While Habibi's interpretation of the Arab stance at Khartoum as one that affirmed their unwavering support for Palestinian rights would eventually prove to be overly optimistic, it nonetheless reflected his ongoing desire to see the Palestinian issue as part of the Arab cause. Both Khamis and Habibi worried that if the Arab countries abandoned the Palestinian cause, Israel's aggression and occupation would go unchecked.

Yet Rakah's veteran political leaders struggled to walk a tightrope. On the one hand, they concurred with Arab officials and Palestinians as a whole in denouncing Israel's occupation of the lands conquered in 1967. On the other hand, Rakah's old guard in particular disagreed strongly with commonly accepted Arab and Palestinian formulations that positioned Israel as an imperialist base. Tubi, Habibi, and other Palestinian communist leaders maintained Israel's legitimacy within the territory allocated to it in the 1947 UN Partition Plan and had largely accepted the existence of Israel's expanded borders. But with the ascent of the PLO, which considered Israel's very existence to be illegitimate, Palestinian citizens were becoming increasingly familiar with alternative decolonizing discourses that publicly called into question previously held assumptions about Israel's legitimacy.

This shift in public discourse sometimes put Rakah leaders into conflict with their own constituents, who were beginning to see more parallels between 1948 and 1967 than their leaders cared to admit. During a question-and-answer session with Rakah Knesset member Tawfiq Tubi in March 1968, the veteran communist leader was asked about comparisons between Palestinians in Israel and those in the territories conquered in 1967. "Are the Arabs of Israel under occupation? Have you been under occupation since 1948?" an audience member asked. Tubi, holding firm to the communist position since Israel's founding, replied:

> In 1948 Rakah members and I supported the UN resolutions [to partition Palestine] because they addressed the just claims of both peoples and sought to evacuate the British occupiers. 1948 is not 1967. [The former] established an independent state, Israel, whose founding was in accordance with the UN resolutions. And within the state of Israel I have struggled for the independence of the country and for the rights of the Arab people.[23]

Tubi's comments reaffirmed his party's long-standing position that recognized the state of Israel and the rights of the Jewish people to sovereignty within that state.

But as the younger generation of Palestinian intellectuals on both sides of the Green Line were shifting the frame of discussion, veteran political leaders such as Tubi were pushed into a defensive crouch. Another audience member asked, "What about Acre, which was not within the borders of an Israeli state according to the 1947 UN Resolution? Don't [its] residents feel they have been under occupation for nineteen years?" Tubi replied (perhaps somewhat testily), "You are ignoring an important and irrefutable difference. The establishment of the state of Israel in 1948 was a just act and the War of Independence differs from the June War of Aggression.... Today, we have before us a cease-fire and an occupation that are the result of an unjust war. That is why we demand a withdrawal from the occupied areas."[24]

The pushback Tubi received from audience members who openly questioned the legitimacy of Israel's territorial expansion beyond the areas allocated in the UN Partition Plan was the first of its kind to appear on the pages of *al-Ittihad*. The exchange came as a younger generation of Rakah organizers, including Darwish and Qasim (who joined the party shortly after he was released from prison in 1967), took over more editorial functions at the paper. The paper's willingness to publish the exchange not only reflected an editorial shift away from party dogmatism but also indicated that a growing political assertiveness among Palestinians under Israeli rule was emerging despite Rakah's leadership, not because of it.

In sum, while Rakah political leaders sought to undo the changes that happened as a result of the 1967 war, they did not want to reopen the issues related to the 1948 war, such as the loss of Palestine and the creation of the refugee problem. Such an analysis was in keeping with the traditional communist position going back to the NLL, as well as the statist framework of the Khartoum Resolution and the UN Security Council Resolution. But it differed from the increasingly decolonizing framework of Palestinian groups that were calling for national liberation through armed struggle. Thus, despite Rakah's proclamations of support for the Palestinian cause, its party leaders had different ideas of how that cause should be championed. The generation gap that started to emerge in the mid-1960s had come to a head.

"SHALL WE THANK THE OCCUPATION?"

Ironically, the Israeli occupation of the remainder of historic Palestine provided the first opportunity in nearly two decades for Palestinian citizens of Israel to overcome their physical isolation from their fellow Palestinians. As the curfews eased in the months following the war, Palestinians began to venture across the Green Line to visit family and friends they had not seen in years. They also became acquainted with writings from the Arab world on a scale much larger than before, ushering in cultural interactions that would accelerate quickly in the following years.

For those old enough to remember Palestine before 1948, the occupation provided a chance to be reunited with friends and family. Shortly after the war, as Hanna Abu Hanna drove through the West Bank for the first time since his youth, he was struck by how much larger and more modern the West Bank towns had become. His wife was tearfully reunited with her sister in Ramallah after a twenty-year separation, and he surprised his friend Salih by dropping in on him unannounced. Upon seeing his long lost friend, Salih asked Abu Hanna ruefully, "Shall we thank the occupation, in whose shadows this meeting occurs? Yet it is the reason for our separation in the first place."[25] By citing Israel's occupation of Palestinian territory as a cause for both reuniting and separating the Palestinians, Salih's comment once again discursively linked the events of 1967 with those of 1948.

For those too young to remember pre-1948 Palestine, or for those without family or friends across the Green Line, the opening up of East Jerusalem and the West Bank was an opportunity to become immersed in an environment where the Arabic language and culture reigned supreme. Writer Salman Natur remembered his first visit to East Jerusalem as an eighteen-year-old, shortly after the 1967 war, as a life-changing experience. "Upon seeing a copy of the [Egyptian] newspapers *al-Ahram* or *al-Jumhuriyya*, or the [Lebanese] journals *al-Adab* or *al-Adib*, I felt at that time as if I was embracing the Arab world." Recalling the busy Salah al-Din commercial area in East Jerusalem, Natur remarked, "In these stores you don't hear anything around you except Arabic, and everything you see is written in Arabic, and the people are calling out in the [open air] market [selling] Arab goods. . . . It was as if I stepped through a large portal and entered the Arab world."[26]

These cultural encounters were not unidirectional. Palestinian cultural producers in the West Bank in particular were influenced by the resistance poets. Like their counterparts in exile, for the previous two decades writers in the West Bank had written works that were largely characterized by grief over the loss of Palestine or personal pain and suffering. Nablus-based poet Fadwa Tuqan, who before 1967 had been known in the Arab world for poems that expressed her personal sorrow and frustrations, found her political voice after the war, thanks in large part to her encounters with the resistance poets. She recalls in her memoir traveling from the West Bank to Haifa a few months after the occupation began to visit the Palestinian poets there, whose work she had read as a result of Kanafani's writings. Her early visits grew into a close friendship between Tuqan, Darwish, Qasim, and others, and her meetings with them lifted her spirits during the dark days after the fall of the West Bank: "For me, they were specks of light in the pitch-black darkness of the occupation. [Sitting] among these writers and poets . . . I found myself. At the same time, a peculiar transformation found its way into my soul and my thoughts, as if I were touched by a miracle! As I returned [home] from an evening gathering, feelings of relief would flutter in me as if it were the fluttering of flowers."[27]

But such encounters soon faced obstacles. Israeli authorities banned several Palestinian writers in Israel from traveling to the occupied territories,[28] while distribution of *al-Ittihad* and *al-Jadid* was deemed illegal in the West Bank and Gaza Strip.[29] In addition, the more Tuqan was invited to participate in literary and cultural events in Jerusalem, Nazareth, and elsewhere, the more she found herself slapped with orders from the military authorities that kept her confined to her hometown of Nablus on the exact day of the event.[30] Earlier Israeli attempts to limit the reach of Darwish, Qasim, and other Palestinian writers within the state were now expanded to try to limit the reach of Palestinian writers under occupation.

Despite such attempts to limit their encounters, Palestinian intellectuals on either side of the Green Line continued to meet with each other and become acquainted with one another's work. Nablus-based novelist Sahar Khalifeh wrote that "1967 introduced us—West Bank intellectuals and activists—to the poetry of Palestinians 'inside,' those who had lived in the Israeli state since 1948. Those poets, particularly Mahmoud Darwish and Samih al-Qassem [*sic*] were our dream and inspiration."[31] The inspiration that Khalifeh and Tuqan drew from their encounters with the Palestinian resistance poets, coupled with their own standing as prominent West Bank intellectuals and their contacts with intellectuals in the region, would soon lead to wider Arab cultural reassessments about the role of resistance poetry in the cultural and intellectual struggle against Israel.

UNDERSTANDING THE BATTLE IN THE CULTURAL REALM

Once Arab intellectuals started to emerge from their state of shock, many called for broader self-introspection and began to search for answers that could help them understand why such a massive, sudden, extensive defeat had occurred. They also sought out a new heroic model that could replace the discredited one of Nasser-led pan-Arab nationalism. For many, the rise of Palestinian armed resistance, embodied by the fedayeen guerrilla fighters, proved to be the new source of inspiration for which they longed. But several Arab intellectuals concluded that reversing the 1967 defeat needed more than guerrilla warfare, especially given Israel's overwhelming military superiority and the fact that (initially at least) Palestinians in the newly occupied territories showed little interest in mass resistance.[32] For these intellectuals, the underlying political and cultural factors that contributed to the defeat must be addressed and rectified.[33]

On the cultural level, the 1967 defeat reignited simmering debates in the Arab world regarding the relationship between tradition (*asala*) and modernity (*muʿasira*). Egyptian journalist and thinker Ahmad Bahaʾ al-Din, for example, contended that "Israel defeated us because we did not adopt scientific methods, neither in warfare nor in the organization of our political, social, and economic lives."[34] Such sentiments were echoed by Syrian philosopher Sadiq Jalal al-ʿAzm, who argued that becoming fully "modern" was "an indispensable tool for liberation and agency."[35] While such analyses rarely interrogated such binaries as "modernity" and "tradition," they did reflect their authors' perceptions that something needed to change in the Arabs' intellectual and cultural approaches to the world around them.

This need for change included the Arab approach to understanding Israel. Given their pre-1967 appraisal of Israel as a weak, fleeting entity, most Arabs did not feel the need to learn much about the Jewish state. Despite the advent in the mid-1960s of the Institute for Palestine Studies and the PRC, both of which were dedicated to producing knowledge about Israeli culture and society, before the June War their analyses rarely entered into broader Arab discussions. Instead, learning about Israel in Arab states was left largely to the military and intelligence services that treated what little knowledge they gained as classified information.[36] This secretive approach was compounded by Arab intellectuals themselves, whose writings on Israel and Zionism were, according to intellectual historian Ibrahim Abu Rabiʿ, "either propagandistic in nature . . . or marked by complete naivety and riddled with clichés that were not helpful for the average citizen."[37]

After the war, Arab thinkers came to recognize the glaring gaps in their knowledge. As Egyptian cultural analyst Rajaʾ al-Naqqash wrote, after the defeat it became clear that "the Arabs know little about Israel and what happens inside it, whereas the Israelis know everything about the Arabs. It was incumbent upon the Arabs to know their enemy well so they could confront it."[38] On the one hand, this sudden, urgent desire to "know thy enemy" reflected a utilitarian approach to understanding Israel as part of the political struggle against it; on the other hand, it also suggested the beginnings of a broader project of self-reflection in which Arab intellectuals would look at Israel as a mirror against which to assess their own state of affairs.

Moreover, these intellectuals had to grapple with the fact that, despite international condemnation of Israel's aggression in the June War, the state still received widespread sympathy, especially in many liberal Western corners. As a result, they started to argue more forcefully that their struggle against Israel had to be waged on the cultural front as well as the political and military ones. An example of this realization was on display in spring 1968, as intellectuals from throughout the Arab world gathered in Beirut for a conference on "The Arab Writer and the Battle against Zionism." Participants discussed ways in which Arab intellectuals and cultural producers could effectively counter Zionist propaganda on the world stage. While a few participants invoked crude stereotypes about Jews, most offered sober assessments of their confrontation with the state of Israel as part of a larger anticolonial struggle. Syrian literary historian ʿUmar al-Daqqaq, for example, argued that Israel "understands well that instruments of war alone are not enough to protect its artificial existence in Palestine. . . . Thought, culture, literature and art are all effective weapons that it deploys readily against the Arabs." He argued that Arabs could not effectively compete on a world stage as long as "our thought is limited and our literature is emaciated," especially since Western thought is predisposed against Arabs to begin with. To change this situation, Daqqaq argued, Arab "culture, thought and literature need to have a high level of maturity," and the best way to do so was by developing and mobilizing in-depth writings around the issue of Palestine.[39] Several other conference participants echoed the need to place Palestine at the forefront of their political and intellectual commitments.

In the months following the June defeat, Arab intellectuals also searched for new heroes they could turn to for inspiration. They were searching for heroes who could offer nuanced, clear-eyed assessments of Israeli politics, culture, and society and who could reassure them that Palestinian identity was firm. While the Palestinian guerrilla forces offered some measure of hope, it also seemed, at least initially, that the valiant figures these intellectuals were looking for could be found among the resistance poets.

THEIR POETRY DOES NOT WEEP

While intellectuals in the region searched for answers that could help them explain the defeat, poets took it upon themselves to mourn the losses of the war. Many adopted a self-flagellating tone, most prominently Nizar Qabbani, who lamented, "Arab children, / Don't read about our windowless generation, / We are a hopeless case. / We are as worthless as a watermelon rind / . . . / Arab children, / Spring rain, / Corn ears of the future, / You are a generation / That will overcome defeat."[40] Qabbani's verses, among the most well known to emerge in the immediate aftermath of the war, reflected a view shared by many that the current generation of Arabs was beyond redemption and they would have to wait until the next generation of youth arises for some glimmer of hope. But not all Arab critics were content with such a despondent tone. Moroccan novelist, journalist, and cultural commentator ʿAbd al-Karim Ghallab wrote that Qabbani's poetry represented a contempt for rational thought. "Tragedy is in need of a new literature," Ghallab wrote, "that moves beyond emotions . . . and that will work vigorously towards reclaiming the stolen land."[41] Ghallab longed for a more resolute approach to the June defeat, one that did not lament the circumstances they faced but sought to change them.

The Palestinian writers in Israel proved to be just what critics such as Ghallab were searching for. Once again, the Palestinian writers in exile—particularly Ghassan Kanafani—played an important role in introducing Arab readers to the more thoughtful appraisals of the Palestinians inside the Green Line. Writing two months after the war, Kanafani contrasted the recent work of the resistance poets with that of other Arab writers. According to Kanafani, the former "does not mourn or weep, it does not surrender or become hopeless, it does not contradict itself or go through fits of hysteria." Rather, he said, it has "a deep awareness of the dimension of the battle in whose depth it has found itself, and for this reason it has avoided the relapses into romanticism that most Arab poetry has witnessed in these times."[42] In other words, Kanafani argued, the Palestinian resistance poets were already doing precisely what critics were calling for—offering a steadfast approach to the challenges at hand that would lead Arabs to effectively contest Israeli claims.

Consequently, Arab media outlets that had largely ignored these poets began devoting enormous attention to them. In December 1967 the Beirut-based weekly *al-Anwar* published poetic responses to the June War by Darwish, Qasim, and Zayyad that did not bear any of the self-flagellation that Qabbani had displayed.[43] Two months later *al-Adab* ran Egyptian critic Rajaʾ al-Naqqash's review of Darwish's 1966 anthology, *A Lover from Palestine*. In his review, Naqqash declared that Arab intellectuals had a responsibility to "present this literature to the world" because it would move "even the hearts of those who have not heard anything about the cause itself."[44] Not only was Darwish's poetry stirring in and of itself, Naqqash argued, but it could also help bring greater awareness to the Palestinians' cause.

Naqqash's emphasis on positioning Darwish's poetry within the global contestation for hearts and minds also reflected ongoing Arab intellectual concerns with matters related to decolonization. The April 1968 *al-Adab* conference that brought together Arab intellectuals to discuss the need to combat Zionism at the cultural level also featured five papers that focused on the duty of progressive writers and intellectuals to combat colonialism and imperialism. Presenters included Cairo University Arabic literature professors and literary critics ʿAbd al-ʿAziz al-Ahwani and Suhayr al-Qalamawi,[45] along with Lebanese leftist critic Husayn Muruwwah, Syrian novelist Hani al-Rahib, and Sudanese poet Muhammad Muhammad Ali.[46] They all insisted that the Arab writer had a duty to use the pen to help combat the ongoing imperial and colonial projects against them, of which Israel was but one—albeit important—component. Kanafani's essay in the same issue of *al-Adab* discussing the dimensions of Palestinian resistance poetry further connected that poetry with the broader project of cultural decolonization in the Arab world. Kanafani insisted that part of what made the works of Darwish, Qasim, and other Palestinian writers so relevant to contemporary Arab discussions was their "ability to transform suffering into revolutionary drive."[47] For Kanafani, the Palestinian poets in Israel were putting into practice exactly the kind of revolutionary writing that was needed at this crucial cultural and political juncture.

Arab readers were further introduced to the work of the resistance poets through a wave of studies and anthologies that appeared throughout 1968. In May the Cairo-based monthly *al-Hilal* reprinted in full Darwish's latest anthology, *End of the Night* (*Akhir al-Layl*), which included poems written shortly before and immediately after the 1967 war.[48] Meanwhile, in Beirut, the avant-garde literary journal *Shiʿr* (Poetry) published several Palestinian poems that had appeared previously in *al-Ittihad*, *al-Jadid*, and *al-Mujtamaʿ* that had been smuggled into Beirut via the West Bank and Jordan.[49] Kanafani also completed a new book on Palestinian resistance literature that was updated to include a fuller range of poets and more documentary evidence of the isolation they faced,[50] while the book-printing arm of *al-Adab* reprinted copies of the poets' earlier and newest anthologies. In Damascus, Palestinian poet and radio broadcaster Yusuf al-Khatib published his anthology, *Poetry of an Occupied Nation*, which included selections of poems by Darwish, Qasim, Zayyad, and others, as well as several poems Khatib had previously read on air.[51] Overall, Arab radio programs began devoting more time to the broadcasts discussing the lives and works of resistance poets: the Voice of Palestine broadcasts expanded their recitations of resistance poetry, while the still-popular *Voice of the Arabs* radio program featured a profile of Qasim's life and work.[52] In short, while Arabs would have found little information about these poets before 1967, by 1968 they had a plethora of options from which to choose. For the resistance poets, their dream of garnering the attention of Arab audiences had finally materialized.

With little prior knowledge about the conditions of the Palestinians in Israel, Arab commentators often turned to the Palestinian armed struggle to make legible the resistance poetry they encountered. In Nizar Qabbani's ode "To the Poets of the Occupied Land," the poet declared, "We, the defeated poets / we the strangers of history and of the sorrow of the grief-stricken / we learned how the letter can take the shape of a knife."[53] Similarly, the Egyptian weekly *Rose al-Youssef* carried a feature on Qasim, accompanied by an illustration that depicted him as a guerrilla fighter.[54] These early depictions of the resistance poets as engaged in something akin to armed revolutionary struggle reflected a rather narrow understanding of their poetry as being the literary equivalent of a guerrilla movement. Over the coming months, however, as critics took a closer look at the resistance poets, that image would become complicated by the nuances that the poets presented to their Arab interlocutors.

In sum, during the first year after the June War Palestinians on both sides of the Green Line were able to physically meet each other (with restrictions), but the encounter between Palestinians in Israel and the rest of the Arab world was still overwhelmingly mediated through texts and the radio. Yet the longing of Palestinian resistance poets and intellectuals to meet face-to-face with their Arab counterparts and their fellow Palestinians living in exile was only magnified as a result of the war. Historically, the quadrennial World Youth Festivals had provided an opportunity for such encounters, though Arab suspicions had sometimes cast a pall over earlier gatherings. Now that so many Arab intellectuals were themselves eager to meet the resistance poets they had been reading about, the upcoming festival in Sofia, Bulgaria, seemed to be the perfect opportunity to do so. While the festival was an important turning point in the relationship between Palestinians in Israel and other Palestinians and Arabs, it was not a straightforward one.

THE POLITICS OF PARTICIPATION

The Seventh International Festival of Youth and Students, held in Sofia from July 26 to August 6, 1968, marked a turning point in the relationship between Palestinians in Israel, Palestinians in exile, and the Arab world. As in previous years, the festival was sponsored by the Komsomol (the youth wing of the Communist Party of the Soviet Union) to celebrate and promote "freedom and friendship" among Soviet bloc countries and to draw leftist activists from around the world more firmly into the Soviet orbit. The festivals were lively events, consisting of an opening ceremony, sports competitions, folklore performances, art and cultural displays, and some political events. The Moscow-based International Preparatory Committee (IPC) determined how many seats would be allocated to each delegation, while planning committees in each country chose who would be included as part of their respective delegations. As chief sponsor, the Soviet Union covered delegates' expenses, including travel and accommodations. For many attendees, it was their first trip abroad.[55]

The politics of participation were not new to festival organizers, though the Arab-Israeli conflict had not factored much into the planning of previous festivals.[56] Israeli delegations had participated since 1949 with members from the CPI, Mapai, and Mapam. Likewise, the IPC had extended invitations to delegations from Egypt, Syria, and Lebanon throughout the 1950s, who were joined by inaugural Iraqi and Algerian FLN (Front de Libération Nationale; National Liberation Front) delegations at the 1959 festival in Vienna. Generally, Israeli and Arab delegations avoided each other, though some positive interactions between Palestinian members of the Israeli delegation and their Arab counterparts (especially from communist parties) had taken place.

In addition, unlike previous festivals that had focused mainly on cultural and sporting events, the IPC for the Sofia festival was set to include a much larger number of political events, including seminars, rallies, and conferences.[57] This shift reflected the heightened political tensions that were a result of not only the 1967 war but also the momentous events of "global 1968." In the months leading up to the festival, students and activists around the world looked across national borders for inspiration and solidarity as they demanded greater freedom and opportunity at home.[58] Earlier in the year, widespread opposition to the American escalation of the Vietnam War, growing impatience with the lingering vestiges of colonialism, and various domestic economic and political grievances had led to massive street protests in cities across Europe, North America, Asia, Africa, and Latin America. Demonstrators called not only for improvements in their own lives but also for fundamental changes to the world order.[59] It was in the midst of this tumultuous climate that about twenty thousand delegates from around the world began making their way to Sofia.

In keeping with the restive mood of that summer, the festival's main themes were solidarity with the people of Vietnam and with anticolonial movements throughout the world, including in the Middle East. Since the Soviet Union and Bulgaria had cut diplomatic ties with the Israeli government in response to Israel's invasion and occupation of Arab lands,[60] the IPC decided to disinvite all Israeli delegates belonging to political parties that had supported the war. That left only the Rakah party, which had opposed the war from the beginning and continued to call for Israel to withdraw from the occupied territories, to be extended an invitation. There was also a question of Palestinian representation: Since the first festival in 1945, Palestinians had never had an independent delegation of their own. Throughout the 1950s and 1960s a few individual Palestinians had attended as part of other Arab delegations, but with the rise of the PLO and Fatah's defiant stand at Karamah just a few months earlier, Arab committees petitioned the IPC to allow an independent Palestinian delegation to attend. Counter-pressure from the committees of Romania (the only Eastern bloc country not to break diplomatic ties with Israel after the June War[61]) and Czechoslovakia (many of whose intellectuals disagreed with their government's anti-Israel stance[62]) led the IPC to ultimately reject the Arab proposal, though eventually a compromise was reached whereby a joint Palestinian-Jordanian delegation would be allowed to participate.[63] But the planning of the Sofia festival also came amid renewed Arab calls for a total boycott of Israel, itself based on a literal reading of the Khartoum Resolution. As the various Arab planning committees weighed their responses to the IPC's decisions, representatives of the Algerian and Syrian committees said they would boycott the festival itself over its decision to allow any Israeli participation whatsoever. Palestinian groups in exile tried to convince such hard-liners that Arabs could best support the Palestinian cause by participating in the festival and meeting with the Rakah delegation. They argued that it was more important that Palestine was represented at the festival for the first time as a country and that the Palestinian flag would be waving at an international event. Rather than use the festival as an opportunity for grandstanding, the Palestinians argued, it should be used "as a pulpit to inform in a practical way the youth of the world about this cause." Most Arab delegates also concluded that since the only Israelis participating were from Rakah and not from Zionist parties, they should not miss this important opportunity to share their perspectives with the world. These arguments ultimately persuaded the Syrian committee, leaving only Algeria to boycott the festival.[64]

The next question that Arab committees had to answer was the extent to which they could or should embrace the members of the Israeli delegation, especially Darwish and Qasim. Once again, Palestinians in exile sought to demystify the Palestinians behind the Green Line for the Arab delegates, arguing that there was no need to boycott Palestinians just because they held Israeli passports. In Damascus, Palestinian planning committee member Faysal Hurani tried to convince his colleagues of this point ahead of the festival. But the head of the Syrian delegation declared that the Syrians would have nothing to do with any member of the Israeli delegation, including Darwish and Qasim, and he warned of serious consequences if the delegates did anything that was not preapproved.[65] Meanwhile, in Amman, as members of the Jordanian delegation criticized the poets for being communists and for recognizing Israel, some of the Palestinian members—who understood well what it meant to possess the passport of one country while longing for another—argued that just as Palestinians in Jordan recognize Jordanian rule over them, yet they still identify as Palestinians, so too was that the case of the Palestinians in Israel. As one delegate put it, "They are Palestinians whether they are there [inside the Green Line] or not."[66]

Unaware of the controversy surrounding their attendance, the Palestinian Rakah delegates embarked on a rickety Greek ship at Haifa's port filled with joy. As Qasim recalled, it was the first trip abroad for him and most of his colleagues, and they were especially excited because "we were going to meet up with our brothers and comrades from the Arab people after a compulsory estrangement that lasted twenty years, during which we did not meet a single Arab from our larger nation."[67] They would soon have their chance.

FRIENDSHIP AND FREEDOM

Delegates arriving at Sofia's airports and train stations were met by scores of Bulgarian children greeting them with flowers. During the day of the opening ceremony, as delegates walked several miles along the route to the Vasil Levski National Stadium in the city center, people lined the streets, threw flowers, and cheered, while planes flew in formation above. Wearing keffiyehs around their necks, Palestinian delegates and their hosts chanted together in Bulgarian, "Mir mir drujba drujba!" (peace peace friendship friendship), signaling the global ascendency of the Palestinian cause.[68] And in a sign of how far Israel's reputation had fallen among leftists in the aftermath of the June War, when delegates from Egypt and other Arab countries passed along the streets, they and the crowd chanted, "Viva Egypt! Viva Jordan! Viva Arabs! Zionist Assassins! Zionist Fascists! Zionist Imperialists! Arab Palestine! Fatah!"[69]

Despite the denunciations of Zionism as the ideological underpinning of Israel's aggressive actions, the seventy-four-member Rakah delegation, comprising Palestinian and Jewish Israelis, was received warmly. Unlike other delegates who joyfully displayed their national pride, the Rakah delegates decided to proceed along the route to the stadium solemnly, walking without musical instruments or songs, holding two large placards, each with a simple message emblazoned in Hebrew and English: "Arab land for Arabs" and "With the Arab people against the Israeli occupation." As they arrived at the stadium, other delegates stood up and cheered them as they marched by. The Palestinian-Jordanian delegation, along with that of South Yemen (which was dominated by communists), was especially welcoming to the Rakah members.[70]

As happy as they were to be at the festival, Qasim and Darwish were also cautious. They knew that in 1959 Rashid Husayn was accosted by members of the Lebanese delegation after he had walked behind the hated blue-and-white flag at the Vienna festival's opening procession. Seeking to avoid such a scene, Darwish and Qasim decided ahead of time to walk at some distance behind the delegation during the opening procession, so as not to be seen walking directly behind the Israeli flag. They also decided to fold and drape their Rakah-issued blazers over their forearms (despite the chilly breeze) to hide the party's emblem, which Qasim worried might "inflame some of the Arab delegates."[71] They were right to be concerned: the Syrian Baʿth delegation, which had boycotted the opening procession altogether and gone directly to the stadium, cursed the Rakah delegates as they walked by, denouncing them as assassins and chanting the classic Arab nationalist motto, "Arab Palestine!"[72]

The calculations Darwish and Qasim made, and the reactions they faced at Sofia, highlighted the acute dilemma they faced. While they wished to be embraced by Arab delegates, and by extension the Arab world, they knew that they could not do so if they were seen as being too closely affiliated with Israel. Despite their championing of Palestinian, Arab, and global anticolonial causes while still holding on to their Israeli citizenship, they recognized that such a position was not yet intelligible in many Arab circles. As a result, Darwish and

Qasim decided to avoid doing anything that would risk their ability to meet with their fellow Arabs and Palestinians.

Other Rakah delegates sought to share their knowledge about Israeli politics and society to help Arabs develop a more nuanced appraisal of the country. At a plenary session discussing the political crisis in the Middle East, Rakah delegation leader George Tubi roundly criticized Israel's actions in the 1967 war as serving imperialist aims and argued that its occupation of Arab lands only exacerbated Israel's strategic problems.[73] But Tubi also chastised the Arabs for employing overheated rhetoric, warning that, "the irresponsible and chauvinistic propaganda in several Arab quarters, which does not distinguish between the people in Israel and the regressive government that is allied with imperialism, provided a pretext for the war and helped the Eshkol-Dayan-Begin government deceive large portions of world public opinion with regard to the aggressive nature of this war."[74] Tubi hoped that he could persuade Arab delegates to moderate their tone so they would not provide Israel with an opportunity to continue its aggressive actions while simultaneously claiming a posture of self-defense. Tubi believed that he could help Arabs be more strategic in their confrontation with Israel while also contributing to peace in the region. By refusing to fully embrace Arab framings of the conflict, which he saw as oversimplified and overheated, Tubi was also seeking to add nuance to Arab discussions of their confrontation with Israel. As subsequent developments revealed, he achieved only limited success.

In addition to political forums, cultural events were a major part of the festival.[75] Members of Rakah and other delegations sang songs and performed folk dances, while members of the PLO Arts, Cultural, and History Division in Beirut set up a poster display in central Sofia showing the history of Palestine and its conflict with the Zionists. They also displayed Palestinian artists' works, including those of famed Ibrahim Shammout.[76] In addition, various delegations organized poetry nights with readings by well-known poets, and Arab students studying in Sofia arranged for a Palestinian poetry night featuring Darwish and Qasim. At the latter event, attendees packed the large conference room and flowed out into the hallway; they were so excited to hear the famous resistance poets that they kept calling for more poems to be recited, extending the event far past its allotted two hours.[77]

The enthusiastic reactions Darwish and Qasim received at their poetry night reflected the celebrity status they had achieved. Several delegates who encountered them in Sofia excitedly recited lines of their poetry, while *al-Adab* editor and publisher Suhayl Idris proudly told them that they had joined the elite "Millionaire Club" because each of their anthologies had sold more than a million copies throughout the Arab world.[78] For other attendees, the poets were seen as key representatives of the larger Palestinian struggle. Jordanian Haydar Rashid recalled that he was excited to meet Darwish and Qasim, who already had the reputation of "defying the large Israeli prison" and had become a "clear example of steadfastness [*sumud*] on the land [by] refusing to leave it in any way." When Rashid encountered the Rakah delegation, he asked which one was Darwish; when the young poet identified himself, Rashid embraced him warmly.[79]

So great was the interest in speaking with the resistance poets that some of the delegates from Syria defied the orders of their superiors so they could meet them (a risky thing to do under the Baʿthist regime, to be sure). Syrian students who were studying abroad met with the poets clandestinely at a local student's home, where they spoke about the Palestinian people and listened to some of the poets' works.[80] At the festival itself, a few Palestinian members of the Syrian delegation secretly met Darwish and Qasim in their dormitory.[81] They understood the difference between the poets' national identity and their identity cards in a way that the Baʿthist officials were unwilling or unable to do.

In addition to the great interest in meeting Darwish and Qasim, the poets themselves were eager to meet other Palestinians and Arabs. When Darwish met Ibrahim Shammout (whom Darwish had been on the lookout for), the poet embraced the artist tightly, saying, "We, the forgotten on the inside, finally meet you."[82] When he heard that famed Iraqi poet Muhammad Mahdi al-Jawahiri was in town, Qasim went with Darwish and their roommate, attorney Muhammad Miʿari, to Jawahiri's hotel room one morning for a "secret" meeting. The elderly poet, surprised at their insistence on wanting to meet him, nonetheless graciously welcomed them. He was further puzzled when they insisted on taking a picture with him, even though he was still in his sleeping gown (*dishdasheh*). It was the opportunity of a lifetime, the young poets insisted, and without it, their participation in the festival would be incomplete. Jawahiri posed with Darwish and Qasim while Miʿari snapped the picture. After the picture was taken, Jawahiri had one request: that they not publish the picture, lest it raise the suspicions of Iraq's feared Baʿthist security apparatus.[83]

Thus, despite the enthusiastic celebrations and the warm embraces, the Sofia festival did not ultimately alleviate the suspicions that many Arabs, especially the hard-line Baʿthists, still had about the Palestinians in Israel. In many ways

Photo 4. Iraqi poet Muhammad Mahdi al-Jawahiri stands between Samih al-Qasim (right) and Mahmoud Darwish (left) at the 1968 World Youth Festival in Sofia, Bulgaria. Source: The National Album of Muhammad Samih al-Qasim. Copyright The Palestinian Museum. Reprinted with permission.

the festival only added to the confusion about this group. Part of the confusion stemmed from the unique political position of the Rakah party and its famous poets, which defied easy categorization. On the one hand, the party agreed with the position held by all Arab nationalists in vehemently opposing Israel's attacks during the 1967 war and its occupation of Arab lands. Moreover, the poems of Darwish and Qasim, with their bold declarations of Palestinians' steadfastness and their call for the emancipation of all peoples, embraced a vocabulary of decolonization that resonated widely with the festival's attendees. On the other hand, neither the Rakah party nor the resistance poets adopted fully the specific decolonizing logic as laid out in the Palestinian National Charter, which had been amended less than two weeks prior to the Sofia conference. The charter's call for armed struggle as the only way to liberate Palestine (Article 9) and its declaration that Jews constituted a religious group but not a national one (Article 20) were at odds with how Rakah leaders and intellectuals understood the conflict between Israelis and Palestinians.[84] While they all agreed that Zionist ideology was a root cause of the conflict, Palestinian intellectuals in Israel, who had been living with Jews for the past two decades, were much more willing to countenance a future settlement that included large numbers of Israeli Jews once they were freed from the ideological constraints of Zionist logic and were willing to live in total equality with the Palestinians. For Arab intellectuals who conflated Jews with Zionists and saw all Israelis as foreign interlopers, such a willingness to accommodate an ongoing Jewish presence on Arab land seemed illogical. As the Sofia conference wound down, participants would continue to mull over the meaning and significance of their encounters.

STANDING BETWEEN TWO BUILDINGS

The Rakah delegates were deeply affected by the conference. Several expressed joy that, for the first time in their lives, the shroud of isolation was lifted from them. After returning from the conference, Miʿari said that the displays of solidarity "convince you that despite all the forces of evil and aggression and spuriousness in the world, [things are] all right."[85] But others were troubled by the confusion on display among their fellow Arabs. Poet Mahmud al-Dasuqi sought to impress on Arabs that he indeed identified as a Palestinian Arab, despite the doubts raised by his Israeli passport.[86] In a poem published in the East Jerusalem–based *al-Quds* newspaper, Dasuqi dedicated his piece to those Arabs he met in Sofia who kept asking "whether I consider myself a part of the Palestinian Arab people." Dasuqi repeatedly declared throughout the poem that despite twenty years of sequestration, "I am a Palestinian Arab."[87] Dasuqi's insistence on being identified as a Palestinian Arab highlights his pain at having his identity called into question, while his publication of the poem in an East Jerusalem–based paper illustrates his desire to reach a wider Palestinian audience.

After the festival Palestinian intellectuals in exile once again defended their fellow Palestinians inside the Green Line to a wider Arab audience. Historian and PLO executive committee member Ahmad Sidqi al-Dajani, who had delivered a speech in Libya introducing this community back in 1961, chastised those Arab delegates he met at Sofia who said that the Palestinian Rakah delegates should renounce their passports and refuse to return to their country. Such comments "reveal the blatant ignorance about the circumstances of our brothers in their occupied country and their heroic struggle throughout the past twenty years," Dajani wrote in the widely circulating Cairo-based newspaper *al-Jumhuriyya*. He compared the condition of Palestinians in Israel to those of other colonized Arab peoples before them, writing, "There is no need to rush to condemn an Arab hero simply because he carries an Israeli passport that has been imposed on him, as long as this Arab believes in and works towards liberating his land. After all, the Italian passport was forced upon Libya for a time, and the French passport was forced upon Algeria for a time. That imposition only increased the fighters' determination as they fought while carrying the enemy's passports."[88]

By comparing the Palestinian citizens of Israel to the indigenous peoples of Libya and Algeria—the two countries in the Arab world that experienced European settler-colonialism most directly—Dajani invoked a "transcolonial sensibility" that positioned Palestine as a metaphor of decolonization.[89] Yet his robust defense of this group of Palestinians nonetheless revealed a lingering tension that remained between two different logics of decolonization. Dajani's comparison reflected his understanding of the Palestinian-Israeli conflict, common in Arabic nationalist circles at the time, as one between a settler-colonial regime and the indigenous people resisting it. But it was not a position that the Rakah party, or any of the Palestinian delegates from Israel, fully articulated themselves. While they insisted on their "Palestinianness" (as emphatically declared in Dasuqi's refrain, "I am a Palestinian Arab"), acknowledged that Palestine was a victim of imperialist machinations, and had spent years declaring their solidarity with colonized people around the world, they did not explicitly position Israel as a colonial regime or themselves as revolutionary fighters. Rather, they adopted a broader understanding of decolonization that called for an emancipatory future that embraced all peoples. This tension between wanting to be considered a part of the Palestinian Arab people but not adopting the settler-colonial paradigm that had become dominant in Arab nationalist discourses left the resistance poets in an ambiguous position.

Darwish in particular reflected this ambiguity. He had felt the tug of both his Palestinian and Israeli identities during the festival, a strain that came to a head when he examined the ten-story dormitories that housed the visiting delegates. Each tower accommodated four delegations: the Palestinian-Jordanian one was housed with those from Mexico, Panama, and Colombia. No Arab delegation shared a tower with Israel.[90] As Darwish recalled, this spatial division epitomized the contradictions in his life: "What does it mean to stand in Sofia between two buildings, one flying the Palestinian flag and the other, the Israeli? And are you capable of embodying the Palestinian spirit under the Israeli flag? Or, can you be a thing and its opposite at the same time? And beyond all that, who are you?"[91] Darwish's contemplative questions suggest that, despite the accolades he received as a poet engaged in resistance akin to that of the anticolonial guerrillas of the era, he struggled against such clear-cut understandings of his struggle. Darwish's questions also echoed wider Arab discussions that emerged in the aftermath of the Sofia festival about whether or not the poets were truly engaged in resistance against a settler-colonial regime.

RESISTANCE OR OPPOSITION?

The encounters at the Sofia festival sparked vibrant debates in Arab cultural and intellectual circles regarding the role that poets such as Darwish and Qasim were playing, both in the Palestinian anticolonial resistance movement and in the larger Arab cultural transformations in the wake of the June War. At stake was the question of whether these poets could truly be considered as engaged in resistance if they accepted Israel's existence and carried its passport. This was part of the larger debate regarding how to treat the challenge of the Zionist state in the wake of the defeat. Should Arabs try to eliminate the state, as they had talked about doing before 1967? Should they focus on ending the occupation of lands taken over in 1967? Or should they focus on asserting Palestinian and Arab self-confidence to ensure that the military defeat would not lead to a total collapse of the Palestinian liberationist project?

How one answered these questions often affected how one viewed the poetry emanating from inside the Green Line. In 1968–1970, a series of studies emerged in Arabic literary journals that explored the relationship between literature and resistance, focusing in particular on the Palestinian resistance poets. For those who longed for a restoration of Arab self-confidence after such a humiliating defeat, the poets' ability to challenge Zionist narratives and their refusal to accept the status quo were a source of inspiration. According to Iraqi critic ʿAbbas Khadr, in their work one finds "a limitless self-confidence, an amazing challenge to the hostile powers, and an insistence on transforming torture into a revolutionary drive."[92] Thus, for Khadr, expressing confidence in the face of oppression was itself a form of resistance. Lebanese Marxist writer and critic Muhammad al-ʿItani wrote that Darwish and Qasim's resistance poetry "returned to us some of the confidence in ourselves at a critical moment in the history of our nation and of our struggle."[93]

But not everyone was convinced that Darwish, Qasim, and their colleagues could be considered the Arab revolutionary vanguard. After all, Darwish in particular had presented a sympathetic face of Israeli society to a region that had had little exposure to such images. His latest anthology included a poem,

"Rita and the Rifle," that described his love for a Jewish Israeli woman,[94] while another poem, "A Soldier Dreams of White Lilies," recalled Darwish's conversation with an Israeli soldier returning from the 1967 war who confessed to the poet his aversion to combat and his desire to live in peace.[95] For Arab critics who were introduced to Darwish through his defiant verses in *A Lover from Palestine* and who believed total revolution was the only path for full decolonization, such sentiments muddied the waters. Syrian critic and poet Adunis, who was an especially vocal advocate of the need for total Arab social transformation in the aftermath of the war, asked, "Is there resistance poetry in the occupied lands? I am not convinced. By resistance poetry I mean, first, poetry that the citizen carries on his lips and in his heart like a fighter carries his gun. And second, I mean poetry that is working to create its times."[96] Adunis argued that, in the wake of the 1967 war, Arabs needed to fundamentally overturn all their preexisting beliefs and poetic styles.[97] For him, in terms of both content and style, the resistance poets did not go far enough.

Whether their assessments of this poetry were positive or negative, Arab critics generally contrasted it to poetry emanating from the Arab world. This juxtaposition made the resistance poets uncomfortable, especially since they saw themselves as part and parcel of the Arab literary scene, not set apart from it. In his famous 1969 essay "Save Us from This Relentless Love," Darwish tried to convince Arab critics that, despite their physical isolation, he and his fellow poets should not be seen as culturally sequestered from the region:

> Our poetry is not at all cut off from the poetic movement in Arab countries.... It is an inseparable part of it and one of many streams of a great river. We were raised by Arab poets old and new, and we attempted to join them through a contemporary poetic style after we learned about the leaders of this poetry in Iraq, Egypt, Lebanon and Syria. We cannot but consider ourselves students of those poets. It is not difficult for the critic even today to see the fingerprints of those poets in the majority of our work.[98]

Embedded in Darwish's essay was an appeal that he and his fellow Palestinian poets in Israel be embraced as part of the Arab literary family of contemporary free verse poets with which they identified so closely for all these years.

But it would not be that simple. Darwish's essay triggered another round of debates, this time on the pages of *al-Hadaf*, the Beirut-based paper of the Marxist-nationalist resistance group known as the Popular Front for the Liberation of Palestine (PFLP) and edited by Kanafani. The terms of the debate were largely a reprise of the one that ensued the previous year over the role that resistance poetry played in the broader cultural and ideological struggle against Zionism. While those who praised the resistance poets stressed that the oppressive environment in which the poets operated was itself a form of resistance,[99] Adunis held firm to his conviction that this was not actually resistance poetry but was in fact reformist (*islahi*) poetry since it did not urge "the total, fundamental transformation of Arab life."[100] Egyptian critic Ghali Shukri likewise expressed doubt about the appropriateness of the "resistance" label, despite the high artistic level of their poems, since they continued to live within Israel.[101] For Shukri, true Palestinian resistance poetry needed to emanate from a position outside one's homeland and could not emerge from within it.[102]

Darwish took a broader definition of resistance than the ones adopted by Adunis and Shukri. "Resistance poetry as I understand it," Darwish wrote, "is an expression of refusing the status quo, filled with a deep sense . . . of the unreasonableness of continuing the current situation and the need to change it, and belief in the possibility of change. . . . Resistance poetry, by its nature, is revolutionary poetry."[103] Qasim seems to have found the whole discussion a bit imprudent. As he told an interviewer in 1970, "I currently avoid using the word 'resistance' because some critics have stirred up a tempest in a teacup over this thing."[104] As Darwish and Qasim saw it, the label given to this poetry was less important than its function, which was to challenge hegemonic Israeli discourses, thereby "seizing the power of self-representation" for themselves.[105]

These discussions were also part of a larger debate about the definition of Palestinian resistance poetry itself. Did it need to be the literary equivalent of armed struggle, or could it express wider dimensions of decolonization? Did it need to call for a total overthrow of the existing order, or could it simply lay out a vision for a better world? Critics of Darwish and Qasim adopted a rather narrow definition of resistance that overlooked the complex ways in which the Israeli social and cultural milieu had affected the resistance poets as well as the nuanced ways in which the poets challenged Israeli framings of the conflict. Their detractors also underestimated the level of repression that the Palestinian citizens of Israel faced in the years after the June War.

"A MISERABLE ECHO"

As Arab critics were debating the extent to which resistance poetry was truly resistant, Palestinian citizens were struggling to come to grips with their tenuous position in an increasingly repressive Israeli environment. While the occupation of the remainder of historic Palestine had led to a reunification between Palestinians on both sides of the Green Line, the concomitant rise in attacks against Israelis by Palestinian guerrilla forces contributed to fears that Palestinian citizens might also participate in such attacks. As a result, despite lifting the military government at the end of 1966, Israel continued to impose restrictions on its Palestinian citizens that were often as tight as those in place during the period of military rule.[106] Throughout 1969 and 1970 Darwish and Qasim were repeatedly arrested, jailed, and/or placed under various forms of detention, accused of posing a risk of the state. The repression led them, and Palestinian intellectuals more broadly, to increasingly see parallels between the treatment of Palestinians in Israel and the treatment of Palestinians under Israeli occupation.

The occupation also brought with it heightened political tensions that drew Palestinians inside the Green Line into the Arab-Israeli conflict much more directly than before. In September 1968 three bombs planted in garbage cans exploded near the central bus station in Tel Aviv, killing one man and injuring fifty-one others. The bombs were assumed to be the work of fedayeen, and within minutes, Jewish Israeli mobs began attacking anyone they assumed to be Arab—primarily Palestinian passersby and vendors who were in fact Israeli citizens. Later that afternoon, the angry mobs moved south to the predominantly Palestinian town of Jaffa, attacking cars with Gaza Strip or West Bank license plates. Between fifty and one hundred Palestinian men from both Israel and the occupied territories were arrested and held overnight before the perpetrators were deemed to be a group of men from the West Bank town of Hebron.[107]

In addition, Israel recorded nearly one hundred apprehensions of young Palestinian citizens seeking to join commando groups in the first half of 1969 alone. Although not a high percentage of the overall population, the figure was higher than all apprehensions during the previous twenty years combined.[108] Fearing that Palestinians on both sides of the Green Line would collaborate to form armed groups to attack civilians, Israeli forces undertook sweeps of politically active Palestinians, trying to discover what networks (if any) existed between them. It is unclear whether any actual cells were disrupted or plots thwarted. But such wide-sweeping arrests and imprisonment had the unintended consequence of introducing politically active Palestinians under occupation to those politically active inside Israel, where they could share their ideas and be reunited in a different sort of way.

Samih al-Qasim experienced this phenomenon firsthand during the spring of 1969. His phone at the *al-Ittihad* office rang, and the voice of a well-known police officer on the other end called him in for questioning. When Qasim arrived, several members of Haifa's police force began peppering him with questions around one central theme: "Which figures did you meet in the West Bank and other [Occupied] Territories?" They accused him of collaborating to blow up an oil platform in Haifa's bay, a charge Qasim vehemently denied. He was then taken to Damun prison as the investigation continued; there, he met twenty prisoners from the Golan Heights, three from the Gaza Strip, and one from the West Bank. Qasim passed the time in detention by discussing Marxist and Hegelian dialectics with a prisoner from Golan, while another prisoner insisted Qasim recite some of his poems. When he paused to think about his circumstances, Qasim had a "strong, almost uncontrollable urge to cry," not out of sorrow but out of joy. After years of writing about the need for Arab unity and lamenting the barriers that kept Palestinians in Israel from having contact with other Arabs, it was in prison, Qasim realized, that they were finally "carrying out a unique type of 'Arab unity.'"[109]

Perhaps recognizing that such "unity" was taking place in prisons, the Israeli authorities soon resorted to other types of confinement. In addition to being forbidden from traveling to the West Bank or Gaza Strip, several Palestinian intellectuals and cultural producers in Israel were placed under a sunset-to-sunrise curfew (as continued to happen with Darwish[110]), or forbidden to have contact with Arabs in nearby areas (as happened to Qasim[111]). They were also required to inform the police if they changed residences and could be arrested for failing to do so (as happened to Salim Jubran[112]).

Such measures were not new, but they were enforced at a time in which Palestinians in exile were taking increased notice as part of their political project of integrating Palestinians inside the Green Line into their struggle. Beginning in late 1968, the PRC-published *Yawmiyyat Filastiniyah* (Palestinian journal), a multivolume compendium listing daily events relevant to the Palestinian cause, began adding more entries about the Palestinians in Israel than it had in previous years. These included reports from the Hebrew and Arabic press in Israel about the arrests and trials of several Palestinian poets, intellectuals, and political organizers in Israel, mirroring the reports of similar measures carried out against Palestinians in the occupied territories.[113] By placing these reports alongside one another, the editors of the PRC compendia were making clear that for them, the Palestinians in Israel were indeed engaged in acts of anticolonial resistance akin to those of other Palestinians. Such placement also contributed to an emerging political vocabulary that placed all Palestinian activists, regardless of citizenship, within the broader discursive framework of anticolonial resistance.

The poets, too, saw the crackdown against them as indicative of a broader Israeli policy toward Palestinians as a whole. As Darwish argued in a 1969 essay, "We must first recognize that this escalation is a miserable echo of a miserable occupation in the Arab territories occupied after June 5. The link between chasing after Arabs in Israel, the escalation of resistance in the occupied territories, and the failure of the occupation in gaining the consent of the occupied people has turned into a deep connection." But Darwish also struck a note of defiance in his essay, insisting that despite the persecution, Palestinian citizens of Israel will "remain in this country because it is their country."[114] Despite Darwish's insistence on toughing it out, he was already questioning his own position in Israel and feeling the pull of Arab world.

LOCATIONS AND POSITIONS

While still under confinement in fall 1969,[115] Darwish received a special invitation from the Soviet Union to attend a series of international literary events in Moscow. The Israeli government granted him a special permit that allowed him to go directly to the airport.[116] Shortly before his trip, Darwish discussed with Abu Hanna the possibility of moving to an Arab country. Abu Hanna told the young poet that they needed to fight the good fight from within their country, and Darwish seemed to concur.[117] Darwish spent several months in Moscow, where he met writers from all over the world. Among the highlights was a meeting with famed Palestinian poet Abu Salma, who had fled to Damascus in 1948 and whose poems Darwish had greatly admired.

The came the shock: Rather than return to Israel, Darwish flew to Cairo instead. To everyone's great surprise, on February 11, 1971, Darwish convened a press conference in which he announced he was taking up residence in the Egyptian capital. In contrast to Israel's draconian policies of detention and isolation, Darwish argued, being in Egypt made him feel that "I did not leave my country, but rather that I moved from the smaller country to the larger country."[118] Anticipating the objections that he would hear from those accusing him of abandoning the Palestinian cause, Darwish declared, "Even though I changed my location, I did not change my position."[119]

Despite his insistence that he had made a personal decision in reaction to the constant harassment he faced at home, Darwish's choice to leave was widely criticized in Arab and Palestinian circles. This was especially true in

Photo 5. Mahmoud Darwish (left) stands next to Abu Salma and Hanna Naqqara (right). Moscow, 1969. Source: The National Album of Muhammad Samih al-Qasim. Copyright The Palestinian Museum. Reprinted with permission.

light of his poetry and earlier statements that emphasized his and his people's steadfastness. The front page of the Lebanese paper *al-Hawadith* ran Darwish's picture with a banner headline above it proclaiming, "I wish he would return to Israel." Below it, an essay (widely speculated to be written by Kanafani) called on Darwish to return to Israel: "We are in the stage of return and insistence on staying. The stage of emigration has forever passed. I wish you would return to Israel, to prison. I wish you would return, no matter the price you will pay in terms of your freedom and even in terms of your art and poetry. Return, for you chose and you cannot renege."[120] The essay reflected a sense of personal betrayal that many of Darwish's champions felt, especially after they had worked so hard to convince Arab intellectuals that remaining in Israel was in fact a form of resistance, not acquiescence. The writer's insistence that Darwish return "to prison" in order to serve as the vanguard for Palestinian revolutionaries who were commencing "the stage of return," even at the expense of his own artistic development, brought to the fore the resistance poets' complicated relationship with other Palestinians and Arabs. In becoming one of the most famous symbols of the Palestinian struggle for liberation, Darwish was being called on to more fully take up the role of revolutionary hero, even though he had not sought that role.

At least some of the Palestinian intellectuals back home seemed to understand Darwish's dilemma. As one commentator in *al-Ittihad* wrote, "We are certain that we need Mahmoud Darwish more here, among us. But the rulers of our country have no one to blame but themselves for the conclusion that Mahmoud Darwish reached."[121] This commentator (widely believed to be Habibi) recognized that the constant struggle to overcome his internal and external isolation had taken a heavy toll on Darwish, especially as he had become the most celebrated—and the most sanctioned—of all the Palestinian resistance poets in Israel. With the Arab world beckoning, it was not surprising that Darwish looked for a way to escape his imprisonment.

CONCLUSION

Darwish was not alone in experiencing this heavy burden of isolation. Around the time that he decided to move to Cairo, Samih al-Qasim issued a revision of his essay "Poets, Not Diplomats," which he had penned seven years earlier. The title of his revised piece, "Poets *and* Diplomats," reflected Qasim's conclusion that he and his fellow poets had no choice but to play a central role in connecting their community to the wider Palestinian and Arab worlds. Qasim argued that Israel had erected "two iron curtains:" the first was between Palestinians "who resided behind the tanks" and those who "resided in the front lines against them," while the second was between Palestinians in Israel and the Arab world. Offering a cautiously optimistic reading of the struggle in which he and his fellow poets were engaged, Qasim wrote, "We do not claim to have succeeded in demolishing the two iron curtains, but we have opened up more than one breach, stirred more than one conscience, affected more than one mind, and mobilized more than one person." Despite their modest successes, however, such efforts took a heavy toll on the poets. Qasim wrote, "This task may appear easy on the surface, but in reality it is an oppressive calling, one that . . . makes you occasionally feel compelled to lock yourself up in a room and scream—scream so that you don't go insane!"[122]

Qasim's essay captured well the challenges that poets and intellectuals in Israel faced in the aftermath of the 1967 war. The occupation had allowed Palestinians on either side of the Green Line to reconnect with one another after two decades of isolation. As a result, Palestinians in Israel had greater exposure to Palestinian liberationist discourses, while Palestinians under occupation and in exile learned that steadfastness and cultural pride were possible in the face of an onerous military rule. Seeking to disrupt this reconnection, Israel soon clamped down on cultural producers, especially the poets, renewing the terms of their confinement and preventing them from participating in cultural and literary events across the Green Line. Despite the clampdowns, the circulation of Palestinian poetry and essays from inside Israel continued through radio, Arab cultural journals, and reprints of their poetry collections. Their defiant verses inspired Palestinians and Arabs still reeling from the shock of the 1967 defeat.

These rapidly changing dynamics also meant that by this time, the previous strategies that Palestinian intellectuals had adopted to mitigate their isolation from the region, such as accessing regional Arabic texts and reprinting texts in local Arabic publications, were woefully inadequate. The generally warm reception that the resistance poets in particular received at the World Youth Festival at Sofia whetted their appetite for more face-to-face contact with other Palestinians and Arabs, though it was complicated by their differing conceptions of what Palestinian decolonization entailed and how it was to be defined. The discussions about the role of the resistance poets in Palestinian decolonization at the festival itself, and the debates that unfolded afterward on the pages of regional cultural journals, confirmed to the resistance poets the need for more face-to-face encounters with their fellow Palestinians and Arabs, but it came at a time of increasingly harsh Israeli measures meted out to politically active Palestinians under their rule.

For Darwish at least, the joys of meeting other Palestinians and Arabs made the sorrows of confinement at home all the more acute. But his decision to move to Cairo illustrated the price that Palestinian citizens of Israel would need to pay in order to fully overcome their isolation from the Arab world. After taking up residence Cairo (and later Beirut), Darwish became internationally acclaimed as "the national poet of Palestine"; he served as a key figure in the PLO and traveled frequently throughout the Arab world. But he was not able to step foot into the land of his birth for the next twenty-two years.[123] Yet even as Darwish and other poets, intellectuals, and political figures in Israel were increasingly celebrated in the Arab world for their numerous modes of cultural and political resistance, the community as a whole would continue to face scrutiny for decades to come.

CONCLUSION

In 2007 researchers at the Haifa-based Mada al-Carmel Palestinian Research Center issued a statement laying out what they envisioned for the Palestinian citizens of Israel. In describing the community's history, the "Haifa Declaration" explained:

> Despite the setback to our national project and our relative isolation from the rest of our Palestinian people and our Arab nation since the *Nakba*; despite all the attempts made to keep us in ignorance of our Palestinian and Arab history; despite attempts to splinter us into sectarian groups and to truncate our identity into a misshapen "Israeli Arab" one, we have spared no effort to preserve our Palestinian identity and national dignity and to fortify it. In this regard, we reaffirm our attachment to our Palestinian homeland and people, to our Arab nation, with its language, history, and culture, as we reaffirm also our right to remain in our homeland and to safeguard it.[1]

This passage summarizes well the means by which Israeli leaders tried to isolate the state's Palestinian citizens from one another, from other Palestinians, and from the Arab world, as well as Palestinian citizens' refusal to accept this state of affairs. This book sheds light on the specific, deliberate, and concrete ways in which intellectuals, cultural producers, and political organizers actively resisted these policies of sequestration.

I elucidate several strategies that multiple generations of Palestinians in Israel deployed between 1948 and 1971 to foster a sense of connection with those living beyond their border. In the aftermath of the Nakba, with the catastrophic loss of the vast majority of the Palestinian leadership and intelligentsia, Palestinian members of the Communist Party of Israel (the only legal non-Zionist party at the time that accepted Palestinians as equal members) reprised two strategies of resistance they had previously deployed during the Mandate period: organizing protests and utilizing local Arabic publications to disseminate narratives that challenged colonial discourses and informed readers about events at home and abroad. But as their access to regional print material was suddenly interrupted, they also had to develop new strategies to access texts from the Arab world. With some help from their Iraqi Jewish allies, they brought in newspapers, literary journals, and poetry collections from abroad (sometimes surreptitiously) and reprinted this material in locally produced Arabic newspapers and journals.

As Arab nationalist and Third World decolonization movements arose in the latter half of the 1950s, intellectuals and political organizers both in and out of the CPI developed these strategies further. They established nonpartisan organizations that spoke against Israeli policies with one voice and organized protests that signaled popular support for Arab and Third World causes of the day. However, because the Israeli military regime restricted large-scale demonstrations, they turned increasingly to poetry to signal their support for other peoples' struggles. Poetry festivals provided a platform for poets to express their views and for listeners to become acquainted with expressions of anticolonial solidarity. In addition, much of this poetry was published in the local Arabic press, especially in *al-Ittihad* and *al-Jadid*, where it garnered an audience far beyond those in attendance. During the heyday of pan-Arab nationalism and Third World revolution in the late 1950s and early 1960s, much of this poetry was devoted to celebrating the anticolonial struggles for freedom in the region and around the world. But disappointment with the Arab revolutionary projects, coupled with the rise of the Palestinian nationalist movement in the mid-1960s, led poets to turn their attention to poems that emphasized their peoples' steadfastness and defiance in the face of Israeli policies of marginalization and erasure.

Despite these deep engagements with regional and global developments, for most of this period the contributions that Palestinian intellectuals in Israel made to broader political and cultural discussions rarely reached audiences beyond the Green Line. To overcome this obstacle, and to signal their joint struggles with Palestinians in exile, intellectuals sent open letters and memoranda to international bodies. Especially notable was the memorandum issued by the pan-Arab nationalist Ard Group in 1964, which played a significant role in raising awareness among Palestinian and some Arab intellectuals about the plight of the Palestinians behind the barbed wire. The Ard memorandum also challenged pervasive beliefs in the region that the Palestinians in Israel were either passive victims of Israeli policies or traitors to the Arab cause. Its success in reaching a larger Arab audience was due in large part to the efforts of a younger generation of Palestinian intellectuals in exile, who were themselves establishing political organizations and research institutes that were aimed at learning more about the Palestinian people as a whole.

The production and circulation of written texts—including newspapers, journals, and poetry collections—played a key role in facilitating and mediating these interactions. Yet as important as these texts were, they could not replace direct contact with other Arabs. Seeking greater face-to-face contact with their counterparts in the region and beyond, some Palestinian intellectuals were able to participate in international gatherings and festivals. Largely sponsored by the Soviet Union, they allowed some politically connected Palestinians to travel abroad and meet colleagues in Europe or the USSR. The most popular of these were the quadrennial World Youth Festivals, which brought together leftist intellectuals and activists from around the world. The 1968 festival in Sofia, Bulgaria, proved to be especially significant in helping Palestinian Rakah delegates, especially Mahmoud Darwish and Samih al-Qasim, meet with Palestinian and Arab intellectuals who were in turn eager to connect with them. But by this time, as Israeli authorities became ever more fearful of the growing Palestinian resistance movement, they tightened their grip on Palestinian writers and intellectuals in Israel, limiting their ability to travel and meet with one another. For Darwish, at least, the push of Israeli restrictions and the pull of his newfound adulation in the Arab world led him to self-imposed exile in Cairo. In addition, Israeli authorities banished Ard cofounders Sabri Jiryis and Habibi Qahwaji on suspicion of illicit activity, whereupon they moved to Beirut and Damascus, respectively. Thus, a final "strategy" for Palestinians to overcome their isolation was to leave Israel altogether.

In addition to demonstrating the strategies that Palestinian intellectuals in Israel deployed and the audiences they tried to reach, this book also elucidates how they were perceived by their fellow Palestinians and Arabs. I argue that despite their deep engagement with the political and cultural developments of the region, prior to 1967 Palestinians in Israel were largely ignored by Arab intellectuals. The lack of direct contact, coupled with incessant Israeli propaganda that described the "Arab Israelis" as a content minority in the Jewish state, led many Arabs to regard those Palestinian who accepted Israeli citizenship as turncoats. In this climate of deep suspicion and hostility, Palestinian intellectuals in exile were the first to raise awareness about the growing Palestinian resistance developing inside Israel. Ghassan Kanafani's 1966 groundbreaking study on Palestinian resistance literature in particular began to draw attention to the presence of literary and cultural resistance in Israel. But it was not until Arab intellectuals called for self-introspection and reassessment in the wake of the June 1967 defeat that Kanafani's call to look to the Palestinians in Israel—especially the resistance poets—as a model of cultural resistance in the face of Israeli hegemony gained traction.

At the same time, the Israeli occupation of the remainder of historic Palestine in 1967 opened up an avenue for Palestinians on either side of the Green Line to reconnect with one another. Moreover, intellectuals and cultural producers who had been following one another's work through journals and the radio developed a strong desire to meet face-to-face. The 1968 World Youth Festival in Sofia was an especially momentous opportunity to do so, and it helped catapult festival participants Mahmoud Darwish and Samih al-Qasim to pan-Arab stardom.

But not all Arabs shared in this adulation. Some critics continued to denounce the Palestinians in Israel for choosing to remain under Zionist rule, for accepting Israeli citizenship and passports, and for refusing to initiate a mass insurrection against Israel to help Palestinian and Arab guerrilla forces overthrow the state. At the heart of these debates were differing notions of what decolonization meant in the context of Palestine. While the dominant Palestinian anticolonial discourse stressed armed struggle to achieve national liberation, Palestinian intellectuals in Israel, especially the resistance poets, called for a broader conceptual framework of decolonization that envisioned all peoples living with equality, dignity, and freedom.

The early 1970s saw a shift in the relationship between Palestinian citizens of Israel and the Arab world. The climate of discovery that had characterized the previous years gave way to a period of deepening collaboration as Jiryis became director of the PRC in Beirut and Qahwaji published several studies on Israeli treatment of the Palestinian minority with the center. Meanwhile, poets Darwish and Rashid Husayn (who had moved from Israel to the United States in 1966) both became spokesmen for the PLO. Their experiences as citizens of Israel allowed them to share with the Arab world insights about the inner workings of Israeli politics and society with more expertise, insight, and institutional weight behind them. As a result, by the mid-1970s, the political vocabulary of Palestinian liberation included more fully the Palestinians in Israel.

This vocabulary translated into action in 1976. In response to Israel's refusal to reconsider seizing thousands of acres of Palestinian-owned land around the Jewish town of Carmiel in the western Galilee, Palestinian communities across Israel organized a series of strikes and demonstrations set for March 30, which they dubbed "Land Day." Protesters were met with heavy police and military violence, leading to six Palestinian citizens being killed, about one hundred wounded, and hundreds more arrested and often beaten before being released.[2] In the weeks leading up to the Land Day protests, regional Arab papers and broadcasts devoted extensive coverage to the planned events,[3] while on Land Day itself Palestinian activists in the West Bank, Gaza Strip, and throughout the region organized solidarity demonstrations.[4] Unlike the numerous earlier protests organized by Palestinians in Israel that had gone unnoticed in neighboring countries, this time regional Arab newspapers gave extensive coverage to the protests and killings.[5] In many ways, Land Day solidified the relationship between Palestinians in Israel and the Palestinian national body: it has entered into the collective memory of Palestinians all over the world who continue to commemorate Land Day every March 30.[6]

In addition to continuing to organize mass protests, Palestinians in Israel also formed political groups along more explicitly Palestinian nationalist lines. In 1984 the Progressive List was founded, which emphasized Palestinian national identity. Although it failed to build the infrastructure needed to garner significant electoral victories, its ideas resonated widely with Palestinian intellectuals, laying the groundwork for more successful nationalist parties to emerge in the 1990s. The best known was the National Democratic Alliance (also known as Balad or Tajammuʿ), headed until 2007 by well-known political philosophy professor Azmi Bishara. It called for Israel to be a "state of all its citizens," to end the occupation of Palestinian territories, to recognize the Palestinian refugees' right to return, and to preserve the cultural and historical identity of the Palestinians in Israel—all positions that were well within the Palestinian national consensus.[7]

Ironically, just as nationally conscious Palestinians in Israel were aligning themselves more fully as part of the Palestinian people, the Palestinian national movement excised them from the national agenda. The PLO's embrace of the two-state solution, as embodied by the 1988 Palestinian Declaration of Independence and by PLO chairman Yasser Arafat's signing of the Oslo Accords in 1993, meant that its focus was on establishing a Palestinian state in the occupied territories, not on achieving full rights for all Palestinians.[8] As a result, the growing national demands of the Palestinian citizens of Israel were largely unacknowledged in the one political body that was supposed to represent Palestinians worldwide.

The dawn of the new century brought about significant changes. The collapse of the Camp David 2 talks in 2000, followed by the immense violence of the Second Intifada from 2000 to 2005, led many Palestinians to reassess whether their focus on state-building efforts was indeed the best route toward liberation. In addition, the October 2000 Israeli police killings of thirteen unarmed Palestinian citizens of Israel who were marching in solidarity with their fellow Palestinians in the occupied territories led intellectuals and organizers on both sides of the Green Line and beyond to emphasize the intersectionality of their struggles. They were aided in this endeavor by new modes of communication, especially satellite television and the Internet, which Palestinians took advantage of to communicate with one another and to keep informed about events happening across their borders.[9]

The Second Intifada also highlighted the ongoing Israeli perception of Palestinian cultural production as a threat. In 2002 Israeli soldiers stormed the preeminent Khalil Sakakini Cultural Center in Ramallah, seizing a computer, destroying artwork, and ransacking Mahmoud Darwish's manuscripts. Shortly afterward, as the world-renowned poet surveyed the damage to his office at the center, he said, "I know [the Israelis] are strong and can invade and kill anyone. But they can't break or occupy my words. That is one thing they can't do. My poetry is the one way I have to resist them. I have to deal with this with the pen, not by stones."[10] The episode confirmed an observation that Darwish had presciently made forty years earlier: while colonial projects try to erase the culture of the people they seek to colonize, those people will utilize cultural productions to resist the attempted erasures.

It is a lesson that Palestinian intellectuals and cultural producers in the Gaza Strip, who as of this writing are entering the second decade of a crippling blockade, have taken to heart. Despite the profound isolation they face, they have turned to cultural and artistic productions to make their voices heard. Like their Palestinian counterparts inside the Green Line, writers,[11] singers,[12] visual artists,[13] television creators,[14] and others have turned to cultural works out of a spirit of steadfastness and to give their community something beautiful that can sustain them during these difficult times. While they do not face the same Arab suspicions as the subjects of this study, those living in Gaza are nonetheless eager for the world to recognize their individual humanity and to see them as more than just victims.

Have Palestinian citizens of Israel overcome their isolation? Yes and no. At the discursive level at least, they have become fully integrated into the Palestinian national narrative. Their cultural productions—especially poetry, novels, hip-hop, and film—enjoy wide circulation and acclaim throughout the region. Their social and political concerns have also become integrated into the Palestinian national agenda: the 2005 boycott, divestment, and sanctions (BDS) platform, endorsed by hundreds of Palestinian civil society groups, lists full equality for Palestinian citizens of Israel as one of its three central demands.[15]

In terms of overcoming their physical isolation, however, the picture is still quite grim. Palestinian citizens of Israel who are active in the public sphere are routinely barred from entering the occupied territories, while Palestinian cultural producers living under occupation are frequently denied entry into Israel.[16] And while Palestinians holding Israeli passports may travel to Jordan, Egypt, and a few other Arab countries,[17] traveling to neighboring Lebanon and Syria can carry serious penalties once they return.[18]

As a result of these dynamics, there remains a great deal of confusion in the Arab world about how to regard this community. On the one hand, Arab satellite channels laud those individuals who risk their lives to help their fellow Palestinians, such as Knesset member Haneen Zoabi and Islamic movement leader Raed Salah, who were on board a Turkish humanitarian aid ship trying to deliver food and medicine to the besieged Palestinians in Gaza when they came under Israeli military assault.[19] On the other hand, such Palestinians are often presented as being exceptionally defiant rather than part of broader community engaged in various forms of resistance. Adding to this blurred picture, often those who do come into Arab public view find that their Israeli citizenship is obscured. Such was the case for Manal Moussa and Haitham Khalailah, two Palestinian citizens of Israel who competed in the 2014 Arab Idol singing competition in Beirut and who were identified solely as being Palestinian.[20] While highlighting their "Palestinianness" reflected in large part their own self-identity, obscuring their Israeli citizenship status does little to demystify this community to the wider Arab world.

In addition to ongoing misperceptions that Palestinians living inside the Green Line face from abroad, their status within the state continues to be quite tenuous. This tenuousness was highlighted in 2015 when police forces raided the family home of Dareen Tatour, who was until then a little-known poet and photographer living in the Galilean city of al-Rayna. After nearly a month behind bars, she was indicted on charges of incitement to violence and support for a terrorist organization, based largely on an Arabic poem she had uploaded to YouTube titled "Resist, My People, Resist Them."[21] After three more months in prison, she was forced to move to an apartment nearly forty miles away from her hometown without phone or Internet access.[22] But in a sign of the growing international interest in the rights of Palestinian cultural producers, more than three hundred prominent writers and intellectuals from around the world signed a petition in support of her release,[23] while PEN America described her arrest as a "worrying escalation in Israeli repression."[24] The campaign succeeded in pressuring the authorities to allow Tatour to return to her hometown after six months, where she was to remain under house arrest for the duration of her trial. In describing her circumstances, Tatour acknowledged the historical precedent of her arrest: "Back in the '60s, all the poets, like Mahmoud Darwish, were arrested." But she also expressed dismay that the draconian measures used to try to silence poets so many years ago were still being deployed. "In this century, I never expected this," she admitted. "I didn't know that democracy was not for everyone in Israel."[25] Like Darwish, Zayyad, Qasim, and other Palestinian cultural producers before her, Tatour learned that a high price was to be paid for Arabic expressions of support for the Palestinians.

In many ways the discursive contestations laid out in these pages have come back to the fore. Debates about Palestinian citizens' loyalty (or lack thereof) to Israel, the state's role in uplifting its Palestinian citizens, and the meaning of peace between Arabs and Jews are as contested today as ever before. More than fifty years after Darwish first recited "Identity Card," his poem continues to loom large over cultural and political debates in the country. In July 2016 an educational program on Israeli Army Radio featured a discussion of Darwish's famous poem, prompting right-wing culture and sports minister Miri Regev to denounce the station for "providing a platform to the Palestinian narrative that opposes the existence of Israel as a Jewish democratic state."[26] Two months later, rapper Tamer Nafar and spoken-word artist Yossi Tsabari featured the poem as part of their onstage performance at the Israeli Ophir film awards ceremony. As the late Darwish's voice was heard saying, "Record, I am an Arab," Nafar (a Palestinian citizen) and Tsabari (of Yemeni Jewish extraction) raised black-gloved fists in the Black Power salute as they affirmed their shared Arab identity in the face of Israeli attempts to co-opt and erase it.[27] In addition to demonstrating the ongoing relevance of Darwish's poem, Nafar and Tsabari's performance—especially their salute—indicates the parallels that Palestinians and some Mizrahim in Israel see between their own condition and that of African Americans. As this book makes clear, the parallels they draw have deep historical roots—roots that have yet to be fully explored.

Meanwhile, in the span of less than a decade the Arab world has witnessed a series of revolutions, counterrevolutions, civil wars, and strategic realignments. It has also seen the rise of a millennial generation that is transnationally connected through social media in ways that earlier generations of Arabs could not have dreamed of. And as these young Arabs chart a path toward dignity in the face of enormous obstacles, I hope that Palestinians living inside the Green Line will be included more fully in these transnational projects of liberation.

NOTES

INTRODUCTION

1. Rashid Husayn, "The Exaggerations of the Lebanese Delegation," *al-Mirsad*, August 13, 1959, 3; Latif Duri, "We and the Arab Delegations in Vienna," *al-Mirsad*, August 20, 1959, 3.

2. Latif Duri, "With Members of the Arab Delegations in Vienna (2)," *al-Mirsad*, August 27, 1959, 2.

3. Ibid. Djamila Bouhired was a fighter in Algeria's war for independence against France. News of her captivity and torture by the French had recently made international headlines, and Egyptian filmmaker Youssef Chahine's popular 1959 biopic *Jamila Buhayrid* made her a household name in the region as a symbol of Arab anticolonial resistance. Khouri, *Arab National*.

4. Duri, "With Members," 2.

5. Husayn, "The Exaggerations of the Lebanese Delegation," *al-Mirsad*, August 13, 1959, 2.

6. Ibid.

7. Rashid Husayn, "Letter to Lebanon," *al-Fajr* 1, no. 11 (August 1959): 6.

8. Husayn was referring to the Egyptian military and popular resistance against British and French paratroopers who landed in Port Said during the 1956 Suez Crisis, the July 1958 revolution in Iraq that overthrew the pro-Western Hashemite monarchy, and the May 1958 nationalist uprisings in Lebanon against a pro-Western president. For more on their significance in Arab imaginaries of decolonization, see Louis and Owen, *Revolutionary Year*; Louis, *Ends*; Yaqub, *Containing*.

9. For population figures, see McCarthy, *Population*, 37.

10. The precise number of Palestinian refugees has been a point of dispute since 1948. Benny Morris draws on Israeli archival material to give an estimated figure of around 700,000 (Morris, *Refugee Problem Revisited*, 602–604), while Rashid Khalidi, drawing on UN reports from that period, argues the number was likely well over 750,000 (Khalidi, *Iron Cage*, 225n3).

11. Tiberias, Safed, Beisan, and Beersheba were completely depopulated of their Arab population, while Jaffa, Haifa, Acre, Ramlah, and Jerusalem saw the number of

Arab residents decrease dramatically after the war. Kamen, "After the Catastrophe I," 459–461; Pappé, *Ethnic Cleansing*, 91–103.

12. Khalidi and Elmusa, *All That Remains*.
13. Peretz, *Israel*, 33–44.
14. Robinson, *Citizen Strangers*, 68–90.
15. Ibid., 96–112.
16. Morris, *Israel's Border Wars*.
17. Anton Shammas, "The Morning After," *New York Review of Books*, September 29, 1988.
18. Robinson, *Citizen Strangers*; Jiryis, *Arabs in Israel*.
19. Feiler, *From Boycott*, 24–34.
20. Kamen, "After the Catastrophe II," 101–103.
21. For an overview and criticism of this scholarship, see Pappé, *Forgotten Palestinians*, 276–280; Saʽdi, "Modernization"; and Rabinowitz, "Oriental Othering."
22. Zureik, *Palestinians*; Lustick, *Arabs*.
23. Smooha, *Orientation*; Reiter, *National Minority*; R. Cohen, *Strangers*; Peleg and Waxman, *Israel's Palestinians*; Haklai, *Palestinian Ethnonationalism*.
24. Abu-Baker and Rabinowitz, *Coffins*; Rouhana, *Palestinian Citizens*; Ghanem, *Palestinian-Arab Minority*.
25. Robinson, *Citizen Strangers*; H. Cohen, *Good Arabs*; and Pappé, *Forgotten Palestinians*. These works build on the earlier, groundbreaking work of Joel Beinin, particularly Beinin, *Red Flag*.
26. Abu-Lughod, "Pitfalls."
27. The Palestinian Authority's Cultural Ministry has founded a national archive in Ramallah, but its holdings are still quite slim.
28. In September 1982 Israeli forces seized the extensive archival collections of the Palestine Research Center (PRC) in Beirut and shipped the holdings to Tel Aviv. Five months later the PRC building was heavily damaged by a car bomb that killed eight employees and wounded several others. As part of a 1983 prisoner-exchange deal with the Palestine Liberation Organization (PLO), Israel returned an unknown portion of the archives, which was shipped to Algeria. Once the PRC was reestablished in Cyprus in 1985, several attempts were made to transport the archival material from Algeria to Cyprus, but they failed. The material is now presumed to be lost. See Samih Shabib, "Palestine Research Center: The Lost Memory," jiyis.net, June 13, 2005, http://tinyurl.com/zxhq5f6. Shabib headed the PRC's documentation office from 1981 to 1993.

In August 2001, Israeli police forces raided the Orient House in East Jerusalem, confiscating a significant portion of its archives. As of this writing, the Orient House remains shut down. While many of its documents are currently housed in the Israel State

Archives, the fate of its remaining archival collection is unclear. For more on the current status of this and other Palestinian archival and library collections, see Librarians and Archivists with Palestine, http://librarianswithpalestine.org.

In addition, during the 1948 war an estimated seventy thousand books were seized by Israeli forces from the personal collections and libraries of Palestinians, along with an untold number of their private papers. A significant portion of this material made its way into the holdings of the National Library of Israel with the call number AP ("Abandoned Property"). See Brunner, *Great Book Robbery*.

29. See El Shakry, "History without Documents."

30. An added challenge is that that many of the records in the Israel State Archives pertaining to the 1948 war and to the Palestinians were declassified in the late 1990s and early 2000s but have since been reclassified. Recently scholars have grown concerned that as the Israel State Archives digitizes its collections, it may further reclassify previously declassified material. See Hazkani and Gratien, "Politics of 1948;" Di-Capua, "Intimate History;" and Hofstadter and Yavne, "Point of Access."

31. Said, *World*, 35.

32. Williams, *Culture*, 49.

33. Gramsci, "The Intellectuals," 5–23.

34. About 80 percent of the Palestinians who remained in Israel were villagers who had been engaged in agriculture prior to 1948. Because of ongoing Israeli land confiscations, large numbers of farmers (and their children) would become part of Israel's labor class. See Kamen, "After the Catastrophe II," 90.

35. Gramsci defines traditional intellectuals "of the rural type" as including priests, lawyers, notaries, teachers, and doctors who mediated between peasants and the state ("The Intellectuals," 14). Yet several of the lawyers and teachers discussed in the pages that follow identified more closely with the organic intellectuals than the traditional ones.

36. Scott, "Temporality," 173.

37. Ibid. Scott elaborates on these ideas in *Refashioning* and *Conscripts*.

38. This trend began to change only in the mid-1970s as subsequent generations of Palestinian writers in Israel increasingly shifted to Hebrew. Notable writers include Siham Daoud, Sayed Kashua, Atallah Mansour, Salman Natur, and Anton Shammas. See Shakour, "Arab Authors."

39. Noorani, "Redefining Resistance," 83–86.

40. Historian Derek Penslar, for example, places Israel's first two decades of statehood firmly within a postcolonial context, though he acknowledges that some early state policies toward Palestinian citizens shared elements with colonial rule. See Penslar, *Israel*, 90–111.

41. Robinson, *Citizen Strangers*.
42. Nassar, "My Struggle."
43. Wilder, *Freedom Time*, 4.
44. Prashad, *Darker Nations*; Dubinsky et al., *New World Coming*.
45. On these earlier circulations, see Polsgrove, *Ending*; and James, *George Padmore*.
46. See also Bhandar and Ziadah, "Acts and Omissions."
47. Ghanem, "Palestinians in Israel," 139.
48. Makhoul, "Ha ezrachim."

CHAPTER 1

1. E. Habibi, "Ana huwa," 186.
2. During the Mandate period, Palestine's government high schools taught only through the tenth grade. Students wishing to complete their final two years of high school could either try to gain admission into the government's highly competitive Government Arab College (which accepted only the top one or two students annually from each government high school) or the Rashidiya College in Jerusalem or attend a private high school. Habibi had hoped for a spot in the Arab College but was edged out by his close friend Ihsan ʿAbbas, who went on to become a preeminent professor of Arabic literature at the American University of Beirut. Fortunately for Habibi, his family had the means to send him to a private school. See ʿAbbas, *Ghurbat*, 107.
3. E. Habibi, "Ana huwa," 186; Budeiri, *Palestine*, 72–73, 201n107.
4. Ibid., 183.
5. Gershoni and Jankowski, *Redefining*, 49–51.
6. E. Habibi, "Ana huwa," 182. On translations of Russian literature to Arabic (particularly those associated with a radical outlook, see Khuri-Makdisi, *Eastern Mediterranean*, 51; and H. al-Khatib, *Harakat al-tarjama*, 15–16.
7. Nordbruch, "Defending," 219–238.
8. E. Habibi, "Ana huwa," 183.
9. Ibid., 182.
10. Throughout this chapter I use the term "Palestinian Arab" (ʿArab filastin) to describe the Arab inhabitants of Palestine, as this was the most common phrase they used to describe themselves during the Mandate period (R. Khalidi, *Palestinian Identity*, 175).
11 Tuma, *Yawmiyat shaʿb*, 62–88.
12. Dallasheh, "Nazarenes."
13. Kalisman, "Schooling."
14. R. Khalidi, *Iron Cage*; Essaid, *Zionism*; Bunton, *Colonial*.
15. Mattar, *Mufti*. Western and Arab scholarship is replete with historiographical debates about Hajj Amin's positions and decisions during the Mandate period. While he was undoubtedly a towering figure over the Palestinian politics and society, such

debates can obscure other important perspectives and dynamics from this period. See Wildangel, "More Than the Myth," 101–126.

16. Matthews, *Confronting*.

17. The Arab East (*al-Mashriq* in Arabic) refers to the areas east of Egypt, including Greater Syria (present-day Syria, Lebanon, Jordan, and Israel/Palestine), and Iraq.

18. "Jund" refers to the military administrative districts of the Umayyad and Abbasid eras.

19. Gerber, "Palestine," 563–572; Gerber, *Remembering*, 48–56.

20. For Qurʾanic references to Jerusalem, see 5:21 and 17:1. Genres of works that discuss these terms include Qurʾanic exegesis, *fadaʾil al-Quds* (merits of Jerusalem) works, travelogues, and historical works. See R. Khalidi, *Palestinian Identity*, 29–30; Gerber, "Palestine," 567.

21. Doumani, *Rediscovering*, 68–75.

22. M. Seikaly, "Haifa," 103; Büssow, *Hamidian Palestine*, 438–450.

23. Hourani, *Arabic Thought*, 95–102; Schumann, *Liberal Thought*; Kendall, "Between Politics," 330–343.

24. Hourani, *Arabic Thought*; Schumann, *Nationalism and Liberal Thought*.

25. Khuri-Makdisi, *Eastern Mediterranean*, 1–6.

26. Buheiry, *Intellectual*; Khuri-Makdisi, *Eastern Mediterranean*, 35–51.

27. ʿAtwat, *Al-Ittijahat*, 64; Ayalon, *Reading*, 49–50.

28. While the first systematized effort to determine literacy rates in Palestine was not undertaken until 1932, some literacy rates between the turn of the twentieth century and World War I were estimated to hover at around 2–3 percent. See Ayalon, *Reading*, 16, 22.

29. Historian Rashid Khalidi cites an observer from 1912 who lamented that readers of the *al-Hilal* and *al-Muqtataf* in Palestine "are counted in the dozens," while hundreds or thousands of people in the country read light and satirical Arabic magazines (Khalidi, *Palestinian Identity*, 56).

30. Rashid Khalidi found the Khalidi and al-Aqsa libraries in Jerusalem to contain bound volumes of near-complete runs of *al-Hilal* and *al-Muqtataf*, along with several other important Nahda-era journals (Khalidi, *Palestinian Identity*, 54).

31. ʿAtwat, *Al-Ittijahat*, 65; Ayalon, *Reading*, 57–58.

32. Although Russian schools were closed during World War I, their influence continued through locally produced journals in Palestine. See Abu Hanna, *Rihlat al-bahth*.

33. Citing Ottoman archival records, Selçuk Akşin Somel argues that more government schools opened in Palestine during the late nineteenth century than almost anywhere else in the Ottoman Empire, with more than 150 rural primary schools in the Jerusalem district alone. See Somel, *Modernization*, 111. This is a significant upward revision of previous estimates that placed the number of government primary schools in Palestine at 95 by 1914. See Tibawi, *Arab Education*, 20.

34. Between 1882 and 1894 two government secondary schools were established, one in Acre and one in Jerusalem. Campos, *Ottoman Brothers*, 71.

35. Khalidi, "Society and Ideology," 125.

36. In the late nineteenth century these numbered upward of one hundred in the Jerusalem district alone. Büssow, *Hamidian Palestine*, 455.

37. Ami Ayalon estimates that by 1914, some 20–28 percent of Palestinian Arab children had received at least some schooling in state or private schools, though it is unclear how readily they were able to interact with, for example, periodical texts. See Ayalon, *Reading*, 22.

38. Campos, *Ottoman Brothers*; Abu-Manneh, "Arab-Ottomanists"; Kayali, *Arabs and Young Turks*.

39. R. Khalidi, *Origins of Arab*; Muslih, *Origins of Palestinian*.

40. In Palestine, thirty-two Arabic newspapers and journals were founded between 1908 and 1914. R. Khalidi, *Palestinian Identity*, 227n59. Dozens more emerged in Syria, Lebanon, and (to a lesser extent) Iraq during this period. See R. Khalidi, "Press," 22–42.

41. Ayalon, *Press*, 148–151.

42. *Al-Quds*, considered the most widely read newspaper at this time, had a circulation rate of roughly fifteen hundred copies. Other papers typically had runs of a few hundred copies. See R. Khalidi, *Palestinian Identity*, 56, 227n61.

43. R. Khalidi, *Palestinian Identity*, 56–57.

44. Ayalon, *Reading*, 117–124.

45. M. Seikaly, "Haifa," 17, 22.

46. R. Khalidi, *Palestinian Identity*, 88.

47. Charles, "Colonial Discourse," 135.

48. Lockman, *Comrades*, 26–29.

49. According to historian Justin McCarthy, in 1298 AH (1880–1881 CE) Palestine's population comprised 399,334 Muslim citizens, 14,731 Jewish citizens, and 42,089 Christian citizens, for a total of 456,929. By 1914 those numbers had risen to 594,820; 37,489; 81,012; and 722,143, respectively. See McCarthy, *Population*, 10.

50. Hillman, "Of Snake-Catchers," 7–9. See also R. Khalidi, *Palestinian Identity*, 101.

51. Cited in Hillman, "Of Snake-Catchers," 2, 21–22.

52. Shafir, *Land*.

53. When residents of the Galilean village of al-Fula learned in 1910 that their village land had been sold to the Jewish National Fund (JNF) and that they would be evicted, the villagers appealed the decision to their provincial governor, Damascene Arabist Shukri al-ʿAsali, who wrote several articles in widely circulating Arab newspapers detailing the plight of al-Fula's residents, denouncing Zionism as a threat to the entire region, and asserting the historical

connections of the local population to their land. Even after the peasants were expelled, news of the ongoing resistance by al-Fula's evicted residents continued to be reported in the local and regional press for another year. See R. Khalidi, *Palestinian Identity*, 107–110.

54. Ghandour, *Discourse*; Fischer-Tiné and Mann, *Colonialism*.

55. Roberts, "Rethinking," 90–93.

56. See full text of Balfour Declaration at http://avalon.law.yale.edu/20th_century/balfour.asp.

57. Muslih, *Origins*, 115–154.

58. Covenant of the League of Nations available at http://avalon.law.yale.edu/20th_century/leagcov.asp#art22. At the San Remo Conference in April 1920, the Mandates of Palestine (including Transjordan) and Iraq were awarded to Britain, and the Mandates of Lebanon and Syria to France. That July France sent troops to Damascus, defeated Faysal's forces at the Battle of Maysalun, and forcibly took full control over Syria.

59. While Transjordan was initially conceived of as part of the Palestine Mandate in 1920, the Transjordan memorandum, approved by the League of Nations on September 15, 1922, led to the effective separation of Transjordan from the regulations set forth in the Palestine Mandate.

60. "French Mandate." See also Meouchi and Sluglett, *British and French Mandates*.

61. Text of Palestine Mandate available at http://avalon.law.yale.edu/20th_century/palmanda.asp.

62. R. Khalidi, *Iron Cage*, 32–33.

63. British authorities increased the number of elementary schools in rural areas of Palestine to expand basic literacy rates, but they resisted Palestinian requests to establish more secondary schools in the area so they could maintain what they saw as a necessary urban-rural divide. Miller, *Government*, 90–101.

64. Darwazah, *Mudhakkirat*, 1:522, 542.

65. Naqqara, "Mudhakkirat," 18–28.

66. Ibid., 32.

67. Ibid.

68. Ibid., 39, 44.

69. Ibid., 46–52. See also Kalisman, "Bursary"; B. Anderson, *American University*.

70. Naqqara, "Mudhakkirat," 67.

71. See text of the Palestine Mandate at http://avalon.law.yale.edu/20th_century/palmanda.asp.

72. Abu El-Haj, *Facts*; Feiner, *Haskalah*; and Sand, *Invention*.

73. Demichelis, "From Nahda," 264–281.

74. Dawn, "Formation," 76–77.

75. For a list of history textbooks during the Mandate period, including their authors and scopes, see Harte, "Contesting," 183–187.

76. Prior to 1927 the Arab College was known as the Men's Teacher Training College, one of only two government teacher training colleges in Palestine (the other being the Women's Teacher Training College in Ramallah). Davis, "Commemorating Education," 200n20.

77. Tibawi, *Arab Education*, 199–200.

78. Davis, "Commemorating Education," 195; Demichelis, "From Nahda," 269.

79. Harte, "Contesting," 144.

80. Miller, *Government*, 95.

81. T. Khalidi, "Palestinian Historiography," 63–69.

82. Najjar, *Sahafat*, 89–96, 112–115. For more on Palestinian political factionalism during this period, see Lesch, *Arab Politics*, 96–99; and R. Khalidi, *Iron Cage*, 65–75.

83. Barakat, "*Thawrat*," 38–96; Najjar, *Sahafat*, 119–124.

84. During the week of rioting, 67 Jews in Hebron and 20 in Safed were among the 133 Jews killed. H. Cohen, *Year Zero*, xxi, 122–165, 188–206.

85. Of the 116 Palestinians killed during this period, at least 20 were bystanders killed by lynching, revenge attacks, or indiscriminate British fire, mainly in Jaffa and Jerusalem. Ibid., xxi, 1–121.

86. Barakat, "*Thawrat*," 158–207.

87. Najjar, *Sahafat*, 124–134.

88. Matthews, *Confronting*, 171–215.

89. Cited in Matthews, *Confronting*, 218. See also C. Anderson, "From Petition," 225–235.

90. Ayalon, *Press*, 98–100; Matthews, *Confronting*, 95–96, 163–164; Najjar, "Arabic Press," 98–100.

91. The Arab Revolt was a series of protests launched by Palestinian Arabs against British rule, beginning with a six-month general strike in April 1936 and evolving into militant acts against British and Jewish targets, largely in the northern countryside, until it was harshly suppressed by British forces in 1939.

92. Najjar, *Sahafat*, 207–208.

93. Ibid., 245.

94. The earliest available studies on literacy rates were conducted by the British in 1931, which put the literacy rate at 25 percent among Muslim males and 3 percent among Muslim females, 72 percent and 44 percent among Christian males and females, respectively, and 93 percent and 73 percent among Jewish males and females, respectively. Cited in R. Khalidi, *Palestinian Identity*, 225n33. See also Ayalon, *Reading*, 16–17. Much of the discrepancy between literacy rates among Muslim and Christian Palestinians can be accounted for by the urban-rural divide. Overall, a much higher percentage of the Christian and Jewish populations lived in or near towns and cities, where they had much greater access to educational opportunities.

95. Ayalon, *Reading*, 40, 103–108.

96. Cited in Najjar, *Sahafat*, 214.

97. After Muhammad ʿIzzat Darwazah, the first al-Najah director and a cofounder of the Istiqlal Party, was expelled from Palestine in 1937 for his nationalist activities, he closely followed press coverage of the revolt in the regional papers, noting in particular articles that expressed support for the Palestinians and that reported on solidarity actions in Egypt, Lebanon, Syria, and elsewhere. Darwazah, *Mudhakkirat*, 3:40, 67, 252, 515.

98. For statistics on the British blocking of newspapers, see Najjar, *Sahafat*, 434–436.

99. Swedenburg, *Memories*, 116. On regional fund-raising and support for the revolt, see Lesch, *Arab Politics*, 131–154.

100. Lahav, "Israel's Press Law," 265–313.

101. Matthews, *Confronting*, 170.

102. Yaghi, *Al-Adab*, 26–41; Yaghi, *Fi'l-adab*, 23–33.

103. Abu Hanna, *Thalathat shuʿaraʾ*.

104. Ibrahim Tuqan, "Tafaʾul wa-amal" [Optimism and hope], in Tuqan, *Diwan Ibrahim Tuqan*, 50–53.

105. *Al-Jamiʿah al-ʿ arabiyya*, June 4, 1928, cited in Najjar, *Sahafat*, 118.

106. Of the twenty-five Arabs and two Jews sentenced to death for their involvement in the 1929 riots, only these three men were not given a reprieve, leading many Palestinian Arabs to view their executions as being politically motivated. See Barakat, "*Thawrat*," 291–301; Barakat, "Criminals," 55–72; and H. Cohen, *Year Zero*, 243–245.

As a schoolboy Habibi was deeply affected by news of the hangings, especially since Hijazi was the brother of his Arabic teacher (Habibi, "Ana huwa," 186). But Habibi later concluded that the three hanged men should not be deemed national heroes since they had participated in the killing of Jews. See Swedenburg, *Memories*, 73.

107. Barakat, "*Thawrat*," 303.

108. Ibrahim Tuqan, "Al-thulathaʾ al-ahmar" (Red Tuesday), in Tuqan, *Diwan Ibrahim Tuqan*, 42–45; Barakat "*Thawrat*," 305; H. Cohen, *Year Zero*, 246.

109. Abu Hanna, *Thalathat shuʿaraʾ*, 68–69.

110. Ibid., 69–72; Najjar, *Sahafat*, 271–272.

111. "To the Arab Kings," reprinted with an introduction in *al-Ittihad*, December 1, 1948. See also Abu Hanna, *Thalathat shuʿaraʾ*, 118.

112. Khuri-Makdisi, *Eastern Mediterranean*.

113. *Al-Ittihad*, December 1, 1948.

114. Naqqara, "Mudhakkirat," 110.

115. Abu Hanna, *Zill al-ghayma*, 187.

116. Ibid., 249.

117. S. Seikaly, *Men of Capital*.

118. Abu Hanna, *Mahr al-buma*, 35.

119. By 1946 an estimated 67 percent of school-age children in towns and cities were in school, but only 20 percent of rural children (Abu-Ghazaleh, *Palestinian Arab*, 76). The overall literacy rate rose to 35 percent among Muslim males and 7 percent among Muslim females, and 85 percent and 65 percent among Christian males and females, respectively (Ayalon, *Reading*, 17).

120. Abu Hanna, who attended the Arab College from 1943 to 1946, was among these graduates. For a complete list, see Nijm, *Dar al-muʿallimin*.

121. The Khalidi Library was established in Jerusalem around 1900 as the country's first public library (Ayalon, *Reading*, 46–47). While a student at the Arab College, Abu Hanna frequented the Khalidi Library (along with the Arab College Library) to read the latest regional periodicals and books from the Arab world and Europe (Abu Hanna, *Mahr al-buma*, 39). The Jerusalem bookstore of Bulus and Wadiʿ Said (the uncle and father, respectively, of Palestinian American academic Edward Said) also carried books from Arab and European publishers. See Ayalon, *Reading*, 51–52.

122. The papers' official circulation numbers had risen from four thousand to six thousand daily copies each in the mid-1930s to seven thousand to ten thousand daily copies each by the mid-1940s. Ayalon, *Reading*, 64.

123. Ibid., 102.

124. Najjar, *Sahafat*, 286; Stanton, "This Is Jerusalem," 138.

125. Najjar, *Sahafat*, 292.

126. Habibi, "Ana huwa," 183.

127. Abu Hanna, *Mahr al-buma*, 36.

128. Stanton, "Part of Imperial."

129. Najjar, *Sahafat*, 286–287.

130. Khuri-Makdisi, *Eastern Mediterranean*.

131. Membership levels at each club varied, ranging from one hundred to more than three thousand, with some of the more active members of the Palestinian intelligentsia belonging to multiple clubs. Palestinian cultural historian Adnan Abu Ghazaleh, himself an attendee of these clubs in the late 1940s, observed that by then club culture was so strong that nearly every educated Palestinian Arab belonged to at least one. See Abu-Ghazaleh, *Arab Cultural*, 96–97.

132. Abu Hanna, *Mahr al-buma*, 39.

133. Naqqara, "Mudhakkirat," 110–111.

134. A few women gave speeches at these social clubs, including Nazarene schoolteacher and poet Najwa Qaʿwar (Kawar). See N. Farah, *A Continent*, 32; and Robson, "The Making," 41.

It appears that the lack of female speakers was due to an oversight and the relative paucity of women in intellectual circles rather than overt hostility to the idea of women speaking at such venues. Naqqara notes that Abu Salma had noticed the lack of gender diversity in the Arab Orthodox Club's speaking roster and made a point of inviting more women to speak, including Qaʿwar. See Naqqara, "Mudhakkirat," 111.

135. Abu Hanna, *Thalathat shuʿaraʾ*, 72–73; Najjar, *Sahafat*, 271–272.

136. Abu Hanna, *Mahr al-buma*, 42; Abu Hanna, *Thalathat shuʿaraʾ*, 75.

137. Khuri-Makdisi, *Eastern Mediterranean*.

138. Budeiri, *Palestine Communist Party*, 5–6.

139. Lockman, *Comrades and Enemies*, 116–145.

140. Muhammad Najati Sidqi (1905–1979) was born to a Muslim family in Jerusalem, where he also attended primary and secondary schools. After the fall of the Ottoman Empire, he accompanied his father to Syria and Cairo while the latter was engaged in Arab nationalist politics. After his return to Palestine a few years later, Sidqi began working in the post office, where he grew close to the communist movement and eventually became a party leader. See Sidqi, *Mudhakkirat*, 13.

141. Hen-Tov, *Communism*, 59.

142. Sidqi, *Mudhakkirat*, 29–30; Kirasirova, "The 'East'"; and Matusevich, "Harlem Globe-Trotters," 213–218.

143. Unlike the First and Second Internationals, the Third International did not posit the national and class identities of colonized peoples as being mutually exclusive. As Joseph Stalin himself declared to the KUTV class of 1925: "Proletarian culture does not abolish national culture, it gives it context. On the other hand, national culture does not abolish proletarian culture, it gives it form." Cited in Spring, *Pedagogies*, 43–44.

144. Sidqi, *Mudhakkirat*, 37–38. Wall newspapers, which were single sheets of newsprint plastered on a wall in a public setting, were quite common in the Soviet Union during this period. See Shneer, *Yiddish*, 94–95.

145. The close connection between literary and political content in such journals goes back to the late nineteenth century. See Kendall, "Between Politics."

146. Hanna Abu Hanna, "Introduction," in Sidqi, *Mudhakkirat*, 1–2. On the salience of these topics (especially Darwinism) during this period, see Elshakry, *Reading Darwin*.

147. On regional discourses, see Dawn, "Formation."

148. Sidqi quit the PCP in 1939 to protest the German-Soviet nonaggression pact, which Sidqi believed betrayed the communists' firm antifascist stance. In addition to his position at NEBS, Sidqi wrote essays for the Egyptian students' journal, *Iqraʾ* [Read] on the lives and works of Russian realist writers Pushkin and Chekhov, familiarizing a new generation of Arab readers with them. See Abu Hanna, "Introduction," in Siqdi, *Mudhakkirat*, 15.

149. Ismael and Ismael, *Communist Movement*; Ismael, *Rise and Fall*; Ismael, *Communist Movement*; Budeiri, *Palestine Communist Party*, 92.

150. Budeiri, *Palestine Communist Party*, 92.

151. Tubi, *Masiratuhu*; Karkabi, "Imil Tuma." Regarding the trend of Orthodox

Palestinian students attending Anglican missionary schools in Jerusalem, see Robson, *Colonialism*, 134.

152. Budeiri, *Palestine Communist Party*, 72.

153. R. Khalidi, *Iron Cage*, 108.

154. Bashkin, *Other Iraq*, 73–79; Batatu, *Old Social Classes*, 439–462.

155. ʿAbd al-Rahim Mahmud was one of the leftist-nationalists who fled to Iraq and returned under the general amnesty. See Abu Hanna, *Thalathat shuʿaraʾ*, 73.

156. Budeiri, *Palestine Communist Party*, 88.

157. Lockman, *Comrades and Enemies*, 303–307.

158. Budeiri, *Palestine Communist Party*, 108, 211n52.

159. *Al-Tariq* was launched in October 1941 by leftist intellectuals Raʿif Khuri and ʿUmar Fakhuri, among others. Its central platform was leftist opposition to fascism and Nazism, though it hosted intellectual debates on a wide range of issues. See Nordbruch, "Bread, Freedom." On the influence of *al-Tariq* on Habibi, see E. Habibi, "Ana huwa," 182.

160. Fuʾad Nassar (1914–1976) was an early PCP leader who joined the revolt in 1936, becoming a rebel commander in the Hebron district. He evaded capture by the British by fleeing to Iraq, where he grew close to members of the Iraqi Communist Party before his return to Palestine in 1943. Abu Hanna, *Mahr al-buma*, 43.

161. Budeiri, *Palestine Communist Party*, 105–108, 139–144, 212n60; Nahas, *Israeli Communist*, 11–26.

162. These included the League of Arab Students (later known as the League of Arab Intellectuals) and the Rays of Hope Society, both of which attracted members with leftist, pan-Arab orientations. See Budeiri, *Palestine Communist Party*, 129–132; Lockman, *Comrades and Enemies*, 284–285.

163. Lockman, *Comrades and Enemies*, 112; Dallasheh, "Nazarenes," 44.

164. Budeiri, *Palestine Communist Party*; Lockman, *Comrades and Enemies*; Dallasheh, "Nazarenes."

165. Abu Hanna, *Mahr al-buma*, 43.

166. Bulus Farah was born in 1910, went to work as a laborer in Haifa at age fifteen, joined the PCP in the early 1930s, and returned from his study at the KUTV in 1938. By the early 1940s he was a PCP Central Committee member, but his Arab nationalist views put him at odds with others in the PCP leadership, and he was expelled from the Central Committee in 1942. Subsequently he became a senior NLL figure. B. Farah, *Min al-ʿuthmaniya*; Lockman, *Comrades and Enemies*, 284–285; Budeiri, *Palestine Communist Party*, 103–108.

167. Naqqara, "Mudhakkirat," 113.

168. Ibid., 112–115.

169. Budeiri, *Palestine Communist Party*, 117, 148–149.

170. *Al-Ghad* was launched in May 1938 in Bethlehem by the nonpartisan League of Arab Students but was suspended by the government in 1941 in part because of its

criticism of the British educational policies. In 1941 the group changed its name to the League of Arab Intellectuals, whose members included Habibi, Tuma, and Tubi. Musallam, *Folded Pages*, 126–130.

171. Socialist realism, promoted by the Soviet Union beginning in the 1930s, built on the Russian social realism of the nineteenth century but called for clearer didactic and propagandistic messages that celebrated communist ideals to inspire the working classes to rise up against the bourgeoisie and usher in a new, revolutionary society.

172. Budeiri, *Palestine Communist Party*, 134–138; 222n185; Abu Hanna, *Mahr albuma*, 61.

173. Budeiri, *Palestine Communist Party*, 132–139.

174. UNGA, Third Session, *Resolution 181*.

175. McCarthy, *Population of Palestine*, 37; W. Khalidi, *From Haven*, 843.

176. Essaid, *Zionism*, 6.

177. Report of Sub Committee 2 to the UNGA regarding UNSCOP proposals, completed November 11, 1947, cited in W. Khalidi, *From Haven*, 645–702.

178. Statement of the Secretariat of the NLL, December 3, 1947, cited in Budeiri, *Palestine Communist Party*, 158.

179. *Al-Ittihad*, December 14, 1947, cited in Budeiri, *Palestine Communist Party*, 229n440.

180. Tuma maintained his opposition to partition and was subsequently expelled from the party. Budeiri, *Palestine Communist Party*, 158–159.

181. Particularly notorious was the Dayr Yasin massacre on April 8, 1948, in which Zionist forces killed 125 Palestinian villagers. News of the massacre spread quickly throughout Palestine, inducing many to flee ahead of advancing Zionist (and later Israeli) forces. See Pappé, *Ethnic Cleansing*, 90–91; Morris, *Refugee Problem Revisited*, 237–240.

182. R. Khalidi, *Iron Cage*, 131.

183. Of the mobilized armies of Transjordan, Iraq, Egypt, and Syria, only the latter two entered territory that had been designated in the Partition Plan as part of the Jewish state. Transjordan's King ʿAbdallah was primarily interested in securing eastern Palestine for himself (not in attacking Israel), while the Iraqi forces were quickly pushed back in the West Bank. A fifth military force, that of Lebanon, was mobilized along the country's southern border but did not cross over into Israel. See Rogan and Shlaim, *War for Palestine*; R. Khalidi, *Iron Cage*, 131–132; Morris, *Righteous Victims*, 218–233.

184. Pappé, *Ethnic Cleansing*; W. Khalidi, *From Haven*; Morris, *Refugee Problem Revisited*.

185. The last Armistice Agreement was between Israel and Syria on July 20, 1949. See UNSC, Third Session, *Israeli-Syrian*.

186. On the circumstances leading to their exile, see Naqqara, "Mudhakkirat," 161–171; Habibi, "Ana huwa," 190.

187. Habibi presents a fictionalized account of his return in his novel, *The Secret Life of Saeed the Pessoptimist* (10–11). He later explained that the path of return depicted in the novel was accurate, though the main character was satirized. See Habibi, "Ana huwa," 190.

188. In 1948 Cyprus Air was still running flights between the two cities (via Nicosia), mainly for employees of British and multinational companies. Naqqara, "Mudhakkirat," 179.

189. Even before Israel's (quite loose) definition of infiltration was legally formulated 1954, the authorities were eager to prevent displaced Palestinians from returning to their homes. See Korn, "From Refugees"; and Robinson, *Citizen Strangers*, 74–86.

190. Naqqara, "Mudhakkirat," 182–264.

191. Ibid., 163.

192. Morris, *Refugee Problem Revisited*, 389–390.

193. Segev, *1949*, 52–57; Pappé, *Ethnic Cleansing*, 207–208.

194. Naqqara was eventually able to petition for his family to return as part of a limited family reunification program, but he was unable to regain possession of his apartment in the German Colony or his belongings. Naqqara, "Mudhakkirat," 162.

195. Morris, *Refugee Problem Revisited*, 418–419; Pappé, *Ethnic Cleansing*, 152–153.

196. Morris, *Refugee Problem Revisited*, 420.

197. On the expulsions of the villages around Nazareth, see Khalidi and Elmusa, *All That Remains*, 344–354.

198. On internal refugees, see Masalha, *Catastrophe Remembered*; and Slyomovics, *Object of Memory*.

199. Abu Hanna, *Mahr al-Buma*, 136–137.

200. H. Cohen, *Good Arabs*, 4.

201. For a map of Palestinian towns and villages that remained, especially in the Galilee, see Robinson, *Citizen Strangers*, 32; and Landau, *Arabs in Israel*, 301.

CHAPTER 2

1. Kusa served on Haifa's Arab Higher Committee, the main decision-making political body of the Palestinian leadership. See W. Khalidi, "Fall of Haifa."

2. Ilyas Kusa, "The Israeli Government's Stance towards the Arab Minority," *al-Yawm*, August 22, 1950. See also Jon Kimche, "The Arabs in Israel," *Jerusalem Post*, July 10, 1950.

3. Michael Assaf, "A Reply," *al-Yawm*, August 22, 1950.

4. Robinson, *Citizen Strangers*, 70–72.

5. Kamen, "After the Catastrophe I," 460; Robinson, *Citizen Strangers*, 31, 39.

6. Kamen, "After the Catastrophe I," 460.

7. The number of Palestinians who returned to Israel without permission is unclear; one estimate placed the figure at about one thousand every month during 1949. See Robinson, *Citizen Strangers*, 78.

8. Kamen, "After the Catastrophe I," 462.

9. Robinson, *Citizen Strangers*, 74–82.

10. These laws originated with the earlier Emergency Law of 1936 and the Defense Law of 1939, both of which were aimed at suppressing Arab unrest against the Mandate authorities during the 1936–1939 Arab Revolt. Jiryis, *Arabs*, 2.

11. For a detailed list of these and other articles and provisions encompassed within the laws of the military government, see ibid., 7–26.

12. Kamen, "After the Catastrophe II," 99–101. As the Jewish population in these cities and towns increased, they were gradually transitioned to civilian rule. Acre was the last "mixed" city to be transitioned to civilian rule, in June 1951. See Robinson, *Citizen Strangers*, 39.

13. Ghanem, *Palestinian-Arab*; Abu-Baker and Rabinowitz, *Coffins*.

14. H. Cohen, *Good Arabs*.

15. Dallasheh, "Persevering," 13–14. See also Dallasheh, "Troubled Waters."

16. For example, in February 1950 the CPI-affiliated Arab Workers' Congress in Nazareth organized about four hundred unemployed workers to strike in front of the military governor's office, calling for "work and bread" and requesting a meeting with the military governor to lodge their complaints. Although the exact details were later disputed, there was general agreement that police used live ammunition to break up the protests, wounding two people. See *al-Ittihad*, February 26, 1950; *al-Yawm*, February 28, 1950; and Dallasheh, "Nazarenes," 62.

17. Beinin, *Red Flag*, 142. By 1957 the CPI would increasingly call into question the legitimacy of Israel's borders. See Robinson, *Citizen Strangers*, 183–184.

18. While they did not use the terms *qawmi* and *watani* explicitly in their political analyses, their views bore a striking resemblance to those of their Iraqi leftist counterparts who challenged their pan-Arab nationalist rivals with an appeal to Iraqi territorial patriotism. See Bashkin, *Other Iraq*, 127–156.

19. Official membership numbers were kept secret, but estimates generally place the number of members in the low hundreds. By the 1960s the party had between one thousand and three thousand members, of whom about four hundred were Palestinian. See Kaufman, *Arab*, 50.

20. I use the term "establishment" advisedly to refer to figures who worked in Israeli government institutions and/or the quasi-official Histadrut labor union. For more on the use of this term, see Snir, "Forget Baghdad!," 146n18.

21. In 1950–1951, following passage of a series of anti-Jewish laws and episodes of violence against them, about 120,000 Iraqi Jews (some 95 percent of the total population) were evacuated to Israel. See Weingrod, "Styles," 527.

22. Levy, *Poetic Trespass*; Eyal, *Disenchantment*.

23. B. Farah, *Min al-ʿuthmaniya*, 199–200.

24. On the concept of "textual encounters," see Gribetz, *Defining Neighbors*, 10–12.

25. The failure of Israel's first membership bid to the United Nations (due in part to international concerns over Israel's refusal to allow refugees to return) led state leaders to rule out expelling additional Palestinians, fearing further derailment. Even after Israel was admitted to the UN in May 1949, state officials worried that any attempt to rid the country of large numbers of additional Palestinians could lead to global interference in Israeli affairs. See Robinson, *Citizen Strangers*, 37–39.

26. Iraqis made up the vast majority of early Arab Jewish immigrants. In addition, between 1948 and 1951 about twenty-four thousand Moroccans and thirty-one thousand Libyans immigrated to Israel, and some forty-four thousand Yemeni Jews were airlifted as well. See Stillman, *Jews*, 155–157; and Weingrod, "Styles," 528. Additional waves of Jewish immigration from Arab countries would follow in subsequent years.

27. Peretz, "Early State," 92.

28. Avida, "Broadcasting," 325.

29. Immediately after the war, Israel took over the PBS's Jerusalem station, renaming it Kol Israel in Hebrew, Sawt Isra' il in Arabic, and the Voice of Israel in English. See Stanton *"This Is Jerusalem,"* 195–196.

30. See *Haqiqat al-Amr*, September 1, 1949, for a sample of the weekly Arabic radio schedule.

31. Kabha and Caspi, *Palestinian Arab*, 63–64.

32. Peled, "Other Side."

33. Kabha and Caspi, *Palestinian Arab*, 64.

34. El-Asmar, *To Be an Arab*, 75.

35. With an official figure of thirty-five hundred to five thousand copies per issue, *al-Yawm* had by far the largest circulation rate (Assaf, "Arabic Press," 23–24). In 1961 Assaf estimated *al-Ittihad*'s circulation to be one thousand to two thousand copies per issue (ibid.), though historian Joel Beinin places the rate in 1956 (the earliest available figures) at around eighteen hundred to twenty-eight hundred copies per issue. See Beinin, *Red Flag*, 242.

36. Rejwan, *Outsider*, 66.

37. This policy had been largely decided on by the end of 1948. See Morris, "Crystallization."

38. *Al-Yawm*, March 15, 1949. This was part of a larger international debate under way at this time about the fate of the Palestinian refugees. See Peretz, *Israel*, 19–32.

39. For a more recent iteration of this argument, see Karsh, *Palestine Betrayed*. Several aspects of Karsh's thesis and methodology have been criticized. See Smith, "Review"; and H. Cohen, "Review."

40. Jiryis, *Arabs*, 58–65; Abu Hussein and McKay, *Access Denied*, 70–71; and Forman and Kedar, "From Arab Land."

41. *Al-Yawm*, March 7, September 18 and 29, 1951; January 13 and 30, July 7 and 21, August 11, 1952; January 22, March 15, April 29, 1953; November 16, 1954. In Is-

raeli legal and political discourse these internal refugees became known as "present-absentees" whose land was still subject to confiscation. See Masalha, *Catastrophe Remembered*; H. Cohen, "Internal Refugees," 43.

42. *Al-Yawm*, July 21, 1952. See also Saba's letter dated January 13, 1952.

43. See Assaf, "Freedom of Thought," *al-Yawm*, March 25, 1955.

44. From 1949 through 1953 the "Free Platform" section ran nearly every Thursday. Beginning in 1954 it ran more sporadically. It is unclear if the number of letters diminished as other publications emerged, or if Assaf was uninterested in running overtly critical letters.

45. Murqus, *Aqwa*, 99. Nimr Murqus was born in Nazareth to a Catholic family in 1930 and attended Nazarene primary schools and the government's secondary school in Acre. After graduation in 1946, he worked as a primary school teacher in the village of Daliat al-Karmal outside Haifa. During the 1948 war he fled briefly to Beirut, sneaking back on foot in mid-August to the Shaghur region near Acre before it fell to Israeli forces. See ibid., 34–98.

46. Cited in Beinin, *Red Flag*, 53. See also Murqus, *Aqwa*, 99, for his recollection of the leaflet's contents.

47. Beinin, *Red Flag*, 53–54; Murqus, *Aqwa*, 99–100.

48. Murqus, *Aqwa*, 99. Murqus recalls spending up to a quarter of his teacher's salary on Arabic books and journals during his monthly trips to Haifa during the mid-1940s (82).

49. Siham Daoud, interview with author, Haifa, May 17, 2007. Tubi had been elected to the Knesset in 1949 on the CPI list and therefore had some diplomatic immunity. Listing him as the primary editor would have given Habibi (who was not a Knesset member until 1951) and the other editors some protection from the authorities.

50. According to a 1957 Central Committee report, the CPI devoted about 80 percent of its funds to publications. Although party leaders would not disclose funding levels or sources beyond membership dues and subscriptions, some sources point to revenue that was the by-product of trade relations between Israel and communist bloc countries (per an agreement with the Soviet Union) as an additional source. See Kaufman, *Arab National*, 144–145n9, 147n34.

51. See, for example, "It Is Not the Jewish People Who Oppress the Arab Minority; Rather, It Is the Government That Oppresses the Jewish People," *al-Ittihad*, April 5, 1955.

52. *Al-Ittihad*, April 18, May 15, July 17, September 18, 1949; February 3, May 26, June 30, 1951.

53. *Al-Ittihad*, August 4, 1951.

54. Lahav, "Israel's Press Law," 275–277.

55. Kamen, "After the Catastrophe II," 102–103; Kabha and Caspi, *Palestinian Arab*, 74–75.

56. Daoud, interview with author; Tubi, *Masiratuhu*, 132.

57. Tubi, *Masiratuhu*, 132. On the revival of this practice, see Robinson, *Citizen Strangers*, 144.

58. Tubi, *Masiratuhu*, 132.

59. Daoud, interview with author.

60. Daoud became a writer and political leader in the Communist Party in the 1970s, where she worked closely with Habibi. She now serves as the official director of Habibi's literary legacy.

61. In addition to *al-Ittihad,* the CPI published a Hebrew-language weekly, *Kol Ha-am*, along with publications in several other languages. They, too, were censored, especially *Kol Ha-am*.

62. Haddad wrote openly of requesting permission from Bechor Shitrit to launch his journal and the latter's willingness to help. See Michel Haddad, "*Al-Mujtamaʿ*s Word," *al-Mujtamaʿ* 1, no. 3 (November 1954): 2–3.

63. For more on Haddad, see Hoffman, *My Happiness*, 222–224.

64. Di-Capua, "Arab Existentialism," 1062.

65. Ibrahim, *Hanna Naqqara*, 279–283.

66. "In the People's Battle, Let Us Unsheathe the Weapon of Literature," *al-Jadid* 1, no. 1 (November 1953): 3.

67. See, for example, Taha Husayn's essays in *al-Yawm*, January 15 and 29, 1954; and ʿAbbas al-ʿAqqad, "Arab Writers in a New World," *al-Yawm*, April 29, 1955.

68. Michel Haddad, "Towards a Better Society," *al-Mujtamaʿ* 1, no. 1 (September 1954): 1.

69. ʿAdnan Abu al-Saʿud, "The Culture of Arab Citizens in Israeli Society," *al-Mujtamaʿ* 2, no. 1 (January 1955): 8.

70. In contrast to *al-Jadid*, few of *al-Mujtamaʿ*s Palestinian contributors produced a larger body of published work that could shed more light on their intellectual outlook.

71. On the relationship between the Education Ministry officials in charge of Arab education and the state security apparatus, see H. Cohen, *Good Arabs*, 139–149.

72. Ibid., 140–141.

73. Marʿi, *Arab Education*; Abu-Saad, "Present Absentees."

74. Murqus, *Aqwa*, 110–111.

75. Marʿi, *Arab Education*, 20–21. Marʿi puts the percentage of the Arab school-age population in elementary schools at 30 percent in 1946, a rate that increased to 59 percent in 1955. Sabri Jiryis, however, places the percentage of the Arab school-age population at 44.1 percent in 1955–1956. These are more modest figures than those of Marʿi and, according to Jiryis, far behind the percentage of Jewish school-age children enrolled in elementary school, which he placed at 91.4 percent in 1955–1956. See Jiryis, *Arabs*, 149.

76. *Al-Yawm*, September 22, 1953; "Talk of the Month: Fathers Worship the Road to School," *al-Jadid* 2, no. 10 (October 1955): 4–7.

77. See, for example, letters to *al-Yawm* on May 5 and August 25, 1953; August 21, 1954. See also "Talk of the Month: Fathers Worship." These discrepancies have continued into the twenty-first century. See Golan-Agnon, "Separate."

78. Ramzi Khuri, "Arab Education Is in Crisis and Arab Teachers Are in a Jungle," *al-Jadid* 1, no. 10 (August 1954): 45–49.

79. H. Cohen, *Army*.

80. Eyal, *Disenchantment*; H. Cohen, *Good Arabs*.

81. The Druze, who live primarily in modern-day Syria, Lebanon, and Israel/Palestine, follow an offshoot of Isma'ili Shi'i Islam. In 1952 the Israeli security services denied the petition of Druze teachers to be allowed a three-day vacation in observance of the Muslim Eid al-Fitr holiday marking the end of Ramadan, arguing the Druze were not Muslims. See H. Cohen, *Good Arabs*, 170.

82. See Eyal, *Disenchantment*, 260n36, n38, for more on these studies. See also Lustick, *Arabs*, especially 209–211.

83. For more on Niqula (1912–1974), see Greenstein, "Palestinian Revolutionary."

84. Jabra Niqula, "The Druze," *al-Jadid* 2, no. 12 (December 1955): 13.

85. Ibid., 14–15.

86. See also Suleiman, *Arabic Language*, for a discussion of the linguistic basis for defining Arab identity beginning in the late nineteenth century.

87. For more on CPI treatments of early Islamic figures and events, see Nassar, "Marginal."

88. Sonn, *Interpreting Islam*.

89. Emile Tuma and Ibrahim Khayyat, "The Revolt against 'Uthman," *al-Jadid* 3, no. 1 (December 1955): 7–10, 52–55; "The Zanj Revolt," *al-Jadid* 2, no. 1 (November 1954): 17–18, 55–58; and "The Qaramites," *al-Jadid* 2, no. 8 (June 1955): 8–12, 51–52.

90. On earlier iterations of this interpretation, see Dawn, "Formation."

91. Ibrahim Khayyat, "Jamal al-Din al-Afghani," *al-Jadid* 1, no. 10 (August 1954): 20–26. For similar Mandate-era discourses, see Dawn, "Formation," 73.

92. See *al-Yawm*, October 20, April 28, and March 3, 1950, respectively.

93. *Al-Yawm*, June 23, 1953.

94. Furani, *Silencing*, 261n21.

95. Hanna Abu Hanna, interview with author, Haifa, May 22, 2007. For more on the role of the Quakers in the initial aftermath of the 1948 war, see Gallagher, *Quakers*.

96. Sasson Somekh, interview with the author, Tel Aviv, May 30, 2007. For more on Iraqi Jewish engagement with Arab discourses prior to their arrival in Israel, see Bashkin, *New Babylonians*.

97. Snir, "Arabic Journalism"; Snir, "Till Spring Comes."

98. Shohat, "Sephardim"; Samir, *Forget Baghdad*; Bashkin, *Impossible Exodus*; Roby, *Mizrahi Era*.

99. Jayyusi, *Trends*, 574–575.

100. On the Wathba and the role of the communists in it, see Batatu, *Old Social Classes*, 545–565.

101. DeYoung, *Placing*, 189–190.

102. Jayyusi, *Trends*, 585–591.

103. Ibid., 577.

104. DeYoung, *Placing*, 191–196; Jayyusi, *Trends*, 565–566.

105. Jayyusi, *Trends*, 564–565.

106. Sasson Somekh, interview with author, Tel Aviv, May 30, 2007; Hoffman, *My Happiness*, 207–209.

107. Hanna Abu Hanna, "Oh Revolution of the Free," *al-Ittihad*, November 22, 1948. See also Hoffman, *My Happiness*, 257.

108. "To the Arab Kings," *al-Ittihad*, December 1, 1948. The poem was still published anonymously at this time.

109. Smethurst, *New Red*, 41–42.

110. Ibrahim Khayyat, "From Iraq: 'The Martyr's Wound' by the Great Iraqi Poet Muhammad Mahdi al-Jawahiri," *al-Ittihad*, March 31, 1950. See also Muhammad Mahdi al-Jawahiri, "In Memory of the Fahd, the Martyr," *al-Ittihad*, February 17, 1951; "To the Fighters," *al-Ittihad*, August 4, 1951; "Stalingrad," *al-Ittihad*, November 3, 1951; and "Precious Blood," *al-Ittihad*, November 6, 1953.

111. Ibrahim Khayyat, "Contemporary Iraqi Poetry," *al-Ittihad*, June 2, 1951.

112. Jayyusi, *Trends*, 577.

113. "Humanity Is the Goal and Subject of Literature: From the Speech of Emile Habibi at the al-Jadid Conference," *al-Jadid* 1, no. 3 (January 1954): 38, 41.

114. Zayyad, *al-Sira*, 1–3.

115. Tawfiq Zayyad, "Abadan and History," *al-Ittihad*, July 7, 1951. Iran's popular prime minister Muhammad Mosaddegh formally nationalized Iran's oil industry, but a diplomatic crisis ensued, and in 1953 the United States and United Kingdom orchestrated a coup that removed Mosaddegh and reversed the nationalization efforts.

116. Tawfiq Zayyad, "Egypt 1951," reprinted in Zayyad, *Diwan Tawfiq Zayyad*, 83–88.

117. Zayyad, *Al-sira*, 5.

118. Ibid., 5–8. This was not the only time Zayyad was imprisoned. Until the lifting of the military government in 1966, Zayyad was arrested and jailed numerous times, and even when he was out of jail, he was either placed under a sunset-to-sunrise curfew or prevented from traveling outside "Area T" (Nazareth, its environs, and Acre) without a travel permit (6).

119. Bashkin, *Other Iraq*; Snir, "Forget Baghdad!"

120. David Semah (b. 1933) was a contemporary of Somekh, who soon became a well-regarded leftist poet of Arabic verses. See Snir and Einbinder, "'We Were Like,'" 168.

121. Cited in Somekh, *Life after Baghdad*, 32–33.

122. Michael (b. 1926) had recently arrived from Iraq, where he had been active in the Iraqi Communist Party. Snir, "Forget Baghdad!"

123. "Conference of the Friends of Progressive Arabic Literature in Tel Aviv," *al-Jadid* 1, no. 8 (June 1954): 51.

124. It is unclear why this was the case, though the travel restrictions imposed by the military government (especially on known communists) made it likely that other Palestinians would not have had permission to go to Tel Aviv.

125. Somekh, *Life after Baghdad*, 33.

126. See, for example, *al-Jadid* 1, no. 10 (August 1954); 1, no. 11 (September 1954); and 2, no. 4 (February 1955).

127. Samir Marid (pseudonym for Sami Michael), "Hebrew Literature and the Zionist Ideology," *al-Jadid* 1, no. 11 (September 1954): 12–13.

128. Ibrahim Khayyat, "Brotherhood in Iraqi Poetry," *al-Jadid* 2, no. 10 (October 1955): 8–12.

129. On narratives of the Farhud, see Bashkin, *New Babylonians*, 100–140.

130. Shaʿshuʿ was born in 1926 in Baghdad and worked as a journalist and jurist before immigrating to Israel, where he wrote poems in fulsome praise of the state. See Snir, "Forget Baghdad!," 146–148.

131. See, for example, Shaʿshuʿ's poetic tribute to *al-Yawm* in honor of its fifth anniversary: "A Gift and a Greeting," *al-Yawm*, September 25, 1953.

132. "Between Two Poets," *al-Mujtamaʿ* 1, no. 1 (September 1954): 12.

133. "Arab-Jewish Brotherhood Festival," *al-Jadid* 2, no. 2 (February 1955): 17–18.

134. "Arab-Jewish Brotherhood Festival," *al-Jadid* 2, no. 4 (April 1955): 55–56.

135. "Brotherhood Festival," *al-Jadid* 2, no. 5 (May 1955): 52–54. Abu Hanna was the only Palestinian speaker listed at the Tel Aviv festival (perhaps due to government-imposed travel restrictions). Among the progressive Jewish Israeli literary figures who spoke at the festival were Nathan Alter, Alexander Ben, S. Yizhar, Moshe Smilansky, and Yehuda Borla.

136. "Friends of Progressive Arabic Literature in Tel Aviv," *al-Jadid* 2, no. 4 (April 1955): 52–54.

137. Shaʿshuʿ had insisted that the group be called the League of *Arabic* Poets rather than the League of *Arab* Poets to highlight their affiliation with the Arabic language rather than with Arab national identity. When the league split (largely along ethnonational lines) less than two years later, the predominantly Palestinian group renamed themselves the League of Arab Poets. See Qahwaji, *Al-ʿarab fi zill*, 282–83.

138. The Iraqi Jewish teachers were Zaki Binyamin and Shalom Katib; the Palestinian teachers were Yusuf Nakhleh, ʿIsa Lubani, Habib Qahwaji, George Najib Khalil, Mahmud ʿAbd al-Fattah, and Jamal Qaʿwar. Student members were Rashid Husayn, Shakib Jahshan, Ahmad Tawfiq, Habib Shweiri, Faraj Nur Salman; the journalist was ʿIsam al-ʿAbbasi. See "*Al-Mujtamaʿ* and the Poets' League," *al-Mujtamaʿ*, 2, no. 4 (April 1955): 4. See also Hoffman, *My Happiness*, 230–231.

139. S. Sasun (pen name of Sasson Somekh), "The Conference of Arab Poets in Nazareth," *al-Jadid* 2, no. 4 (April 1955): 56–57; Qahwaji, *Al-ʿarab fi zill*, 282–283; Snir, "Forget Baghdad!," 147.

140. See "First Arab Literary Festival in Haifa," *al-Yawm*, June 3, 1955.

141. Lubani was born in 1924 in Mujaydal near Nazareth and attended Nazareth schools before becoming a teacher in that town.

142. Al-ʿAbbasi was born 1924 to a Palestinian family in Beirut, attended high school at the Bishop Gobat School (a couple of years behind Tuma and Tubi), then worked as an editor for the popular newspaper *Filastin* while publishing poems in NLL publications. After 1948 he taught Arabic in high school in Haifa while he continued his creative pursuits.

143. "On the Arab Literary Festival in Haifa," *al-Jadid* 2, no. 6 (June 1955): 56.

144. See Yasir Suleiman's discussion of Kusa's 1955 petition objecting to the lack of Arabic on official Israeli bills of exchange in Suleiman, *Arabic, Self and Identity*, 24–29. On Kusa's disbarment, see Hadawi, *Israel and the Arab Minority*, 13.

145. See, for example, Jamal Qaʿwar, "Seven Years," *Al-Mujtamaʿ* 1, no. 4 (December 1954): 30.

146. Qahwaji, *Al-ʿarab fi zill*, 283.

CHAPTER 3

1. "On May 1st Police Turn Nazareth into a Battlefield," *al-Ittihad*, May 2, 1958.
2. For a photograph of this sign, see Robinson, *Citizen Strangers*, 187.
3. Schwarz, *Arabs in Israel*, 16.
4. Robinson, *Citizen Strangers*, 183–187.
5. Schwarz, *Arabs in Israel*, 22.
6. Amnon Kapeliuk, "The Nazareth Events and the Lesson We Can Learn from Them," *al-Mirsad*, May 15, 1958; "Red Heckling Provokes Nazareth May Day Clash," *New York Times*, May 2, 1958; Schwarz, *Arabs in Israel*, 15–34.
7. "On May 1"; Beinin, *Red Flag*, 202.
8. "Potential Fifth Column," *Jerusalem Post*, May 11, 1958; "Red Heckling."
9. Murqus, *Aqwa*, 223.
10. "The Arab Masses, with the Support of Forces for Freedom in Israel and the World, Oppose the Police Brutality That Exposes the Reality of Ben-Gurion's Regime," *al-Ittihad*, May 6, 1958.
11. ʿIsam al-ʿAbbasi, "The Arrogant One's Brutality Is a Sign of His Weakness," *al-Ittihad*, May 2, 1958.
12. Lubin, *Geographies of Liberation*.
13. The term "horizontal solidarity" was first coined by political leaders and Négritude cofounders Aimé Césaire and Leopold Senghor. See Césaire, "Culture and Colonization," 129–130; Senghor, "Some Thoughts," 189–190.

14. Robinson, *Citizen Strangers*, 165–166; Pappé, "Uneasy Coexistence," 625–626.

15. Ibn Khaldun (pen name of Emile Tuma), "The Refugees and National Security," *al-Ittihad*, April 3, 1956. See also Nassar, "Palestinian Citizens."

16. Robinson, *Citizen Strangers*, 167.

17. Ibrahim, *Shajarat al-maʿrifa*; Furani, *Silencing*, 58.

18. Massive protests held in Jordan in December 1955 had succeeded in preventing King Hussein from signing on to the British-sponsored military defense agreement known as the Baghdad Pact. Ibrahim, *Shajarat al-maʿrifa* 189; Jankowski, *Nasser's Egypt*, 78–81.

19. *Al-Jadid* printed it anyway, along with an account of its rejection. See Hanna Ibrahim, "Greetings to the Jordanian People," *al-Jadid* 3, no. 3 (March 1956): 27–29.

20. Hanna Ibrahim, interview with author, al-Biʿna, May 23, 2007; Furani, *Silencing*, 59–60.

21. Jankowski, *Nasser's Egypt*; Aburish, *Nasser*.

22. Prashad, *Darker Nations*. See also Nassar, "'My Struggle.'"

23. Murqus, *Aqwa*, 133.

24. Beinin, *Red Flag*, 87–93, 107–113.

25. Ibid., 164–172.

26. N. Farah, *Continent*, 68.

27. Abu Hanna, *Khamirat al-ramad*, 25.

28. Y. Sayigh, *Armed Struggle*, 61–62; Laron, "Logic Dictates."

29. Podeh, "Demonizing," 78; Kyle, *Suez*, 115–116; Love, *Suez*, 129–130.

30. For excerpts of Nasser's nationalization speech and the reaction to it, see Love, *Suez*, 345–350.

31. El-Asmar, *To Be an Arab*, 43.

32. Salim Jubran, interview with author, Nazareth, May 24, 2007.

33. Laron, "Logic Dictates," 80–84; Love, *Suez*, 433–476; Kyle, *Suez*, 135–152.

34. Kyle, *Suez*, 455–511; Love, *Suez*, 598–619.

35. R. Khalidi, "Consequences," 380–384.

36. Jankowski, *Nasser's Egypt*, 83–86.

37. Jubran, interview with author. While Jubran's contention that the Palestinians in Israel loved Nasser "more than anyone else" may be a bit overstated, the widespread support Nasser received in these quarters was clear.

38. The most comprehensive accounts of the massacre can be found in E. Habibi, *Kafr Qasim*; and Robinson, "Local Struggle."

39. "From Kafr Qasim to Port Said," *al-Ittihad*, November 23, 1956. For similar arguments, see "The Policy of the Kafr Qasim Massacre Was Shattered at the Gates of Port Said," *al-Ittihad*, December 11, 1956; and Tawfiq Tubi, "After the Massacre," *al-Ittihad*, December 31, 1956.

40. On April 9, 1948, members of the Zionist military groups Irgun (IZL) and Stern

Gang (LEHI)—in coordination with the Haganah's commander in Jerusalem—attacked and killed about 120 Arab residents in the Palestinian village of Dayr Yasin (Deir Yassin), west of Jerusalem. See W. Khalidi, *Dayr Yasin*; Khalidi and Elmusa, *All That Remains*, 289–292; Morris, *Righteous Victims*, 207–209; Morris, *Refugee Problem Revisited*, 237–240; Pappé, *Ethnic Cleansing*, 90–91. News of this and other massacres induced thousands of Palestinians to flee their villages. For many Palestinians, the Dayr Yasin massacre came to symbolize Zionist brutality but also served a warning not to allow subsequent massacres to terrorize Palestinians into leaving their homes.

41. Tubi, "After the Massacre." Tubi was referring here to the October 1953 raid on the West Bank village of Qibya that killed sixty-nine villagers (mainly women and children); the April 1954 attack on the West Bank village of Nahalayn that killed nine villagers (including one woman); the February 1955 raid on Gaza that killed thirty-six Egyptian soldiers, a seven-year-old Palestinian boy, and an adult; and the August–September 1955 raid on Khan Yunis in the southern Gaza Strip that killed seventy-two Egyptians and Palestinians. For more on each of these raids, see Morris, *Israel's Border Wars*, 244–247, 300–304, 324–334, 350–351, respectively.

42. For more on the poetry of the Kafr Qasim massacre, see Nassar, "Affirmation," chap. 3.

43. N. Farah, *A Continent*, 48–49.

44. Qahwaji, *Al-ʿArab fi zill*, 283.

45. ʿIsa Lubani, "Sad Nights and a Smiling Dawn," *al-Jadid* 4, no. 3 (March 1957): 26–29.

46. For more on Palestinian discourses around the refugee issue, see Nassar, "Palestinian Citizens."

47. Nimr Murqus, "A Harvest of Poems, or, Portraits of a People," *al-Jadid* 4, no. 7 (July 1957): 15–20.

48. Hanna Abu Hanna, "The Land," cited in Murqus, "A Harvest," 17. The Abu al-Hayjas were among the thousands of internally displaced Palestinians whose land was confiscated by the Israeli state. This case was particularly ironic because the Abu al-Hayjas were relegated to an unrecognized village overlooking their former lands while their village became an artists' colony for Jewish Israelis. See Slyomovics, *Object of Memory*.

49. Murqus, "A Harvest," 16. See also Sabbagh, "Arabic Poetry," 80–82.

50. Boullata and Ghossein, *World of Rashid*, 25–30. For an English translation of his poem, see Rashid Hussein, "A Song of Asia," *New Outlook* 1, no. 11 (June 1958): 35–36.

51. Rashid Husayn, "From the Triangle to the Galilee," in Murqus, "A Harvest," 17. See also Qahwaji, *Al-ʿArab fi zill*, 284–285.

52. Rashid Husayn, "A Letter from My Cousin in Jordan," in Murqus, "A Harvest," 17.

53. Cited in Furani, *Silencing*, 107.

54. Qahwaji, *al-ʿArab fi zill*, 285.

55. Ibid., 286; N. Farah, *A Continent*, 72.

56. Michael Assaf, "Journal," *al-Yawm*, September 5, 1957. See also "Talk of the Month: The League of Arab Writers and Intellectuals," *al-Jadid* 4, no. 8–9 (August–September 1957): 4–5.

57. He recalls this incident in Darwish, "Lahum," 4.

58. Ibid., 5.

59. S. Qasim, *Innaha mujarrad*, 40, 67–68.

60. Ibid., 69.

61. Ibid., 72–73.

62. Darwish, "Lahum," 5.

63. Ibid.

64. For more on how schools were especially targeted to disseminate official Israeli narratives during Independence Day celebrations, see Robinson, *Citizen Strangers*, 143–148.

65. Mahmoud Darwish, "Hayati," 54.

66. Ibid., 62–63.

67. Qahwaji contends that in the 1956–1957 school year only 47.6 percent children between the ages of five and fourteen were attending school. In addition, Palestinian students had a much lower high school matriculation rate than Jewish students, and that year Palestinians accounted for only 0.6 percent of university students in Israel. See Qahwaji, *al-ʿArab fi zill*, 210–212; Al-Haj, *Education*, 103–108, 193.

68. Qahwaji, *al-ʿArab fi zill*, 283. Qahwaji was born in 1931 in the northern Galilean village of Fassuta (near Acre), graduated from a nationalist high school in nearby Bassa, and went on to study at the National College in Aley, Lebanon, before returning to Palestine to become a teacher.

69. Ibid., 287.

70. "The League of Arab Writers and Intellectuals," 46.

71. ʿAdnan Abu Saʿud, "Arab Culture and Arab Literature," *al-Jadid* 4, no. 8–9 (September–October 1957): 52–56.

72. Robinson, *Citizen Strangers*, 269n138.

73. In fall 1956 Syrian intelligence discovered plans by the CIA to stage a coup to overthrow the Baʿth and install a more Western-friendly regime. See Seale, *Struggle for Syria*, 270–282.

74. *Al-Ittihad*, February 11, 1958, cited in Beinin, *Red Flag*, 201.

75. Murqus, *Aqwa*, 185–186.

76. Stora, *Algeria*, 33–68; Malley, *Call from Algeria*; Shepard, *Invention of Decolonization*.

77. For a sample of *al-Ittihad* headlines regarding Algeria between 1955 and 1957, see Robinson, *Citizen Strangers*, 238n134.

78. See *al-Ittihad*, February 26, 1958, for a report on the execution of Algerians in French jails.

79. Laskier, "Israel and Algeria," 2–3.
80. *Al-Ittihad*, February 11, 1959; Robinson, *Citizen Strangers*, 184.
81. Abu Hanna, *Khamirat al-ramad*, 69; Beinin, *Red Flag*, 199.
82. *Al-Ittihad*, March 4, 1958.
83. Ibid. See also Hanna Abu Hanna, "Letter to Jamila, *al-Ittihad*, February 11, 1958; Rashid Husayn, "To Jamila," in Husayn, *Diwan Rashid Husayn*, 496–499.
84. Robinson, *Citizen Strangers*, 182–187.
85. Eliahu Agassi, "Towards Positivity," in *Fi mahrajan al-adab*, 1–2.
86. ʿAbdallah Muhammad Yunis, "Peace, Delightful Peace, and the Call to It," in *Fi mahrajan al-adab*, 104. First place went to Sami Mizighit, principal of the Kafr Yasif high school, for his poem "To Israel: Thoughts of an Arab Citizen on the Occasion of Its Tenth Anniversary," in ibid., 101–103.
87. Mahmoud Darwish, "Sister," *al-Jadid* 5, no. 5 (May 1958): 23.
88. Muhammad Khass, "A Nationalist Conference in the Language of Poetry," *al-Jadid* 5, no. 7 (July 1958): 52.
89. Mahmoud Darwish, "The Martyr," *al-Jadid* 5, no. 7 (July 1958): 19–22.
90. Cited in Hoffman, *My Happiness*, 263.
91. For the circumstances that led to the revolution and for details of the coup itself, see Batatu, *Old Social Classes*, 765–804.
92. Tripp, "Iraq and the 1948 War," 138; Murqus, *Aqwa*, 187.
93. Ibrahim, *Shajarat al-maʿrifa*, 204.
94. Kerr, *Arab Cold War*.
95. According to the declaration distributed after the founding meeting on July 6, the Popular Front's demands included (1) allowing villagers to return to their villages; (2) ending land confiscation and returning confiscated land to its owners; (3) canceling military government and "lifting of national repression"; (4) ending racial discrimination (*al-tamyiz al-ʿunsuri*) among citizens; (5) using Arabic for official business; and (6) allowing the 1948 refugees to return. *Al-Ittihad*, July 8 and September 26, 1958; Beinin, *Red Flag*, 202–203.
96. Most of the paper's initial attention had been on attracting Arab Jewish readers, with exposés on the poor conditions of transit camps and lack of employment opportunities. See *al-Mirsad*, April 4, May 29, June 12, and 26, August 7, 1952. See also Magal, "Al-Mirsad."
97. El-Asmar, *To Be an Arab*, 65–66; Beinin, "Knowing Your Enemy," 114.
98. See Batatu, *Old Social Classes*, 808–820, 849–862.
99. "*Al-Ittihad*'s Word: Diligence in Opposing Imperialism Is the Way to Arab Unity," *al-Ittihad*, February 3, 1959.
100. Batatu, *Old Social Classes*, 870–889.
101. *Al-Ittihad*, March 10, 1959.

102. Abu Hanna, *Khamirat al-ramad*, 46; Ibrahim, *Shajarat al-maʿrifa*, 205; Murqus, *Aqwa*, 188–189.

103. Rashid Husayn, "Reports and Views," *al-Fajr* 1, no. 6 (March 1959): 16.

104. Hanna Abu Hanna, "Debate, Not Enmity," *al-Jadid* 6, no. 4 (April 1959): 15–18.

105. These discursive contestations bore a striking resemblance to those happening simultaneously in Iraq, further highlighting how local debates reflected regional dynamics. See Bashkin, "Hybrid Nationalisms."

106. See Rashid Husayn, "To Hanna Abu Hanna," *al-Fajr* 1, no. 8 (May 1959): 19–23; Hanna Abu Hanna, "A Final Word," *al-Jadid* 6, no. 6–7 (June–July 1959): 37–42; and Rashid Husayn, "The Middle East between Nasser and Kassem: The Case against Kassem," *New Outlook* 2, no. 9 (June 1959): 37–40.

107. Abu Hanna, *Khamirat al-ramad*, 44–45.

108. After his 1954 imprisonment, Zayyad was jailed several more times, including in 1958. See Zayyad, *al-Sira*, 8–9.

109. Tawfiq Zayyad, "One of the 'Agents,'" *al-Ittihad*, March 31, 1959.

110. Murqus, *Aqwa*, 189.

111. Ibrahim, *Shajarat al-maʿrifa*, 205.

112. Ibid., 206.

113. Mapai was the prime beneficiary of the voting trends in that election (gaining seven seats), while Mapam held steady with nine seats. For more on the 1959 election results and their implications for the three parties, see Beinin, *Red Flag*, 218–221; Landau, *Arabs in Israel*, 122–129, and Nahas, *Israeli Communist Party*, 40–41.

114. Emile Habibi, "Regarding the Results of the Fourth Knesset Elections," *al-Ittihad*, November 6, 1959.

115. Y. Sayigh, *Armed Struggle*, 71–75.

116. Zelkovitz, *Students and Resistance*, 16–20.

117. Y. Sayigh, *Armed Struggle*, 83–87.

118. Shemesh, *Palestinian Entity*, 3–5.

119. Zelkovitz, *Students and Resistance*, 18.

120. Y. Sayigh, *Armed Struggle*, 68; Shemesh, *Palestinian Entity*, 8.

121. Qahwaji, *Al-qissa al-kamila*, 18–19.

122. For discussions of the formation of the Ard Group and its relationship to the Popular Front and the CPI, see El-Asmar, *To Be an Arab*, 67–78; Jiryis, *Arabs in Israel*, 130; Landau, *Arabs in Israel*, 92–107; and Zureik, *Palestinians in Israel*, 172–175.

123. Qahwaji, *Al-qissa al-kamila*, 21–22.

124. Ibid.

125. Ibid.

126. Ibid., 23–25.

127. On circulation statistics, see Nassar, "Palestinian Citizens," 48.

128. Landau, *Arabs in Israel*, 103.

129. To be sure, some articles did simply toe the official UAR line. See, for example, "An Important Speech by President Gamal Abdel Nasser Inaugurating the Project to Build the High Dam," *Sirr al-ard* [Secret of the land], November 30, 1959; "Numbers Talk: The Gross National Product Doubles over Ten Years in the [United] Arab Republic," *Abna' al-ard* [Sons of the land], November 23, 1959; and "Agricultural Socialism," *Kifah al-ard* [Struggle of the land], December 7, 1959.

130. "Science Day in the United Arab Republic and Our Science Reality in Israel," *Abna' al-ard*, November 23, 1959. See also "Education, and Education!" *Sarkhat al-ard* [Scream of the land], December 21, 1959.

131. Baransi, *Al-nidal al-samit*, 22–23.

132. Salih Baransi, "Arab Unity: The Only Way to Solve the Palestinian Issue," *Kalimat al-ard* [Word of the land], October 31, 1959.

133. "The Believer Is Not Bitten by the Animal Twice," *Kalimat al-ard*, October 31, 1959.

134. Hanna Abu Hanna, interview with author.

135. "'We Have No Orders' and 'Abd al-Karim Qasim," *Wahdat al-ard* [Unity of the land], January 16, 1960. The title is a reference to the distinctive Iraqi phrase *maku awamir* (we have no orders), which was what Iraqi soldiers deployed to Palestine in summer 1948 allegedly said when asked why they were not protecting villages from Israeli advances. The phrase soon acquired notoriety in Palestinians' bitter recollections of Arab betrayal. See Tripp, "Iraq and the 1948 War," 138; and Murqus, *Aqwa*, 187.

136. Mahmud Saruji, "An Open Letter to the Interior Minister," *Sirr al-ard*, November 30, 1959.

137. "The Arab Victor [Nasser] on the Day of Victory Speaks at the Courageous Port Sa'id on the Third Anniversary of Victory Day, the Day the Aggressors Withdrew," *Shadha al-ard* [Fragrance of the land], December 28, 1959.

138. The minister argued that Salih Baransi, who was listed as the paper's editor in chief on the application, did not hold a high school matriculation certificate (*bagrut*), a requirement under Israeli press law. Qahwaji, *Al-qissa al-kamila*, 30–31.

139. Mahmud Saruji, "An Open Letter: To the Esteemed Interior Minister," *Nada al-ard* [Call of the land], January 25, 1960, 5; Qahwaji, *Al-qissa al-kamila*, 30–31.

140. Fouzi El-Asmar, interview with author, Bethesda, Maryland, September 7, 2012. El-Asmar wrote for the paper and helped with its publication.

141. Qahwaji, *Al-qissa al-kamila*, 27.

142. Badawi, "Commitment in Contemporary Arabic Literature," 23–24.

143. Fouzi El-Asmar, interview with author.

144. I thank Joel Beinin for bringing this point to my attention. On Israeli acquisitions of pre-1948 Palestinian material, see Brunner, *Great Book Robbery*.

145. Rashid Husayn, "A Guest in Jail," *al-Mirsad*, March 3, 1960, reprinted in Husayn, *Kalam mawzun*, 72–81. Husayn was released the next day without charge.

146. Muhammad Miʿari, interview with author, Haifa, May 21, 2007.

147. These included three collections by Jawahiri and two by Sayyab. Salim Jubran, interview with author.

148. Ibid.

149. Hanna Abu Hanna, interview with author,

150. Langston Hughes, "Negro" and "Rivers," *al-Jadid* 8, no. 9 (September 1961): 52.

151. Emile Tuma, "The Intellectual Struggle in Literature, Cinema and Song," *al-Jadid* 6, no. 1 (January 1959): 7–13. See also "Tashkent: The Bandung of Literature," *al-Ittihad*, October 21, 1958.

152. Nazik al-Malaʾika, "Greetings to the Republic," *al-Fajr* 2, no. 6 (June 1959): 7, and "We and Jamila," *al-Fajr* 3, no. 9 (September 1960): 21; ʿAbd al-Wahhab al-Bayati, "Broken Pitchers," *al-Fajr* 3, no. 1 (January 1960): 21.

153. Hoffman, *My Happiness*, 287.

154. Rejwan, *Outsider*, 62–64.

155. "Histadrut In as Part Owner of 'Al Yaum,'" *Ner* 12, no. 1–2 (November–December 1960): 29.

156. Classical works included Andalusian love poetry and stories of the pre-Islamic Arab hero ʿAntar. Featured modern writers included Taha Husayn and Saʿid ʿAql. Hoffman, *My Happiness*, 287–288; Jubran, interview with author.

157. Jubran, interview with author.

158. "Literature between Freedom and Commitment," *al-Hadaf* 1, no. 12 (September 1961): 11–15.

159. Lorch, "An Israeli View," 29; Segre, "Philosophy and Practice;" Levey, "Israel's Strategy."

160. Nassar, "My Struggle."

161. Ibid., 83–84.

162. Byrne, *Mecca of Revolution*, 70–95.

163. Rashid Husayn, "Here You Are, the Other Jamila," *al-Fajr* 2, no. 10 (September 1960): 10–12.

164. Fouzi Yusuf El-Asmar, "Algeria in Arab-Israeli Poetry," *al-Fajr* 2, no. 10 (September 1960): 23–25.

165. For reports on such gatherings, including accounts of CPI leaders meeting with Arab communist delegations, see "The Communist Centennial Conference," *al-Jadid* 3, no. 2 (February 1956); Emile Tuma, "The Twenty-Fifth Conference of Orientalists," *al-Ittihad*, September 2, 1960.

166. Ismael, *Communist Movement in the Arab World*. A partial exception was the Iraqi Communist Party, though it, too, was soon marginalized by Qasim.

167. See Rashid Hussein, "I Am an Israeli Arab," *New Outlook* 5, no. 12 (December 1961): 36.

168. Ibid., 39.

169. Fayez Sayegh (Fayiz Sayigh) (1922–1980) was born in Syria, then moved to Tiberias, Palestine, with his family as a child. He earned a BA and MA from the American University of Beirut in 1941 and 1945, respectively, then earned a PhD in philosophy from Georgetown University in 1949. In addition to holding several diplomatic and academic posts, he founded and served as first director-general of the Palestine Research Center in 1965.

170. Jamiʿat al-duwal al-ʿarabiyya, idarat Filastin, *Idtihad al-ʿarab fi israʾil*. See also the English translation: League of Arab States: Palestine Department, "Report on Persecution of the Arabs in Israel." While these reports do not list an author, my assertion that Fayez Sayegh wrote them stems from the numerous similarities to a report in which he is listed as author. See F. Sayegh, *Mihnat al-ʿarab*.

171. Sami Hadawi (1904–2004) was born in Jerusalem and served as a land value assessor in Palestine during British Mandate rule. After 1948 he worked as a land value assessor for the Jordanian government, subsequently with the United Nations Palestine Conciliation Commission, where he documented the value of Palestinian land losses.

172. Hadawi, *Israel and the Arab*.

173. *Violations of Human Rights*; on distribution at the UN by Arab delegates, see Robinson, *Citizen Strangers*, 191.

174. Ahmad Sidqi al-Dajani (1936–2003) was born in Jaffa, Palestine, and fled with his family to Latakia, Syria, in 1948. He was a schoolteacher while working toward a bachelor's degree in history from the University of Damascus, which he completed in 1959. He moved to Libya in 1960, then to East Jerusalem in 1964, where he was one of the founding members of the Palestine Liberation Organization. A few years later he moved to Cairo, where he earned a PhD in history in 1969. There he remained active in Palestinian politics and wrote numerous academic and policy studies.

175. For more on this episode, see Nassar, "Palestinian Citizens."

176. Dajani, *Min al-muqawama*, 164–167. The two sources Dajani cited were Schwarz, *Arabs in Israel*, and Peretz, *Israel and the Palestine Arabs*.

177. El-Asmar, *To Be an Arab*, 82–85; El-Asmar, interview with the author.

CHAPTER 4

1. Mahmoud Darwish, "Ten Years," *al-Jadid* 9, no. 12 (December 1962): 4.

2. Beinin, *Red Flag*, 217. The phrase "an imperialist base" was a common Arab nationalist formulation for describing Israel, though it was studiously avoided by CPI leaders because it was seen as denying Israel's legitimacy.

3. Notable studies include Q. Husyan, *Al-mawt waʾl-hayat*; Yaghi, *Fiʾl-adab al-filastini al-hadith*; Yaghi, *Shiʿr al-ard al-muhtalla*.

4. Smooha, *Orientation and Politicization*; Rouhana, *Palestinian Citizens*.
5. Yaqub, *Containing Arab Nationalism*.
6. Barnhisel, *Cold War Modernists*.
7. Laugesen, "Books for the World," 136–139.
8. Badawi, "Commitment," 39; Di-Capua, "Arab Existentialism," 1083–1084.
9. Badawi, "Commitment," 36; Klemm, "Different Notions," 61–62n51.
10. Di-Capua, "Homeward Bound."
11. Di-Capua, "Arab Existentialism," 1083–1085.
12. Kadhim, *Poetics of Anti-colonialism*.
13. Gohar, "Integration of Western Modernism."
14. See, for example, the debate on socialist realism in literature between Husayn Muruwwah and his critics in *al-Jadid* 9, no. 4–5 (April–May 1963): 29–31.
15. According to my tally, from 1960 to 1967, Darwish published forty-eight poems in *al-Ittihad* and *al-Jadid*, sixteen of which subsequently appeared in his poetry collections.
16. Nabulsi, *Majnun al-turab*; Naqqash, *Mahmoud Darwish*; Dik, *Mahmoud Darwish*; Hasan, *Qadiyat al-ard*; Altoma, *Abʿad al-tahhaddi*.
17. Darwish's essays in *al-Jadid* were collected in *Shayʾ ʿan al-watan*.
18. Throughout 1958 *al-Ittihad* and *al-Jadid* ran numerous poems in celebration of the Arab revolutions that were submitted anonymously or pseudonymously. The style and aesthetics of those works indicate they were composed by novice poets. See Nassar, "Affirmation and Resistance," chap. 3.
19. Mahmoud Darwish, "Incidentally," *al-Ittihad*, July 27, 1962.
20. Mahmoud Darwish, "A New Plot against Arab Culture," *al-Ittihad*, February 9, 1962.
21. Mahmoud Darwish, "Writers Are Calling Their People," *al-Ittihad*, August 4, 1961.
22. Mahmoud Darwish, "Thoughts in Jail," *al-Ittihad*, September 1, 1961. See also "The Release of Mahmoud Darwish," *al-Ittihad*, August 25, 1961.
23. Mahmoud Darwish, "Once Again: The Histadrut and Arabic Literature," *al-Ittihad*, February 2, 1962.
24. Mahmoud Darwish, "Is There Really Lethargy?" *al-Ittihad*, October 19, 1962.
25. Mahmoud Darwish, "Three Words on a Single Topic," *al-Ittihad*, August 3, 1962.
26. Mahmoud Darwish, "ʿAbd al-Wahhab's Latest Book: Words Don't Die," *al-Ittihad*, December 15, 1961; "Africa in a Poetry Collection," June 1, 1962; "Three Poets from Angola," *al-Ittihad*, September 22, 1961.
27. Mahmoud Darwish, "Incidentally," *al-Ittihad*, July 27, 1962.
28. Mahmoud Darwish, "The Ice Will Not Melt This Way," *al-Ittihad*, December 28, 1962.
29. See Somekh, "Reconciling."

30. In 1960 the Israel Lands Authority issued a law placing state-owned lands and lands held by the Jewish National Fund under its jurisdiction. Beinin, *Red Flag*, 224. See also Forman, "Liberal Reform."

31. Falah, "Israeli 'Judaization' Policy."

32. This area comprised several villages, including Dayr al-Asad, Majd al-Kurum, Nahaf, and al-Biʿna. See Abu Hussein and McKay, *Access Denied*, 87.

33. "Move Carmiel South by Two Kilometers and Bring Jewish-Arab Friendship Closer by Hundreds of Kilometers," *al-Ittihad*, August 13, 1963; "Al-Ittihad's Word: The Peasants of Shaghur Have a Right to Harvest Their Lands," *al-Ittihad*, November 19, 1963.

34. Mahmoud Darwish, "Our Beloved Land," *al-Ittihad*, December 14, 1962.

35. The line "They like communism" was in the original poem but taken out of the 1973 reprint of Darwish's anthology as well as subsequent editions.

36. Mahmoud Darwish, "Identity Card," *al-Jadid* 10, no. 7 (July 1963): 21; collected in *Awraq al-zaytun*, reprinted in *Diwan Mahmoud Darwish*, 1:71–74. For more on this poem, see ʿAtwat, *Al-Ittijahat al-wataniyya*, 225–227; Nabulsi, *Majnun al-turab*, 157–167. For translations, see Aruri and Ghareeb, *Enemy of the Sun*, 2–4.

37. On Darwish learning to read—and becoming acquainted with the classics of Arabic literature—from his grandfather, see Darwish, *Journal*, 19.

38. Darwish, "Hayati," 63.

39. *Al-Ittihad*, November 3, 1964, cited in Robinson, "Local Struggle," 409.

40. See Samih al-Qasim, "An Elegy for Badr Shakir al-Sayyab," *al-Ittihad*, January 22, 1965.

41. Qasim would join the communist Rakah party in 1967, after the June War.

42. See "In Two Words," *al-Ittihad*, December 25, 1964.

43. Samih al-Qasim, "Poets, Not Diplomats," *al-Ittihad*, December 31, 1964.

44. Robinson, *Citizen Strangers*, 190–192.

45. See S. Qasim, *Mawakib al-shams*; and Darwish, *ʿAsafir bila ajniha*. Both collections consisted primarily of solidarity poetry and were not included by the poets in their subsequent collective anthologies.

46. Kassis, "Samih al-Qasim," 45

47. Samih al-Qasim, "Hayati," 74.

48. Qasim, *Aghani al-durub*; Darwish, *Awraq al-zaytun*.

49. Qasim, "Hayati," 71.

50. Ibid.

51. An exception was made for one visit to their families per year.

52. Kassis, "Samih al-Qasim," 45; Darwish, *Journal*, 69–73.

53. Kassis, "Samih al-Qasim," 45–46.

54. Mahmoud Darwish, "Thoughts from the First Prison: The Dowry for Words," *al-Jadid* 12, no. 8–9 (August–September 1965): 6–8.

55. Darwish, *Diwan Mahmoud Darwish*, 1:82.

56. Ibid., 1:93–97, 102–103, 115–116, 138–140.

57. Hout, *My Life*, 43–46.

58. Quoted in ibid., 52–53.

59. Cited in Y. Sayigh, *Armed Struggle*, 98.

60. Ibid., 100–104; Zelkovitz, *Students and Resistance*, 33–34.

61. "Opening Conference in Jerusalem of the Palestinian Entity Conference," *al-Ittihad*, May 29, 1964; "Ittihad's Word," *al-Ittihad*, June 2, 1964. See also "Sovereign 'Palestine' Declared," *Jerusalem Post*, June 3, 1964.

62. "New Paths to Peace between Israel and the Arabs," *New Outlook* 7, no. 3–4 (March–April 1963): 66–67, cited in Landau, *Arabs in Israel*, 104.

63. Dallasheh, "Political Mobilization," 28.

64. I thank Leena Dallasheh for generously sharing a copy of the complete Ard memorandum with me. Selections are also reprinted in Landau, *Arabs in Israel*, 228–230.

65. Ibid., 229.

66. Ibid. The memorandum's invocation of the "Arab national movement" here is a reference to Arab nationalism in general, not the ANM specifically.

67. Habib Qahwaji, "The Complete Story of the Ard Movement," *Shuʾun Filastiniyah* 1, no. 1 (March 1971): 116–117. *Shuʾun Filastiniyah* was the flagship academic journal of the Palestine Research Center. Also of note is that the journal's inaugural issue included an article on the Ard movement, marking its full integration into the Palestinian national research agenda.

68. Jiryis, *Arabs in Israel*, 132; Landau, *Arabs in Israel*, 103.

69. Muhammed Watad, "Why Was El Ard Banned?," *New Outlook* 7, no. 7 (September 1964): 44–48.

70. Juhayna (pen name of Emile Habibi), "The Ard Group," *al-Ittihad*, July 17, 1964.

71. Jiryis, *Arabs in Israel,* 131; see also Landau, *Arabs in Israel*, 102.

72. Cited in Landau, *Arabs in Israel*, 102–103. Jiryis has slightly different wording, along with what appears to be his own interpretation mixed in with the original text of the clause. See Jiryis, *Arabs in Israel*, 132.

73. *Al-mithaq al-qawmi al-filastini* [The Palestinian National Charter], http://www.palestine-studies.org/sites/default/files/uploads/files/28-5-1964b.pdf.

74. Sabri Jiryis was born in 1938 to a Christian family in village of Fassuta, near the Lebanese border. He graduated from Terra Santa high school in Nazareth and was among the first sizable cohorts of Palestinian students to enter Hebrew University, from which he graduated with a master's degree in law in 1962. After obtaining a license to practice law in 1965, he worked as an attorney in Haifa. See his website at http://jiryis.net/about-me/.

75. Jiryis, *Arabs in Israel*, 132; Landau, *Arabs in Israel*, 99.

76. Dallasheh, "Political Mobilization," 31.

77. Landau, *Arabs in Israel*, 99–100.

78. Full text of resolution at http://cns.miis.edu/nam/documents/Official_Document/2nd_Summit_FD_Cairo_Declaration_1964.pdf. See also Juhayna, "The Palestinian Arab People," *al-Ittihad*, October 16, 1964.

79. United Nations General Assembly, Third Session, *Resolution 194 (III)*.

80. See Zilbershats, "International Law."

81. Beinin, *Red Flag*, 243–244.

82. Fatah began launching raids into Israel on January 1, 1965.

83. *Al-Ittihad*, May 17 and 28, 1965.

84. On the transformation of the CPI's formulation regarding the Palestinian refugees during the 1950s, see Nassar, "Palestinian Citizens."

85. *Al-Ittihad*, November 3, 1964.

86. Tawfiq Tubi, "Who Stands in the Way of a Peaceful Resolution to the Palestinian Issue?," *al-Ittihad*, May 14, 1965.

87. See *al-Ittihad*, October 12, November 19, and December 17, 1965, for coverage of the debates. A full account of the resolutions introduced and ultimately passed. See United Nations General Assembly, Twentieth Session, *Report of the Special Political Committee*.

88. *Al-Ittihad*, October 15, 19, 22, and 29,1965.

89. The Ard leaders also put forward a list for the 1965 elections, but the authorities refused to let the group run its own slate. Landau, *Arabs in Israel*, 100–101.

90. Ahmad, *Al-Muʿadhdhabun*, 6–7.

91. Cited in ibid., 174.

92. See *al-Jihad*, July 16, 1964; *al-Manar*, July 17, 28, 1964; *al-Difaʿ*, July 19, July 28, 1964. Clippings in Maktab Jamiʿat al-Duwal al-Arabiyah bi-al-Quds, Miscellaneous Records, 1964–1967 File Box MQ 2/3/3, courtesy of the Hoover Institution on War, Revolution, and Peace.

93. "Behind the Barbed Wire: Al-Ard Is One of Tens of Arab Organizations," *Filastin*, September 15, 1964.

94. The bureau was shut down in 1967 when Israel occupied East Jerusalem. See "*Al-Wasat* Spoke with Its First and Last Director: The Story of the Arab League Bureau in Occupied Jerusalem," *al-Wasat*, August 5, 1996, https://tinyurl.com/j6fdflu.

95. Memorandum dated August 10, 1964, Maktab Jamiʿat al-Duwal al-Arabiyah bi-al-Quds, MQ 2/3/3-55. A follow-up memorandum was sent out on August 13, 1964, that included an interview with al-Ard's leader, Mansur Kardosh; see MQ 2/3/3-59. At least one reply came from the Syrian embassy in Amman requesting additional information about the group. See MQ 2/3/3-106.

96. MQ 2/3/3-314, 326, 349, 372, 386.

97. *Filastin*, December 31, 1964.

98. Examples include F. Sayigh, *Al-diblumasiyya al-sahyuniyya*; Kadi, *Al-histadrut*; S. Habibi, *Al-suhuf al-israiliyya*; and Kayyali, *Al-kibutz*.

99. Jiryis, *Arabs in Israel*, 91–118.

100. Meric Dobson, "Preface," in Jiryis, *Arabs in Israel*, xii.

101. "Al-Adab's Roundtable: Palestine and Literature," *al-Adab* 12, no. 3 (March 1964): 4.

102. Khatib, *Diwan al-watan al-muhtall*, 5.

103. Mahmoud Darwish, "A Lover from Palestine," *al-Adab* 14, no. 6 (June 1966): 1–2.

104. Ghassan Kanafani, "Resistance Literature in Occupied Palestine," *al-Adab* 14, no. 7 (July 1966): 1–3, 65–69. The article was a portion of the introduction of his book by the same name. Ghassan Kanafani was born in 1936 to a Muslim family in Acre. In 1948 he fled with his family to Syria. After completing high school in Damascus in 1952, Kanafani enrolled in the Arabic literature program at the University of Damascus, while also working with Palestinian children in refugee camps. Kanafani was expelled from the university because of his involvement in the ANM movement and spent a few years in Kuwait. In 1960 he moved to Beirut, where he worked as a journalist and editor for pro-Nasser papers. His 1962 novel, *Men in the Sun*, earned him critical praise as a novelist and cultural critic. A leading political thinker affiliated with the leftist PFLP, he was killed by Israeli forces in a car bomb in 1972. See Bashkin, "Nationalism as a Cause," 92–97.

105. Kanafani, *Adab al-muqawama*, 5.

106. Ibid., 11–12.

107. Ibid., 13–18.

108. Ibid., 30.

109. Ibid., 31–32.

110. Ibid., 41.

111. Ibid, 43–44.

112. The most famous of these is "Huna baqun" (Here we shall remain), which appeared as "'Ala sudur mudtahidayna" [On the chests of our persecutors] in *al-Ittihad*, September 14, 1965. Kanafani cited and praised it in *Adab al-muqawama*, 48, 94–97. It also appears in Zayyad's collection *Ashiddu 'ala aydikum* [I pull on your hands] (Beirut: Dar al-'Awda, 1969 [Nazareth: n.p., 1967]) and is translated as "The impossible" in Elmessiri, *Palestinian Wedding*, 151–152, and Hijjawi, *Poetry of Resistance*, 16–18.

113. Tawfiq Zayyad, "Key Observations regarding Arabic Revolutionary Poetry in Israel," *al-Jadid* 13, no. 8–9 (August–September 1966): 6.

CHAPTER 5

1. 'Abbas Zayn al-Din, "Memories across Sixty Years: With Mahmoud Darwish under a Single Tent," *al-Jabha* online, March 26, 2010.,www.aljabha.org/index.asp?i=49902.

2. Hurani, *Al-Jary ila al-hazima*, 457–461.

3. Chamberlin, *Global Offensive*, 18–33.

4. Rouhana, *Palestinian Citizens*, 66–73.

5. Smooha, *Arabs and Jews*; Ashkenazi, *Palestinian Identities*.

6. Louis and Shlaim, *The 1967 Arab-Israeli War*; Quigley, *Six-Day War*; Raz, *Bride and the Dowry*.

7. Amin, *Al-muthaqqafun*, 16.

8. According to a September 1967 Israeli census, an estimated 600,000 Palestinians lived in the West Bank, 66,000 lived in East Jerusalem, and 356,000 lived in the Gaza Strip. Cited in Raz, *Bride and the Dowry*, 5.

9. Baev, "Eastern Europe," 184.

10. Shlaim, *Iron Wall*, 258–259.

11. Sela, *Decline*, 108.

12. Raz, "Generous Peace Offer."

13. See United Nations Security Council, *Resolution 242 (1967)*.

14. Y. Sayigh, *Armed Struggle*, 179.

15. Hout, *My Life*, 67.

16. Darwish, "Hayati," 59.

17. Muhammad Khass, "One Year since the June War," *al-Ittihad*, June 7, 1968; Hasan, *Mahmoud Darwish*, 29–30.

18. "Al-Ittihad's Word: Let Peace Prevail over War," *al-Ittihad*, June 27, 1967.

19. "Representative Tawfiq Tubi Condemns the Political Detentions," *al-Ittihad*, June 30, 1967.

20. *Al-Ittihad*, June 9 and 16, 1967.

21. Saliba Khamis, "Talk of the Month: The Events of the Last Few Weeks," *al-Jadid* 14, no. 7–8 (July–August 1967): 4–6. See also Raz, *Bride*, 53–78.

22. Juhayna, "The Khartoum Conference and Israel's Office Stance," *al-Ittihad*, September 8, 1967.

23. "Question and Answer Session with Comrade Tawfiq Tubi," *al-Ittihad*, March 15, 1968.

24. Ibid.

25. Abu Hanna, *Khamirat al-ramad*, 130–133.

26. Salman Natur, interview with Rawan Damin, "Taht al-Mijhar: Ashab al-bilad (2)" [Under the microscope: Owners of the country, part 2], *al-Jazeera*, October 28, 2010, https://www.youtube.com/watch?v=jHpiFtq4q-Y.

27. Tuqan, *Al-rihlatu al-asʿab*, 21.

28. Salman Natour, interview with the author, Haifa, May 21, 2007.

29. Tuqan, *Al-rihlatu al-asʿab*, 17.

30. Ibid., 23.

31. Johnson and Khalifeh, "Uprising of a Novelist," 24.

32. Raz, *Bride*, 96–98.

33. Abu Rabiʿ, *Contemporary Arab Thought*, 8.

34. Amin, *Al-muthaqqafun*, 19–26.
35. Kassab, *Contemporary Arab Thought*, 77.
36. Kayyal, "'A Hesitant Dialogue,'" 56.
37. Abu Rabiʿ, *Contemporary Arab Thought*, 53.
38. Naqqash, *Mahmoud Darwish*, 6.
39. ʿUmar al-Daqqaq, "The Arab Writer and the Fight against Zionism," *al-Adab* 16, no. 4 (April 1968): 40–42.
40. Qabbani, "Footnotes on the Book," 97–101.
41. ʿAbd al-Karim Ghallab, "Literature of Tragedy, Not Literature of Return," *al-Adab* 16, no. 4 (April 1968): 45–46.
42. Ghassan Kanafani, "Dimensions and Positions in Palestinian Resistance Literature," *Mulhiq al-anwar al-usbuʿi*, August 13–20, 1967, reprinted in *al-Adab* 16, no. 4 (April 1968): 131.
43. Cited in ibid.
44. Rajaʾ al-Naqqash, "Mahmoud Darwish: 'A Lover from Palestine,'" *al-Adab* 16, no. 2 (February 1968): 4.
45. ʿAbd al-ʿAziz al-Ahwani, "The Arab Intellectual and the New Colonialism," *al-Adab* 16, no. 4 (April 1968): 10–14; Suhayr al-Qalamawi, "The Arab Writer and the Fight against Imperialism," *al-Adab* 16, no. 4 (April 1968): 17–20.
46. Husayn Muruwwah, "The Arab Writer and the Fight against the New Colonialism," *al-Adab* 16, no. 4 (April 1968): 50–52; Hani al-Rahib, "The Writer's Message in the Fight against Imperialism," *al-Adab* 16, no. 4 (April 1968): 25–28; Muhammad Muhammad Ali, "The Arab Writer and the New Colonialism," *al-Adab* 16, no. 4 (April 1968): 78–86.
47. Kanafani, "Dimensions and Positions," 135.
48. Mahmoud Darwish, "End of the Night," *al-Hilal* 76, no. 5 (May 1968): 123–178.
49. "Poems from behind the Barbed Wire," *Shiʿr*, no. 28 (Spring 1968): 9.
50. Kanafani, *Al-adab al-filastini*.
51. Y. Khatib, *Diwan*.
52. Halayhil, "Samih al-Qasim."
53. Nizar Qabbani, "To the Poets of the Occupied Land," reprinted in *al-Ittihad*, May 14, 1968. It is important to note that in introducing the poem to their readers, the editors of *al-Ittihad* took issue with Qabbani describing them as the poets of "the occupied land." According to the editors, "We understand the term 'occupied land' to be the lands that Israel occupied in the June 1967 aggression. We do not accept this term when it carries the meaning of not recognizing the right of the Israeli people to their country." The need to include the explanatory footnote likely reflected a combination of the political views of the veteran Rakah leaders and concern over Israeli censorship.
54. Halayhil, "Samih al-Qasim."
55. Rutter, "Look Left," 194; Mohyeddin Abdulaziz, interview with author, Tucson,

Arizona, May 8, 2014. Abdulaziz attended the Sofia festival as part of the Palestinian-Jordanian delegation.

56. Rutter, "Look Left," 196.

57. Ibid., 198–199.

58. Katsiaficas, *Imagination of the New Left*, 3; Dubinsky et al., *New World Coming*.

59. Suri, *Power and Protest*.

60. Baev, "Eastern Europe," 184.

61. Ibid.

62. Golan, *Czechoslovak Reform Movement*, 237, 246.

63. Lutfi al-Khuli, "The First Comprehensive Arab Encounter with World Public Opinion after the June 5 War," *al-Ahram*, September 1, 1968, reprinted in *al-Ittihad*, September 28, 1968.

64. Ibid.

65. Hurani, *Al-jary ila al-hazima*, 457–461.

66. Abdulaziz, interview with author.

67. Samih al-Qasim, "1968, Rakah, Sofia: Resistance Poets, Site of the Flag," *al-Jabha*, April 30, 2011, www.aljabha.org/?i=59322.

68. Jamil ʿAbd al-Qadir Shammout, "The World Youth Festival," www.lydda.com/34.htm.. See also Chamberlin, *Global Offensive*.

69. Salim and Tawila, "A Comedy," 6.

70. "The Israeli Delegation Receives Great Attention at the Festival, *al-Ittihad*, August 2, 1968; Hurani, *al-Jary ila al-hazima*, 467.

71. S. Qasim, *Innaha mujarrad*, 88. The emblem appeared to be a flaming torch with Hebrew lettering around it. For a photograph of the Rakah uniform with the emblem, see *al-Ittihad*, July 26, 1968.

72. Hurani, *Al-jary ila al-hazima*, 467.

73. Salim and Tawila, "A Comedy," 7.

74. "The Youth Festival Stands in Solidarity with the Struggle of the Arab Peoples," *al-Ittihad*, August 6, 1968.

75. George Tubi, "The Israeli Delegation [Stands] against Aggression and Expansion and in Favor of Peace," *al-Ittihad*, September 6, 1968.

76. Shammout, "World Youth Festival."

77. Abdulaziz, interview with author.

78. S. Qasim, "Resistance Poets."

79. Haydar Rashid, "Mahmoud Darwish," *al-ʿArab al-Yawm*, August 12, 2008.

80. Ahmad al-Ghufari, "With Mahmoud Darwish and Samih al-Qasim Forty Years Ago," *al-Nur*, no. 420 (August 2008). The paper is the official organ of the Syrian Communist Party. The website from which this article was retrieved (in 2010) is no longer functional.

81. S. Qasim, "Resistance Poets."

82. Shammout, "World Youth Festival."

83. S. Qasim, *Innaha mujarrad*, 87; S. Qasim, "Resistance Poets"; Rawaʾ al-Jasani, "With Jawahiri, Away from Politics and Literature (15)," *al-Akhbar*, April 5, 2014, http://www.iraqicp.com/index.php/sections/platform/13080-15.

84. Full text at http://avalon.law.yale.edu/20th_century/plocov.asp.

85. Muhammad Miʿari, "Those Returning from the Festival Talk to *al-Ghad* Readers," *al-Ghad*, no. 7 (August 1968): 10–11.

86. Mahmud al-Dasuqi (Mahmoud al-Desouqi) was born in 1934 in al-Tiba and completed high school in Nazareth in 1955. He studied journalism and economics at Tel Aviv University and has published (traditionally structured) poetry from the 1960s until today. Abu Hamad, *Aʿlam*, 421–422; Furani, *Silencing*, 62–63.

87. Mahmud Dasuqi, "Ana Filastini" [I am a Palestinian], *al-Quds*, December 15, 1968.

88. Ahmad Sidqi al-Dajani, "The Arab Heroes in the Occupied Land," *al-Jumhuriyyah*, September 26, 1968, reprinted in Dajani, *Min al-muqawama*, 152–155.

89. Harrison, *Transcolonial Maghreb*.

90. Shammout, "World Youth Festival."

91. Darwish, *Journal*, 156.

92. Khadr, *Adab al-Muqawama*, 103.

93. Muhammad al-ʿItani, "They Returned Them to Us and Returned Us to Ourselves," *al-Tariq* 27, no. 11–12 (November–December 1968): 16.

94. Darwish, "Rita wa'l-bunduqiyya" (Rita and the rifle), in *Akhir al-layl* [The end of night], reprinted in *Diwan Mahmoud Darwish*, 1:186–188.

95. Darwish, "A Soldier Dreams of White Lilies," *al-Ittihad*, July 1967. This poem appeared as "Jundi yahlam bi'l-zanabiq al-baydaʾ," in *Akhir al-layl*, reprinted in *Diwan Mahmoud Darwish*, 1:189–195. The soldier was Shlomo Sand, who became a professor of European history at Tel Aviv University.

96. Adunis, "Poems That the Masses Clasp like Bread and Bullets," *al-Tariq* 27, no. 11–12 (November–December 1968): 15.

97. Jayyusi, "Modernist Poetry," 171–173.

98. Mahmoud Darwish, "Save Us from This Relentless Love," *al-Jadid* 16, no. 6 (June 1969): 3. Darwish's essay was reprinted in the Beirut-based leftist journal *al-Taliʿa* 5, no. 9 (September 1969): 113–116.

99. M. Sufyan, "Is It Resistance Poetry, or Only Opposition Poetry?," *al-Hadaf* 1, no. 18 (November 1969): 18–19.

100. Adunis, "Poetry and Revolution," *al-Hadaf* 1, no. 20 (December 1969): 18–19.

101. Suzan al-Sharif, "Poetry of the Occupied Land between Resistance and Opposition: An Interview with Ghali Shukri," *al-Hadaf* 1, no. 21 (December 1969): 18–19.

102. Shukri, *Adab al-muqawama*, 428–429.

103. Mahmoud Darwish, "Reply," *al-Hadaf* 1, no. 21 (December 1969): 19.

104. "A Literary Interview with Samih al-Qasim," *al-Adab* 17, no. 10 (October 1970): 5.

105. Ashcroft, "Representation and Its Discontents," 116.

106. Jiryis, *Democratic Freedoms in Israel*; Zureik, *The Palestinians in Israel*.

107. *Al-Ittihad*, September 6, 1968; James Feron, "Fatal Bombing in Tel Aviv Stirs Mob Attack on Arabs," *New York Times*, September 5, 1968.

108. Peretz, "Arab Palestine," 330. Azmi Bishara estimates that the attempts to militarize young Palestinian youth inside and have them join armed struggle groups yielded a few hundred total throughout its entire duration. See Bishara, *Al-ʿarab fi israʾil*, 118.

109. "A Page from the Thoughts of Samih al-Qasim," *al-Jadid* 16, no. 7 (July 1969): 30–32. He was released several weeks later with no charges filed against him.

110. Darwish, "Lahum," 7.

111. See the August 23, 1969, report of Qasim being confined to his hometown, along with forty other politically active Druze, and forbidden from having any contact with Druze in the Golan Heights in *al-Yawmiyat al-filastiniyya*, 10:165.

112. In March 1970 Jubran was sentenced to two months in jail and fined one hundred Israeli pounds (about twenty-nine dollars) for failing to inform the police that he moved from one apartment to another in Haifa. See ibid., 11:234.

113. See, for example, the entry from February 2, 1970, that reports on the sentencing of several men from the West Bank and Gaza Strip for various resistance-related activities. The same paragraph notes that Samih al-Qasim had an upcoming trial in which he stood accused of publishing verses deemed seditious by the Israeli censor. See ibid., 11:76.

114. Mahmoud Darwish, "Something on the Homeland," *al-Jadid* 16, no. 9–10 (September–October 1969): 3–4.

115. Darwish was ordered by the northern military governor not to leave Haifa, to check in with the police daily, and to remain in his apartment from sunset to sunrise daily. See http://www.darwishfoundation.org/atemplate.php?id=51.

116. Abu Hanna, *Khamirat al-ramad*, 49.

117. Ibid.

118. Naqqash, *Mahmoud Darwish*, 268–273.

119. "I Changed My Location, but I Did Not Change My Position," *al-Ahram*, February 11, 1971.

120. Cited in Naqqash, *Mahmoud Darwish*, 274.

121. "Mahmoud Darwish Did Not Leave," *al-Ittihad*, reprinted in Naqqash, *Mahmoud Darwish*, 318.

122. Samih al-Qasim, "Poets and Diplomats," *al-Jadid* 18, no. 1–2 (January–February 1971): 1–2.

123. Darwish returned to the West Bank city of Ramallah in 1993, where he took up residence, and visited family and friends in Israel until shortly before his death in 2008.

CONCLUSION

1. Mada al-Carmel, "The Haifa Declaration."
2. Pappé, *The Forgotten Palestinians*, 129–134.
3. "Land Day Takes a Prominent Place in Foreign, Arab and Local Newspapers and Broadcasts," *al-Ittihad*, March 5, 1976.
4. Solidarity protests organized by Palestinian activists were held in Damascus, Cairo, and Amman. Additional solidarity actions took place in Pakistan and Malaysia. See "Echoes of Land Day in the Region and the World," *al-Ittihad*, March 31, 1976.
5. Ibid.
6. Sorek, *Palestinian Commemoration*.
7. Ghanem, *Palestinian-Arab Minority*, 111–112.
8. Bishara, "The 1948 Arabs," 43–68.
9. Khalili, *Heroes and Martyrs*; Jamal, *Arab Public Sphere in Israel*.
10. William Dalrymple, "A Culture under Fire," *The Guardian*, October 2, 2002, https://www.theguardian.com/artanddesign/2002/oct/02/art.artsfeatures
11. Abu Saif, *The Book of Gaza*; Alareer, *Gaza Writes Back*.
12. The most famous recent singer to emerge from Gaza is Mohammed Assaf, who in 2013 won the Arab Idol singing competition. Assaf's unlikely rise to fame is depicted in the 2015 Hany Abu-Assad film, *The Idol*.
13. Eduardo Soteras Jalil, "Gaza Artists," *al-Jazeera English*, March 22, 2015, http://www.aljazeera.com/indepth/inpictures/2015/03/gaza-artists-150317062737303.html; "We Paint for the People of Gaza," *UNRWA*, October 2, 2015, http://www.unrwa.org/newsroom/features/"we-paint-people-gaza"; Amelia Smith, "Artists Challenge the Blockade by Building a Virtual Bridge between Gaza and London," *Middle East Monitor*, February 8, 2016, https://www.middleeastmonitor.com/20160208-artists-challenge-the-blockade-by-building-a-virtual-bridge-between-gaza-and-london/.
14. Sophie McNeill, "Gaza Comedy Group Bas Ya Zalameh Records Skits about War in Effort to Make Gazans Laugh," *ABC News (Australia)*, July 13, 2015, http://www.abc.net.au/news/2015-07-13/gaza-comedy-group-bas-ya-zalameh-try-to-make-light-of-conflict/6616760; Iyad Qatrawi, "Candid TV Show Comes to Gaza," *al-Monitor*, June 22, 2016, http://www.al-monitor.com/pulse/originals/2016/06/gaza-comedy-hidden-camera-program.html.
15. See full text at http://www.bdsmovement.net/call.
16. The impact of these restrictions on Palestinian hip-hop artists in Israel, the West Bank, and the Gaza Strip is poignantly captured in Jackie Salloum's 2009 documentary, *Slingshot Hip Hop*.
17. Arab countries to which Israeli citizens are allowed to travel include Bahrain, Egypt, Jordan, Mauritania, Morocco, Oman, Qatar, Tunisia, and the UAE.
18. In 2001 Knesset member Azmi Bishara faced legal sanction and a Knesset vote to strip him of his diplomatic status after he returned from Syria, where he had attended

Hafez al-Assad's funeral and praised Hezbollah as a resistance force. Bishara also stood accused of trying to help Palestinian citizens of Israel enter Syria illicitly to meet with their family members who had fled or been expelled to that country in 1948. The charges were later dropped. See Louër, *To Be an Arab*, 85–86.

In 2014 Palestinian Israeli journalist Majd Kayyal was arrested and interrogated for several days by the Israeli GSS (Shin Bet) after his return from a conference in Beirut honoring the fortieth anniversary of the *as-Safir* newspaper, to which Kayyal regularly contributed. See Jack Khoury and Gill Cohen, "Israeli Arab Journalist Arrested upon Return from Beirut Visit," *Haaretz*, April 17, 2014, http://www.haaretz.com/news/diplomacy-defense/1.585994

19. In May 2010 Israeli commandos forcibly boarded the Turkish ship *Mavi Marmara* in international waters. The confrontation that ensued left ten Turkish humanitarian workers dead. In 2013 Israeli prime minister Benjamin Netanyahu apologized for the loss of life, and in 2016 Israel paid twenty million dollars in compensation to the families of the victims. See "Israel Pays Turkey $20 Million in Compensation over the Mavi Marmara Assault," *Middle East Monitor*, October 1, 2016, https://www.middleeastmonitor.com/20161001-israel-pays-turkey-20m-compensation-over-mavi-marmara-assault/.

20. Yael Marom, "Representing Palestine, Not Israel: Arab Idol's Contestants from Israel," *972mag*, September 26, 2014, http://972mag.com/representing-palestine-not-israel-arab-idols-contestants-from-israel/97025/.

21. For an English translation of the poem, see mlynxqualey, "The Poem for Which Dareen Tatour's under House Arrest: 'Resist, My People, Resist Them,'" Arabic Literature (in English), April 27, 2016, https://arablit.org/2016/04/27/the-poem-for-which-dareen-tatours-under-house-arrest-resist-my-people-resist-them/.

22. Gideon Levy and Alex Levac, "In 2016 Israel, a Palestinian Writer Is in Custody for Her Poetry," *Haaretz*, May 21, 2016, http://www.haaretz.com/israel-news/.premium-1.720418.

23. See Jewish Voice for Peace, https://jewishvoiceforpeace.org/dareen/#signers.

24. "Detention of Poet Dareen Tatour Signals Worrying Escalation in Israeli Repression," *PEN America*, June 17, 2016, https://pen.org/press-release/2016/06/17/detention-poet-dareen-tatour-signals-worrying-escalation-israeli.

25. Nigel Wilson, "Israel Prosecutes a Palestinian over YouTube Poem," *al-Jazeera*, June 20, 2016, http://www.aljazeera.com/news/2016/06/israel-prosecutes-palestinian-poet-youtube-poem-160619085525624.html.

26. "Broadcast on Palestinian Poet Darwish Puts Army Radio in Crosshairs," *Times of Israel*, July 20, 2016, http://www.timesofisrael.com/broadcast-on-palestinian-poet-darwish-puts-army-radio-in-crosshairs/.

27. Regev was again outraged at the inclusion of Darwish's poem and walked out during the performance. See Lisa Goldman, "The Minister of Culture Who Knows Nothing about Democracy," *972mag*, September 27, 2016, http://972mag.com/the-minister-of-culture-who-knows-nothing-about-democracy/122217/.

BIBLIOGRAPHY

NEWSPAPERS AND PERIODICALS

al-Adab (Beirut)
al-Adib (Beirut)
al-Anbaʾ (Jerusalem)
al-Ard (Nazareth)
al-Darb (Haifa)
al-Difaʿ (Jaffa/East Jerusalem)
al-Fajr (Tel Aviv)
Filastin (Jaffa/East Jerusalem)
Filastin (Kuwait)
al-Ghad (Haifa)
al-Hadaf (Beirut)
al-Hadaf (Tel Aviv)
Ha-Olam ha-zeh-Hadha al-ʿAlam (Tel Aviv)
Haqiqat al-Amr (Tel Aviv)
al-Hilal (Cairo)
al-Ittihad (Haifa)
al-Jadid (Haifa)
Jerusalem Post (Jerusalem)
Kalimat al-Marʾa (Tel Aviv)
Majallat al-Akhbar al-Durziya (Jerusalem)
Majallat al-Akhbar al-Islamiya (Jerusalem)
Majallat al-Dirasat al-Filastiniya (Beirut)
Mawaqif (Beirut)
Mifgash-Liqaʾ (Tel Aviv)
al-Mirsad (Tel Aviv)
al-Mujtamaʿ (Nazareth)
Ner (Tel Aviv)
New Outlook (Tel Aviv)
New York Times (New York)

al-Rabita (Nazareth)
Ruz al-Yusuf (Cairo)
Sawt Filastin (Damascus)
Shiʿr (Beirut)
Shuʾun Filastiniya (Beirut)
al-Taliʿa (Beirut)
al-Tariq (Beirut)
al-Wasit (Nazareth)
al-Yawm (Jaffa)

GOVERNMENTAL AND INTERGOVERNMENTAL PUBLICATIONS

League of Arab States: Palestine Department. *Idtihad al-ʿarab fi israʾ il* [The persecution of Arabs in Israel]. [Cairo]: Dar al-tibaʿa al-fanniyya, 1955.

———. *Report on Persecution of the Arabs in Israel*. Cairo: Dar al-hana, 1956.

Maktab Jamiʿat al-Duwal al-Arabiyah bi-al-Quds [League of Arab States, Jerusalem Bureau], Miscellaneous Records, 1964–1967. File Box MQ 2/3/3. Courtesy of the Hoover Institution on War, Revolution and Peace.

Statistical Abstracts of Israel, 1959–1966. Tel Aviv: Central Bureau of Statistics, 1966.

United Nations General Assembly, Third Session. *Resolution 181 (II): Future Government of Palestine* (A/RES/181 [II]), November 29, 1947. https://unispal.un.org/DPA/DPR/unispal.nsf/0/7F0AF2BD897689B785256C330061D253.

———. *Resolution 194 (III): Palestine—Progress Report of the United Nations Mediator* (A/RES/194 [III]), December 11, 1948. https://unispal.un.org/DPA/DPR/unispal.nsf/0/C758572B78D1CD0085256BCF0077E51A.

United Nations General Assembly, Twentieth Session. *Report of the Special Political Committee* (A/6115*), November 23, 1965. https://unispal.un.org/DPA/DPR/unispal.nsf/0/425EEA6E57021A058525694B006E6D83.

United Nations Security Council. *Israeli-Syrian General Armistice Agreement* (S/1353), July 20, 1949. https://unispal.un.org/DPA/DPR/unispal.nsf/0/E845CA0B92BE4E3485256442007901CC.

United Nations Security Council, 1382nd Meeting. *Resolution 242 (1967)* (S/RES/242), November 22, 1967. https://unispal.un.org/DPA/DPR/unispal.nsf/0/7D35E1F729DF491C85256EE700686136.

INTERVIEWS

Mohyeddin Abdulaziz, Tucson, AZ, May 8, 2014
Hanna Abu Hanna, Haifa, May 22, 2007
Siham Daoud, Haifa, May 21, 2007
Fouzi El-Asmar, Bethesda, MD, September 7, 2012

Hanna Ibrahim, al-Biʿna, May 23, 2007
Salim Jubran, Nazareth, May 24, 2007
Muhammad Miʿari, Haifa, May 21, 2007
Salman Natour, Haifa, May 21, 2007
Samih al-Qasim, al-Rama, May 23, 2007
Sasson Somekh, Tel Aviv, May 30, 2007

OTHER SOURCES

ʿAbbas, Ihsan. *Ghurbat al-raʿiy: Sira dhatiyya* [The shepherd's exile: An autobiography]. Amman: Dar al-shuruq, 1996.

Abu-Baker, Khawla, and Dan Rabinowitz. *Coffins on Our Shoulders: The Experience of the Palestinian Citizens of Israel*. Berkeley: University of California Press, 2005.

Abu El-Haj, Nadia. *Facts on the Ground: Archaeological Practice and Territorial Self-Fashioning in Israeli Society*. Chicago: University of Chicago Press, 2008.

Abu-Ghazaleh, Adnan. *Arab Cultural Nationalism in Palestine during the British Mandate*. Beirut: Institute for Palestine Studies, 1973.

———. *Palestinian Arab Cultural Nationalism: 1919–1960*. Beltsville, MD: Amana Books, 1991.

Abu Hamad, ʿIrfan. *Aʿlam min ard al-salam* [Luminaries from the land of peace]. Haifa: Sharikat al-abhath al-ʿilmiyya wa'l ʿamaliyya, 1979.

Abu Hanna, Hanna. *Khamirat al-ramad: Sira* [Yeast of the ashes: A biography]. Haifa: Maktabat kull shayʾ, 2004.

———. *Mahr al-buma: Sira* [Dowry of the owl: A life]. Haifa: Maktabat kull shayʾ, 2004.

———. *Rihlat al-bahth ʿan al-turath* [A journey in search of heritage]. Haifa: Al-wadi li'l-tibaʿa wa'l-nashr, 1994.

———. *Thalathat shuʿaraʾ: Ibrahim Tuqan, ʿAbd al-Rahim Mahmud, Abu Salma* [Three poets: Ibrahim Tuqan, ʿAbd al-Rahim Mahmud, Abu Salma]. Haifa: Matbaʿat al-wadi, 1995.

———. *Zill al-ghayma: Sira* [The cloud's shade: A biography]. Beirut: Al-muʾassasa al-ʿarabiyya li'l-dirasat wa'l-nashr, 2001.

Abu Hussein, Hussein, and Fiona McKay. *Access Denied: Palestinian Land Rights in Israel*. London: Zed Books, 2003.

Abu-Lughod, Ibrahim. "Review: The Pitfalls of Palestiniology." *Arab Studies Quarterly* 3, no. 4 (1981): 403–411.

Abu-Manneh, Butrus. "Arab-Ottomanists' Reactions to the Young Turk Revolution." In *Late Ottoman Palestine: The Period of Young Turk Rule*, edited by Yuval Ben-Basset and Eyal Ginio, 145–164. London: I. B. Tauris, 2011.

Abu Rabiʿ, Ibrahim. *Contemporary Arab Thought: Studies in Post-1967 Arab Intellectual History*. London: Pluto Press, 2004.

Abu-Saad, Ibrahim. "Present Absentees: The Arab School Curriculum in Israel as a Tool for De-educating Indigenous Palestinians." *Holy Land Studies: A Multidisciplinary Journal* 7, no. 1 (2008): 17–43.

Abu Saif, Atef, ed. *The Book of Gaza: A City in Short Fiction*. Manchester, UK: Carcanet Press, 2014.

———. *The Drone Eats with Me: A Gaza Diary*. Manchester, UK: Carcanet Press, 2015.

Aburish, Said K. *Nasser: The Last Arab*. New York: Thomas Dunne, 2013.

Ahmad, Hamid Isma'il Sayyid. *Al-muʿadhdhabun fi'l-ard al-muqaddasa: Al-ʿarab fi israʾil* [The tormented in the Holy Land: The Arabs in Israel]. [Cairo]: Dar al-qawmiyyah li'l-tibaʿ wa'l-nashr, 1966.

Alareer, Refaat, ed. *Gaza Writes Back: Short Stories from Young Writers in Gaza, Palestine*. Washington, DC: Just World Books, 2014.

Al-Haj, Majid. *Education, Empowerment and Control: The Case of the Arabs in Israel*. Albany: State University of New York Press, 1995.

Altoma, Salih. *Abʿad al-tahhaddi fi shiʿr Mahmoud Darwish* [The aspects of challenge in the poetry of Mahmoud Darwish]. Beirut: Majallat mawaqif, 1970.

Amin, Jalal. *Al-muthaqqafun al-ʿarab wa israʾil* [Arab intellectuals and Israel]. Cairo: Dar al-shuruq, 1998.

Anderson, Betty S. *The American University of Beirut: Arab Nationalism and Liberal Education*. Austin: University of Texas Press, 2011.

Anderson, Charles W. "From Petition to Confrontation: The Palestinian National Movement and the Rise of Mass Politics, 1929–1939." PhD diss., New York University, 2013.

Araj, Rumzi, Jackie Reem Salloum, Waleed Zaiter, and Suhell Nafar. *Slingshot Hip Hop*. [New York]: Fresh Booza Production, 2009.

Aruri, Naseer, and Edmund Ghareeb, eds. *Enemy of the Sun: Poetry of Palestinian Resistance*. Washington, DC: Drum & Spear, 1970.

Ashcroft, Bill. "Representation and Its Discontents: Orientalism, Islam and the Palestinian Crisis." *Religion* 34 (2004): 113–121.

Ashkenazi, Abraham. *Palestinian Identities and Preferences: Israel's and Jerusalem's Arabs*. New York: Praeger, 1992.

Assaf, Michael. "The Arabic Press in Israel." *International Communication Gazette* 7 (1961): 23–24.

ʿAtwat, Muhammad ʿAbd ʿAbdalla. *Al-ittajahat al-wataniyya fi'l-shiʿr al-filastini al-muʿasir, 1918–1968* [Nationalist directions in contemporary Palestinian poetry, 1918–1968]. Beirut: Dar al-afaq al-jadid, 1998.

Avida, Mordechai. "Broadcasting in Israel" [Organization and special functions of the three broadcasting services]. *Middle Eastern Affairs* 3 (1952): 321–328.

Ayalon, Ami. *The Press in the Arab Middle East: A History*. New York: Oxford University Press, 1995.

———. *Reading Palestine: Printing and Literary, 1900–1948*. Austin: University of Texas Press, 2004.

Badawi, M. M. "Commitment in Contemporary Arabic Literature." In *Critical Perspectives on Modern Arabic Literature, 1945–1980*, edited by Issa J. Boullata, 23–44. Washington, DC: Three Continents Press, 1980.

Baev, Jordan. "Eastern Europe and the Six Day War: The Case of Bulgaria." In *The Soviet Union and the June 1967 Six Day War*, edited by Yaacov Ro'i and Boris Morozov, 172–197. Stanford, CA: Stanford University Press, 2008.

Barakat, Rana. "Criminals or Martyrs? Let the Courts Decide! British Colonial Legacy in Palestine and the Criminalization of Resistance." *Omran*, no. 6 (Autumn 2013): 55–72.

———. "*Thawrat al-buraq* in British Mandate Palestine: Jerusalem, Mass Mobilization and Colonial Politics, 1928–1930." PhD diss., University of Chicago, 2007.

Baransi, Salih. *Al-nidal al-samit: Thalathun sana taht al-ihtilal al-sihyuni* [The silent struggle: Thirty years under Zionist occupation]. Beirut: Dar al-taliʿa liʾl-tibaʿ waʾl-nashr, 1981.

Barnhisel, Greg. *Cold War Modernists: Art, Literature, and American Cultural Diplomacy*. New York: Columbia University Press, 2015.

Bashkin, Orit. "Hybrid Nationalisms: Watani and Qawmi Visions in Iraq under ʿAbd al-Karim Qasim, 1958–61." *International Journal of Middle East Studies* 43, no. 2 (2011): 293–312.

———. *Impossible Exodus: Iraqi Jews in Israel*. Stanford, CA: Stanford University Press, 2017.

———. "Nationalism as a Cause: Arab Nationalism in the Writings of Ghassan Kanafani." In *Nationalism and Liberal Thought in the Arab East: Ideology and Practice*, edited by Christoph Schumann, 92–112. London: Routledge, 2010.

———. *The New Babylonians: A History of Jews in Modern Iraq*. Stanford, CA: Stanford University Press, 2012.

———. *The Other Iraq: Pluralism and Culture in Hashemite Iraq*. Stanford, CA: Stanford University Press, 2009.

Batatu, Hanna. *The Old Social Classes, and the Revolutionary Movements in Iraq: A Study of Iraq's Old Landed and Commercial Classes and of Its Communists, Baathists, and Free Officers*. Princeton, NJ: Princeton University Press, 1978.

Beinin, Joel. "Knowing Your Enemy, Knowing Your Ally: The Arabists of Hashomer Hatsa'ir (MAPAM)." *Social Text* 9, no. 3 (1991): 100–121.

———. *Was the Red Flag Flying There? Marxist Politics and the Arab-Israeli Conflict in Egypt and Israel, 1948–1965*. Berkeley: University of California Press, 1990.

Bhandar, Brenna, and Rafeef Ziadah. "Acts and Omissions: Framing Settler Colonialism in Palestine Studies." *Jadaliyya*, January 16, 2016. http://www.jadaliyya.c.jadaliyya.com/pages/index/23569/acts-and-omissions_framing-settler-colonialism-in-.

Bishara, Azmi. *Al-ʿarab fi israʾ il: Ruʾ ya min al-dakhil* [The Arabs in Israel: A view from within]. Beirut: Markaz al-diarasat al-wahda al-ʿarabiyya, 2008.

———. "The 1948 Arabs: A Comprehensive Discussion with Knesset Member Azmi Bishara on the Oslo Predicament and the Latest Developments." *Majallat al-dirasat al-filastiniyah* [Journal of Palestine studies] 7, no. 28 (Fall 1996): 43–68.

Boullata, Kamal, and Mirène Ghossein, eds. *The World of Rashid Hussein*. Detroit, MI: Arab-American Association of University Graduates, 1979.

Brunner, Benny. *The Great Book Robbery*. DVD. Directed by Benny Brunner. Amsterdam: 2911 Foundation, 2012.

Budeiri, Musa. *The Palestine Communist Party, 1919–1948: Arab and Jew in the Struggle for Internationalism*. 1979. Reprint, Chicago: Haymarket Books, 2010.

Buheiry, Marwan R., ed. *Intellectual Life in the Arab East: 1890–1939*. Beirut: Center for Arab and Middle East Studies, 1981.

Bunton, Martin. *Colonial Land Policy in Palestine, 1917–1936*. Oxford: Oxford University Press, 2007.

Büssow, Johann. *Hamidian Palestine: Politics and Society in the District of Jerusalem, 1872–1908*. Leiden, Netherlands: Brill, 2011.

Byrne, Jeffrey James. *Mecca of Revolution: Algeria, Decolonization, and the Third World Order*. Oxford: Oxford University Press, 2016.

Campos, Michelle. *Ottoman Brothers: Muslims, Christians, and Jews in Early Twentieth-Century Palestine*. Stanford, CA: Stanford University Press, 2010.

Césaire, Aimé. "Culture and Colonization." *Social Text* 28, no. 2 (2010): 127–144.

Chamberlin, Paul. *The Global Offensive: The United States, the Palestine Liberation Organization, and the Making of the Post–Cold War Order*. Oxford: Oxford University Press, 2012.

Charles, Asselin. "Colonial Discourse since Christopher Columbus." *Journal of Black Studies* 26, no. 2 (November 1995):134–152.

Cohen, Hillel. *Army of Shadows: Palestinian Collaboration with Zionism, 1917–1948*. Translated by Haim Watzman. Berkeley: University of California Press, 2008.

———. *Good Arabs: The Israeli Security Agencies and the Israeli Arabs, 1948–1967*. Translated by Haim Watzman. Berkeley: University of California Press, 2010.

———. "The Internal Refugees in the State of Israel: Israeli Citizens, Palestinian Refugees." *Palestine-Israel Journal of Politics, Economics, and Culture* 9, no. 2 (2002): 43.

———. "Review of Efraim Karsh's *Palestine Betrayed*." *American Historical Review* 116, no. 2 (2011): 545–546.

———. *Year Zero of the Arab-Israeli Conflict: 1929*. Translated by Haim Watzman. Waltham, MA: Brandeis University Press, 2015.

Cohen, Ra'anan. *Strangers in the Homeland: A Critical Study of Israel's Arab Citizens*. Sussex, UK: Academic Press, 2009.

Dajani, Ahmad Sidqi al-. *Min al-muqawama ila al-thawra al-shaʿbiyya fi filastin* [From resistance to popular revolution in Palestine]. [Cairo]: Maktabat al-anjlu al-misriyya, 1969.

Dallasheh, Leena. "Nazarenes in the Turbulent Tide of Citizenships: Nazareth from 1940 to 1966." PhD diss., New York University, 2012.

———. "Persevering through Colonial Transition: Nazareth's Palestinian Residents after 1948." *Journal of Palestine Studies* 45, no. 2 (2016): 8–23.

———. "Political Mobilization of Palestinians in Israel: The al-ʾArd Movement." In *Displaced at Home: Ethnicity and Gender among Palestinians in Israel*, edited by Rhoda Ann Kanaaneh and Isis Nusair, 21–38. Albany: State University of New York Press, 2010.

———. "Troubled Waters: Citizenship and Colonial Zionism in Nazareth." *International Journal of Middle East Studies* 47, no. 3 (2015): 467–487.

Darwazah, Muhammad ʿIzzat. *Mudhakkirat Muhammad ʿIzzat Darwazah* [The memoirs of Muhammad ʿIzzat Darwazah]. 6 vols. Beirut: Dar al-gharb al-islami, 1993.

Darwish, Mahmoud. *Akhir al-layl* [The end of night]. Beirut: Dar al-ʿawda, 1967).

———. *ʿAsafir bi-la ajnihah* [Birds without wings]. Acre: n.p., 1960.

———. *ʿAshiq min filastin* [A lover from Palestine]. 2nd ed. Beirut: Dar al-adab, 1969.

———. *Awraq al-zaytun* [Grape leaves]. Haifa: [Matbaʿat al-ittihad al-taʿawuniyah], 1964.

———. *Diwan Mahmoud Darwish* [Anthology of Mahmoud Darwish]. 2 vols. Beirut: Dar al-ʿawda, 1993.

———. "Hayati, qadiyati, shiʿri" [My life, my cause, my poetry]. *Al-Tariq* 27, no. 10–11 (November–December 1968): 48–65.

———. *Journal of an Ordinary Grief*. Translated by Ibrahim Muhawi. Brooklyn, NY: Archipelago Books, 2012.

———. "Lahum al-layl w'al-naharu li" [They have the night, but the day is mine]. *Al-Adab* 18, no. 4 (April 1970): 3–6.

———. *The Music of Human Flesh: Poems of the Palestinian Struggle*. Translated by Denys Johnson-Davies. London: Heinemann, 1980.

———. *Shayʾan al-watan* [Something about the homeland]. Beirut. Dar al-ʿawda, 1971.

Davis, Rochelle. "Commemorating Education: Recollections of the Arab College in Jerusalem, 1918–1948." *Comparative Studies of South Asia, Africa and the Middle East* 23, no. 1–2 (2003): 190–204.

Dawn, C. Ernest. "The Formation of Pan-Arab Ideology in the Interwar Years." *International Journal of Middle East Studies* 20, no. 1 (1988): 67–91.

De Young, Terri. *Placing the Poet: Badr Shakir al-Sayyab and Postcolonial Iraq*. Albany: State University of New York Press, 1998.

Demichelis, Marco. "From Nahda to Nakba: The Government Arab College of Jerusalem and Its Palestinian Historical Heritage in the First Half of the Twentieth Century." *Arab Studies Quarterly* 37, no. 3 (Summer 2015): 264–281.

Di-Capua, Yoav. "Arab Existentialism: An Invisible Chapter in the Intellectual History of Decolonization." *American Historical Review* 117, no. 4 (2012): 1061–1091.

———. "Homeward Bound: Ḥusayn Muruwwah's Integrative Quest for Authenticity." *Journal of Arabic Literature* 44, no. 1 (2013): 21–52.

———. "The Intimate History of Collaboration: Arab Citizens and the State of Israel." *Middle East Research and Information Project*, May 2007. http://www.merip.org/mero/interventions/intimate-history-collaboration.

Dik, Nadi Sari. *Mahmoud Darwish: Al-shiʿr waʾl-qadiya* [Mahmoud Darwish: The poetry and the cause]. Amman: Dar al-karmal, 1995.

Doumani, Beshara. "Rediscovering Ottoman Palestine: Writing Palestinians into History." *Journal of Palestine Studies* 21, no. 2 (1992): 5–28.

———. *Rediscovering Palestine: Merchants and Peasants in Jabal Nablus, 1700–1900*. Berkeley: University of California Press, 1995.

Dubinsky, Karen, Catherine Krull, Susan Lord, Sean Mills, and Scott Rutherford, eds. *New World Coming: The Sixties and the Shaping of Global Consciousness*. Toronto: Between the Lines, 2009.

El Shakry, Omnia. "'History without Documents': The Vexed Archives of Decolonization in the Middle East." *American Historical Review* 120, no. 3 (2015): 920–934.

Elad-Bouskila, Ami. *Modern Palestinian Literature and Culture*. London: Frank Cass, 1999.

El-Asmar, Fouzi. *To Be an Arab in Israel*. Beirut: Institute for Palestine Studies, 1978.

Elmessiri, Abdelwahhab, ed. *The Palestinian Wedding: A Bilingual Anthology of Contemporary Palestinian Resistance Poetry*. Washington, DC: Three Continents Press, 1982.

Elshakry, Marwa. *Reading Darwin in Arabic, 1860–1950*. Chicago: University of Chicago Press, 2014.

Essaid, Aida. *Zionism and Land Tenure in Mandate Palestine*. London: Routledge, 2013.

Eyal, Gil. *Disenchantment of the Orient: Expertise in Arab Affairs and the Israeli State*. Stanford, CA: Stanford University Press, 2006.

Falah, Ghazi. "Israeli 'Judaization' Policy in the Galilee." *Journal for Palestine Studies* 20, no. 4 (Summer 1990): 69–75.

Farah, Bulus. *Min al-ʿuthmaniya ila al-dawla al-ʿibriya* [From the Ottoman era to the Hebrew state]. Nazareth: Maktabat al-sawt, 1985.

Farah, Najwa Kawar. *A Continent Called Palestine: One Woman's Story*. London: SPCK, 1996.

Feiler, Gil. *From Boycott to Economic Cooperation: The Political Economy of the Arab Boycott of Israel*. London: Frank Cass, 1998.

Feiner, Shmuel. *Haskalah and History: The Emergence of a Modern Jewish Historical Consciousness*. Portland, OR: Littman Library of Jewish Civilization, 2004.

Fi mahrajan al-adab [At the Literary Festival]. Tel Aviv: Histadrut, 1958.

Fischer-Tiné, Harald, and Michael Mann. *Colonialism as Civilizing Mission: Cultural Ideology in British India*. London: Anthem Press, 2004.

Forman, Geremy. "Liberal Reform in an Illiberal Land Regime: The Land Settlement Ordinance Amendment of 1960." *Israel Studies* 15, no. 1 (2010): 47–72.

Forman, Geremy, and Alexander (Sandy) Kedar. "From Arab Land to 'Israel Lands': The Legal Dispossession of the Palestinians Displaced by Israel in the Wake of 1948." *Environment and Planning D: Society and Space* 22, no. 6 (2004): 809–830.

"French Mandate for Syria and the Lebanon." Supplement, *American Journal of International Law: Official Documents* 17, no. 3 (July 1923): 177–179.

Furani, Khaled. *Silencing the Sea: Secular Rhythms in Palestinian Poetry*. Stanford, CA: Stanford University Press, 2012.

Gallagher, Nancy. *Quakers in the Israeli-Palestinian Conflict: The Dilemmas of NGO Humanitarian Activism*. Cairo: American University in Cairo Press, 2007.

Gerber, Haim. "'Palestine' and Other Territorial Concepts in the 17th Century." *International Journal of Middle East Studies* 30, no. 4 (1998): 563–572.

———. *Remembering and Imagining Palestine: Identity and Nationalism from the Crusades to the Present*. London: Palgrave Macmillan, 2008.

Gershoni, Israel, and James P. Jankowski. *Redefining the Egyptian Nation*. Cambridge: Cambridge University Press, 2002.

Ghandour, Zeina B. *A Discourse on Domination in Mandate Palestine: Imperialism, Property, Insurgency*. London: Routledge, 2010.

Ghanem, Asʿad. *The Palestinian-Arab Minority in Israel, 1948–2000: A Political Study*. New York: State University of New York Press, 2001.

———. "The Palestinians in Israel: Political Orientation and Aspirations." *International Journal of Intercultural Relations* 26, no. 2 (2002): 135–152.

Gohar, Saddik M. "The Integration of Western Modernism in Postcolonial Arabic Literature: A Study of Abdul-Wahhab Al-Bayati's Third World Poetics." *Third World Quarterly* 29, no. 2 (2008): 375–390.

Golan, Galia. *The Czechoslovak Reform Movement*. Cambridge: Cambridge University Press, 1971.

Golan-Agnon, Daphna. "Separate but Not Equal: Discrimination against Palestinian Arab Students in Israel." *American Behavioral Scientist* 49, no. 8 (2006): 1075–1084.

Gramsci, Antonio, "The Intellectuals." In *Selections from the Prison Notebooks of Antonio Gramsci*. Edited and translated by Quintin Hoare and Geoffrey Nowell Smith, 3–23. New York: International Publishers, 2012.

Greenstein, Ran. "A Palestinian Revolutionary: Jabra Nicola and the Radical Left." *Jerusalem Quarterly* 46 (2009): 32–48.

Gribetz, Jonathan Marc. *Defining Neighbors: Religion, Race and the Early Zionist-Arab Encounter*. Princeton, NJ: Princeton University Press, 2014.

Habibi, Emile. "Ana huwa al-tifl al-qatil" [I am the fallen child]. Interview with Mahmoud Darwish and Elias Khoury. *Al-Karmal* 1, no. 1 (Winter 1981): 180–198.

———. *Kafr Qasim: Al-majzara, al-siyasa* [Kafr Qasim: The massacre, the politics]. Haifa: Dar al-ittihad li'l-nashr, 1976.

———. *The Secret Life of Saeed the Pessoptimist*. Translated by Salma Khadra Jayyusi and Trevor LeGassick. 1985. Reprint, Northampton, MA: Interlink, 2003.

Habibi, Salwa. *Al-suhuf al-israʾ iliyya* [Israeli newspapers]. Beirut: Munazzamat al-tahrir al-filastiniyya—markaz al-abhath, 1966.

Hadawi, Sami. *Israel and the Arab Minority*. New York: Arab Information Center, 1959.

Haklai, Oded. *Palestinian Ethnonationalism in Israel*. Philadelphia. University of Pennsylvania Press, 2011.

Halayhil, ʿAlaaʾ. "Samih al-Qasim: Afnaytu ʿumri fi khidmat al-qasida, wa qasidati aham min al-watan!" [Samih al-Qasim: I gave my entire life to poetry, and my poetry is more important than the nation!]. Qadita.net, September 19, 2012. http://www.qadita.net/featured/sameeh-alqasem/.

Harlow, Barbara. *Resistance Literature*. New York: Methuen, 1987.

Harrison, Olivia. *Transcolonial Maghreb: Imagining Palestine in the Era of Decolonization*. Stanford, CA: Stanford University Press, 2015.

Harte, John. "Contesting the Past in Mandate Palestine: History Teaching for Palestinian Arabs under British Rule, 1917–1948." PhD diss., School of Oriental and African Studies, 2009.

Hasan, ʿAbd al-Karim. *Qadiyat al-ard fi shiʿr Mahmoud Darwish* [The land issue in the poetry of Mahmoud Darwish]. Damascus: n.p., 1975.

Hasan, Dib ʿAli. *Mahmoud Darwish: Rihlat al-shiʿr waʾl-hayat* [Mahmoud Darwish: A journey of poetry and life]. Beirut: Dar al-manara li'l-tibaʿ waʾl-nashr, 2002.

Hazkani, Shay, and Chris Gratien. "The Politics of 1948 in Israeli Archives." Ottoman History Podcast, no. 166, July 19, 2014. http://www.ottomanhistorypodcast.com/2014/07/the-politics-of-1948-in-israeli-archives.html.

Hen-Tov, Jacob. *Communism and Zionism in Palestine during the British Mandate*. New Brunswick, NJ: Transaction Books, 2012.

Hijjawi, Sulafa. *Poetry of Resistance in Occupied Palestine*. Baghdad: Al-Jumhuriya Printing House, 1968.

Hillman, Susanne. "Of Snake-Catchers and Swamp-Drainers: Palestine and the Palestinians in Central European Zionist Discourse, 1891–1914." *Holy Land Studies*. 8, no. 1 (2009): 1–29.

Hoffman, Adina. *My Happiness Bears No Relation to Happiness: A Poet's Life in the Palestinian Century*. New Haven, CT: Yale University Press, 2009.

Hofstadter, Noam, and Lior Yavne. *Point of Access: Barriers for Public Access to Israeli Government Archives*. Akevot Institute for Israeli-Palestinian Conflict Research, April 2016. http://akevot.org.il/wp-content/uploads/2016/05/Point-of-Access-English.pdf.

Hourani, Albert. *Arabic Thought in the Liberal Age, 1798–1939*. 1962. Reprint, Cambridge: Cambridge University Press, 1983.

Hout, Shafiq al-. *My Life in the PLO: The Inside Story of the Palestinian Struggle*. Edited by Jean Said Makdisi and Martin Asser. Translated by Hader al-Hout and Laila Othman. New York: Pluto Press, 2011.

Hurani, Faysal. *Al-Jary ila al-hazima: Shahada* [Rushing to defeat: A testimony]. Ramallah: Muwatin: The Palestinian Institute for the Study of Democracy, 2001.

Husyan, Qusayy al-. *Al-mawt wa'l-hayat fi shiʿr al-muqawama* [Death and life in resistance poetry]. Beirut: Dar al-Raʾid al-ʿArabi, n.d.

Husayn, Rashid. *Diwan Rashid Husayn* [Anthology of Rashid Husayn]. Beirut: Dar al-ʿAwda, 1999.

———. *Kalam mawzun* [Weighted words]. Nazareth: Lajnat jamʿ turath Rashid Husayn, 1982.

Ibrahim, Hanna. *Shajarat al-maʿrifa: Dhikrayat shab lam yatagharrab* [Tree of knowledge: Memories of a young man who did not emigrate]. Acre: Muʾassasat al-aswar, 1996.

Ismael, Tareq Y. *The Communist Movement in Egypt, 1920–1988*. Syracuse, NY: Syracuse University Press, 1990.

———. *The Rise and Fall of the Communist Party of Iraq*. Cambridge: Cambridge University Press, 2008.

Ismael, Tareq Y., and Jacqueline S. Ismael. *The Communist Movement in Syria and Lebanon*. Gainesville: University Press of Florida, 1998.

Jamal, Amal. *Arab Minority Nationalism in Israel: The Politics of Indigeneity*. London: Routledge, 2011.

———. *The Arab Public Sphere in Israel: Media Space and Cultural Resistance*. Bloomington: Indiana University Press, 2009.

James, Leslie. *George Padmore and Decolonization from Below: Pan-Africanism, the Cold War, and the End of Empire*. New York: Springer, 2014.

Jankowski, James. *Nasser's Egypt, Arab Nationalism, and the United Arab Republic*. Boulder, CO: Lynne Rienner, 2002.

Jayyusi, Salma Khadra. "Modernist Poetry in Arabic." In *Modern Arabic Literature*, edited by Muhammad Mustafa Badawi, 132–179. Cambridge: Cambridge University Press, 1992.

———. *Trends and Movements in Modern Arabic Poetry*. 2 vols. Leiden, Netherlands: Brill, 1977.

Jiryis, Sabri. *The Arabs in Israel.* Translated by Meric Dobson. Beirut: Institute for Palestine Studies, 1969.
———. *Democratic Freedoms in Israel.* Translated by Meric Dobson. Beirut: Institute for Palestine Studies, 1972.
Johnson, Penny, and Sahar Khalifeh. "Uprising of a Novelist: Penny Johnson Interviews Sahar Khalifeh." *Women's Review of Books* 7, no. 10–11 (1990): 24.
Kabha, Mustafa, and Dan Caspi. *The Palestinian Arab In/Outsiders: Media and Conflict in Israel.* London: Valentine Mitchell, 2011.
Kadhim, Hussein N. *The Poetics of Anti-colonialism in the Arabic Qasidah.* Leiden, Netherlands: Brill, 2004.
Kadi, Laila. *Al-histadrut* [The Histadrut]. Beirut: Munazzamat al-tahrir al-filastiniyya—markaz al-abhath, 1966.
Kalisman, Hilary Falb. "Bursary Scholars at the American University of Beirut: Living and Practising Arab Unity." *British Journal of Middle Eastern Studies* 42, no. 4 (Fall 2015): 599–617.
———. "Schooling the State: Educators in Iraq, Palestine and Transjordan, c. 1890–1960." PhD diss., University of California, Berkeley, 2015.
Kamen, Charles. "After the Catastrophe I: The Arabs in Israel, 1948–51." *Middle Eastern Studies* 23, no. 4 (October 1987): 453–495.
———. "After the Catastrophe II: The Arabs in Israel, 1948–51." *Middle Eastern Studies* 24, no. 1 (January 1988): 68–109.
Kanafani, Ghassan. *Al-adab al-filastini al-muqawim taht al-ihtilal, 1948–1968* [Palestinian resistance literature under occupation, 1948–1968]. Beirut: Institute for Palestine Studies, 1968.
———. *Adab al-muqawama fi filastin al-muhtalla, 1948–1966* [Resistance literature in occupied Palestine]. Beirut: Dar al-adab, 1966.
Karkabi, Zahi. "Imil Tuma: Shaʻla mudiʼa la tantafiʼ" [Emile Tuma: A glowing flame that is not extinguished]. *Al-Jabha*, August 27, 2005. http://www.aljabha.org/?i=14628.
Karsh, Efraim. *Palestine Betrayed.* New Haven, CT: Yale University Press, 2010.
Kassab, Elizabeth Suzanne. *Contemporary Arab Thought: Cultural Critique in Comparative Perspective.* New York: Columbia University Press, 2010.
Kassis, Shawqi. "Samih al-Qasim: Equal Parts Poetry and Resistance." *Journal of Palestine Studies* 44, no. 2 (Winter 2015): 43–51.
Katsiaficas, George N. *The Imagination of the New Left: A Global Analysis of 1968.* Cambridge, MA: South End Press, 1987.
Kaufman, Ilana. *Arab National Communism in the Jewish State.* Gainesville: University Press of Florida, 1997.
Kayali, Hasan. *Arabs and Young Turks: Ottomanism, Arabism, and Islamism in the Ottoman Empire, 1908–1918.* Berkeley: University of California Press, 1997.

Kayyal, Mahmud. "'A Hesitant Dialogue with the Other': The Interactions of Arab Intellectuals with the Israeli Culture." *Israel Studies* 11, no. 2 (2006): 54–74.

Kayyali, ʿAbd al-Wahhab al-. *Al-kibutz: Al-mazaraʿ al-jamaʿiyya fi israʾ il* [The kibbutz: The cooperative farms in Israel]. Beirut: Munazzamat al-tahrir al-filastiniyya—markaz al-abhath, 1966.

Kendall, Elisabeth. "Between Politics and Literature: Journals in Alexandria and Istanbul at the End of the 19th Century." In *Modernity and Culture: From the Mediterranean to the Indian Ocean*, edited by Leila Tarazi Fawaz and Christopher Alan Bayly, 330–343. New York: Columbia University Press, 2002.

Kerr, Malcolm. *The Arab Cold War, 1958–1964*. London: Oxford University Press, 1965.

Khadr, ʿAbbas. *Adab al-Muqawama* [Resistance literature]. Cairo: Dar al-katib al-ʿarabi, 1968.

Khalidi, Rashid. "Consequences of the Suez Crisis in the Arab World." In *Suez 1956: The Crisis and Its Consequences*, edited by William Roger Louis and Roger Owen, 377–392. Oxford: Clarendon Press, 1989.

———. *The Iron Cage: The Story of the Palestinian Struggle for Statehood*. Boston: Beacon Press, 2007.

———. *Palestinian Identity: The Construction of Modern National Consciousness*. New York: Columbia University Press, 1997.

———. "Perceptions and Reality: The Arab World and the West." In *A Revolutionary Year: The Middle East in 1958*, edited by William Roger Louis and Roger Owen, 181–208. London: I. B. Tauris, 2002.

———. "The Press as a Source for Modern Arab Political History." *Arab Studies Quarterly* 3, no. 1 (Winter 1981): 22–42.

Khalidi, Rashid, Lisa Anderson, Muhammad Muslih, and Reeva S. Simon, eds. *The Origins of Arab Nationalism*. Rev. ed. New York: Columbia University Press, 1993.

Khalidi, Tarif. "Palestinian Historiography: 1900–1948." *Journal of Palestine Studies* 10, no. 3 (1981): 59–76.

Khalidi, Walid. *Dayr Yasin: Al-jumuʿah, 9 nisan/abril 1948* [Dayr Yasin: April 9, 1948]. Beirut: Muʾassasat al-dirasat al-filastiniyah, 1999.

———. "The Fall of Haifa Revisited." *Journal of Palestine Studies* 37, no. 3 (2008): 30–58.

———. *From Haven to Conquest: Readings in Zionism and the Palestine Problem until 1948*. 1971. Reprint, Washington, DC: Institute for Palestine Studies, 1987.

Khalidi, Walid, and Sharif S. Elmusa. *All That Remains: The Palestinian Villages Occupied and Depopulated by Israel in 1948*. Washington, DC: Institute for Palestine Studies, 1992.

Khalili, Laleh. *Heroes and Martyrs of Palestine: The Politics of National Commemoration*. Cambridge: Cambridge University Press, 2007.

Khatib, Husam al-. *Harakat al-tarjama al-filastiniya min al-nahda hatta awakhir al-*

qarn al-ʿishrin [The Palestinian translation movement from the Nahda to the end of the twentieth century]. Amman: Al-muʾassasa al-ʿarabiyya li'l-dirasat wa'l-nashr, 1995.

Khatib, Yusuf al-, ed. *Diwan al-watan al-muhtall* [Anthology of the occupied country]. Damascus: Dar filastin li'l-taʾlif wa'l-tarjama wa'l-nashr, 1968.

Khouri, Malik. *The Arab National Project in Youssef Chahine's Cinema*. Cairo: American University of Cairo Press, 2010.

Khuri-Makdisi, Ilham. *The Eastern Mediterranean and the Making of Global Radicalism, 1860–1914*. Berkeley: University of California Press, 2010.

Kirasirova, Masha. "The 'East' as a Category of Bolshevik and Comintern Ideology: The Arab Section of the Communist University of the Toilers of the East." *Kritika: Explorations in Russian and Eurasian History* 18, no. 1 (2017): 7–34.

Klemm, Verena. "Different Notions of Commitment (*Iltizam*) and Committed Literature (*al-adab al-multazim*) in the Literary Circles of the Mashriq." *Arabic and Middle Eastern Literatures* 3, no. 1 (2000): 51–62.

Korn, Alina. "From Refugees to Infiltrators: Constructing Political Crime in Israel in the 1950s." *International Journal of the Sociology of Law* 31, no. 1 (2003): 1–22.

Kyle, Keith. *Suez*. London: Weidenfeld & Nicolson, 1991.

Lahav, Pnina. "Israel's Press Law." In *Press Law in Modern Democracies: A Comparative Study*, edited by Pnina Lahav, 265–313. New York: Longman, 1985.

Landau, Jacob. *The Arabs in Israel: A Political Study*. London: Oxford University Press, 1969.

Laron, Guy. "'Logic Dictates That They May Attack When They Feel They Can Win': The 1955 Czech-Egyptian Arms Deal, the Egyptian Army, and Israeli Intelligence." *Middle East Journal* 63, no. 1 (2009): 69–84.

Laskier, Michael M. "Israel and Algeria amid French Colonialism and the Arab-Israeli Conflict, 1954–1978." *Israel Studies* 6, no. 2 (2001): 1–32.

Laugesen, Amanda. "Books for the World: American Book Programs in the Developing World, 1948–1968." In *Pressing the Fight: Print, Propaganda, and the Cold War*, edited by Greg Barnhisel and Catherine Turner, 126–144. Amherst: University of Massachusetts Press, 2010.

Lesch, Ann Mosely. *Arab Politics in Palestine, 1917–1939*. Ithaca, NY: Cornell University Press, 1979.

Levey, Zach. "Israel's Strategy in Africa, 1961–1967." *International Journal of Middle East Studies* 36, no. 1 (2004): 71–87.

Levy, Lital. *Poetic Trespass: Writing between Hebrew and Arabic in Israel/Palestine*. Princeton, NJ: Princeton University Press, 2014.

Lockman, Zachary. *Comrades and Enemies: Arab and Jewish Workers in Palestine, 1906–1948*. Berkeley: University of California Press, 1996.

Lorch, Netanel. "An Israeli View of the Third World." In *Israel in the Third World*, edited by Michael Curtis and Susan Auerlia Gitelson, 27–30. New Brunswick, NJ: Transaction Books, 1976.

Louër, Laurence. *To Be an Arab in Israel.* New York: Columbia University Press, 2007.

Louis, William Roger. *Ends of British Imperialism: The Scramble for Empire, Suez, and Decolonization.* London: I. B. Tauris, 2006.

Louis, William Roger, and Roger Owen, eds. *A Revolutionary Year: The Middle East in 1958.* Washington, DC: Woodrow Wilson Center Press, 2002.

Louis, William Roger, and Avi Shlaim, eds. *The 1967 Arab-Israeli War: Origins and Consequences.* Cambridge: Cambridge University Press, 2012.

Love, Kennett. *Suez: The Twice-Fought War.* New York: McGraw-Hill, 1969.

Lubin, Alex. *Geographies of Liberation: The Making of an Afro-Arab Political Imaginary.* Chapel Hill: University of North Carolina Press, 2014.

Lustick, Ian. *Arabs in a Jewish State: Israel's Control of a National Minority.* Austin: University of Texas Press, 1980.

Mada al-Carmel. *The Haifa Declaration.* May 2007. http://mada-research.org/en/files/2007/09/haifaenglish.pdf.

Magal, Aryeh. "*Al-Mirsad*: Mapam's Voice in Arabic, Arab Voice in Mapam." *Israel Studies* 15, no. 1 (Spring 2010): 115–146.

Makhoul, Manar. "Ha ezrahim ha palstiniyim shel yisraʾel: Ha teptahut shel shem" [Palestinian citizens of Israel: The development of a name]. In *Ha palstiniyim be yisraʾel: ʿIyunim be historiah, politikah ubehavarah* [Palestinians in Israel: Studies in history, politics, and society], vol. 2, edited by Areej Sabbagh-Khoury and Nadim N. Rouhana, 5–16. Haifa: Mada al-Carmel, 2015.

Malley, Robert. *The Call from Algeria: Third Worldism, Revolution, and the Turn to Islam.* Berkeley: University of California Press, 1996.

Marʿi, Sami Khalil. *Arab Education in Israel.* Syracuse, NY: Syracuse University Press, 1978.

Masalha, Nur. *Catastrophe Remembered: Palestine, Israel and the Internal Refugees.* London: Zed Books, 2005.

Mattar, Philip. *The Mufti of Jerusalem: Al-Hajj Amin al-Husayni and the Palestinian National Movement.* New York: Columbia University Press, 1992.

Matthews, Weldon. *Confronting an Empire, Constructing a Nation: Arab Nationalists and Popular Politics in Mandate Palestine.* London: I. B. Tauris, 2006.

Matusevich, Maxim. "Harlem Globe-Trotters: Black Sojourners in Stalin's Soviet Union." In *The Harlem Renaissance Revisited: Politics, Arts and Letters*, edited by Jeffrey O .G. Ogbar, 211–244 . Baltimore: Johns Hopkins University Press, 2010.

McCarthy, Justin. *The Population of Palestine: Population History and Statistics in the Late Ottoman Period and the Mandate.* New York: Columbia University Press, 1990.

Meouchi, Nadine, and Peter Sluglett. *The British and French Mandates in Comparative Perspectives / Les Mandats français et anglais dans une perspective.* Leiden, Netherlands: Brill, 2004.

Miller, Ylana. *Government and Society in Rural Palestine, 1920–1948.* 1985. Reprint, Austin: University of Texas Press, 2014.

Minns, Amina, and Nadia Hijab. *Citizens Apart: A Portrait of the Palestinians in Israel.* London: I. B. Tauris, 1990.

Moreh, Shmuel. *Fihrist al-matbuʿat al-ʿarabiyya fi israʾil, 1948–1972* [Index of Arabic publications in Israel, 1948–1972]. Jerusalem: Hebrew University Press, 1974.

Moreh, Shmuel, and Mahmud al-ʿAbbasi. *Tarajim wa-athar fi'l-adab al-ʿarabi fi israʾil, 1948–1986* [Biographies and writings in Arabic literature in Israel, 1948–1966]. 3rd ed. Shafa ʿAmr: Dar al-mashriq li'l-tarjama wa'l-tibaʿa wa'l-nashr, 1987.

Morris, Benny. *The Birth of the Palestinian Refugee Problem Revisited.* Cambridge: Cambridge University Press, 2004.

———. "The Crystallization of Israeli Policy against a Return of the Arab Refugees: April–December, 1948." *Journal of Israeli History* 6, no. 1 (1985): 85–118.

———. *Israel's Border Wars, 1949–1956.* Oxford: Clarendon, 1993.

———. *Righteous Victims: A History of the Zionist-Arab Conflict, 1881–1998.* New York: Knopf, 2000.

Murqus, Nimr. *Aqwa min al-nasyan: Risala ila ibnati* [Stronger than oblivion: A letter to my daughter]. Tarshiha: Matbaʿat makhul wa-hazbun, 2000.

Musallam, Adnan A. *Folded Pages from Local Palestinian History in the 20th Century: Developments in Politics, Society, Press and Thought in Bethlehem in the British Era, 1917–1948.* Bethlehem: WIAM: Palestine Conflict Resolution Center, 2002.

Muslih, Muhammad Y. *The Origins of Palestinian Nationalism.* New York: Columbia University Press, 1988.

Nabulsi, Shakir. *Majnun al-turab: Dirasa fi shiʿr wa-fikr Mahmoud Darwish* [Obsessed with the soil: A study of the poetry and thought of Mahmoud Darwish]. Beirut: Al-Muʾassasa al-ʿarabiyya li'l-dirasat wa'l-nashr, 1987.

Nahas, Dunia. *The Israeli Communist Party.* London: Croon Helm, 1976.

Najjar, Aida Ali. "The Arabic Press and Nationalism in Palestine, 1920–1948." PhD diss., Syracuse University, 1975.

———. *Sahafat filastin wa'l-haraka al-wataniyya fi nisf qarn, 1900–1948* [The Palestinian press and the nationalist movement during a half century, 1900–1948]. Beirut: Al-muʾassasa al-ʿarabiyya li'l-dirasat wa'l-nashr, 2005.

Naqqara, Hanna. "Mudhakkirat" [Memoirs]. In *Hanna Naqqara: Muhami al-ard wa'l-shaʿb* [Hanna Naqqara: Attorney of the land and the people], edited by Hanna Ibrahim. Acre: Manshurat dar al-aswar, 1985.

Naqqash, Rajaʾ al-. *Mahmoud Darwish: Shaʿir al-ard al-muhtalla* [Mahmoud Darwish: Poet of the occupied land]. Cairo: Dar al-hilal, 1971.

Nassar, Maha. "Affirmation and Resistance: Press, Poetry and the Formation of National Identity among Palestinian Citizens of Israel, 1948–1967." PhD diss., University of Chicago, 2006.

———. "The Marginal as Central: *Al-Jadid* and the Development of a Palestinian Public Sphere, 1953–1970." *Middle East Journal of Culture and Communication* 3, no. 3 (November 2010): 333–351.

———. "'My Struggle Embraces Every Struggle': Palestinians in Israel and Solidarity with Afro-Asian Liberation Movements." *Arab Studies Journal* 22, no. 1 (Spring 2014): 74–101.

———. "Palestinian Citizens of Israel and the Discourse on the Right of Return, 1948–59." *Journal of Palestine Studies* 40, no. 4 (Summer 2011): 45–60.

Natur, Salman. "Taht al-mijhar: Ashab al-bilad (2)" [Under the microscope: Owners of the country, part 2]. Al-Jazeera, October 28, 2010. https://www.youtube.com/watch?v=jHpiFtq4q-Y.

Nijm, Muhammad Yusuf. *Dar al-muʿallimin waʾl-kulliya al-ʿarabiya fi bayt al-maqdis* [The (Men's) Teacher (Training) College and Arab College in Jerusalem]. Beirut: Dar sadir, 2007.

Noorani, Yaseen. "Redefining Resistance: Counterhegemony, the Repressive Hypothesis and the Case of Arabic Modernism." In *Counterhegemony in the Colony and Postcolony*, edited by John Chalcraft and Yaseen Noorani, 75–99. London: Palgrave Macmillan, 2007.

Nordbruch, Götz. "Bread, Freedom, Independence: Opposition to Nazi Germany in Lebanon and Syria and the Struggle for a Just Order." *Comparative Studies of South Asia, Africa and the Middle East* 28, no. 3 (2008): 416–427.

———. "Defending the French Revolution during World War II: Raif Khoury and the Intellectual Challenge of Nazism in the Levant." *Mediterranean Historical Review* 21, no. 2 (2006): 219–238.

Pappé, Ilan. *The Ethnic Cleansing of Palestine*. Oxford: Oneworld, 2006.

———. *The Forgotten Palestinians*. New Haven, CT: Yale University Press, 2011.

———. *The Making of the Arab-Israeli Conflict, 1947–1951*. London: I. B. Tauris, 1992.

———. "An Uneasy Coexistence: Arabs and Jews in the First Decade of Statehood." In *Israel: The First Decade of Independence*, edited by S. Ilan Troen and Noah Lucas, 617–658. Albany: State University of New York Press, 1995.

Peled, Alisa. "The Other Side of 1948: The Forgotten Benevolence of Bechor Shalom Shitrit and the Ministry of Minority Affairs." *Israel Affairs* 8, no. 3 (2002): 84–103.

Peleg, Ilan, and Dov Waxman. *Israel's Palestinians: The Conflict Within*. Cambridge: Cambridge University Press, 2011.

Penslar, Derek. *Israel in History: The Jewish State in Comparative Perspective*. London: Routledge, 2008.

Peres, Yochanan, Avishai Ehrlik, and Nira Yuval-Davis. "National Education for

Arab Youth in Israel: A Comparative Analysis of Curriculum." *Jewish Journal of Sociology* 12, no. 2 (1970): 147–163.

Peretz, Don. "Arab Palestine: Phoenix or Phantom?" *Foreign Affairs* 48 (January 1970): 322–333.

———. "Early State Policy towards the Arab Population, 1948–1955." In *New Perspectives on Israeli History: The Early Years of the State*, edited by Laurence J. Silberstein, 82–102. New York: New York University Press, 1991.

———. *Israel and the Palestine Arabs*. Washington, DC: Middle East Institute, 1958.

Podeh, Elie. "Demonizing the Other: Israeli Perceptions of Nasser and Nasserism." In *Rethinking Nasserism: Revolution and Historical Memory in Modern Egypt*, edited by Elie Podeh and Onn Winkler, 72–99. Gainesville: University Press of Florida, 2004.

Polsgrove, Carol. *Ending British Rule in Africa: Writers in a Common Cause*. Manchester, UK: Manchester University Press, 2009.

Prashad, Vijay. *The Darker Nations: A People's History of the Third World*. New York: New Press, 2008.

Qahwaji, Habib. *Al-ʿarab fi zill al-ihtilal al-israʾ ili mundhu 1948* [Arabs in the shadow of Israeli occupation since 1948]. Beirut: Munazzamat al-tahrir al-filastiniyya—markaz al-abhath, 1972.

———. *Al-qissa al-kamila li-harakat al-ard* [The complete story of the Ard movement]. Jerusalem: Dar al-ʿArabi, 1978.

Qasim, Samih al-. *Aghani al-durub* [Songs of the paths]. Nazareth: Matbaʿat al-hakim, 1964.

———. "Hayati, Qadiyati, Shiʿri" [My life, my cause, my poetry]. *Al-Tariq* 27, no. 10–11 (November–December 1968): 70–79.

———. *Innaha mujarrad minfada: Sira* [It is only an ashtray: A life]. Haifa: Dar raya li'l-nashr, 2011.

———. *Mawakib al-Shams* [Processions of the sun]. Nazareth: Matbaʿat al-hakim, 1958.

Quigley, John. *The Six-Day War and Israeli Self-Defense: Questioning the Legal Basis for Preventive War*. Cambridge: Cambridge University Press, 2012.

Rabinowitz, Dan. "Oriental Othering and National Identity: A Review of Early Israeli Anthropological Studies of Palestinians." *Identities: Global Studies in Culture and Power* 9 (2002): 305–324.

———. *Overlooking Nazareth: The Ethnography of Exclusion in the Galilee*. Cambridge: Cambridge University Press, 1997.

Raz, Avi. *The Bride and the Dowry: Israel, Jordan, and the Palestinians in the Aftermath of the June 1967 War*. New Haven, CT: Yale University Press, 2012.

———. "The Generous Peace Offer That Was Never Offered: The Israeli Cabinet Resolution of June 19, 1967." *Diplomatic History* 37, no. 1 (2013): 85–108.

Reiter, Yitzhak. *National Minority, Regional Majority: Palestinian Arabs versus Jews in Israel*. Syracuse, NY: Syracuse University Press, 2009.

Rejwan, Nissim. *Outsider in the Promised Land: An Iraqi Jew in Israel*. Austin: University of Texas Press, 2006.

Roberts, Nicholas. "Rethinking the Status Quo: The British and Islam in Palestine, 1917–1929." PhD diss., New York University, 2010.

Robinson, Shira. *Citizen Strangers: Palestinians and the Birth of Israel's Liberal Settler State*. Stanford, CA: Stanford University Press, 2013.

———. "Local Struggle, National Struggle: Palestinian Responses to the Kafr Qasim Massacre and Its Aftermath, 1956–66." *International Journal of Middle East Studies* 35 (2003): 395–412.

Robson, Laura. *Colonialism and Christianity in Mandate Palestine*. Austin: University of Texas Press, 2011.

———. "The Making of Palestinian Christian Womanhood: Gender, Class, and Community in Mandate Palestine." *Journal of Levantine Studies* 4, no. 1 (2014): 41–63.

Roby, Bryan K. *The Mizrahi Era of Rebellion: Israel's Forgotten Civil Rights Struggle, 1948–1966*. Syracuse, NY: Syracuse University Press, 2015.

Rogan, Eugene, and Avi Shlaim, eds. *The War for Palestine: Rewriting the History of 1948*. Cambridge: Cambridge University Press, 2001.

Rouhana, Nadim. *Palestinian Citizens in an Ethnic Jewish State*. New Haven, CT: Yale University Press, 1997.

Rutter, Nick. "Look Left, Drive Right: Internationalisms at the 1968 World Youth Festival." In *The Socialist Sixties: Crossing Borders in the Second World*, edited by Anne E. Gorsuch and Diane P. Koenker, 193–212. Bloomington: Indiana University Press, 2013.

Sabbagh, Hani Raji. "Arabic Poetry in Israel: The Developing Expressions of the Identity and Aspirations of the Arabs in Israel." PhD diss., University of Michigan, 1986.

Saʿdi, Ahmad. "Modernization as an Explanatory Discourse." *British Journal of Middle Eastern Studies* 24, no. 1 (1997): 25–48.

Said, Edward. *The World, the Text and the Critic*. Cambridge, MA: Harvard University Press, 1983.

Salim, Jamal, and ʿAbd al-Sattar al-Tawila. "A comedy at the Sofia festival" [*Mahzala fi mahrajan sufia*]. *Ruz al-Yusuf* 2096 (August 12, 1968): 6–7.

Samir. *Forget Baghdad*. DVD. Directed by Samir. Seattle, WA: AFD/Typecast, 2003.

Sand, Shlomo. *The Invention of the Jewish People*. London: Verso, 2009.

Sayigh, Fayiz, *Al-diblumasiyya al-sahyuniyya* [Zionist diplomacy]. Beirut: Munazzamat al-tahrir al-filastiniyya—markaz al-abhath, 1966.

———. *Mihnat al-ʿarab fi'l-ard al-muqaddasah* [The persecution of Arabs in the Holy Land]. [Cairo]: Dar al-tibaʿa al-fanniyya, 1956.

Sayigh, Yezid. *Armed Struggle and the Search for State: The Palestinian National Movement, 1949–1993*. Oxford: Oxford University Press, 1997.

Schumann, Christoph, ed. *Liberal Thought in the Eastern Mediterranean: Late 19th Century until the 1960s*. Leiden, Netherlands: Brill, 2008.

———, ed. *Nationalism and Liberal Thought in the Arab East: Ideology and Practice*. London: Routledge, 2010.

Schwarz, Walter. *The Arabs in Israel*. London: Faber & Faber, 1959.

Scott, David. *Conscripts of Modernity: The Tragedy of Colonial Enlightenment*. Durham, NC: Duke University Press, 2004.

———. *Refashioning Futures: Criticism after Postcoloniality*. Princeton, NJ: Princeton University Press, 1999.

———. "The Temporality of Generations: Dialogue, Tradition, Criticism." *New Literary History* 45, no. 2 (Spring 2014): 157–181.

Seale, Patrick. *The Struggle for Syria: A Study of Post-war Arab Politics, 1945–1958*. London: Oxford University Press, 1966.

Segev, Tom. *1949: The First Israelis*. 1986. Reprint, New York: Owl Books, 1998.

Segre, D. V. "The Philosophy and Practice of Israel's International Cooperation." In *Israel in the Third World*, edited by Michael Curtis and Susan Auerlia Gitelson, 7–25. New Brunswick, NJ: Transaction Books, 1976.

Seikaly, May. "Haifa at the Crossroads: An Outpost of the New World Order." In *Modernity and Culture from the Mediterranean to the Indian Ocean*, edited by Leila Tarazi Fawaz and C. A. Bayley, 96–111. New York: Columbia University Press, 2002.

Seikaly, Sherene. *Men of Capital: Scarcity and Economy in Mandate Palestine*. Stanford, CA: Stanford University Press, 2016.

Sela, Avraham. *The Decline of the Arab-Israeli Conflict: Middle East Politics and the Quest for Regional Order*. Albany: State University of New York Press, 2012.

Senghor, Leopold. "Some Thoughts on Africa: A Continent in Development." *International Affairs* 38, no. 2 (1962), 189–190.

Shafir, Gershon. *Land, Labor and the Origins of the Israeli-Palestinian Conflict, 1882–1914*. Berkeley: University of California Press, 1996.

Shakour, Adel. "Arab Authors in Israel Writing in Hebrew: Fleeting Fashion or Persistent Phenomenon?" *Language Problems & Language Planning* 37, no. 1 (2013): 1–17.

Shammas, Anton. "The Morning After." *New York Review of Books* 35, no. 14 (1988): 47–52.

Shemesh, Moshe. *The Palestinian Entity, 1959–1974: Arab Politics and the PLO*. London: Psychology Press, 1988.

Shepard, Todd. *The Invention of Decolonization: The Algerian War and the Remaking of France*. Ithaca, NY: Cornell University Press, 2008.

Shlaim, Avi. *The Iron Wall: Israel and the Arab World*. New York: W. W. Norton, 2001.
Shneer, David. *Yiddish and the Creation of Soviet Jewish Culture: 1918–1930*. Cambridge: Cambridge University Press, 2004.
Shohat, Ella. "Sephardim in Israel: Zionism from the Standpoint of Its Jewish Victims." *Cultural Politics* 11 (1997): 39–68.
Shukri, Ghali. *Adab al-muqawama* [Resistance literature]. Cairo: Dar al-maʿarif, 1970.
Sidqi, Najati. *Mudhakkirat Najati Sidqi* [Najati Sidqi's memoirs]. Edited by Hanna Abu Hanna. Beirut: Institute for Palestine Studies, 2001.
Slyomovics, Susan. *The Object of Memory: Arab and Jew Narrate the Palestinian Village*. Philadelphia: University of Pennsylvania Press, 1998.
Smethurst, James Edward. *The New Red Negro: The Literary Left and African-American Poetry, 1930–1946*. New York: Oxford University Press, 1999.
Smith, Charles D. "Review of Efraim Karsh's *Palestine Betrayed*." *Middle East Journal* 65, no. 1 (Winter 2011): 155–158.
Smooha, Sammy. *Arabs and Jews in Israel*. Vol. 1, *Conflicting and Shared Attitudes in a Divided Society*. Boulder, CO: Westview, 1989.
———. *The Orientation and Politicization of the Arab Minority in Israel*. Haifa: University of Haifa Press, 1984.
Snir, Reuven. "Arabic Journalism as a Vehicle for Enlightenment: Iraqi Jews and the Arabic Press during the Nineteenth and Twentieth Centuries." *Journal of Modern Jewish Studies* 6, no. 3 (November 2007): 219–237.
———. "'Forget Baghdad!': The Clash of Literary Narratives among Iraqi-Jews in Israel." *Orientalia Suecana* 53 (2004): 143–163.
———. "'Till Spring Comes': Arabic and Hebrew Literary Debates among Iraqi-Jews in Israel (1950–2000)." *Shofar: An Interdisciplinary Journal of Jewish Studies* 24, no. 2 (2006): 92–123.
Snir, Reuven, and Susan Einbinder. "'We Were like Those Who Dream': Iraqi-Jewish Writers in Israel in the 1950s." *Prooftexts* 11, no. 2 (May 1991): 153–173.
Somekh, Sasson. *Life after Baghdad: Memoirs of an Arab-Jew in Israel, 1950–2000*. Sussex, UK: Academic Press, 2012.
———. "'Reconciling Two Great Loves': The First Jewish-Arab Literary Encounter in Israel." *Israel Studies* 4, no. 1 (1999): 1–21.
Somel, Selçuk Akşin. *The Modernization of Public Education in the Ottoman Empire, 1839–1908: Islamization, Autocracy, and Discipline*. Leiden, Netherlands: Brill, 2001.
Sonn, Tamara. *Interpreting Islam: Bandali Jawzi's Islamic Intellectual History*. Oxford: Oxford University Press, 1996.
Sorek, Tamir. *Palestinian Commemoration in Israel: Calendars, Monuments, and Martyrs*. Stanford, CA: Stanford University Press, 2015.

Spring, Joel. *Pedagogies of Globalization: The Rise of the Educational Security State.* London: Routledge, 2006.

Stanton, Andrea. "Part of Imperial Communication: British-Governed Radio in the Middle East, 1934–1949." *Media History* 19, no. 4 (2013): 421–435.

———. *"This Is Jerusalem Calling": State Radio in Mandate Palestine.* Austin: University of Texas Press, 2013.

Stillman, Norman. *The Jews of Arab Lands in Modern Times.* Philadelphia: Jewish Publication Society, 2003.

Stora, Benjamin. *Algeria, 1830–2000: A Short History.* Ithaca, NY: Cornell University Press, 2001.

Suleiman, Yasir. *The Arabic Language and National Identity: A Study in Ideology.* Edinburgh: Edinburgh University Press, Edinburgh, 2003.

———. *Arabic, Self and Identity: A Study in Conflict and Displacement.* Oxford: Oxford University Press, 2011.

Suri, Jeremi. *Power and Protest: Global Revolution and the Rise of Détente.* Cambridge, MA: Harvard University Press, 2009.

Swedenburg, Ted. *Memories of Revolt: The 1936–1939 Rebellion and the Palestinian National Past.* 1995. Reprint, Fayetteville: University of Arkansas Press, 2003.

Tibawi, Abdul Latif. *Arab Education in Mandatory Palestine: A Study of Three Decades of British Administration.* London: Luzac, 1956.

Torstrick, Rebecca. *The Limits of Coexistence: Identity Politics in Israel.* Ann Arbor: University of Michigan Press, 2000.

Tripp, Charles. "Iraq and the 1948 War." In *The War for Palestine: Rewriting the History of 1948*, edited by Eugene Rogan and Avi Shlaim, 125–149. Cambridge: Cambridge University Press, 2007.

Tubi, Tawfiq. *Masiratuhu* [His journey]. Haifa: Dar al-Raya, 2012. http://www.aljabha.org/files/tobi-book.pdf.

Tuma, Emile. *Yawmiyat shaʿb: Thalathun ʿaman ʿala al-ittihad* [Journal of a people: Thirty years of al-Ittihad]. Haifa: Matbaʿat al-ittihad al-taʿawuniyah, 1974.

Tuqan, Fadwa. *Al-rihlatu al-asʿab: Sira dhatiyya* [The most difficult journey: An autobiography]. Amman: Dar al-shuruq li'l-nashr wa'l-tawziʿ, 1993.

Tuqan, Ibrahim. *Diwan Ibrahim Tuqan* [Ibrahim Tuqan's poetry collection]. Beirut: Dar al-masira, 1984.

Violations of Human Rights in Israel. New York: Arab Information Center, 1961.

Weingrod, Alex. "Styles of Ethnic Adaptation: Interpreting Iraqi and Moroccan Settlement in Israel." In *Israel: The First Decade of Independence*, edited by Ilan S. Troen and Noah Lucas, 523–542. Albany: State University of New York Press, 1995.

Wildangel, René. "More Than the Mufti: Other Arab-Palestinian Voices on Nazi Germany, 1933–45 and Their Postwar Narratives." In *Arab Responses to Fascism and*

Nazism: Attraction and Repulsion, edited by Israel Gershoni, 101–126. Austin: University of Texas Press, 2014.

Wilder, Gary. *Freedom Time: Negritude, Decolonization and the Future of the World*. Durham, NC: Duke University Press, 2015.

Williams, Raymond. *Culture and Materialism*. 1980. Reprint, London: Verso, 2005.

Yaghi, ʿAbd al-Rahman. *Al-adab al-filastini al-hadith* [Contemporary Palestinian literature]. [Cairo]: Dar al-kitab al-ʿarabi, 1969.

———. *Fi'l-adab al-filastini al-hadith qabla al-nakba wa baʿdaha* [On contemporary Palestinian literature before the Nakba and after]. Kuwait City, Kuwait: Sharikat Kazima li'l-Nashr wa'l-Tarjama wa'l-Tawziʿ, 1982.

———. *Shiʿr al-ard al-muhtalla fi'l-sittinat: Dirasa fi'l-madamin* [Poetry of the occupied land during the sixties: A content analysis]. Kuwait City, Kuwait: Sharikat kazima li'l-nashr wa'l-tarjama wa'l-tawziʿ, 1983.

Yaqub, Salim. *Containing Arab Nationalism: The Eisenhower Doctrine and the Middle East*. Chapel Hill: University of North Carolina Press, 2004.

Yawmiyat al-filastiniyya, al- [Palestinian journal]. Beirut: Markaz al-abhath al-filastiniyya, 1965–1970.

Zayn al-Din, ʿAbbas. "Memories across Sixty Years: With Mahmoud Darwish under a Single Tent." *Al-Jabha*, March 26, 2010. www.aljabha.org/index.asp?i=49902.

Zayyad, Tawfiq. *Ashiddu ʿala aydikum* [I pull on your hands]. 2nd ed. Beirut: Dar al-ʿAwda, 1969.

———. *Diwan Tawfiq Zayyad* [Poetry collection of Tawfiq Zayyad]. Beirut: Dar al-ʿawda, 1985.

———. *Al-sira al-dhatiya, 1929–94* [Autobiography, 1929–94]. [Nazareth]: Mu'assasat Tawfiq Zayyad, 1994.

Zelkovitz, Ido. *Students and Resistance in Palestine: Books, Guns and Politics*. London: Routledge, 2014.

Zilbershats, Yaffa. "International Law and the Palestinian Right of Return to the State of Israel." In *Israel and the Palestinian Refugees*, edited by Eyal Benvenisti, Chaim Gans, and Sari Hanafi, 191–218. Berlin: Springer, 2007.

Zureik, Elia. *The Palestinians in Israel: A Study in Internal Colonialism*. London: Routledge & Kegan Paul, 1979.

INDEX

Page numbers in *italics* indicate illustrations. The prefix al- is suppressed for alphabetical sorting purposes; thus Sami al-Qasim will be found in the Qs.

al-ʿAbbasi, ʿIsam, 74, 77, 79, 90, 109, 211n138, 212n142
ʿAbbas, Ihsan, 141, 194n2
ʿAbbud, Marun, 16, 26, 58, 107
Abd al-Fattah, Mahmud, 211n138
ʿAbd al-Quddus, Ihsan, 109
Absentee Property Law (1950), 54
Abu Ghazaleh, Adnan, 200n131
Abu Hanna, Hanna: adaptation of resistance strategies by, 45; on Algerian independence, 92; on Arab-Jewish relations, 74; on Ard movement, 103; Siham Daoud compared, 57; Darwish's departure from Israel and, 177; June 1967 war and, 156; at Khalidi Library, Jerusalem, 121n200; League of Arab Poets and, 74; leftist discourse, exposure to, 37, 39, 40; Mandate period shaping, 18, 24; in *Nakba,* 43, 44; on Gamal Abdel Nasser, 83; on pan-Arab nationalists versus communists, 96–97; poetry of, 33–34, 67, 70, 87, 89, 92–93, 109; at social clubs, 36; as student radio broadcaster, 35, 37; at Tel Aviv brotherhood festival, 74, 211n135
Abu al-Hayja family, 87, 214n48
Abu Rabiʿ, Ibrahim, 158
Abu Salma (ʿAbd al-Karim Karmi), 31, 32–33, 36, 41, 67, 145, 177, *178,* 200–201n134

Abu Saʿud, ʿAdnan, 59, 90
Abu-Lughod, Ibrahim, 8
al-Adab (Literatures), 66, 105, 106, 141, 142, 156, 160, 161, 167
Adunis (Syrian critic and poet), 173, 174
al-Afghani, Jamal al-Din, 62–63
African Americans, 37, 68, 189
African nations, independence in, 108
Agassi, Eliahu, 93, 120
al-Ahram, 105, 156
al-Ahwani, ʿAbd al-ʿAziz, 161
Algerian war of independence, 2, 78, 79, 90, 92, 93, 108–109, 121–122
ʿAli ʿUthman, 30
ʿAli, Taha Muhammad, 107
Amin, Jalal, 150
anticolonialism. *See* decolonizing discourse
al-ʿAqqad, ʿAbbas, 16, 35, 58
Arab, definition of, 61–62
Arab Book Company, 105, 106
Arab citizens of Israel. *See* Palestinians in Israel
Arab College, Jerusalem, 34–35, 36, 39, 194n2, 198n76, 200n121
Arab East, role of Palestine in, 19–20
Arab Idol, 187, 231n12
Arab Information Center (AIC), 110
Arab League, 5, 110, 139–140, 141, 153
Arab modernism, 12, 20, 50, 57–60, 158

257

Arab National Movement (ANM), 99, 101, 102, 225n104
Arab nationalism. *See* pan-Arab nationalism
Arab Revolt (1936-1939), 15, 30, 32, 33, 37–38, 68, 198n91
Arab Summit (1964), 130, 138
Arab views of Palestinians in Israel: Arab knowledge about Israel, recognition of need for, 157–158; awareness of resistance literature inside Palestine, 141–144, 146; in decolonizing period, 109–111; "discovery" of resisting Palestinians by other Arabs, 7; disputes about definition of Palestinian resistance and, 147–149, 184; from early 1970s to present day, 184–189; June 1967 war and aftermath, 7, 147, 148, 162, 176–177; after Sofia Festival, 170–172; at Sofia Festival, 146–147, 162, 164–170, 183; suspicion, hostility, and lack of knowledge, 41–44, 49–52, 183–184; at World Youth Festivals generally, 1–3, 7, 10, 80, 109, 162
"The Arab Writer and the Battle against Zionism" (Beirut Conference, 1968), 159, 161
Arab Writers' Conference, 106–107
Arabic, use of, 11–12
Arabism, 20, 79
Arab-Jewish relations: differing views Palestinians in and outside of Israel on, 169–170; ethno-religious strife, rejection of framework of, 17, 38, 41, 45; in mid-1960s, 122, 132; NLL vision of, 41; in post-*Nakba* period, 50–51, 71–75
Arafat, Yasser, 186
archival materials, Palestinian, 9, 105, 192–193n28, 193n30
Ard movement: awareness of, outside Israel, 147; in decolonizing period, 98, 99–105, 104, 112; exile of cofounders from Israel, 148, 183; in mid-1960s (as Ard Group), 132–136, 137, 139–141, 144, 182–183, 223n67, 224n95
armed resistance movement, 7, 99, 147–148, 151–152, 157, 169, 175, 230n108
Armistice Lines (Green Line), 4
El-Asmar, Fouzi, 84, 105, 109, 112
Assaf, Michael, 46–47, 49, 53, 54, 88
al-ʿAzm, Sadiq Jalal, 158

Baghdad Pact, 82, 94, 213n18
Bakdash, Khalid, 37, 38–39, 42, 95
Balfour, Arthur James, and Balfour Declaration (1917), 23–25, 27
Baha al-Din, Ahmad, 109, 158
Bandung Conference, 82, 83, 87
Baransi, Salih, 102, 132, 218n138
al-Bayati, ʿAbd al-Wahhab, 66–67, 117, 121
Baydas, Khalil, 21
Begin, Menachem, 167
Ben, Alexander, 211n135
Ben-Gurion, David, 83, 84
Binyamin, Zaki, 211n138
Bishara, Azmi, 185, 231–232n18
bookstores, 35, 39–40, 51, 200n121
Borla, Yehuda, 211n135
Bouhired, Djamila, 2, 92, 108, 191n3
Boupacha, Jamila, 108
bourgeois nationalism, 16, 36, 40, 74
Boy Scouts, 28, 29
boycott, divestment, and sanctions (BDS) platform, 187
Breasted, Henry, 27
British Mandate, 15–45; Arab Revolt (1936-1939), 15, 30, 32, 33, 37–38, 68, 198n91; Balfour Declaration (1917) and League of Nations, 23–24, 197nn58–59; decolonizing discourse under, 15–18, 22–24; education under, 18, 24–28, 194n2, 197n63; intellectual life in 1940s Palestine, 34–36; interwar years, importance of, 15–18; leftist discourse, emergence of, 18, 20–21, 36–

39, 44–45; organizations, role of, 5, 18, 38–41; press and print material, 18, 20–22, 28–31; riots (1929), 29, 32, 198n85, 199n106; social clubs and radio programming, 18, 35–36, 200n131

Carmiel, 123, 126, 185
Césaire, Aimé, 13, 212n13
Charles, Asselin, 22
Citizenship Law (1952), 4
Cold War, 100, 116, 119, 140
colonialism. *See* decolonizing discourse
committed literature, 66, 80, 90, 105, 107, 117
communism and communists: Anglo-American imperialism, denunciations of, 54–57, 76; Marxism, 15, 38, 40, 44, 62–63, 66, 69, 70, 102, 117, 172, 173; pan-Arab nationalism versus, 81, 94–98; Third International (Comintern), 36, 37, 38, 201n143. *See also* leftist discourse; *specific communist parties*
Communist Party of Israel (CPI): Arabic and Hebrew, use of, 11–12; Ard movement and, 99–100, 102–103, 105; in decolonizing period, 78–79, 81, 82–83, 85, 86, 90, 92, 108, 109, 112–113; on definition of Arab, 61; on education, 60–61; May Day rally (1958), Nazareth, 78–79, 81, 90; in mid-1960s, 114, 115, 118, 119–120, 122–123, 126, 127, 131, 133–134, 136, 137; on modernism and modernization, 58; number of members in, 205n19; pan-Arab nationalists versus, 81, 95–98; in post-*Nakba* period, 49–51, 52, 55–57, 64, 67–69, 71–73, 75, 76; press and publications, 6, 90, 104, 105, 115, 207n50, 208n61; split into Jewish and Palestinian parties, 137; state framework, working within, 100; strategies of resistance, 182; strategies of resistance used by, 5; at World Festival of Youth and Students, 2; at World Youth Festivals, 163
Communist University of the Toilers of the East (KUTV), 37, 201n143, 202n166
Cullen, Countee, 68
cultural production. *See* literature; poetry

al-Dajani, Ahmad Sidqi, 111, 170–171, 220n174
Dallasheh, Leena, 48
Daoud, Siham, 57, 193n38, 208n60
al-Daqqaq, ʿUmar, 159
Darwazah, Muhammad ʿIzzat, 25, 199n97
Darwish, Mahmoud: Arab modernism and, 12; decolonizing discourse of, 118–123; in decolonizing period, 80, 88, 93–94, 109, 112; departure from Israel, 7, 149, 177–179, *178*, 180; disputes about definition of Palestinian resistance and, 172–174; *End of the Night*, 161; "Identity Card," 124–126, 188; June 1967 war and, 152–153, 156, 157, 160–161; Kanafani on, 142–143, 161; on land confiscations, 123–126; "A Lover from Palestine" (poem), 129–130, 142, 144; *A Lover from Palestine* (book of verse), 129, 143, 160, 173; on Palestinian literature, 114–115, 118–123; photos of, *129, 169, 178*; in PLO, 180, 184; Qasim compared, 126; as resistance poet, 6; return to Israel, 186, 230n123; "Save Us from This Relentless Love" (essay), 173, 177; at Sofia Festival, 7, 146, 165, 166–169, *169*, 171–172, 180, 183; state efforts to control, 115, 119–120, 127–130, 143, 157, 175, 176, 188, 230n115
al-Dasuqi, Mahmud, 170, 229n86
Dayan, Moshe, 167
Dayr Yassin massacre (1948), 85, 114, 143, 203n181, 213–214n40

decolonizing discourse: Anglo-American imperialism, denunciations of, 54–57, 76; under British Mandate, 15–18, 22–24; continuing validity of, 44, 45; engagement of Palestinian Israelis with, 5, 6, 9; "imperialist base," controversy over regarding Israel as, 115, 154, 220n2; "internal colonialism" of Palestinians in Israel, 8; leftist discourse, emergence of, 37; in mid-1960s, 115, 118–123; Palestinian national identity, groups promoting, 135–136; positioning Palestinians in Israel in context of, 12–14; in post-*Nakba* period, 49; questions relating to, 3; responding to Zionist and British colonial discourses, 22–24; after Sofia Festival, 171; at World Youth Festivals, 2; Zionism and imperialism, relationship between, 131–132

decolonizing period (1956-1960), 78–113; Algerian war of independence, 78, 79, 90, 92, 93, 108–109; Arab views of Palestinians in Israel during, 109–111; Ard movement, 98, 99–105, *104*, 112; education in, 89–90, 215n67; intellectuals, defining, 89–90; Iraqi revolution (1958), 3, 5, 79, 94, 191n8; Israeli state self-representation during, 93, 107–109, 112; Kafr Qasim massacre (1956), 85–86, 90, 111; May Day rally (1958), Nazareth, 78–79, 81, 90, 94; Gamal Abdel Nasser as inspiration in, 5, 78, 81, 82, 213n37; pan-Arab nationalists versus communists in, 81, 94–98; poetry and poetry festivals in, 79, 80, 81, 86–89, 92–94, 107, 109, 111–112; press and print material in, 90, 95, 101, 105–108, 112; Suez Crisis (1956-1957), 3, 5, 80, 83–85, 90, 103, 111, 114, 191n8; UAR, 79, 90, 91–92, 94–96, 98, 99, 101; "Year of Africa" (1960), 108; younger cohort of intellectuals emerging in, 79–81, 84, 88–89

Defense Law (1939), 103, 127, 205n10
demographics and population of Palestine/Israel, 47, 196n49, 226n8
Di-Capua, Yoav, 58
al-Difaʿ, 35, 52, 53
Druze, 61, 126, 127, 209n81
Dulles, John Foster, 84

education: under British Mandate, 18, 24–28, 194n2, 197n63; in decolonizing period, 89–90, 215n67; literacy rates in Palestine, 22, 30, 31, 34, 195n28, 197n63, 198n94, 200n119; under Ottoman rule, 21–22, 195n33, 196n37; in post-*Nakba* period, 60–61, 208n75
Education Ordinance (1933), 28
Egypt: British military presence in, 22, 70; in UAR, 79, 90, 91–92, 94–96, 98, 99, 101.116–117. *See also* June 1967 war; Nasser, Gamal Abdel; Suez Crisis
Emergency Law (1936), 103, 127, 205n10
Eshkol, Levi, 133, 137, 167

al-Fajr (The dawn), 2–3, 95, 96, 107, 108, 109, 112, 126
Fakhuri, ʿUmar, 202n159
Farah, Bulus, 40, 51, 200n121, 202n166
Fatah, 99, 130, 137, 151–152, 164, 166
al-Fayturi, Muhammad, 121
Fayyad, Tawfiq, *129*
Feraoun, Mouloud, 121
Filastin, 35, 52, 53
Franklin Book Programs, 116, 117, 119
Friends of Progressive Arabic Literature in Tel Aviv, 72, 74
al-Fula tenant farmers, 23, 196–197n53

General Union of Palestinian Students (GUPS), 99, 101, 102
al-Ghad (The morrow), 40–41, 62, 67, 202–203n170
Ghallab, ʿAbd al-Karim, 160
Gramsci, Antonio, 10, 193n35

Green Line (Armistice Lines), 4

Habib, Ghassan, 137
Habibi, Emile: Ihsan ʿAbbas and, 141; adaptation of resistance strategies by, 45; on Algerian independence, 92; on Ard movement/Group, 103, 134; Siham Daoud compared, 57; on Darwish's departure from Israel, 179; as editor, 207n49; education of, 15, 194n2; on elections of 1959, 98; on Khartoum Resolution, 153–154; leftist discourse, exposure to, 38, 39; on legitimacy of Israel as state, 154; on "literature of the people," 69, 80; Mandate period shaping, 15–16, 24, 199n106; in *Nakba*, 16, 42, 43; NLL and, 39, 40; Palestinian national identity movement, on emergence of, 134, 135; on PLO, 131; on Qasim, 126–127; as radio broadcaster, 16, 35; *The Secret Life of Saeed the Pessoptimist*, 204n187; on UAR, 91–92, 95–96, 98
al-Hadaf (The goal), 107–108, 112, 173
Hadawi, Sami, 110, 220n171
Haddad, Michael, 57, 58–59, 74, 107, 208n62
al-Hawadith (The events), 178
Hebrew, use of, 11–12, 71–72, 193n38
Hebrew University, 25, 69, 105, 106
Hijazi, Fuʾad, 32, 199n106
Hikmet, Nâzim, 68
al-Hilal (The crescent), 20–21, 161, 195nn29–30
Histadrut: in decolonizing period, 78, 89, 90, 93, 107, 112; in mid-1960s, 120, 122, 127; PCP versus, 36; in post-*Nakba* period, 52, 74, 76
history textbooks, Palestinian, 27–28
horizontal solidarity, 81, 212n13
Hughes, Langston, 68, 106
Hurani, Faysal, 146, 165
al-Hurriya (Freedom), 37

Husayn, Rashid: on Arab views of Palestinians in Israel, 1–3, 109–110; in decolonizing period, 80, 87, 88, 96–97, 105–106, 108–110; in League of Arab Poets, 211n138; move to United States and involvement with PLO, 184–185; at World Youth Festival (1959), 1–3, 10, 109, 166
Husayn, Taha, 15–16, 35, 58, 66, 107
al-Husayni, Hajj Amin, 17, 46–47, 194–195n15
Hussein (king of Jordan), 131, 150, 213n18

Ibrahim, Hanna, 82, 87–88, 94, 98
Idris, Suhayl, 168
imperialism. *See* decolonizing discourse
"imperialist base," controversy over regarding Israel as, 115, 154, 220n2
"infiltration," 43, 48, 204n189, 205n7
Institute for Palestine Studies, 140, 141, 158
international conferences and festivals: attendance as strategy of resistance, 6–7, 183; World Youth Festivals, 1–3, 7, 10, 80, 109, 162, 183. *See also* Sofia Festival
Iranian oil industry, nationalization of, 70, 210n115
Iraq: Ard movement and, 103; Baʿthist party in, 168; Communist Party in, 54, 64, 202n160; Farhud (1941), 73; forces during *Nakba*, 218n135; Jewish immigration from, 64, 105, 205n21, 206n26; pan-Arab nationalism in, 205n18; poetry in, 65–67, 69, 72–73; political environment in 1930s and 1940s, 38; post-*Nakba* period, influence in, 51, 64–67; revolution (1958), 3, 5, 79, 94, 191n8; UAR and, 95–96, 99
isolation of Palestinians in Israel: under British Mandate, 41–44; in decolonizing period, 87, 93, 94, 97, 100, 101, 104,

110; from early 1970s to present day, 184–189; June 1967 war and aftermath, 147, 149, 161, 170, 173, 177, 179–180; in mid-1960s, 115, 117–118, 120, 123, 128, 141, 143, 144; occupation reuniting Palestinians in and outside of Israel, 10, 155–157, 175, 176, 184; in post-*Nakba* period, 49–52, 55, 61–63, 75, 77; resistance to, 3–5, 6, 10, 181–189
Israel, Palestinians in. *See* Palestinians in Israel
Israeli Organization for Understanding and Friendship, 122
Israeli State Archives, Palestinian material in, 193n28, 193n30
Istiqlal Party, 17, 29, 35, 199n97
al-ʿItani, Muhammad, 172
al-Ittihad (The union): Arab views of Palestinians in Israel and, 138, 141–142, 146, 147; under British Mandate, 40, 42; on Darwish's departure from Israel, 179; in decolonizing period, 79, 80, 85, 89, 90, *91*, 92, 96, 182, 221n18; June 1967 war and, 152, 153, 157, 161, 227n53; in mid-1960s, 116, 118, 121, 122, 126, 127, 131, 133, 138, 141–142; in post-*Nakba* period, 50, 55–57, 59, 67–68, 70, 71, 76, 206n35

al-Jabali, ʿIzzat, 139
al-Jadid (The new): in decolonizing period, 80, 89, 90, 95, 96, 106, 107, 182, 213n19, 221n18; June 1967 war and, 157, 161; in mid-1960s, 114–118, 121, 126, 127; in post-*Nakba* period, 50, 57–59, 61–64, 68, 69, 71, 72, 74, 76
Jahshan, Shakib, 211n138
Jamjun, Muhammad, 32
al-Jawahiri, Muhammad Mahdi, 65–66, 68, 69, 106–107, 168, *169*
Jawzi, Bandali, 62
Jewish immigration, 17, 29, 41, 43, 71, 105, 123, 205n21, 206n26

Jewish-Arab relations. *See* Arab-Jewish relations
Jiryis, Sabri, 135, 140–141, 148, 152, 183, 184, 223n74
Jubran, Salim, 84, 85, 106, 107, 176, 213n37, 230n112
al-Jumhuriyya (The republic), 156, 170
June 1967 war and aftermath: Arab intellectuals' response to, 157–159, 172, 173; Arab views of Palestinians in Israel and, 7, 147, 148, 162, 176–177; attitudes of Palestinians in Israel toward, 152–155; circumstances of, 150–152; crackdown on Palestinians in Israel after, 174–177; occupation reuniting Palestinians in and outside of Israel, 10, 155–157, 175, 176, 184; poets and intellectuals, challenges faced by, 179–180; resistance poets and, 147, 156–157, 159–162, 179–180. *See also* Sofia Festival

Kafr Qasim massacre (1956), 85–86, 90, 111, 114, 126, 127, 143
Kalila wa Dimna, 121
Kanafani, Ghassan, 142–144, 147, 156, 160, 161, 173, 184, 225n104
Karamah, Battle of, 151–152, 164
Kardush, Mansur, 152, 224n95
Kassis, Shawqi, 128–129
Khadr, ʿAbbas, 172
Khalailah, Haitham, 187
Khalifeh, Sahar, 157
Khamis, Saliba, 153, 154
Khartoum Resolution, 151, 153, 155, 164
al-Khatib, Yusuf, 142, 161
Khayyat, Ibrahim, 69, 72, 73
Khuri, Raʾif, 16, 38, 39, 202n159
Kimche, Jon, 46
Kusa, Ilyas, 46–47, 49, 54, 76, 204n1, 212n144

land, confiscation of, 54, 87, 123–126,

144, 185, 214n48, 216n95, 222n30, 231n4
League of Arab Students (later League of Arab Intellectuals), 40, 202–203n170, 202n162
League of Arab Writers and Intellectuals, 89–90, 111
League of Arabic Pens, 86
League of Arab[ic] Poets, 74–75, 77, 82, 86, 89, 211n137
League of Nations, 23–24, 197nn58–59
Lebanon: Communist Party, 37, 38, 54, 117; uprisings (1958), 3, 191n8
leftist discourse: Anglo-American imperialism, denunciations of, 54–57, 76; Arab history and identity, Marxist interpretation of, 62–64; bookshops, dissemination through, 35, 39–40; emergence of, 18, 20–21, 36–39, 44–45; Marxism, 15, 38, 40, 44, 62–63, 66, 69, 70, 102, 117, 172, 173; socialist realism, 6, 41, 65–69, 72, 76, 88, 114–117, 119, 125, 203n171. *See also* communism and communists
literacy rates in Palestine, 22, 30, 31, 34, 195n28, 197n63, 198n94, 200n119
literature: committed literature, 66, 80, 90, 105, 107, 117; Darwish on, 114–115, 118–123; global awareness of resistance literature inside Palestine, 141–144; Habibi on "literature of the people," 69; mid-1960s, literary landscape of, 116–118; Romanticism, 20, 58, 63–66, 71, 74, 87, 89, 143, 160; socialist realism, 6, 41, 65, 66, 69, 116, 117, 203n171; as strategy of resistance, 6. *See also* poetry; *specific print vehicles and authors*
Lorca, Federico García, 68, 106
Lubani, ʿIsa, 74, 77, 86, 211n138, 212n141
Lumumba, Patrice, 108

Mahmud, ʿAbd al-Rahim, 31, 32, 36, 41, 67, 145, 202n155

al-Malaʾika, Nazik, 66
Mannheim, Karl, 11
Mapai Party, 53, 57, 98, 163, 217n113
Mapam Party, 2, 11–12, 78, 95, 100, 102, 106, 112, 133, 134, 138, 163, 217n113
Marxism, 15, 38, 40, 44, 62–63, 66, 69, 70, 102, 117, 172, 173
Mavi Marmara (Turkish ship), 187, 232n19
May Day rally (1958), Nazareth, 78–79, 81, 90, 94
Meir, Golda, 108
memoranda to international bodies, 7, 115, 132–134, 139, 140, 144, 182–183, 224n95
Miʿari, Muhammad, 106, 168, 170
Michael, Sami, 72, 73, 210n122
mid-1960s, 114–145; Arab-Jewish relations in, 122, 132; decolonizing discourse in, 115, 118–123; global outreach and dissemination of information during, 115–116, 138–144; land, confiscation of, 123–126, 144, 222n30; literary landscape, 116–118; Palestinian national identity, groups promoting, 130–136; poetry in, 115, 118–119, 127–130, 141–145; press and print material in, 114, 116, 139; right of return in, 136–138; younger cohort of intellectuals emerging in, 115, 127
military rule of Palestinian areas of Israel, 48, 56–57, 70, 80, 82, 83, 127, 148, 175, 205n12, 216n95
al-Miqdadi, Darwish, 27–28
al-Mirsad, 95, 109, 112, 133, 142, 216n96
modernism and modernization, 12, 20, 50, 57–60, 158
Moussa, Manal, 187
Muhammad Ali, Muhammad, 161
al-Mujtamaʿ (The society), 50, 57, 58–59, 71, 73, 76, 90, 107, 161, 208n70
al-Muqtataf (The selected), 20–21, 195nn29–30

264 INDEX

Murqus, Nimr, 54, 55, 60, 82–83, 207n45, 207n48
Muruwwah, Husayn, 117, 161, 221n14

Nafar, Tamer, 188–189
Nahda period, 20–22, 33, 44
al-Najah national school, Nablus, 25, 31, 32
Nakba (1947-1949): adaptation of strategies of resistance to, 16–17, 41–45; Arab armies deployed in, 42, 94, 203n183, 218n135; defined, 3–4; refugees and dislocation resulting from, 4, 42–44, 47, 191nn10–11
al-naksa (the setback). *See* June 1967 war
Naqqara, Hanna: adaptation of resistance strategies by, 45; on committed literature, 80; convergence of political and cultural emancipation in career of, 58; leftist discourse, exposure to, 40; Mandate period shaping, 18, 24; in *Nakba*, 43, 204n194; photos of, *91, 178*; poetry, influence of, 32, 94; at social clubs, 36, 200–201n134; teachers, influence of, 25–26
al-Naqqash, Raja', 160–161
Nassar, Fu'ad, 39, 40, 202n160
Nasser, Gamal Abdel: Ard movement and, 98, 99, 101–103, *104*, 112; as inspiration to Palestinians, 5, 78, 81, 82, 213n37; June 1967 war and, 150; on Palestinians in Israel, 138; pan-Arab nationalism and, 91, 94–98, 104, 112–113, 157; PLO and, 131; Suez Crisis (1956-1957), 3, 5, 80, 83–85, 90, 103, 114, 191n8; UAR and, 79, 90, 91–92, 94–96, 98, 99, 101, 116–117, 130
National Democratic Alliance (Balad or Tajammuʿ), 185
National Liberation League (NLL), 39–41, 42, 44, 45, 49, 54, 55, 67, 155
Natur, Salman, 156, 193n38

Near East Broadcasting Service (NEBS), 35, 37, 201n148
Neruda, Pablo, 68, 106
Niqula, Jabra, 61–62, 72
nonpartisan organizations, 5, 40, 80, 89, 111, 140, 182
Noorani, Yaseen, 12
Nuwayhid, ʿAjaj, 35
Nuʿayma, Mikhail, 21

organic intellectuals, 10, 12, 193n35
Orient House archives, 192–193n28
Ottoman Empire, 18–22, 23, 31

Palestine Broadcast program, 142
Palestine Broadcasting Service (PBS), 16, 35, 206n29
Palestine Communist Party (PCP), 15, 36–38, 201n148, 202n160, 202n166
Palestine Liberation Front (PLF), 130–131
Palestine Liberation Organization (PLO), 130–132, 135, 140, 151, 152, 164, 180, 184, 185–186, 192n28, 220n174
Palestine Research Center (PRC), 140, 141, 158, 176, 181, 184, 192n28, 223n67
Palestinian Declaration of Independence, 186
Palestinian National Charter, 135, 169
Palestinian refugees. *See* refugees, Palestinian
Palestinians in Israel, 1–14; 1917-1948 (*See* British Mandate); 1947-1949 (*See Nakba*); 1948-1956 (*See* post-*Nakba* period); 1956-1960 (*See* decolonizing period); in mid-1960s (*See* mid-1960s); 1967-1968 (*See* June 1967 war and aftermath); academic studies of, 7–9; decolonizing discourse, use of, 12–14 (*See also* decolonizing discourse); intellectuals, generational shifts in, 10–12; isolation of, 3–5 (*See*

also isolation of Palestinians in Israel); strategies of resistance developed by, 5–7, 15–18, 44–45, 181–189; tensions and conflicts faced by, 1–3; terms for, 14, 194n10; texts and their audiences, 9–10; transnational analytical framework for studying, 9. *See also* Arab views of Palestinians in Israel; literature; poetry; resistance poetry and resistance poets

pan-Arab nationalism: ANM, 99, 101, 102; Arab East, role of Palestine in, 19–20; Arab history and identity, articles promoting, 62–64; Ard movement, 99–105; under British Mandate, 18; communists versus, 81, 94–98; CPI position on, 50; fall of Ottoman Empire and, 23–24; historical context, 5, 9–10; history textbooks, Palestinian, 27; in Iraq, 205n18; leftist discourse, emergence of, 37; in *Nahda* period, 20; Nasser-led, 91, 94–98, 104, 112–113, 157; Palestinian national identity, groups promoting, 130–131; of Qasim, 126–127; UAR, 79, 90, 91–92, 94–96, 98, 99, 101

Partition Plan (1947), 41–42, 47, 133, 154–155, 203n183

Pinto de Andrade, Mário, 121

poetry: under British Mandate, 18, 31–34; in decolonizing period, 79, 80, 81, 86–89, 92–94, 107, 109, 111–112, 182; free verse, 66–67.124; Iraqi, 65–67, 69, 72–73; June 1967 war and aftermath, challenges posed by, 179–180; League of Arab Poets, 74–75, 77, 211n137; in mid-1960s, 115, 118–119, 127–130, 141–145; in post-*Nakba* period, 65–71, 72–77; as strategy of resistance, 6, 79, 186, 188–189. *See also* resistance poetry and resistance poets; *specific poets*

Popular Front, 94–95, 99–100, 111, 173, 216n95

population and demographics of Palestine/Israel, 47, 196n49, 226n8

Port Said, in Suez Crisis (1956), 3, 84, 85, 103, 114, 191n8

post-*Nakba* period (1948-1956), 48–77; Anglo-American imperialism, denunciations of, 54–57, 76; Arab history and identity, articles promoting, 62–64; Arab-Jewish relations in, 50–51, 71–75; competing Palestinian and Israeli narratives in, 46–52, 75–77; definition of Arab in, 61–62; education in, 60–61, 208n75; ghettoization in, 48, 51; Iraqi influence in, 51, 64–67; loyalty of Palestinian citizens to Israel, 46–47, 49–50; military rule of Palestinian areas, 48, 56–57, 70, 205n12; modernism and modernization, 50, 57–60; poetry in, 65–71, 72–77; press and print material, 51, 52–58, 64, 76; social status and occupations of Palestinians in Israel after, 10, 193n34; state's role in cultural and intellectual development, 50, 52–54; textual encounters with region in, 51–52

press and print material: bookstores, 35, 39–40, 51, 200n121; under British Mandate, 18, 28–31; CPI publications, 6, 90, 104, 105, 115, 207n50, 208n61; in decolonizing period, 90, 95, 101, 105–108, 112; hand copying of, 106; in mid-1960s, 114, 116, 139; under Ottoman rule, 20–22, 196n40; in post-*Nakba* period, 51, 52–58, 64, 76; as strategy of resistance, 5–6, 105. *See also specific newspapers and journals*

Press Ordinance (1933), 29, 30

Progressive List, 185

Qabbani, Nizar, 159–160, 162, 227n53
Qahwaji, Habib, 89, 99–101, 109, 148, 152, 183, 184, 211n138, 215n68
al-Qalamawi, Suhayr, 161

Qasim, ʿAbd al-Karim, (Iraqi leader), 95, 96, 98, 99, 103
al-Qasim, Samih: Arab modernism and, 12; Darwish compared, 126; in decolonizing period, 88–89, 93, 109, 112; disputes about definition of Palestinian resistance and, 172, 174; June 1967 war and, 152–153, 156, 157, 160, 161, 162; Kanafani on, 142, 143, 161; military service, refusal to enlist in, 127–128; pan-Arab nationalism of, 126–127; photos of, *129, 169*; "Poets, not Diplomats" (essay), 126–127, 179; as resistance poet, 6; at Sofia Festival, 7, 146, 165, 166–169, *169*, 183; state efforts to control, 115, 127–130, 157, 175–176, 188, 230n111, 230n113
qawmi. See pan-Arab nationalism
Qaʿwar, Jamal, 73, 76–77, 87, 109, 211n138
Qaʿwar Farah, Najwa, 83, 86, 200–201n134
al-Quds, 170, 196n42

Rabin, Yitzhak, 152
Radio Cairo, 92, 94, 98, 150
radio programming, 18, 35–36, 52, 91, 92, 94, 96, 98, 142, 150, 161–162, 188
al-Rahib, Hani, 161
Rakah Party, 137–138, 146, 147, 152–155, 164–171
Rashid, Haydar, 168
Ratner Commission report, 82
realism, socialist, 6, 41, 65, 66, 69, 116, 117, 203n171
refugees, Palestinian: Absentee Property Law (1950), 54; ANM and, 99; Darwish's departure from Israel, 149, 177–179, *178*, 180; ghettoization of Palestinians within Israel, 48, 51; homogeneity of Israeli state due to, 47; "infiltration" by, 43, 48, 204n189, 205n7; in *Nakba*, 4, 42–44, 47, 191nn10–11; in post-*Nakba* period, 53; right of return, 136–138, 216n95; voluntary emigration/exile, 7, 110
Regev, Miri, 188, 232n27
Rejwan, Nissim, 107
resistance poetry and resistance poets: awareness of, outside Israel, 141–144, 146; disputes about definition of Palestinian resistance and, 147–149, 172–174; early instances of, under British Mandate, 31–34; June 1967 war and, 147, 156–157, 159–162, 179–180; scholarly attention to, 116, 143, 147, 160–162, 184; at Sofia Festival, 146–147, 167–169, 180. *See also specific poets*
resistance strategies, 5–7, 15–18, 44–45, 181–189. *See also specific strategies*
right of return, 136–138, 216n95
riots (1929), 29, 32, 198n85, 199n106
Robinson, Shira, 13
Romanticism, 20, 58, 63–66, 71, 74, 87, 89, 143, 160
Rose al-Youssef, 162
al-Rusafi, Maʿruf, 72–73
Russian literature, Palestinian consumption of, 16, 21, 201n148

Saba, Nicola, 54
Saʿid, Ahmad, 91, 96, 98
Said, Edward, 9, 200n121
Salah, Raed, 187
Salih (friend of Abu Hanna), 156
Samuel, Herbert, 23
Sartre, Jean-Paul, 66
Sayegh, Fayez, 110, 140, 220nn169–170
al-Sayyab, Badr Shakir, 65–66, 69, 117, 126
al-Sayyad, 106
Scott, David, 11
Second Intifada (2000-2005), 186
Semah, David, 71–72, 210n120
"Semitic wave" theory, 27

INDEX 267

Senghor, Leopold, 13, 212n13
Shammas, Anton, 4, 193n38
Shammout, Ibrahim, 167, 168
Shaʿshuʿ, Salim, 73, 211n130, 211n137
Shitrit, Bechor, 53, 208n62
Shiʿr (Poetry), 161
Shukri, Ghali, 174
Shuqayri, Ahmad, 131
al-Sibaʿi, Yusuf, 146
Sidqi, Muhammad Najati, 37, 201n140, 201n148
social clubs, 18, 35–36, 200n131
socialism. *See* communism and communists; leftist discourse
socialist realism, 6, 41, 65–69, 72, 76, 88, 114–117, 119, 125, 203n171
Sofia Festival (1968): aftermath of, 170–172; attitudes towards Palestinians in Israel at, 146–147, 162, 164–170, 183; opening procession, 165–166; political forums and cultural events, 167; politics of participation in, 163–165; resistance poets at, 146–147, 167–169, 180; separation of Israeli and Palestinian dormitories at, 171–172
Somekh, Sasson, 66–67, 71–72
Soviet Union: British Mandate Palestine and, 36, 38, 40, 42, 45; Cold War, 100, 116, 119, 140; Darwish visiting, 177; in decolonizing period, 84, 109; German-Soviet nonaggression pact, 201n148; June 1967 war and, 150; in mid-1960s, 116, 137; in post-*Nakba* period, 55, 56, 63–68, 76, 207n50; socialist realism and, 67, 203n171; wall newspapers in, 201n144; World Youth Festivals and, 1–2, 163, 164, 183
strategies of resistance, 5–7, 15–18, 44–45, 181–189. *See also specific strategies*
Suez Crisis (1956-1957), 3, 5, 80, 83–85, 90, 103, 111, 114, 191n8
Syria: Baʿth Party in, 91, 146, 166, 168, 215n73; Communist Party in, 37, 38, 54; Sofia Festival, delegation at, 146, 166, 168; in UAR, 79, 90, 91–92, 94–96, 98, 99, 101.116–117

al-Taliʿa (The vanguard), 37
al-Tariq (The path), 16, 39, 41, 117, 202n159
Tatour, Dareen, 188
"theory of stages," Marxist, 40
Third Worldism, 13
transnational analytical framework, 9
travel restrictions, 1, 4–5, 6, 11, 49, 56, 80, 88, 112, 127, 157, 176, 183, 187, 211n124, 211n135, 231n17
Tsabari, Yossi, 188–189
Tubi, George, 167
Tubi, Tawfiq, 38, 39, 57, 85–86, 91, 137, 154–155, 207n49, 214n41
Tuma, Emile, 38, 39, 40, 62, 82, 121
Tuqan, Fadwa, 156–157
Tuqan, Ibrahim, 31–32, 65, 145

U Thant, 133
United Arab Republic (UAR), 79, 90, 91–92, 94–96, 98, 99, 101, 116–117, 130
United Kingdom: Anglo-American imperialism, denunciations of, 54–57, 76; Suez Crisis (1956-1957), 3, 5, 80, 83–85, 90, 103, 111, 114, 191n8. *See also* British Mandate
United Nations: Algerian independence, resolution on, 92; Israeli admission to, 206n25; June 1967 war and, 150, 151, 155; Partition Plan (1947), 41–42, 47, 133, 154–155, 203n183; PLO at, 140, 151; right of return at, 136, 137; UNSCOP (UN Special Committee on Palestine), 41
United States: Anglo-American imperialism, denunciations of, 54–57, 76; Cold War, 100, 116, 119, 140; Franklin Book Programs, 116, 117, 119
United States Information Agency (USIA), 116

Voice of the Arabs (radio program), 91, 96, 98
Voice of Israel (radio station), 52, 98, 206n29
Voice of Palestine (radio program), 162

Wasfi, Tawfiq Hasan, 139
Watad, Muhammad, 133, 134
watani (Palestininan/territorial patriotism), 18, 27, 32, 50, 205n18
Wathba demonstrations, 65
Western Wall, Jerusalem, 29
Wilder, Gary, 13
Williams, Raymond, 9
women speakers at social clubs, 36, 200–201n134
World Youth Festivals, 1–3, 7, 10, 80, 109, 162, 183. *See also* Sofia Festival

al-Yawm (Today): in decolonizing period, 90, 98, 107, 112; in post-*Nakba* period, 46, 50, 53–55, 57–59, 63, 71, 73, 75, 206n35
Yawmiyyat Filastiniyah (Palestinian journal), 176
"Year of Africa" (1960), 108
Young Men's Christian Association (YMCA), Jerusalem, 36
Young Turk Revolution, 21, 31
Yunis, ʿAbdallah Muhammad, 93
al-Zayr, ʿAta, 32

Zayyad, Tawfiq, 70–71, 74, 97, 142, 145, 160, 161, 188, 210n118
Zionism: Arab-Jewish relations, as obstacle to, 72, 73; as bourgeois nationalist movement, 40; colonial discourse of, responding to, 22–24; imperialism and, 131–132; Jews conflated with, 154, 170
Zoabi, Haneen, 187
Zuriek, Elia, 8

Stanford Studies in Middle Eastern and Islamic Societies and Cultures

Joel Beinin, *Stanford University*
Juan R. I. Cole, *University of Michigan*

Editorial Board
Asef Bayat, Marilyn Booth, Laurie Brand, Laleh Khalili, Timothy Mitchell, Jillian Schwedler, Rebecca L. Stein, Max Weiss

---

Orit Bashkin, *Impossible Exodus: Iraqi Jews in Israel*
2017

Nahid Siamdoust, *Soundtrack of the Revolution: The Politics of Music in Iran*
2017

Laure Guirguis, *Copts and the Security State: Violence, Coercion, and Sectarianism in Contemporary Egypt*
2016

Michael Farquhar, *Circuits of Faith: Migration, Education, and the Wahhabi Mission*
2016

Gilbert Achcar, *Morbid Symptoms: Relapse in the Arab Uprising*
2016

Jacob Mundy, *Imaginative Geographies of Algerian Violence: Conflict Science, Conflict Management, Antipolitics*
2015

Ilana Feldman, *Police Encounters: Security and Surveillance in Gaza under Egyptian Rule*
2015

Tamir Sorek, *Palestinian Commemoration in Israel: Calendars, Monuments, and Martyrs*
2015

Adi Kuntsman and Rebecca L. Stein, *Digital Militarism: Israel's Occupation in the Social Media Age*
2015

Laurie A. Brand, *Official Stories: Politics and National Narratives in Egypt and Algeria*
2014

Kabir Tambar, *The Reckonings of Pluralism: Citizenship and the Demands of History in Turkey*
2014

Diana Allan, *Refugees of the Revolution: Experiences of Palestinian Exile*
2013

Shira Robinson, *Citizen Strangers: Palestinians and the Birth of Israel's Liberal Settler State*
2013

Joel Beinin and Frédéric Vairel, *editors, Social Movements, Mobilization, and Contestation in the Middle East and North Africa*
2013 (Second Edition), 2011

Ariella Azoulay and Adi Ophir, *The One-State Condition: Occupation and Democracy in Israel/Palestine*
2012

Steven Heydemann and Reinoud Leenders, *editors, Middle East Authoritarianisms: Governance, Contestation, and Regime Resilience in Syria and Iran*
2012

Jonathan Marshall, *The Lebanese Connection: Corruption, Civil War, and the International Drug Traffic*
2012

Joshua Stacher, *Adaptable Autocrats: Regime Power in Egypt and Syria*
2012

Bassam Haddad, *Business Networks in Syria: The Political Economy of Authoritarian Resilience*
2011

Noah Coburn, *Bazaar Politics: Power and Pottery in an Afghan Market Town*
2011

Laura Bier, *Revolutionary Womanhood: Feminisms, Modernity, and the State in Nasser's Egypt*
2011

Samer Soliman, *The Autumn of Dictatorship: Fiscal Crisis and Political Change in Egypt under Mubarak*
2011